THE EMM

THE EMMONS SAGA

A History of the
USS EMMONS (DD457-DMS22)

Edward Baxter Billingsley

iUniverse, Inc.
New York Lincoln Shanghai

THE EMMONS SAGA

***A History of the* USS EMMONS (DD457-DMS22)**

iUniverse books may be ordered through booksellers or by contacting:

iUniverse
2021 Pine Lake Road, Suite 100
Lincoln, NE 68512
www.iuniverse.com
1-800-Authors (1-800-288-4677)

Cover photo courtesy of Navy Art Collection,
Naval Historical Center.
Artist: Dwight C. Shepler

ISBN-13: 978-0-595-36299-8 (pbk)
ISBN-13: 978-0-595-80739-0 (ebk)
ISBN-10: 0-595-36299-0 (pbk)
ISBN-10: 0-595-80739-9 (ebk)

Printed in the United States of America

Contents

Edward Baxter Billingsley, Rear Admiral (Ret) USN

Admiral Billingsley was the USS *Emmons*' third commanding officer. A member of the destroyer's commissioning detail in December, 1941, he had served previously as Engineering Officer and Executive Officer. He was transferred to another command prior to the *Emmons* deployment to the Pacific. Billingsley was captain on D-Day at Normandy, during the bombardment of Cherbourg, and landings at Southern France. He was awarded the Silver Star and Bronze Star for meritorious performance in those engagements. After retirement from the Navy in 1959, he earned a doctorate and taught at the University of South Florida.

Geo. Case Collection

Introduction

Edward Baxter Billingsley, RAdm. (Ret.) USN was the third captain of the destroyer USS Emmons (July 1943-November 1944). Though he held other notable assignments and commands during his thirty-year career, he acknowledged special affection for the Emmons, his first command. He maintained regular contact with crew members after his retirement and was active in originally organizing the Emmons Association.

Having completed a second career as professor of history at the University of South Florida, Admiral Billingsley agreed to write the ship's history. In 1989, after eight years of research into every available source, "*The Emmons Saga*" was completed and published privately by the Emmons Association. His expansive work chronicled the extraordinary involvement of the Emmons and her crew in World War II and brought into focus a striking fact: her life and exploits paralleled the history of the War itself—from her commissioning two days before Pearl Harbor to her sinking in a massive Kamikaze attack April 6, 1945.

Then, 56 years later, an almost incredulous event brought the Emmons seemingly back to life and provided an epilogue for "*The Saga.*" In February 2001, American divers at Okinawa found the wreckage of the *USS Emmons*. They have sent back stirring videos and pictures, insured protection of the resting place of lost shipmates, arranged memorial services over the site and joined the Emmons family as latter-day members.

The Admiral's original work has been augmented in this printing with epilogue chapters XVII and XVIII. They cover eyewitness's accounts of the discovery, subsequent protection and commemoration of the wreck of the *Emmons* and the unique relationship that has evolved among the special people of the Emmons Family.

Preface

This history of the USS *Emmons* (DD457-DMS22) was undertaken at the request of the Emmons Association, an organization of men who served aboard at one time or another during World War II. The purpose is to preserve the memory of a gallant ship, and to honor the shipmates who did not survive her sinking as the result of a Japanese kamikaze attack on April 6, 1945.

It is not the intention to glorify the *Emmons* as a dashing "greyhound" of the battle fleet or her crewmen as superheroes. Rather it is the intention to show her as a working unit of a mighty navy, required to do many different tasks under widely varied conditions, rarely glamorous or exciting. True, there was ever present danger, but by no means always from enemy action. For every day of direct confrontation with the Germans and Japanese, there were months of exposure to the impartial forces of nature which every ship at sea faces. Added to this were the inherent risks involved in the everyday operation of the delicate and complicated equipment packed into the hull of a destroyer.

An attempt is made to show how this one destroyer, the *Emmons,* fitted into the overall picture of a navy and a nation at war, whether in a combat zone or a quiet area—why she was where she was at a particular time, what she did, how she did it, and, where discernable, the results. There is no contention that she was far different from hundreds of other destroyers going through similar experiences, but it has been a goal to show how she became special for the men who served aboard her. An almost impossible goal was to show how the more than six hundred men who served aboard at one time or another gradually began to think of the *Emmons* as "her," a vibrant entity rather than an inanimate mass of steel, wire, paint, guns and machinery.

A major effort is made to show something of the life of the crew, their living conditions, their actions and reactions in different situations—where possible, their thoughts. To show the gradual conversion of raw, untrained youths to reliable, seaworthy sailors is part of this effort. The *Emmons* was the focus of their existence during some of the prime years of their lives. It was they who make this history more than just a factual account of a ship in war.

Many sources have been used in reconstructing the *Emmons* story. Primary sources such as ship's logs, war diaries, action reports, administrative histories, and records of the various Navy Department bureaus, were found in the National Archives, the Naval Operational Archives and Library of the Naval Historical Center, and the Washington National Records Center. A major source was personal interviews with former members of the *Emmons'* crew. Among the latter were taped recordings of the memories of those who attended the reunion of the Emmons Association in Portland, Maine, in October, 1982. An invaluable source has been the hand written reports of the crew members who survived the Kamikaze attack. The latter were compiled and collected under the supervision of Lieutenant John J. Griffin, Jr., USNR, shortly after the sinking while the survivors were still awaiting evacuation from the Okinawa area. They have since been reproduced and distributed to members of the Emmons Association.

Prominent among the secondary accounts used were the writings of Admiral Samuel Eliot Morison, USNR, *(History of the United States Naval Operations in World War II),* Captain S.W. Roskill, R.N. *(The War at Sea),* EH. Hinsley *(British Intelligence in the Second World War),* and Theodore Roscoe *(United States Destroyers Operations in World War II).*

The author is indebted to so many people that it is impossible to acknowledge all by name. Virtually all surviving officers and men contacted provided personal reminiscences and general information from their experiences aboard. David Jensen, the Secretary of the Emmons Association supplied mailing addresses and telephone numbers of members and helped locate nonmembers. Jerry McAlevey, one of the plank owners members of the commissioning crew) and an enthusiastic supporter of the history, initiated and supervised the tape recording of all men attending the biennial reunion at Portland, Maine, in 1982.

Jerry was also responsible for getting *The Emmons Saga* published. Severely handicapped for funds he had to rely heavily on friends in the business. Special thanks must go to Jack Lane, William Paul Harkins and Paul Heikkila of Potomac Graphics for the typesetting, Frank Maguire, Sr. of Horan Engraving for the color separations and printing of the cover, and Boris Mlower for his special technical assistance.

The idea of an *Emmons* history came from Captain Harold M. Heming, U.S.N., Retired, and the second commanding officer. He gave solid support through all phases of its composition and provided much information not available in official records. One of his major contributions was a thorough analysis of the informal survivor reports made shortly after the *Emmons* was sunk. Captain Eugene N. Foss, 2nd, U.S.N.R., Retired, the last commanding officer, was conversant with all operations of the ship, but consulted most frequently on her conversion to a high speed minesweeper and operations in the Pacific. Lieutenant

John J. Griffin, Jr., U.S.N.R., Retired, was gunnery officer at Okinawa. He assumed command after the captain was wounded and the executive officer killed during the battle with kamikazes April 6, 1945, and has been a primary source on that battle and the subsequent attempts to save the ship.

Personnel of the National Archives and other depositories of official records were invariably courteous and helpful. But special mention must be made of the staff of the Naval Historical Center and its head, Dr. Dean C. Allard. Mr. Michael Walker, in charge of World War II documents, was very helpful in solving unresolved questions and running down obscure records pertaining to the *Emmons.*

Two colleagues of the History Department of the University of South Florida, Doctor Charles Wong and Cecil Currey, have been kind enough to review the manuscripts and make valuable suggestions for its improvement. It goes without saying that any errors in the final product are the responsibility of the author alone.

The history could never have been written without the wholehearted support of my wife, Pat, who helped edit the sometimes illegible rough draft and wrote and rewrote it on her personal computer without complaint.

The author presents this history in the name of the Emmons Association, well knowing that it can never fully honor the *Emmons* and the men who served her.

1

A Bath-Built "Boat"

> At 1045, "To the Colors" was sounded. The colors and commission pennant were hoisted, placing the ship in commission.
>
> —*USS* ***Emmons*** *Log, 5 December 1941*

On a crisp New England morning, Friday, December 5, 1941, at the Boston Navy Yard, the USS *Emmons* (DD 457) was commissioned as a working unit of the United States Navy. Two days later the Japanese struck Pearl Harbor and the United States was at war. The *Emmons* was the last naval ship to be commissioned before World War II. Her career almost coincided with the duration of the war. Almost, but not quite. After serving well and faithfully for three years and four months, her career was ended by five Japanese kamikazes off Okinawa on April 6, 1945.

In keeping with the troubled times of late 1941, the commissioning ceremony at Boston was brief and simple, with no frills, not even the usual band to play the national anthem. Twelve officers and 206 enlisted men were paraded aft to hear the Captain of the Yard read dispatches from the Secretary of the Navy and the Chief of Naval Operations directing that the new destroyer be placed in commission. A bugler sounded "To the Colors" as the national ensign and commission pennant were hoisted. Lieutenant Commander Thomas C. Ragan, USN, read his orders to assume command, and, turning to the Executive Officer, Lieutenant Harold M. Heming, USN, ordered the watch to be set. Chief Boatswain's Mate Charles J. Clark piped the order over the ship's loud speaker system. The men of the first section broke ranks and manned their assigned watch stations throughout the ship. The whole ceremony took less than thirty minutes, but the *Emmons* was now a commissioned ship of the United States Navy.

She was conceived and born at a crucial point in the history of the United States and the world. By late 1941, the German Wehrmacht had rolled over Western Europe and was thrusting deep into Russia. Germany's partner in fascism, Italy, was attempting to consolidate control of the Mediterranean. In the West, England had managed to survive the Nazi war machine, but she was hard pressed by Hitler's air and submarine fleets. Since Germany's staggering victories of 1940, the United States had openly sided with the British, and was helping them in every way possible, short of war. Actually, we were engaged in an undeclared war in the North Atlantic. We had taken over control of Greenland and Iceland, and were providing convoy services in the North Atlantic for the vital shipping which carried lend-lease supplies to England. By the time the *Emmons* joined the fleet, one destroyer had been sunk and another damaged on this duty.

But the United States had to be particularly wary of the third member of the Axis team, Japan, which was threatening to establish hegemony over the Western Pacific. That country had taken advantage of Europe's troubles to occupy French Indochina and to announce her ambitious plans for a Greater East Asia Co-Prosperity Sphere. She had already taken over vast areas of China and was in the process of fitting them into her empire.

Japanese aggression did not go unchallenged. When her troops occupied French Indochina in the summer of 1941, President Roosevelt promptly froze all Japanese assets in the United States, and he extended those sanctions after she signed on with the Axis. The increased sanctions forbade all exports to her from this country, including the oil so vital for her military and industrial machines. The President demanded her withdrawal from occupied territory in China and Indochina. Japan countered with demands that her dominance in the Far East be acknowledged and that all trade embargoes be lifted. Diplomatic negotiations which had dragged on throughout the summer worsened during the autumn months. In November, as the *Emmons* neared completion at Bath, Maine, war between the two countries seemed inevitable unless some formula for relieving the tensions could be found.

Even as the new destroyer was being delivered to the Navy at Boston in early December, high level talks between Secretary of State Cordell Hull and Japanese Ambassadors Kichisaburo Nomura and Saburo Kurusu were going on in Washington. The very day the *Emmons* was commissioned it appeared that the talks had reached an impasse. Newspapers gloomily headlined Japan's rejection of our proposals and predicted the talks would be broken off. However, on December 6, the only full day of peace the *Emmons* was ever to know as a commissioned ship, the headlines were more optimistic. It appeared that Japan was willing to soften her hard line. There was hope that a final break could be averted.

It was not to be. Even while the headlines hinted at accommodation, a Japanese carrier task force was steaming silently toward Hawaii. Just two days after the *Emmons* was commissioned, the Japanese struck Pearl Harbor on what President Roosevelt characterized as the "day of infamy." We were at war. Some crew members jokingly claimed the sneak attack on Pearl Harbor had been triggered by the news that this new destroyer was about to join the fleet. Undoubtedly, the Japanese intelligence network had advised the Imperial Navy of the new addition. It is a sure bet that it was noted as one more ship in the major buildup of American naval forces which had started in the early thirties and had accelerated with the outbreak of wars in Europe and Asia. The Japanese perceived this buildup as a threat to their goals in the Far East.

In the ensuing war, the *Emmons* served well and faithfully in two oceans and in many capacities. This is an account of her life and death, her missions and battles, her equipment, her crew who loved her, sometimes hated her, and kept her fighting until the end. From date of commissioning there were days on end of seemingly endless monotony, a few days of the tense anxiety of combat, a few moments of exhilarating triumph—one day of dark despair. In a broad sense, her career was a microcosm of the United States at war, representative of the application of the nation's best technological and industrial genius. In her career was also represented the country's ability to adapt, to change to meet new challenges. Above all, her crew represented the best of America's young manhood.

2.

The *Emmons* was built under the authority of the Naval Construction Act of March 27, 1934, the so-called Vinson-Trammell Act, as extended by the Naval Expansion Act of 1938. The latter became known as the Twenty Percent Expansion Bill.[1] The stated purpose of the Vinson-Trammell Act was to bring the Navy up to strength in underage ships as allowed by the Washington and London Naval Treaties. The expansion was to be accomplished in an orderly fashion over a period of seven or eight years. Another aim was to provide bargaining chips for a new disarmament conference scheduled for the end of 1936. Yet another

1. According to *American Fighting Ships,* vol. 1, p. 303, the *Emmons* was authorized March 27, 1934, date of Vinson-Trammell, but official data sheets in the Naval Historical Center files cite May 17, 1938, date of the Twenty Percent Expansion Bill.

important reason in the depression years of the thirties was to alleviate the unemployment situation in the idle shipyards on both coasts. The Naval Expansion Act of 1938 was passed under the urgent threats of war in both Europe and the Western Pacific.

The problem at the time of Vinson-Trammell was not so much the total number of ships as it was the age of those left over from World War I. While the other signatories of the Washington and London treaties had been replacing their overage ships with modern construction, the United States had failed to keep pace. There were projected shortages in all classes of ships except battleships. The shortage of modern destroyers was particularly acute. It was reported that as of November 1, 1933, only three of 351 existing destroyers were underage by treaty definitions. Those three would be overage by the time the London Treaty expired at the end of 1936. However, 33 were either under construction or in the planning stage. Some of these were being built under leftover World War I authorizations, others under the provisions of an executive order of 1933. The executive order allowed funds voted for the National Industrial Recovery Act to be used for the construction of naval vessels. By contrast, in 1933, the British Empire had 44 underage destroyers out of 160. Twenty-seven more were on the ways. Japan had 60 modern ones out of 102, with 26 more building. Figures for the French and Italians were similar, but those powers were not bound in destroyer tonnage by the London Treaty.

The arguments for and against the two naval expansion acts of 1934 and 1938 reveal a great deal about the economic and politico-diplomatic conditions of the period. The arguments changed little over the four years between the acts. Indeed, they have changed little over the last fifty years. One comparing the debates over defense expenditures in the 1930's and the 1980's cannot help being struck by the similarities. Only the potential enemies and the projected weapons systems have changed. In 1934, when the Vinson-Trammel Act was debated in Congress there was general agreement that Japan was the greatest threat to our peace. Many legislators fretted over our relations with Great Britain, more from fear that we were being used as a cat's paw by our cousins than from any thought of aggression from that source. The rise of Adolph Hitler and the Nazi Party in Germany was casually noted, but they were not then considered a threat to the United States, least of all a naval threat. Senators Borah and Nye and their isolationist colleagues attributed Hitler's rise to the greediness of French munitions manufacturers more concerned for profits than for the well-being of their country—characteristics they as readily attributed to U.S. shipbuilders and munitions manufacturers.

The debates in Congress had as much to do with economic and political questions as with the more direct issue of building the Navy to treaty strength. Differences on strategy and the position of the United States as a world power were also heatedly discussed. Strongest opposition to expansion came from a group of isolationists centered in the Rocky Mountain and Midwestern states who believed that a powerful navy was not necessary for our defense and could only lead to unwanted international involvement. Some even clung to the notion that the shield of two oceans was the only defense needed against external threats. They demanded to know if we had a clearly defined national policy, and if so, what it truly was. Were we planning for offense or defense? Would a first rate navy be more likely to promote peace or to involve us in other's quarrels? Against whom were we arming? Was not the build-up a plot of the munitions manufacturers, more intent on profits than defense? How much was enough? Were we spending money on over-kill? Was the United States preparing to take on the role of world policeman? If so, could we afford the cost?

The true isolationists were joined by senators and representatives who opposed expansion on economic grounds. Still others, under the influence of air power enthusiasts, claimed that we were putting our money on the wrong weapons system. They contended that aircraft had made naval ships obsolescent—money for defense would be more efficiently spent on other arms, preferably airborne. Some legislators simply questioned the monetary cost of a modern navy. Were we not in a period of inflation? Were not skyrocketing costs getting out of hand? Were not Navy Department estimates deliberately understated? Regardless of official estimates, what would be the ultimate cost—in today's jargon, what would be the overrun? In a period of depression, growing deficits, and rising interest rates, what would be the effect of the cost of modernization on the budget and taxes? In short, could the United States afford the cost of a modern navy?

For whatever reasons, the Vinson-Trammell Act became law March 27, 1934, and was expanded by the Twenty Percent Expansion Act on May 17, 1938. Under prodding by the Roosevelt administration, Congress had voted to authorize the modernization of the Navy. Many who had voted for the measures hoped that additional ships would never be necessary. As the world drifted into World War II, they were thankful the bills had been adopted.

3.

The *Emmons* was the sixty-ninth destroyer to be built under authorization of the acts discussed above. She was a 1630 tonner of the *Benson* class.[2] She and her sister ships were among the last to enjoy the niceties of relatively unhurried peacetime construction. Yet she benefited from the latest technological innovations emerging from the European war experience. Unlike later ships her superstructure was neatly faired and deck edges gracefully rounded to lessen resistance to wind and water. Her curved lines were aesthetically pleasing as well as efficient. Propulsion machinery and auxiliaries were virtually fitted by hand to insure reliability and precision. Later ships produced under wartime pressure had to forego such niceties to conserve precious time and manpower. By comparison their lines were boxy and awkward.

The contract to build DD457 was awarded to Bath Iron Works of Bath, Maine, June 12, 1940, at a cost of $4,898,000. As usual in such contracts, provision was made for certain bonuses for exceeding the specifications and penalties for failing to meet them. For example, a bonus was provided for bettering the specifications for fuel oil consumption at full power. Excess time in construction could be penalized. Delivery date for the ship was set at December 12, 1941, eighteen months from date of the contract.

Located on the banks of the Kennebec River, the contractor was favorably known throughout the naval service for the quality of its ships. Known as "The Cradle of Ships," Bath Iron Works was the successor to many smaller yards whose shipwrights had been turning out seaworthy vessels almost from the appearance of the first English settlements in America. Indeed, the first English vessel to be built in America was the pinnace *Victoria,* launched at the abortive fishing settlement of Fort Popham at the mouth of the Kennebec in 1607, long before the Pilgrims landed at Plymouth Rock. When sail gave way to steam, and steel replaced wood, the shipyards along the Kennebec made the changes in stride and continued to maintain their reputation as master shipbuilders.

Almost simultaneously with the organization of the Bath Iron Works in the 1880's the yard began construction of warships for the Navy. In 1893, the BIW-built gunboats *Machais* and *Castine* were commissioned. There followed rams, torpedo boats, a scout cruiser, and even one battleship, the *Georgia.* But the relatively shallow waters of the Kennebec did not provide enough margin of safety for the deep draft ships, and gradually the company concentrated on the destroy-

---

2. Official naval publications place *Emmons* in the *Benson* class of DDs. *Jane's Fighting Ships* lists her in the *Gleaves* class. The Bureau of Ships frequently lumped her with the *Bristol* class for changes in armament and military characteristics. There is little difference between them in general characteristics. Both *Gleaves* and *Bristol* were later variations of the *Benson* class. *Emmons* followed *Gleaves* in machinery characteristics and *Bristol in* armament.

ers which evolved from the torpedo boats developed after the Spanish-American War. During World War I, the Bath yard produced many of the famous "four pipers." When revitalization of the Navy was started in the thirties, the company played a leading role in the development and design of modern destroyers. In cooperation with other shipbuilders and designers, notably the marine design firm of Gibbs & Cox, Bath advanced new ideas and techniques. One of the most important innovations pushed was the use of high pressure, superheated steam. The keel of the *Gleaves,* utilizing this idea in its propulsion plant, was laid at Bath on May 16, 1938. She was delivered in June, 1940, the same month the contract for building the *Emmons* was signed. Every two or three months thereafter, Bath delivered destroyers of the same design to the Navy. The *Emmons* was the seventh of this series following *Niblick, Livermore, Eberle, Woolsey,* and *Ludlow. Macomb* was the eighth.

Throughout the Navy, and especially among destroyer sailors, it was considered good fortune to be assigned to a Bath built "boat." Quality and reliability were assured. The keel of the *Emmons* was laid November 14, 1940. A few weeks earlier on September 3, the keel of an identical twin, USS *Macomb* (DD458) had been laid on an adjacent building way. In spite of the head start the *Emmons* was commissioned nearly two months ahead of the *Macomb.*

While the *Emmons* and the *Macomb* were on the ways at Bath, seven other destroyers were in various stages of construction at other East Coast shipyards. Three were at Federal Shipbuilding and Dry Dock Company of Kearny, New Jersey; two at Boston Navy Yard; and two at the Charleston, South Carolina, Navy Yard. The seven were *Ellyson* (DD454), *Hambleton* (DD455), *Rodman* (DD456), *Forrest* (DD461), *Fitch* (DD462), *Corry* (DD463), and *Hobson* (DD464). They, with the *Emmons* and *Macomb,* would eventually comprise Destroyer Squadron 10. The keels of all nine ships were laid between September 3, 1940, and January 6, 1941, one every 14 days. All were commissioned within a span of 68 days between November 28, 1941, and February 3, 1942, one every seven days.

In Kearny, the building of the *Rodman* merits more than passing note. The *Emmons* and the *Rodman* became sister ships in more than design. After their shakedown cruises they were paired on nearly every patrol and in every action right up to April 6, 1945, when both, sharing the same picket station, were attacked by kamikazes. Men of the *Emmons* formed affection for the *Rodman* second to that for their own ship. As one former Emmonite said, "It seems that each time assignments were given out it was *Emmons* and *Rodman.* The crews of the two destroyers formed affection for each other similar to that between two brothers."

4.

DD457 was named for an eminent nineteenth century naval officer, Rear Admiral George Foster Emmons. As a lieutenant he served with the Wilkes expedition of 1838-1842 which explored the waters of Antartica and the South Pacific, then surveyed and charted the waters of the Pacific Coast of North America. When his ship, the *Peacock,* was wrecked on the bar at the entrance to the Columbia River, Lieutenant Emmons was given command of the land expedition which explored the little known coastal area from the Columbia to San Francisco Bay. Much of this area was then under Mexican jurisdiction, but was of vital interest to the expanding United States. The end of the Mexican War found him off the coast of California aboard the Pacific Squadron flagship, the *Ohio.* During the Civil War, as commanding officer of the *Hatteras,* he captured Cedar Keys, Florida, and Pass Christian, Mississippi, and took twenty prizes. In 1863, he was Captain of the Fleet under Admiral Dahlgren off Charleston. Back in the Pacific as commanding officer of the U.S. Steam Sloop *Ossipee,* he assisted in the formal takeover of Alaska from Russia in 1868. His last command was the Philadelphia Navy Yard. Before his death in 1884, he published *The Navy of the United States, 1775-1853.* A native of Clarendon, Vermont, he would have been pleased to know that a man-of-war bearing his name was built in a New England shipyard.

Frances Emmons Peacock, granddaughter of the admiral, was named sponsor of the ship. At 2 p.m. on a bright summer day, August 23, 1941, she broke a bottle of Great Western Champagne across the bow of DD457, christening it *Emmons* after her distinguished grandfather. As the traditional champagne splattered across the bow the hull came to life. Slowly at first, then with increasing eagerness, the *Emmons,* signal flags flying in the breeze, slid gracefully into the waters of the Kennebec. A crowd of more than 3,000 people, who lined the shores of the river and the Carlton Bridge overlooking the shipyard, let out a cheer as she plunged into the river. Attending tugs greeted her with prolonged whistle blasts as they took control and nudged her safely into the fitting-out berth. The *Emmons* had successfully completed the first step of her voyage to the sea.

Sharing the limelight with the sponsor at the christening ceremony were her brother Thornton Emmons, and her three children, Mary, Janet, and George Emmons, the last named for the admiral. Others in the launching party were

Governor Sumner Sewell of Maine, Archibald M. Main, vice-president of the Bath Iron Works, Commander Joseph M. Kiernan, USN, Supervisor of Shipbuilding at Bath, and one who perhaps had the greatest interest of all, the prospective commanding officer, Lieutenant Commander Thomas H. Temple-ton, USN. He had recently been ordered up from the Bureau of Ships to put the new ship in commission.

Scattered among the spectators at the launching were a number of officers and men who made up the advance guard of the commissioning and fitting-out detail. This detail, when fully assembled, would constitute a cadre around which the full complement would be formed. One of their duties was to assist the Supervisor of Shipbuilding and his technical experts in inspecting the ship and its equipment as it neared completion to insure that navy specifications were met. Their major job was to learn every detail of the ship from the keel up so that when it was turned over to the Navy they could assume its operation without a hitch. A bonus for them was a few months of relatively relaxed duty in pleasant surroundings without the stress and strain of responsibility in the operating forces at sea.

After the launching, the pace of work to complete and outfit the new ship was stepped up under the increasing threat of involvement in war in both the Atlantic and the Pacific. Only a few days before the christening, Roosevelt and Churchill had met off Newfoundland and jointly issued a statement of their goals in the Atlantic Charter. Tension with Japan over her aggressive actions in the Far East continued to escalate.

Although her gun mounts and other armament could not be installed at Bath, the *Emmons* became more and more recognizable as a destroyer. Engines and other equipment necessary for operations at sea were installed and tested by the Iron Works' shipwrights under the watchful eyes of the nucleus crew. As she neared completion, more officers and men were ordered to Bath to augment the commissioning and fitting-out crew. By the time she was ordered to Boston for final acceptance, twelve officers and forty men were attached.

One, however, was not to be permitted to carry out his original orders. Lieutenant Commander Templeton was detached as prospective commanding officer because under new directives of the Navy Department he had become too old for command of a destroyer. As the undeclared war in the Atlantic heated up, especially along the northern convoy routes, the navy brass decided that such rigorous duty should be left to younger, and presumably, more vigorous men. Although Tommy Templeton was only a year over the cut-off age of 41 for destroyer commanders, he was detached. His replacement was a Naval Academy classmate,

Lieutenant Commander Thomas C. Ragan, one of the youngest members of the class of 1924, comfortably under the new age limit, and fresh from duty on the staff of the Naval War College.

5.

Destroyers launched under the shipbuilding program of the 1930's represented the highest state of the art at that time. During the period following World War I, the scant appropriations available to the Navy went—quite reasonably considering the times of construction—into the design and building of major ships such as battleships, cruisers, and aircraft carriers. Submarines had a niche of their own. Smaller ships and support craft had to make do with the crumbs left over. Even so, naval planners were well aware of the need for fast, versatile escort vessels in the make-up of a well balanced fleet. They continually reviewed the anticipated tasks required of destroyers and the characteristics to best meet those requirements within the restricted tonnages allowed under the various disarmament treaties. Obviously, major compromises had to be made to provide maximum versatility. Besides the armament to be carried, speed, maximum endurance, and sea keeping ability under all conditions were central to the equation.

Long before Pearl Harbor, it was apparent that characteristics required for destroyer operations in the Atlantic would differ from those in the Pacific. While DesRon 10 was still under construction, it was decided to arm and equip the nine ships for Atlantic duty. Thus it was that the *Emmons* spent the first three years of her life operating against the Germans and Italians rather than the Japanese. This in spite of the dire need for destroyers in the Pacific. It was not until victory over the German Navy was assured, that she and her sister ships underwent the drastic and dramatic alteration to high speed minesweepers for service in the Pacific.

World War I had emphasized escort and antisubmarine capability. There had been very little ship-to-ship action—practically no antiaircraft action. As World War II approached, it became clear that antisubmarine operations would remain a major job. But the coming of age of aircraft weapons imposed a new and important defense capability on escort ships. Given the make-up of the German, Italian, and Japanese fleets, ship-to-ship action was always a possibility. Indeed, during World War II, many such actions occurred in all theaters. As the Allies gained the upper hand in both oceans, yet another task was found for destroyers, this was gunfire support for amphibious landings against shore targets. Under no circumstances, in peace or in war, was the need for maintenance of stability diminished.

The question of weight remained crucial, as more and heavier armament, brought on by the lessons of the war, was added. In some of the older destroyers it was necessary to add pig lead in their skegs and under their boilers. Fortunately, this was not necessary on the *Emmons,* but weight control was a continuing problem as changes were made to accommodate newer, more efficient—and heavier—anti-aircraft guns and electronic equipment.

How were these diverse requirements met in the *Emmons?* Her vital statistics were: 1,630 tons standard displacement—2,200 full load; length, 348' 2"; beam, 36' 1"; maximum draft, 15' 8"; designed speed, 37.5 knots. It was intended that she would be manned by a complement of nine officers and 199 enlisted men. Living quarters were originally designed to accommodate that number in relative luxury for a destroyer. However, under wartime service there would always be more men aboard than the planned complement.

Originally, the *Emmons* and her sister ships were designed to carry five 5"/38 dual purpose guns for use against both surface and aircraft targets, five 21" torpedoes carried in a quintuple mount plus four reserve torpedoes in ready storage, six .50 caliber machine guns, and two depth charge tracks on the fantail from which 600 pound, barrel-shaped depth charges could be dropped over the stern. Such was the planned armament, but, as the British experiences of the early war years were accumulated and digested, it became apparent to the General Board that it was necessary to increase the flexibility of antiaircraft defense over that provided by the relatively slow 5" guns. This was done by the addition of heavier machine guns capable of picking up attacking aircraft more quickly and of maintaining fire down to zero range. Further, as the German submarine offensive gained strength, it was obvious that the depth charge counterattacks could be made far more effective if the size of the pattern could be increased over that produced by stern drops alone.

Accordingly, early in 1941 directives were issued to change the armament of the *Bristols,* a later variation of the *Bensons,* by replacing the third 5"/38 gun with either four 1.1 inch or an equal number of 40mm machine guns. The latter, the Swedish designed Bofors, had proved highly effective for the British and were favored over the home designed 1.1's, but were in short supply in 1941. The original .50 caliber light machine guns were to be replaced with the more effective and reliable 20mms, patented by the Oerlikon Company of Switzerland. Antisubmarine capability was to be improved by the installation of a "Y" gun amidships on the fantail. This utilized projectile charges to throw 300 pound depth charges to either side of the ship outboard of the pattern made by the stern drops. In the aggregate, the new weapons, associated ammunition, and fire control systems would exceed the weight of the 5" gun removed. To compensate for the extra weight, the four spare torpedoes were to be removed and the superstructure redesigned to lower the center of gravity.

In March, 1941, the above changes were extended to all destroyers of the *Benson-Livermore* classes still under construction. The *Emmons* and *Macomb* at Bath Iron Works were specifically included in the order, but with the stipulation that their delivery was not to be delayed to make the changes. By then virtually all of the work on foundations and magazines had been completed for the *Emmons,* but Bath agreed to do as much as possible to make the shift, subject to availability of the new machine guns, and with the further proviso that any uncompleted installations would be done at the Boston Navy Yard as government responsibility.

Throughout the spring and summer a series of conferences was held to establish the final armament and to pin down the responsibility for accomplishing the transition. The "ultimate" armament decreed for the class was four 5"/38 DP guns, five torpedoes, two twin 40mm mounts with associated directors, four 20mm machine guns—two in the waist and two forward of the bridge superstructure, two depth charge racks on the stern, relocated outboard and lengthened to hold fourteen additional 600 pound depth charges, and a "Y" gun amidships aft with racks for ten 300 pound depth charges.

As for the *Emmons,* at the time of her preliminary acceptance trials, no armament was in place other than the torpedo tubes and the "Y" gun because the guns and equipment to be supplied by the Navy had not yet been delivered. However, the structural work necessary for placement of the guns had been completed. The installations were made at Boston after acceptance by the Navy. Since, as mentioned before, the Bofors guns were in very short supply during the *Emmons'* fitting out period; one quadruple 1.1 was mounted to starboard in the space intended for a twin Bofors. After the shakedown cruise, a single 20mm machine gun was mounted to port in the other space designed to take a twin Bofors. These were only interim measures. Eventually, two twin Bofors were installed as planned. The Oerlikons were eventually increased to a total of seven. Following the shakedown cruise the "Y gun was replaced by six "K" guns placed along the deck edges to port and starboard.

The engineering plant occupied four water tight spaces comprising two engine rooms and two fire rooms. The plant was capable of generating 50,000 horsepower at full power. Four Babcock and Wilcox boilers, two in each fire room, delivered steam at 600 pounds pressure, superheated to 825°F, to two Westinghouse geared turbines. Each turbine drove one of the two propeller shafts. For maximum efficiency, the plant was designed to operate on various combinations of boilers and engines, but under wartime conditions was usually "split" so that one fire room and one engine room operated as a single, independent unit. Thus, if one space were damaged there was a possibility of maintaining power in the remainder. At full power the plant could drive the ship at 37.5 knots or better.

Each engine room held a 200 KW steam generator which powered a countless number of electrically driven appliances and pieces of machinery from coffee pots to gun mounts. Miles of electrical wiring girdled the ship from stem to stern. These vital circuits could be compared to the nervous system of the human body—if the nerves are severed, essential functions stop. However, in the electrical system of a ship alternate circuits are provided to continue operations. There was even a diesel generator to provide standby power if the regular generators were put out of action. Indeed, the entire installation was designed to keep as much of the vital equipment as possible working as long as a single source of power remained. The last resort was good, old-fashioned man power.

So much for the physical characteristics. No matter how good a ship's equipment is, or how artfully put together, it is useless without competent men to run it. In that area the *Emmons* was not lacking. It was her crew which made her more than just another well-built "tin can."

6.

Most of the twelve officers had been ordered to Bath during the summer and autumn of 1941 as part of the commissioning and fitting out detail. A few had been shunted into special training courses to learn the latest about the operation of the new gunnery and electronic installations. Half of the twelve were career officers, graduates of the Naval Academy, or the "trade school," as it was dubbed by reservists throughout the service. The officers included the captain, Lieutenant Commander Thomas C. Ragan, 37 years old, class of 1924. Fresh from an assignment at the Naval War College, he was reported to be the youngest member of his class to be given command of a destroyer. The next senior officer, the executive officer, Lieutenant Harold M. Heming, 35, class of 1930, had been shanghaied from the destroyer *Stack,* which he had helped commission in 1939. Two lieutenants, Annapolis classmates of the class of 1932, were ordered as gunnery and engineer officers. The remaining two career officers were recent graduates of the Academy. Alongside the career officers were six naval reserve officers, all young ensigns commissioned from the Naval Reserve Officers Training Corps units of leading eastern universities.

These twelve officers would see the *Emmons* through the opening months of the war. It was they who, with the leading petty officers, were responsible for the organization and training of the new ship. All were young, well within the age limits prescribed by the Bureau of Navigation for destroyer duty. It was expected that in accordance with BuNav policy the older, more experienced officers and petty officers would be transferred to new construction or other duty as soon as the ship was "shaken down." Therefore, a conscientious program for training replacements within the ship was adopted. As the process of promotion upward and outward created vacancies in the organization, they normally were filled by promotion from below. Thus, each of the first three commanding officers was succeeded by his executive officer. Probably more by chance than by design, the *Emmons'* commanding officers were usually junior to the other COs of DesRon 10, which may have had a great deal to do with the assignments she drew.

As the war progressed, a steady input of new officers gradually replaced most of the plank owners. By the day of final reckoning off Okinawa in 1945, only one of the first twelve officers was left on board. He was the fourth commanding officer, Lieutenant Commander Eugene N. Foss, 2nd, USNR, class of 1934 at Harvard. He had reported aboard at Bath in the summer of 1941 as Ensign Foss. All of the eighteen officers under his command at Okinawa, except one, were naval reservists.

Of the 206 enlisted plank owners aboard, 166 were regular and 40 were reserves. This proportion of regulars to reserves was much higher than in the officer category. As with the officers, the war caused rapid and drastic changes in the crew. At Okinawa, only thirty-two of the plank owners remained on board, and the regulars were outnumbered 180 to 55.

The veteran petty officers of the commissioning crew had been carefully selected on their records for new construction. Not only would they be charged with the upkeep and operation of machinery and equipment entrusted to their care, but they also were responsible for the training and indoctrination of the newly assembled crew in the Navy way. These included personal cleanliness, discipline, responsibility, a sense of integrity, and living in peace with their shipmates in crowded quarters.

The *Emmons* was lucky that her commissioning crew was selected and assembled before war sped up and diluted the process. She had a few months of relative stability before having to cope with the loss of key officers and petty officers. She made good use of that time.

Forty of the senior petty officers on the original roster had been ordered to Bath as part of the commissioning and fitting out detail. They were seasoned chiefs, first and second class, with a wealth of experience in their specialties throughout the fleet. Of equal importance, they had demonstrated superiority in administrative and leadership ability. Most had served aboard destroyers. At Bath their duties were mostly technical. Their foremost job was to familiarize themselves with the complicated machinery and equipment which would be their responsibility once the ship was on its own. They were required to master the details of the installations, their capabilities and limitations, upkeep, and operation. A secondary task was to assist the supervisor of shipbuilding in inspections to insure that all material met naval specifications.

Another important function was to help prepare Watch, Quarter, and Station Bills under the supervision of the executive officer. Thus, long before the ship was commissioned and taken to sea; she was organized—at least on paper. In port and underway watch bills assigned each man of the crew a duty section and a watch station. A general quarter's bill assigned every man a battle station. The ship lacked only warm bodies with names and ratings.

Most of the precommissioning detail was engineers for the simple reason that the engineering plant would necessarily be the first part of the ship to come into use. As a nucleus of the engineering department their duties were to learn every detail of the propulsion plant and its operation under all possible conditions. Soon dubbed "Billingsley's Bilge Divers" after the engineer officer, they spent days crawling through the bilges or swinging from overhead pipes and fittings, tracing out the vital steam, oil, and water lines. They literally memorized the location and markings, even the feel, of hundreds of valves and gauges. When not bilge diving they pored over instruction manuals. By the time of commissioning they could go into unlighted engineering spaces and bring the plant alive by feel alone. The electrician's mates memorized the location and markings of miles of electrical cables from stem to stern, from the generators to the anchor windlass in the bow, to the steering engine in the stern.

Of equal importance during the building period were petty officers from other departments. A chief yeoman was responsible for the never-ending mass of paper work. A chief boatswain's mate was concerned for the ship's boats, the anchor gear, towing gear, rigging, and related lines and equipment. He also had the thankless job of logging in and accounting for the hundreds of pieces of "title B" gear, the portable gear not permanently attached to the hull, such as fire extinguishers, life rafts, whale boats, and tools. Although the guns, torpedoes, and most of the fire control instruments were not put aboard until after commissioning, keeping tabs on the basic structural and electrical installations fell to a chief fire controlman. Similarly, basic communication equipment and preparation for future installations fell to radiomen and a signalman. A boilermaker, a metal smith, and a ship fitter augmented the engineers. A chief pharmacist, inevitably called "Doc" by his peers, rounded out the Bath contingent. Besides monitoring the tiny sick bay, Doc looked after the health of the crew, administering first aid, doling out aspirin, and arranging for transfer to local or naval hospitals the more serious cases of illness.

While the *Emmons* was being readied for sea at Bath, a much larger group of experienced hands was being assembled at the Boston Receiving Station. The men waiting at Boston consisted of a wide variety of petty officers whose expertise could not be efficiently used until the ship was commissioned and in operation—additional gunner's mates, firecontrolmen, radiomen, torpedo men, and signalmen, plus sonarmen, coxswains, quartermasters, cooks, and bakers. These were the men needed to flesh out the blank spaces on the Watch, Quarter, and Station Bills. They came from all over the fleet, but most had served in destroyers of the Atlantic Fleet. A few had experienced the rigors of North Atlantic convoy duty in the undeclared war. The petty officers of this group were augmented by seamen and firemen who for one reason or another had not yet been advanced to petty officer ratings. Many of them had completed their first enlistment, gone on re-enlistment leave, and were available when the *Emmons'* slate was being filled. A very few, unfortunately, were available for reassignment only because they were stragglers or had gotten into disciplinary trouble on their former ships. It was an old navy game to pass along the "problems" when a call came for a new draft.

Many of the petty officers waiting at Boston had recently been promoted and found themselves in excess of the rating structure of their ships. Others were fresh graduates of the Navy's technical schools scattered along the coast. Some had reenlisted under the inducement of special training which would virtually assure promotion. A few, attuned to the relaxed informality of destroyer life, had shipped over expressly for duty in new destroyers. All at Boston eagerly awaited the arrival of their new home where they would have permanent quarters and steady assignments. They were thoroughly tired of shore patrol, cleaning details, working parties, and the many "make-do" jobs typical of a receiving station. On one working party to the navy yard, members of the gunner's gang recall seeing the gun mounts destined for the *Emmons* waiting, like them, for their ship to come in. An early winter storm had left a pristine blanket of snow on each mount. Although they appreciated the artistic beauty of the scene, the gunners were more concerned with what damage the elements might be doing to their future charges. To them the mounts in their too-thin coats of red lead seemed forlorn and neglected, almost naked, exposed to the weather. They yearned to get at them to give them the care they needed.

Perhaps the most interested, and the most apprehensive, group of the commissioning crew consisted of seventy-six recruits of Companies 58 and 60 from the Newport Naval Training Station. Company 60 had distinguished itself by winning Gold Star Hall of Fame Honors for excellence in all phases of competition with other companies in training. Company 58 was not far behind. Almost to a man, the apprentice seamen of the two companies had volunteered in the last weeks of September. After an accelerated training period at boot camp, they found themselves assigned to the *Emmons.* Obviously, the detail officer simply tore out contiguous pages from the training center rolls to fill out the detail for DD457. In the first day's log they are neatly alphabetized from Aksamit, Joseph J., 646 08 72, V-6, AS, USNR, to Young, Harold, 646 08 90, V-6,AS, USNR. They appeared to be as alike as their sailor hats, but beneath the thin veneer of training they were as diverse as the high school population of the United States in the year 1941. For most of them were just out of high school or in the last two years when they enlisted. They were incredibly young, 17, 18, and 19 years of age, with an occasional "old" man of 20 or 21. Only one or two were married, and only a few had started college. Most had never left their place of birth. All but a few came from New York, New Jersey, Pennsylvania, and the New England states. In this respect they had a common background, if the differences between rural and urban upbringing are discounted. Some were products of farms and small towns, but there was a large contingent of youths from urban Philadelphia, New York, Brooklyn, and Boston. Almost without exception, they had enlisted under the drive of patriotism helped along by the urge for adventure. A few, mainly the more mature, confessed they needed a steady job or felt the breath of the new draft on their necks. Some had joined the Navy to avoid being drafted into the Army. Others became sailors because their fathers and uncles had served at sea. Still others signed up under the spell of romantic sea stories spun by friends on leave. Among the boots at the commissioning, naval reservists were a minority, largely because few knew or cared about the various options for service open to them at the time of their enlistment.

7.

For the officers and men at Bath, the summer and fall of 1941 was a busy one and a happy one, the last such relaxed time many of them would enjoy. They were performing a useful and necessary service, but for a time was without the stress of operational responsibility they would find at sea. They became part of the ship which they would eventually have to take to sea. It was only natural that they formed a deep affection for the destroyer taking shape under their eyes.

Most of them were married and brought their families to Bath for a short stay, sometimes at a considerable financial sacrifice. The extra allowance for housing and food did not begin to cover the additional expenses. Decent short term rentals were hard to find during the summer season, and many which were available had to be surrendered when schools reopened in the fall. Some families had to move several times before the *Emmons* left Bath in December. Many could not find quarters with cooking facilities and were obliged to feed themselves and their families in the restaurants and boarding houses of the town. Food was not too costly in 1941, but neither was Navy pay very great. One saving grace was that the New England fare was excellent. Some families found relatively inexpensive housing in the old farmhouses of the countryside or the cottages of outlying towns. Once they got used to commuting over rural roads they found living in the country delightful—that is, until winter set in. As usual, the burden of house hunting and domestic arrangements fell on the shoulders of the wives.

The single crewmen fared somewhat better as far as finding living quarters was concerned. There were a number of small, inexpensive hotels in the downtown area and some boarding houses near the shipyard. Some found adequate rooms for as little as nine dollars a week. The hotels were near a number of good restaurants and small bars. The latter provided such limited night life as the town offered. One restaurant in particular became a hangout for the *Emmons'* crew. Besides its food, it featured slot machines in a back room behind the kitchen. Some joined church groups and participated in their social affairs.

Slot machines and church socials notwithstanding, the fact remains that there was little for unattached men to do after the sun went down. On weekends, many of them made the short drive down the coast to Portland. Some traveled as far as Boston and New York. The sportsmen found plenty to keep them occupied in the "sportsman's paradise" along the coast and streams. In November, several of the leading petty officers were instrumental in getting a recreational program established with the help of the city fathers and the USO. The three senior chief petty officers and one of the junior ensigns were appointed to the committee which got the program underway at the local YMCA.

Whatever the financial cost or inconvenience may have been to the small group of commissioning and fitting out detail and their families, it was well worth while. The families knew that once the ship was ready for sea there would be little time together. The single men realized that opportunities for liberty and leave would be rare. So, they made the most of the few months together during the New England summer and fall. One of the most pleasant experiences was getting acquainted with shipmates and their families. Under the common bond of service aboard the building destroyer, lifetime friendships were formed. Those still living count the days at Bath among the happiest of their lives.

There were many great parties which brought the crew together. The biggest and most memorable was the "Grand Ball" held for Tommy Templeton on his detachment. In keeping with tradition the grand march was led by the senior petty officer and the skipper, each escorting the wife of the other around the ballroom. But most of the get-togethers were informal and took advantage of local attractions. A bowling league met weekly at a local bowling alley for beer and skittles. Boating and picnicking along the coast offered good weekend fun for small groups, as did touring the historic areas surrounding Bath. Fishing was always popular. So was eating at the good seafood restaurants in town and along the shore. As the days shortened, the time-honored New England clam bakes offered a chance for groups to get together.

Suddenly, it was summer no longer. Foul weather gear became the order of the day. Wood heaters were lighted off. The hunters took to the ponds and woods in search of fowl and game. What they bagged was generously shared with their friends. The first snow fell in November, and the families began to drift down to Boston to try to find temporary housing for the next phase in the *Emmons* story.

As the seasons changed so did the *Emmons.* Her bridge, superstructures and hull fittings were completed. Machinery spaces no longer were yawning cavities. Electric cables were connected to the equipment to be driven. Portable equipment was brought on board and stored. No classified communication gear became operable. Galley equipment was cleaned and tested. Living quarters were given their final coats of paint and readied for occupancy.

8.

On a cold, blustery day early in November, after careful dockside tests, lines were cast off and the *Emmons* dropped down the Kennebec under her own power to conduct builder's trials at sea. It was her first taste of the open sea and it was good. One by one, the exacting tests were chalked off. Cautiously, but with no strain, she worked up to full power for the last of the trials. Unfortunately, after an hour and a half at full power, a lubricating oil failure to the port engine forced discontinuance of the trials, and the ship had to return to Bath on one engine for assessment of any possible damage. Gloom was the mood of the day.

Damage proved to be not as serious as it could have been. The turbines were opened and wiped bearings refitted without too much delay. But the preliminary acceptance trials, with the Naval Board of Inspection and Survey observing and recording data, had to be postponed to meet the busy schedule of the Board. The rescheduled trials with the Board of Inspection and Survey in attendance were held off the mouth of the Kennebec on November 26. They were entirely successful. In his report to the Chief of Naval Operations the President of the Board noted that at the time of the trials none of the armament of the *Emmons* was on board except the torpedo tubes and the "Y" gun, because the guns to be supplied by the Navy had not been delivered. He added, however, that the necessary hull work in connection with the extensive armament changes ordered was virtually completed. It was noted that the ship was to be delivered well within the contract time and could take her place as an effective fighting unit of the fleet much sooner than would otherwise have been the case. The Board characterized the workmanship as being of "excellent character throughout," conforming to the "high standard customary" with the builder, the Bath Iron Works.

Following the acceptance trials, the destroyer returned to Bath, where she received her final touchup painting and a thorough cleaning preparatory to delivery. When she sailed, everything was immaculate, even the passageway decks were covered with heavy butcher's paper to prevent soiled shoes from marring their glossy surfaces. On December 3, she left the Kennebec forever on the short voyage to Boston Navy Yard where she was scheduled to get the final acceptance inspection.

The voyage to Boston was uneventful so far as performance of materiel went. Although the ship was the responsibility of the builders until finally accepted, many of the officers and men of the commissioning and fitting out crew went along as passengers. Indeed, the engineering ratings helped the Bath civilians man the propulsion plant, while others stood by the stations which would be their eventual responsibility. Some of the Iron Works officials also went along to negotiate the acceptance terms with the Navy. The story is told that one of the young naval ensigns, zealous for the pristine condition of his future home, spotted one of the civilian passengers nonchalantly leaning back in his chair with his feet propped up on the wardroom table. He officiously ordered the civilian to take his feet off the table. Unperturbed, the offender casually replied, "Son, I own this ship." In a sense he was correct, for until the Navy accepted delivery the ship remained the responsibility of the builder. The civilian was the president of Bath Iron Works, W. S. Newell.

After final inspections at Boston, the DD457 was transferred to the United States on December 5, 1941. The Commandant of the Navy Yard sent the following mailgram to the Chief of Naval Operations on that date:

> EMMONS ACCEPTED AT 0930 EST TODAY X PLACED IN FULL COMMISSION AT 1045 EST THIS DATE WITH LIEUTENANT COMMANDER RAGAN ASSUMING COMMAND

The *Emmons'* active career had begun.

2

Commissioning and Fitting Out

o o o o o o o o o o o o o o o o o o o o o o o o o o o o o o

0630 Stationed special sea detail. 0659 Underway from Pier No. 9, Navy Yard, Boston, Mass.... 1635 Exercised at general quarters. 1650 darkened ship. 1655 Entered international waters. 1717 secured from general quarters....

—***Emmons*** *Log, 22 January 1942*

Saturday, December 6, 1941 was the last full day of peace the *Emmons* was ever to know after the commission pennant was hoisted. For on Sunday, the 7th, the Japanese struck Pearl Harbor.

Following Saturday morning inspection, the liberty party, expecting a normal weekend, left the ship. They scattered throughout New England, visiting family and friends, or staying in Boston to enjoy the sights and pleasures the city offered a sailor on leave. The watch section aboard ship expected nothing more exciting than receipt of a few perishable provisions. On Sunday morning holiday routine was followed. Late reveille allowed a few extra minutes of sleep before the duty section turned out to make up bedding and clean down the decks. Some of the newer members were unable to take advantage of the opportunity—not yet used to the narrow bunks and thin mattresses, they were up and about early. After breakfast, the usual church parties were sent to services of their choice in the yard. Following the on meal off duty personnel settled down to a relaxed Sunday afternoon. Many planned a little extra sack time undisturbed by the noise and grime of navy yard activities. Others tried to catch up on their correspondence with family and girl friends. A few even planned to study.

The relaxed holiday routine was shattered by news of the sneak attack on Pearl Harbor. Mess cooks were still cleaning up after the noon meal when the usual Sunday afternoon radio programs were interrupted to carry the President's announcement of the Japanese assault. Some thought it a hoax, but all too soon the event was confirmed by official dispatches from the communication guard ship. The duty officer had the word passed over the ship's intercom system. The news came more slowly to the ship's company scattered throughout New England on weekend passes, but it didn't take long for the word to get around. Newspaper extras soon appeared on the streets of Boston. Movie houses and amusement centers broke into their programs to repeat the President's announcement of the attack. Total strangers stopped passersby to spread the word.

Captain Ragan happened to be on board that afternoon catching up on paper work. Two days after being commissioned, the ship was virtually without means to defend it. With engines disabled and without guns or ammunition on board, there was little the skipper could do except to order additional sentries posted and to instruct the watch section to take extra precautions against sabotage.

That Sunday, the executive officer, Hal Heming, and his wife Wanda, were guests of Eugene and Winifred Foss at their home in Brookline. They had hardly finished luncheon when the President's message came over the air. There were no details on damage or casualties at Pearl, or on the situation in the remainder of the islands. The Hemings' normal concerns were greatly heightened by fear for the safety of Wanda Heming's family living at Waikiki Beach. Her father was Captain William C. Colbert, senior supply officer on the *Nevada* at Pearl Harbor, and her sister was a coding secretary at the Office of Naval Intelligence in Honolulu. Efforts to reach Hawaii by telephone were futile, so the exec shifted into uniform and reported to his ship not knowing whether his wife's family was safe or not. Happily, their anxiety was relieved later in the day by cables from Honolulu announcing that all were safe.

The engineer officer and his wife had taken advantage of a brilliant autumn day to visit Bunker Hill Monument. Back at ground level after the long climb to the top of the monument, they were greeted by the shrill cries of newsboys hawking extras about the attack.

Many men on weekend liberty struggled with the problem of whether to break off their activities and rush back to the ship or not. Some hastily shifted from civvies to uniform and reported back, only to find that there was little they could do given the state of readiness of the *Emmons* at that point. Seaman Anthony Esposito, on a weekend pass in Peekskill, New York, records that he thought, "Oh, my God, I have to return back to my ship," but adds "then I remembered we didn't have any guns on board. I spent the rest of my weekend at home. I returned to the ship next day and was ready to go to war." Apprentice

Seaman Anthony Siragusa was on a train returning to Boston from overnight liberty to his home in Lawrence, Massachusetts when he got the word.

Reaction aboard was varied. Only a few were really surprised. Most regular navy men following the events of 1941 had expected that sooner or later the United States would be directly involved in the European war. Many veterans were aware of the dangerous situation in the Pacific, although the undeclared war in the Atlantic had served to divert attention from the deteriorating conditions in the West. There were plenty of indications of impending trouble in the accounts of the American-Japanese negotiations. Nevertheless, it was a distinct shock, even to those most aware of the probabilities for war, when the probability became a certainty. The real surprise was the nature of the attack, the chosen target, and the sobering knowledge that the attack had been overwhelmingly successful.

The news had an immediate and personal impact on some. Seaman First Class Louis E. Lakin, who had just been transferred from the *Oklahoma,* recalls his concern for old friends on the battleship at Pearl Harbor. And well he might have had worries; the "Okie" was capsized in the attack. Similarly, First Class Gunner's Mate Richard K. Bransom remembers that his first thoughts were for the safety of many old friends on duty aboard ships at Pearl. Robert R. Reid, then fireman first class, was more immediately affected. He had been advised of the death of his father on Saturday and was making preparations to go home on leave. His leave was cancelled because of the attack. He recalls that he "was ready to fight and kill Japs." And so it went. Whether they realized it or not the lives of everyone on the *Emmons* were drastically altered that Sunday in December. One thing was perfectly clear to every officer and man as he pondered the accounts of the disaster at Pearl: one phase of their naval careers had come to an end. A more demanding one for themselves and their ship had begun.

2.

Considering that the *Emmons* was virtually unarmed, there was relatively little immediate change in life aboard ship. Most of the immediate changes involved increases in security measures. The executive officer found that the Watch, Quarter and Station Bill had to be revised to meet the new situation. Watch sections were beefed up, liberty was a little more precious, and inspections were more rigorous. Right after the attack, the gangway watch was armed with a .45 caliber revolver and armed guards were stationed in the bow and at the stern. Every person coming on board was carefully checked, not even yard workmen were allowed on board without proper identification tags. Anti-sabotage measures, including regular checks on the dockside garbage containers, were taken. There was fear of some sort of underwater attack, but this problem was left largely up to the yard security forces. Censorship of outgoing mail was instituted. From a practical viewpoint, there was little that could be done to defend against a direct attack until the guns were mounted and some ammunition stored aboard. Frequent drills were held to familiarize the crew with their battle stations. Indeed, the duty section had been called to general quarters on Pearl Harbor day, more as a morale gesture than otherwise. Thomas J. Sheppard recounts that when general quarters was sounded that Sunday, he was ordered by the petty officer in charge of his station to report to his assigned gun mount, No. 1, and to remain there until secured. This in spite of the fact that No. 1 mount was then nothing more than an open hole in the forecastle deck. Seaman Lakin, the former *Oklahoma* sailor, quotes one of his officers as saying that if the ship should be attacked by aircraft "we would have to throw potatoes at them as the magazines are empty."

Pearl Harbor served to step up the process of equipping and readying the ship for sea. There was a new sense of purpose among all ranks and ratings. Nor was the sense of urgency confined to naval personnel. Shipyard workers seemed to be just as anxious as the sailors to get the ship finished and to sea in the best condition possible in the shortest time. Among other things, the installation of the guns was stepped up. As the machine guns and 5" mounts became operable, general quarters drills became more realistic to the new crew. When it was considered that the 20mms could actually be fired with some degree of safety, a limited amount of ammunition was brought aboard and the *Emmons* became part of the antiaircraft defenses of Boston, albeit an untested part. Ammunition for the 5" guns was not put on board until the ship was fully ready for sea. From time to time a nervous Defense Command for the area would sound a real air raid warning. At such times the machine guns would be cast loose, ammunition broken out, and all preparations made for actual firing. At the same time, the main battery would be manned and prepared for dry runs on any targets sighted. Of course, all yard work would cease and the civilian workers left the ship for makeshift air raid shelters ashore. The air raid warnings were rare. Fortunately, all proved false. Aside from the interruption of yard work, the alarms proved to be an excellent tonic for keeping the ship's company alert and aware of their ultimate purpose.

The five week fitting out period was one of the busiest and most hectic of *Emmons*'s career. Gradually, everything began to fall into place—guns, communication equipment, navigation gear—the hundred and one things which transformed a stripped down hull into a first class fighting machine. With a few exceptions, she left the navy yard with all equipment intended for destroyers of her class. One cosmetic change from original specifications drastically changed her outward appearance. The neat battleship gray paint so carefully applied at Bath had been replaced by a jigsaw camouflage pattern of angular blacks and grays designed to confuse any enemy trying to estimate her course and speed.

3.

There was more than material change. The frequent drills, were vital for a new ship and crew, now took on a new meaning. From the captain on down, there was now involved more than the usual desire to excel. What had been routine now might mean the difference between survival and death in a showdown with the enemy. Gunner's mates and fire controlmen watched the installation and alignment of the guns with an increased sense of personal stake. Loading drill at the dummy loading machine became the subject of intense rivalry between crews of the 5" guns. Considerable money changed hands on bets between the four crews. Number 2 gun usually retained the lead but was never sure of keeping it.

A similar spirit prevailed in other departments. Quite a bit of competition developed among the seamen to get assigned to the communication division. Not only was advancement assumed to be quicker and more certain, but the watch stations, except for the signalmen, were in relatively comfortable compartments. Communications watch stations were also near the "nerve centers" of the ship—men in those billets prided themselves on knowing "the score." Assignment to sonar and radar billets attracted the scientifically minded. At first the sonar gang had the advantage as the *Emmons* left Bath with its underwater sound gear virtually completed. Not so with the radar equipment. At that time, radar was just beginning to be put aboard all fleet ships, but there simply weren't enough sets to go around. DD457 was originally scheduled to get one of the late SC-2 air search radars, but it was shunted to some other vessel. The ungainly "bedspring" antenna was in place on the foremast on departure from Boston, but was hooked up to a more primitive set. She did not get a modern set until after the shakedown cruise.

There was almost as much competition to get assigned to the engineers as to the communication division. The almost universal fascination of American males with machinery was an important factor. The fact that watch and work stations were not exposed to the weather was another consideration. Not to be caught lagging in preparation for wartime service, the engineers and damage control parties held frequent casualty drills simulating various types of damage and failures, including loss of electrical power to vital equipment. Damage control was no longer a stepchild. Realistic training was handicapped because steam and electricity were not actually generated by the ship's plant, but came from the shipyard. Nearly all drills had to depend on "play acting" under the watchful eyes of senior petty officers. Whenever yard work would permit, the plant would actually be lighted off and secured under various conditions of assumed readiness.

Full use was made of the highly specialized training facilities ashore. Promising candidates were marked and sent to the extended technical schools such as the Sonar School at Key West or the gunnery schools at Norfolk. Local facilities at Boston were utilized for training in antiaircraft defense, submarine attacks, damage control, and fire fighting. In the fire fighting field, the ship was lucky to have an expert on board. Before reporting to the East Coast, Chief Boatswain's Mate Charles J. Clark had taken part in experiments at San Diego in the use of the fog nozzle developed to fight oil and gasoline fires aboard carriers. He also worked with the Boston Fire Department on the use of this device for several weeks before reporting to the *Emrnons.* Many of the special training facilities featured sophisticated mock-ups to make the drills as realistic as possible without the actual use of live ammunition or depth charges. Some made use of advanced electronic devices, somewhat akin to the video games of today, but more attuned to realities of the earthly combat of 1941.

Under the spur of war the process of readying the new destroyer neared an end. In the meantime, the new crew was coming together as a team. The newness too many of living in crowded quarters aboard wore off. Landlubbers learned to live out of foot lockers and sea bags and still keep themselves and their belongings neat and clean. They could sleep in narrow bunks with only a few inches to spare in any direction and still face reveille ready for a full day of housekeeping chores and drills.

At the end of a hard day's work, they would go ashore singly, or in groups, to explore Boston and its attractions, and then back to the ship to start the routine all over again. Of greatest importance, they began to know one another. Lifelong friendships were cemented. Lifelong habits were formed. The *Emmons* had become a second home.

Promotion was rapid. Before the ship left Boston, plank owning apprentice seamen had become seamen second class or firemen third. Many had chosen a route which would lead to a petty officer's rating within a very few months. From time to time a new draft would come aboard from the training station or from the naval schools. A few men, usually in the ratings requiring extensive technical training, would be ordered to other ships or stations. But for the most part the crew remained stable during this period. The total on board increased slowly. By the time the shakedown cruise started, 246 souls were on board, all anxious to get on with the business at hand.

The galley became one of the most important centers of the ship. It was the first area to show signs of life early in the morning before the crew hit the deck. Long before reveille, the sounds and smells originating in the galley would let the morning watch know that their four hour stint was almost over. A few early risers would congregate around the galley hatches looking for a handout. Food was plentiful, if not always prepared the way "mom" would have done it. The galley crew did a good job catering to the appetites of more than 200 hungry men from so many different social and ethnic backgrounds. Complaints were relatively few. When they did come, they were concerned with the preparation and serving rather than the basic quality of the food. For the meat and produce supplied under government contract in the United States was of top quality. Fresh milk, bread, and vegetables were delivered dockside nearly every day. There was never any complaint about quantity. Excerpts from the *Emmons'* log for Friday 26 December indicate the type of fare the crew could anticipate in the closing days of 1941 and the early days of 1942.

> 0930 Received following stores for the general mess, inspected as to quantity by Ens. E. W. Trudeau, USNR, and as to quality by Finch, E. L., CPhM. USN; from General Baking Co.: 250 lbs. white bread. 0950...from G. Slobodkin and Co.: 220 lbs. veal saddles, 336 lbs. beef rumps, 496 lbs. beef chucks, 221 lbs. chicken roast, 109 lbs. beef rib, 125 lbs. beef loin. 1100...from Kellogg Sales Co.: 31 lbs. Rice Crisp, 31 lbs. Rice Flakes, 31 lbs. Wheat Bran, 15 lbs. Puffed Wheat.

The situation became somewhat different at sea and in foreign ports. After a few days at sea fresh produce began to run out. After a few weeks the reefers would be practically empty. The galley then had to fall back on canned goods, and on a few occasions even the dry storerooms yielded little variety. Everyone remembers the scanty Thanksgiving feast of 1942 when franks and sauerkraut had to do for roast turkey and the fixings and the modern version of hardtack for hot buttered rolls. In foreign ports where there was no fleet concentration, the chief commissary steward had to forage for what was available. Sometimes it was excellent, sometimes not so good.

Two typical shipboard activities connected with the commissary outfit were the mess cooks and the coffee "messes." The mess cooks, usually junior seamen under the supervision of the masters-at-arms, were charged with the task of setting up the mess tables before each meal, carrying the food from the galley to the mess compartments, serving it, and keeping it replenished. When the meals were over, they then had to clean up, help wash the dishes, and restore the tables to their storage racks. Lowly as the job sounds, it had many advantages. Mess cooks did not have to stand regular watches, were usually eligible for liberty after the compartments were cleaned, and were paid $5.00 per month extra. On the other hand, they had to get up before reveille, and generally had to take quite a bit of guff from a hungry crew. A bonus was being in a position to hear most of the gossip being passed around at meals—chow lines were second only to the scuttlebutts for rumor mongering.

Coffee aboard ship runs a close second to fuel oil as a prime mover. Aboard every navy ship there is always a variety of coffee "messes" ranging from those officially sanctioned to the more exclusive private ones. One measure of a man's status on board is the coffee group which welcomes him to share its brew. The *Emmons* was no exception. Before long various groups had set up their percolators. Quite naturally the galley was the source for the official distribution to the watches and working parties. "Big Stoop" Ginn, Chief Steward's Mate in charge of the wardroom mess, saw that coffee was always on tap for the watch officers and bridge players. There was always a fresh pot in the chief's quarters. Each engine room and fire room kept the pots boiling while they were manned. Somehow or other each of the shops, such as the electrical workshop and the torpedo shack, got hold of a percolator for the benefit of their gangs. The ground beans were rationed out to the approved customers by commissary petty officers. Semi-official and private groups either had to scrounge for the makings or establish a kitty to make purchases ashore. Some of the more finicky preferred commercial brands to the navy issue, and were careful to keep a good supply on hand, especially before putting to sea for indefinite periods. Tea was available and was sometimes served in lieu of coffee but was never very popular. Not all the beverages introduced on board were legal. Rumor has it that a small but efficient still, utilizing copper tubing and other material intended for maintenance of torpedoes, was rigged up in the torpedo shack to process "torpedo juice" for an exclusive clientele.

If such an apparatus was in operation, it never became a matter of record. Actually, there were very few serious disciplinary cases during the fitting out period or, for that matter, any time later. None the less, captain's mast became an important part of the daily routine. Most of the mast cases involved over leave, varying from a few minutes to a day or more. As the date of sailing came closer and closer, the last few minutes with friends and family became more and more precious. There was a marked increase in the number of absences over leave. As Boston was central to New England and the middle states, and most of the crew came from that area, the crew tended to stretch liberty hours to the breaking point. Too often they gambled on making split-second bus and train connections in an already overloaded transportation system. Too often they lost. Generally, the captain was sympathetic and limited punishment to a warning or loss of a few liberties. In aggravated cases of over leave or other serious breaches of discipline, he did not hesitate to award a deck or summary court. Petty officers involved in serious infractions, especially those threatening the maintenance of discipline, were reduced in rating. The brig was little used except for aggravated offenses and punishments involving confinement on bread and water. Normally, confinement was extended to the limits of the ship. The first deck court to be held on board involved a seaman on his second enlistment who had overstayed his leave by nearly a day and then broke arrest while confined to the ship. He was given five days confinement and loss of pay amounting to $10.00. Unfortunately, this had little effect and he was almost continuously under arrest and confinement for one infraction or another. As usual with habitual troublemakers he removed himself as a problem by missing ship at one of the ports visited after the shakedown cruise. By a process of attrition, the "foul balls" were eliminated, mostly by their own actions in staying over leave when the ship was due to sail. There were few general courts from the *Emmons* during her entire career. Nor were there many repeat offenders once the habitual troublemakers were eliminated. Many of the petty offenders during the fitting out days at Boston went on to become petty officers and contributed greatly to the maintenance of discipline on board.

Most competent petty officers take pride in keeping their men out of trouble as well as seeing that they do their assigned jobs well. The leading petty officers of the *Emmons* were of this breed. If there was no other way, they would not hesitate to place a man on the report. But, as a rule, they preferred to administer justice in their own way, without invoking "The Articles for the Government of the Navy." There were many subtle ways they could accomplish this through the exercise of their authority as a petty officer—watch assignments, working parties, and special details are examples. Sometimes less subtle measures were used. "Big Stoop" Gin soon established his authority over the steward's mates assigned to the wardroom mess. Over six feet and every inch muscle, he is reputed to have preferred settling problems in his domain by administering unofficial justice on the fantail without cluttering up the records with messy, no pun intended, reports. Sometimes peers took care of situations within their own group by highly unorthodox methods. On one occasion, one of the chief petty officers was caught cheating in one of the frequent poker games held in the mess. To have reported him would, at best, have been awkward. Therefore, the mess members in an informal court sentenced him to be banned from the mess except to eat his meals.

Sick bay got its share of business. Most of the sick list involved respiratory problems brought on by the weather and conditions inherent in a crowded ship at a navy yard. Besides the usual colds and sniffles, an occasional case was serious enough to be packed off to the hospital for more careful and personalized treatment than could be provided in the small compartment designated as the sick bay. The chief pharmacist's mate—there was yet no medical officer—was especially careful to see that any cases which might be contagious were removed to the hospital. There was the usual number of accidents from the superficial to the serious. The first serious accident requiring hospitalization occurred when Boiler Maker First Class Lewis E. Shotts, wrestling a 200 pound container of plastic fire clay from the gangway to the fire room hatch, tripped over an air hose and severely cut his hands and back.

Most injuries resulted from falls and burns. Many burn cases involved inexperienced mess cooks whose duties required them to deliver steaming hot coffee over cluttered decks and narrow ladders to the different messes and watch stations. Later, at sea, the number of burns increased when the bearers tried to negotiate rolling decks and steep ladders in all kinds of weather. The passage from the galley to the bridge was particularly hazardous because of the open deck space and long, steep ladders. To ensure a steady supply to the bridge watches, the captain devised a sort of yoke and tray suspended from the neck of the bearers, leaving their hands free to hang on to the hand lines. Sometimes, in extreme weather, all service had to be suspended in the interest of safety. It really didn't matter too much. Few members of the watch would be interested in coffee—or food—under such conditions.

4.

Toward the end of seven weeks of accelerated yard work, the Emmons began preparations for sea. On January 16th, steam was raised and all services from the fitting out dock were discontinued—a symbolic cutting of the umbilical cord. Under her own power she moved to another berth where the only yard services provided were fresh water and telephone connections. At the new berth one day was devoted to taking on a full load of provisions. Another day, 5" and machine gun ammunition, barged in from the Naval Ammunition Depot at Hingham, was taken aboard and struck below to the magazines. It was an "all hands" evolution which took eight hours to complete and lasted until long after sundown. Fuel oil tanks were filled a week before sailing and topped off the night before sailing. Before leaving the yard the ship was "depermed." At Newport, the first port after Boston, she would be "degaussed," or, in sailorese, "degoosed." These steps were designed to neutralize the magnetic field inherent in any steel ship, and thus make them less vulnerable to the magnetic mines then widely used by the Germans. The day before sailing, a large draft of apprentice seamen came aboard. Unlike previous drafts, most of them were classified as reserves rather than regular navy, an indication of the new order of draftees.

Most of the important armament was aboard when the *Emmons* put to sea. All guns, four 5" double purpose, one quadruple 1.1 heavy machine gun mount, and four 20mm machine guns were in place and aligned with their associated fire control instruments. Torpedoes and depth charges were to be picked up at Newport and Yorktown. A new and improved sonar dome had been installed at the last dry-docking. Engines had been fine tuned. Communication gear was in place. Missing, was the modern SC-2 radar she had been scheduled to receive.

Early Thursday morning, January 22, 1942, before sunrise, the *Emmons* got underway to proceed to sea on her own. There was yet much to be done before she could be called ready for war. The first day was spent in Massachusetts Bay calibrating the radio direction finder, compensating the magnetic compass, testing guns, and conducting other tests which could not be done in port. Once more the engines were put through their paces, culminating in an emergency crash stop, from full speed ahead to sternway in less then two minutes. While nothing else was going on the everlasting emergency drills were gone through.

That evening, at sunset, general quarters was set and the ship was darkened. Rounding Cape Cod, she entered international waters enroute to Newport. The weather was moderate and by all normal measures the passage around the Cape was smooth and uneventful. But there was little sleep for most people on board that night from the captain down. It was the first night ever at sea for most of the recruits. Many, who had begun to walk with a roll on liberty in Boston, soon learned there is a big difference between the feel of a destroyer snugly secured alongside a dock and the roll of a destroyer at sea, however gentle. For the old hands it was more or less routine, but even for them, there was a new element—the unknown hazards of war. As the new warship zigzagged along the coast of Cape Cod with all topside lights darkened, many a man paused alongside the rail to peer into the night wondering what was out there and what the future held in store. More than one had to be warned to put out a cigarette or pipe, absent-mindedly lighted in an attempt to regain a sense of normality.

Dawn saw the destroyer approaching the entrance to Narragansett Bay. The first light was greeted with a routine call to general quarters. As they manned their battle stations, most felt that sense of relief and elation at seeing the beginning of a new day which would be repeated many times during the next three years. A hurdle had been gotten over; a new confidence was taking hold.

At Newport, the ship was degaussed by the electrical experts and five new Mark 15-1 torpedoes taken aboard at the Naval Torpedo Station. It may be noted that the torpedoes were the only weapons in the *Emmons'* arsenal which were never fired at any time in anger at an enemy. They were ultimately removed when she was converted to a minesweeper in 1944.

During a four day stopover at Newport, regular liberty was granted to the delight of those who had families in the vicinity, and the many that had gone through boot camp there. It was the last good liberty for many until the ship reached the Canal Zone on her shakedown. Norfolk, next port where liberty could be granted, was far too crowded with sailors from all over. It could hardly be called a good liberty town for the *Emmons'* New England-bred crew. A large draft of men from the Training Station reported on board, the last until she returned from her forthcoming shakedown cruise. This time the detail officer had torn out fourteen names all beginning with D, from Dely to Donovan. All but one were classified as reserves.

Enroute to Norfolk, two new items were added to the growing list of learning experiences. One was incidental to the war, the other common to any ship in any ocean. Between Newport and the Virginia Capes, she was responsible for protecting the battleship *Wyoming* from submarine attack. More zigzagging, more new responsibility for the novice lookouts and sonar men, not to mention the "make-e-learn" young officers of the deck. Protection of the "big boys" involved not only staying in the right position, but frequently meant staying out of the way of the escorted ship. Approaching the Capes, a fog closed in, never a relaxing experience for even the most seasoned seaman. In this case, it was doubly unwelcome because the early model search radar chose that particular time to break down, to the disgust of the skipper and the bridge watch who were beginning to rely on it for station keeping under conditions of reduced visibility. Few of those cursing the fog at that time could imagine that in a few months they would be happy to see an enveloping fog. Fewer still understood that before long absolute reliance would be placed on the maligned radar for running blind, in or out of a fog.

Once clear of the fog, the *Wyoming* went her own way and the *Emmons* stood up Chesapeake Bay to Yorktown where she took on the last of her ammunition, the depth charges and related accessories. From Yorktown she dropped down to the Naval Operating Base at Norfolk to make final preparations for her shakedown cruise to South America. There she joined the U.S.S. *Hambleton* (DD455) with which she was to make the cruise. The *Hambleton,* like the *Emmons,* was destined to be part of DesRon 10. She had been the next destroyer after the *Emmons* to be commissioned, and was the first after Pearl Harbor. Her captain was Lieutenant Commander Forrest Close, a classmate of Tommy Ragan's and his senior by 37 numbers. By virtue of this seniority, "Bony" Close was in command of the two-ship training group when it got underway.

After taking on provisions and topping off fuel, the two new destroyers weighed anchor for Cristobal, Canal Zone, on the first leg of their official shakedown, under the operational control of the Training Command, Atlantic Fleet. As an additional duty they were ordered to escort the merchantman, *Robin Tugford,* to the Canal Zone.

3

South American Shakedown

o o o o o o o o o o o o o o o o o o o o o o o o o o o o o o

Steaming as before.... 0900 Neptunus Rex came on board and was welcomed by the Captain. Initiation of Pollywogs commenced.... 1040 Sighted land (Cape Blanco, Peru), bearing 140° (t), distant 22 miles.... Initiation of pollywogs completed. Total number of pollywogs initiated as shellbacks: 193. Neptunus Rex left the ship.

—***Emmons*** *Log, 9 February 1942*

The *Robin Tugford* was delivered safely and left to join the huge armada of merchantmen waiting to transit the canal. The two destroyers fueled and waited for their turn which came the following afternoon, the 6th of February. An amazing amount of shipping, including warships, was going in both directions, with the preponderant number of ships headed for the Pacific. The canal passage took a little better than seven hours and it was nearly 9 p.m. when the ships secured to the dock in Balboa on the Pacific side. In spite of the late hour an enthusiastic liberty party hit the beach to sample the pleasures of a foreign port—a first for most of them.

Surprisingly, there were no stragglers when the training group got underway the following morning. As the *Emmons* and *Hambleton* stood out to sea, the swept channel was crowded, but once in deep water, the two destroyers headed south leaving most of the traffic to proceed westward to Pearl and the Western Pacific. They were bound for Callao, Peru, on the next leg of their shakedown cruise.

At the same time, two other new destroyers were making their way down the Atlantic Coast of South America. The shakedown ships were lucky to be heading south instead of west at a time when the war was going so badly for the United

States. After the crippling blow at Pearl Harbor, fleet commanders were begging Washington for reinforcements. Why then, were these newest ships heading away from combat zones on what proved to be the last of the glamorous shakedown cruises? The answer lies in the field of diplomacy rather than the field of combat. It was obviously desirable to work the new ships up to combat readiness in relatively safe waters, but there were also important diplomatic reasons for sending the latest and finest warships to South American ports at this particular stage of the war.

While the *Emmons* was outfitting at Boston, the Ministers of Foreign Affairs of the Latin American States were meeting with representatives of the United States Department of State at Rio de Janeiro, to determine what steps to take to fulfill the "one for all and all for one" pledge of the Havana Declaration of Reciprocal Assistance and Cooperation of 1940. The Havana Declaration had expressly stated that "aggression against one American State should be considered aggression against all." The Rio meeting had been called to present a common front against the Axis in view of the attack on the United States. The United States delegates found it inadvisable to push for a unanimous declaration of war by all the American states, but wanted to present a show of hemispheric unity to the rest of the world. Therefore, they supported a strong resolution sponsored by Mexico, Colombia, and Venezuela calling for a diplomatic break with the Axis Powers. At the time of the Rio Conference, the Central American and Caribbean Island Republics had already declared war against the Axis. Mexico, Venezuela, and Colombia had severed relations. Most of the other South American countries supported this action and their governments were taking positive action to end formal relations with the Axis nations.

The solid front was broken by Argentina and Chile, which were unwilling to go that far. Those two nations agreed to accord the United States the privileged status of a nonbelligerent, but not to make a diplomatic break with the Axis. The conferees finally compromised on a mild resolution recommending that the American States "consider" breaking relations with the Axis.

The exposed position of the two southernmost South American countries may have had something to do with their foot-dragging when, in January, 1942, the enemy appeared to be ascendant. Chile, in particular, seems to have concluded that the war was already lost for the allies and felt that its long, exposed coastline made it particularly vulnerable to Japanese submarines. Both countries had strong fascist factions. The Argentine leaders were openly pro-Axis, and remained so until the last few months of the war when an allied victory was certain. Chile was less militantly pro-Axis, but had a large number of Axis sympathizers among its businessmen and army officers. It has been said of the Chilean army that it was "German down to the buttons of their uniforms." On the other hand, the Chilean Navy was pro-British, having been organized and trained in the British tradition from the days of their struggle for independence in the early 1800s. Colombia, Ecuador, and Peru, the other countries visited by the *Emmons* and *Hambleton,* were solidly and enthusiastically behind the United States. In fact, at the time of the visits to Peru and Ecuador, successful negotiations were going on with those two countries for active military cooperation in the war effort. The United States was especially eager to finalize negotiations with Ecuador for use of the Galapagos Islands in defense of the Panama Canal. What better way to demonstrate the capability of the United States to meet its commitment to defend the Pacific Coast than to send two of its newest warships to those shores? There is no sure way to gauge the effectiveness of the cruise in influencing our friends and neighbors. There can be no doubt about one thing, the ships' companies had a wonderful time "showing the flag" while less fortunate contemporaries had to "work up" out of such places as Casco Bay and Guantanamo Bay.

2.

Enroute to Callao the two DDs crossed the equator. The actual crossing was made during the night of 8-9 February, but the ceremonies were delayed until the following morning because no lights were allowed above deck at night. The day before the crossing the *Emmons'* mimeographed newssheet, the "Scuttlebutt," carried dire warnings of the fate in store for the pollywogs aboard. Imaginative proclamations and instructions from Neptunus Rex were interspersed with real news of the war. Most of the latter was bad, but in no way lessened the determination of the shellbacks to see that every member of the crew was fully initiated into the mysteries of Neptune's realm. Preceding an account of allied losses in the Southwest Pacific the following message from NEPTUNUS REX to USS EMMONS appeared in the newssheet:

> REPORTS HAVE BEEN RECEIVED FROM MY ROYAL SCOUTS STATING THAT YOUR VESSEL IS HEADING IN THE GENERAL DIRECTION AND EXPECTS TO ENTER MY DOMAIN IN THE NEAR FUTURE X IN VIEW OF THE FACT THAT YOU CARRY A LARGE AND SLIMY CREW OF LANDLUBBERS AND POLLYWOGS I DEMAND THAT YOU REPORT ONE DAY PRIOR TO ARRIVAL WITHIN MY DOMAIN BY DISPATCH X A MIGHTY WELCOME IS EXTENDED TO ALL OF MY SUBJECTS ON BOARD YOUR SHIP

AND MAY ALL WHO HAVE NOT YET SWORN ALLEGIANCE BEWARE X SIGNED REX

Other dispatches from Neptune alluded disdainfully to the "plow dodging" pollywogs aboard, and ordered that all uninitiated "guttersnipes, hay shakers, lounge lizards, and apple knockers" be put on a "strict diet of marlin spikes, seaweed, rope yarn, and ratline tar" to toughen them up. One item reported the rumor that a baby had been delivered by the royal obstetrician and attributed the somewhat rougher seas that day to Neptune's annoyance that the new heir was a girl. Even so, his majesty did not work up the violent storm usually anticipated in the event a female was added to the royal line—the weather off the Pacific Coast of South America remained relatively mild.

The last communication from Neptune said that through his "underwater listening devices" he had learned that certain "slimy pollywogs" had shown disrespect for his trusty shellbacks and directed that those "toads" be brought before him in person so that their crimes might be rightly punished. This no doubt was caused by the rumor on board that the pollywogs, which greatly outnumbered the shellbacks, planned to stage a revolt. Whatever their intentions, all novices aboard received a summons to appear before the Royal Court to answer for their ignorance and lack of respect for the ways of the sea.

On the appointed day, King Neptune and his court, including the Royal Baby, appeared on board. Mysteriously, they emerged from the after deck house. They proceeded to the bridge where Neptune checked out the skipper and the bridge watch. The captain, himself a pollywog, wisely gave sway to the Royal Party after being assured that Neptune's minions would do nothing to impair the combat readiness of the ship. Accompanied by a loyal handful of shellbacks, the party proceeded to the fantail where Court was held. The pollywogs, from the captain on down, received the full treatment from the shellbacks. An attempted revolt was mercilessly put down by the shellbacks. As usual, experience, plus a genuine respect for tradition, prevailed over the rebels.

Years later, the ceremonies of crossing the line are remembered with awe and pride by the initiates of 1942. Some recall the bitter pills prescribed by the Royal Physician, and the close shaves administered by the Royal Barber. Others remember with disgust having to pay homage to the Royal Baby by kissing "her" huge belly which was generously coated with a nasty solution concocted in sick bay. The worst experience was the tortuous journey on hands and knees through a canvas slop chute filled with garbage. The crawler was encouraged on by prods and straps in the hands of the shellbacks applied to what was assumed to be his rear end. For special cases the diameter of the chute was tightened to slow down the progress of the unhappy pollywog. No one emerged at the end without red stern sheets, and few could sit comfortably for several days. But all emerged as shellbacks with a strange, new sense of belonging to a special group.

3.

Soon after crossing the line, the training group docked at Callao, the port for the Peruvian capital, Lima, which was located eight to ten miles inland. They arrived at a good time. The carnival season was just beginning and a feeling of camaraderie was in the air. Pedro Beltran, Peru's delegate to the Rio Conference, had just returned, and the government had broken diplomatic relations with Germany and her allies. In accordance with agreements made at Rio, Peruvian troops were being withdrawn from disputed territory along the border with Ecuador as a gesture of anti-American solidarity.

The newspapers of Lima featured war news and combat pictures from all battle fronts. Most of the news was bad—an exception being the successful Russian counterattack against the Germans in the Ukraine. In Southeast Asia, the Japanese had overrun the Malay Peninsula and were closing in on Singapore. The Philippines appeared to be doomed, but allied forces were putting up a gallant defense. In the Mediterranean, the Axis had all but cut the British supply lines. In North Africa, the German commander, Rommel, was temporarily bogged down, but was building up his forces for a new thrust toward Tobruk and Egypt.

In spite of the unfavorable news, the Peruvian press was militantly pro-allied. Losses were minimized and the few allied victories played up. The newspapers displayed large photos of allied leaders accompanied by their optimistic statements concerning the progress of the war. One of the leading dailies, *La Cronica,* ran a cartoon depicting the bloodthirsty Japanese bombing defenseless Manila, contrary to all concepts of international law.

La Cronica heralded the arrival of the *Emmons* and *Hambleton* at Callao. The citizens' interest in the military characteristics of the two ships was noted. The editor recorded with gusto, and with some surprise, the warm welcome given the "norteamericanos" by the man in the street of Callao and Lima:

> The demonstrations of cordiality with which our citizens have received the North American sailors signify a new spirit of pan-Americanism. It is eloquent testimony that in Peru there is most fervent friendship for the great democracy of the north, particularly in these historic times when it fights for the liberty of the world and struggles for victory over totalitarianism.

The North Americans know well, then, that they are welcome to Peru, and that our nation also is united for cooperation in the defense of the continent and for the liberty of the democratic nations.

In recognition of the new found solidarity, a series of receptions and dinners were given in honor of the officers of the visiting squadron. In their turn, the officers reciprocated with somewhat more austere affairs aboard their ships. One dinner aboard the *Emmons* was not on the official protocol list, but nonetheless was a huge success. The president of Peru, Manuel Prado y Ugarteche, signaled his approval of the new alliance by attending some of the functions and allowing members of his family to attend others. At one of these, the executive officer of the *Emmons* naively invited the president's daughter to have dinner aboard ship at Callao. Unexpectedly, she accepted. After a few discreet telephone calls, the dinner received the blessing of her parents. The executive officer had forgotten that he was scheduled to attend a dinner party the same evening with the captain. By protocol, the captain should have been aboard to welcome such a distinguished guest, but as he was committed, it was finally agreed that he would attend the dinner ashore while the executive officer remained aboard to act as host. In the long run, the dinner worked out well, without any damage to United States-Peruvian relations. The president's daughter captivated the officers on duty that evening by her graciousness and gave every indication of enjoying her visit to a United States man-of-war.

When the exec escorted her back to the presidential palace, he had the unusual honor of being received by the president. The conversation quite naturally turned to naval subjects. The American officer, himself a former submariner, was impressed by President Prado's knowledge of naval subjects in general, and of submarines in particular. It was apparently no accident that Peru had an outstanding submarine force.

Although liberty had to be curtailed because of wartime restrictions, most of the crew managed to get in at least one visit to Lima where most of the tourist attractions were located. Some few, unfamiliar with the fiery native drinks, pisco and aguardiente, never got beyond Callao. But for those who did, organized tours acquainted them with the ancient monasteries and other evidences of a rich Spanish-Indian civilization which flourished long before the English attempted to settle North America. Relics of the Inca civilization were especially attractive. One of the most popular tours was one which visited pre-Spanish Indian ruins high in the Andes. The ruins were reached by a railway designed and built by an American entrepreneur, Henry Meiggs, "The Yankee Pizarro," in the late nineteenth century. It is one of the marvels of railroad engineering. Where the faces of the mountains were too precipitous to allow even the sharpest of hairpin curves, the ascent was made by alternately going ahead, switching, and backing up the steep right-of-way carved into the rocky sides. Those who made the trip enjoyed the scary ride, but claimed that they felt much safer aboard their ship than hanging over the edges of the Andes.

Most of the events arranged by the Peruvian hosts for the members of the crews of the two ships took place in Callao. Besides tours there were receptions and athletic events. Not surprisingly, the yanks excelled at baseball but did not fare so well in soccer matches with the Peruvian ratings.

A visit to the Grand Plaza in Lima where the cathedral and governmental palaces were located was a must. The tour guides timed their arrival at the plaza to coincide with drills by the magnificent palace guard units. One of the major attractions was the grinning mummy of Francisco Pizarro displayed in a glass case in a special chapel of the cathedral. It was he who conquered the Incas in the 1530s and established Lima as the capital of Spanish America—only to be assassinated by his own quarrelsome followers.

Some citizens who were enthusiastic supporters of the allied war effort extended invitations to the American ratings to visit their homes. The Spanish speaking American sailors enjoyed these visits the most, but even those who couldn't speak the language found a warmth and friendliness in their new found allies that they had not expected.

On the whole, most men preferred to arrange for their own entertainment. Normally, the daylight hours were spent walking around the principal streets just taking in the sights and making frequent stops to buy postcards or haggle for souvenirs. Many bought the excellent wool products of Peru to take back home. Simply walking around the streets and visiting the small shops and markets was a liberal education for the North Americans. As the daylight hours waned, the sight-seers gravitated to the numerous restaurants and cantinas.

In the cantinas the visitors not only learned about new and exotic drinks but they gained firsthand knowledge of cultural differences. One adjustment which was hard for the more bashful to make was to use the open urinals found in the ordinary cantinas. Admittedly, it was very convenient to get off the stools at the bar along one wall of the room and take only a few steps to the open trough along the other wall. It was not that way in Boston or Providence!

Another cultural oddity was *Calle Septembre,* where the prostitutes were concentrated. Here were stalls with large windows facing the street behind which the girls, some incredibly young, patiently sat, displaying their wares. Needless to say, September Street attracted a great number of sightseers, and possibly some customers. The longing for feminine companionship, by those who wanted nothing to do with the girls of September Street, was met in the public dance halls.

Those who strayed away from the business and entertainment centers into the back streets learned about other facets of Peruvian life. Some of the back streets were literally covered with guano, the bird droppings which for years were one of the world's prime sources of agricultural fertilizer. Whole islands off the coast had been built up with the droppings of birds attracted to the area by the marine life of the Humboldt Current through the centuries. The export of guano had been one of Peru's most important exports in the nineteenth century.

Aglow with a sense of continental solidarity, the shake downers departed for Valparaiso, Chile, on Valentine's Day, February 14, 1942. As evidence of the newly cemented ties between Peru and the United States, three especially selected young officers of the Peruvian Navy, Teniente Segundo Alberto Monge V, Alferez de Fragata Able Woll, and Alferez de Fragata Federico Dias G, were ordered on board for training in the latest equipment and tactics of the United States fighting ships. They proved to be good shipmates and were quick to learn the intricacies of a modern destroyer. As an extra bonus, they were invaluable as interpreters with the Chileans, and, in spite of the traditional animosity between Peru and Chile, as instructors in the history of the Pacific Coast countries of South America.

4.

The training group arrived in Valparaiso February 18, after a pleasant voyage of four days. The passage southward had been made several miles to seaward of the normal coastal routes for security reasons and, as usual, the days had been devoted to tactical exercises and drills. By now these were beginning to be routine for the crews, although many rough spots remained to be ironed out. The Peruvian officer passengers enthusiastically joined in the drills, and appeared to enjoy them.

Unlike Peru, there was little interchange with the civilian elements of the Chilean government. For one thing, the capital city, Santiago, about 80 miles by road from the port city, was not as convenient to Valparaiso as Lima was to Callao. For another, Chile had just gone through a presidential election and the winner, Juan Antonio Rios Morales, purportedly pro-allied, had not yet been inducted into office. He was at that time in the process of choosing his cabinet. Neither the outgoing nor the incoming officials were willing to go as far as the Peruvians had gone to show commitment to the Allies. Actually, the Chileans were still trying to determine which way the winds of war were blowing. In mid-January, while negotiations were going on between the United States and Chile for possible military cooperation in defense of the continent, the American ambassador had reported to the State Department that Chile was reluctant to break with the Axis because of fear of Japanese power. The Chileans were demanding exorbitant amounts of equipment, including antiaircraft installations, and the assurance of offshore protection in exchange for a military agreement. The Japanese ambassador had convinced them that Japanese submarines were already operating off their coasts. At a meeting with the minister of defense and senior officers, the Japanese naval attaché was reported to have argued that the United States was unprepared for war and would surely lose. Our naval attaché believed that these representations had had a strong impact on the Chilean military leaders. It is certainly true so as to we were not entirely prepared for war, and at that time things were going badly for us. In spite of all this, the ambassador was able to report that the acting minister of foreign affairs had stated that "if Chile had military equipment she would not only be willing to break relations but would go to war with the Axis."

This was the diplomatic situation when the *Emmons* and the *Hambleton* put into Valparaiso harbor. It should be noted here that whatever impact their visit may have had on the negotiations, it was nearly a year before Chile could be persuaded to make a clean break with the Axis. Given the conditions existing in February, 1942, it is not surprising that nearly all of the official contacts between the destroyers' personnel and the Chileans were confined to naval authorities at the seaport. In true South American style, the latter went all out to make their visitors welcome. Whatever the reaction in Santiago may have been, the Chilean Navy appeared to be entirely sympathetic to the allied cause. As was to be expected from a country with such a long history of naval prowess as Chile, keen interest was expressed in the military hardware of the new warships. Next to the guns, most interest was centered on the radar antenna on the foremast. Many questions were asked about it. Fortunately, most people on board were as much in the dark as to its function as the Chileans, and those who did understand it were indoctrinated to keep their knowledge to themselves.

There was scant mention of the two North American destroyers in the Valparaiso press. However, the papers were openly favorable to the Allies and, with the exception of the German language newspaper; there was a distinct sense of uneasiness at the prospect of an Axis victory. Singapore had fallen after the two ships left Callao, and the Japanese jubilation at their victory was noted. The mounting German submarine offensive in the Caribbean was another cause for comment and concern. *La Union,* in reporting submarine attacks at Aruba, remarked that "the attack on Aruba has alarmed the entire continent." A large picture of President Roosevelt accompanied a statement attributed to him that two United States war aims were that "the weak be protected and the strong just." Nowhere was the bias of the press toward the allies more evident than in two comic strips featuring "El Capitan Wings," depicting the daring exploits of an aviator named Clark, and "Cintella" featuring an equally brave submariner performing all sorts of miraculous rescues. They obviously had been copied from pro-allied syndicated strips, with only the nationality markings changed on the warplanes and subs.

Officers and men of the destroyers were feted at a series of parties and receptions, both official and private. Many were held at Vina del Mar, internationally famous seaside resort near Valparaiso. One of the most memorable events was an *al fresco* luncheon given by the Chilean naval officers for the visiting North American and Peruvian officers. The luncheon lasted well into the afternoon, while the Chileans introduced the truly excellent wines of the country to their guests. The Peruvian officers had many friends and relatives among the international set summering at Vina, and were generous in arranging for their friends among the younger officers of the destroyers to meet them. The outstanding restaurants and casinos of the resort became a favorite spot for the junior officers during the short visit.

The facilities of the beautifully appointed officers' club at the naval headquarters in Valparaiso were opened to the visitors. One outstanding feature was a magnificent marble staircase which featured on its grand landing a huge painting of the defeat of the Peruvian battleship *Huascar* by a superior Chilean squadron during the War of the Pacific in 1879. Indeed, the *Huascar* under Admiral Grau had fought so gallantly against overwhelming odds that the young Peruvian officers described it as a victory for Peruvian honor, if not for Peruvian arms. The feelings they expressed were much the same as those of a Southerner explaining the Battle of Gettysburg. Both Chile and Peru have a strong sense of the importance of sea power in their respective histories.

While the officers were learning about Chilean wines at Vina del Mar, the American sailors were also being made welcome by their Chilean counterparts. The Chileans were even more avid soccer fans than the Peruvians, and the results of the exhibition games were just as one-sided as the games held in Peru for the makeshift naval teams. The Yankees had their innings, however, when it came to baseball. Swimming parties on the glistening Pacific beaches were popular. They were appreciated all the more when the "Scuttlebutt" printed radio accounts of wintry storms back home. The lesson in international finance begun in Peru was continued in Chile. All hands were delighted with, and sometimes fooled by, the apparently favorable rate of thirty *escudos* for one dollar.

A few members of the ship's company were able to get off long enough to visit Santiago. The capital city, with its many elegant public buildings, offered far more cultural and entertainment activities than the port city of Valparaiso. One group, looking for a public dance hall, made the interesting discovery that not all Chilean dance houses confined their activities to drinking and dancing. In the words of one of these tourists: "...In Santiago a cab driver took us out in the country to this large, beautiful house. There was a huge patio with a juke box and dance floor. The patio was completely surrounded by rooms of the girls who were there to entertain. Sensational." It was far different from the dance halls in the land of beans and cod.

Back in Valparaiso, the crewmen were not entirely dependent on their naval hosts for recreation. They explored the fascinating public markets for souvenirs and gifts for family and girl friends back in the states. Some of the best buys were woven goods and semi-precious jewels. Among the more exotic items carted back to the ship were mummified cow udders and handmade artifacts fashioned from the horns of oxen, such as hat racks and lamp stands. Nor were the bars and night spots of Valparaiso neglected. Judging from the records of captain's mast, the port city offered more inducements for staying over leave and enjoying the good life than had any other port of call.

It is probably idle to speculate on the spate of mast reports which were far more numerous than they had been in Peru. The old trilogy of "wine, women, and song" would account for many of the reports, but not all—the log does not record even one instance of "overindulgence in song." Time, and distance from home, may account for some lapses. It had been nearly a month since the ships had left Norfolk. Only a handful of the young men aboard the *Emmons* had ever been away from the United States.

For a few of the mast cases a more subtle reason might be found in the changes resulting from a month at sea under wartime cruising conditions. The long watches under conditions of combat readiness and constant drills had brought on a new sense of confidence and self-reliance in the ship's company. Whether entirely warranted or not, there was a feeling that together they could handle any situation which might arise. A little cockiness had crept in with the legitimate self-esteem. A little cockiness is a good thing. But sometimes, when combined with the fierce patriotism inherent in the American sailor, it can lead to trouble in ports where language problems and different political and cultural values are found. Such differences existed in Valparaiso, where there was considerable anti-American sentiment. Unfortunately, American pride collided with anti-Americanism in some of the bars and bistros of the seaport. Fortunately, no serious injuries were reported and only a few fights ended up as shore patrol reports.

No one knows what the diplomatic results of the visit were—three days is a short time to make much of an impression—but the flag had been shown by the newest and best the United States could afford, at a time when Chile was genuinely doubtful of North America's ability to stop Japan and her partners. The hosts must have appreciated the capabilities of the new destroyers, and they surely knew that there were more where those two came from. For their part, the North Americans left Chile impressed with the wonderful climate, the magnificent scenery, and the evident sympathy of most, if not all, Chileans.

5.

The training ships followed the Humboldt Current north from Valparaiso, taking advantage of the fine weather of the "Ladies Passage" to resume their training exercises. The stretch of water off the coasts of Chile and Peru had been given the name back in the days of sail because of the favorable winds and current, and the usually smooth seas. In this instance the "passage" lived up to its reputation. Each day saw its quota of drills and exercises, executed under nearly ideal conditions. Life at sea became routine, even boring. But the news coming from the Western Pacific and the East Coast of the United States was disturbing. Officers and men of the *Emmons* realized that the ideal conditions of the shakedown cruise could not continue for long.

After a brief pause off Callao to disembark the three Peruvian officers to a waiting tug, the destroyers continued their northwestward course to the next scheduled port, Guayaquil, Ecuador. Guayaquil, the largest city and main port of Ecuador, is located on the Guayas River, several miles up stream from where it empties into the Gulf of Guayaquil. Since the time of Francisco Pizarro, navigation on the Guayas has been known to be dangerous and unpredictable. Swelled by torrential tropical rains during the rainy season, the current varies from six to twelve knots on the ebb tide. The rains sometimes block out the low lying navigational aids, and radar is virtually useless. The difficulties are complicated by literally thousands of floating islands of tropical vegetation torn from the flooded mangrove swamps upstream. Constant watch at anchor must be kept to prevent fouling of the anchor chain by the floating islands. Dragging anchor is a constant danger. Indeed, the first evening at anchor off Guayaquil, the *Emmons* had to raise steam and reset her mud hook to keep from being swept downstream.

Later the same evening, while the tide was still on the ebb, the liberty party returned from shore with the usual quota of men more or less under the weather. While they were milling about on the fantail before going below, a scuffle broke out and one of the older seamen, who had been in disciplinary trouble ever since reporting on board, either jumped or lost his footing and fell overboard. A much later version was that he was knocked overboard during the scuffle. Without giving any thought to their own safety, or the condition of the river, four of his shipmates dived over the side to help him. Others were about to jump when the duty officer came back to the stern in time to order all hands to stand fast. At this point, instead of one man overboard, there were five, none of whom could make much progress against the swift current. Normally, it could have been expected that all five would be lost. But there is an old saying that "God looks after drunks and sailors." On that night some men were carrying double protection.

The key people of the duty watch were in the right spots when the petty officer of the watch sounded the chilling "Man Overboard" alarm. The duty electrician's mate was sipping coffee in the electrical shop and promptly manned the searchlight. He was able to pick up five neatly spaced heads bobbing downstream before they got out of range of its beam. Life rings were dropped over the side but were of no use. The whaleboat had just disembarked another load of men returning from liberty and took off downstream at the first alarm. The coxswain, Seaman Robert W. Charoux, ignored the men closest to the ship and proceeded directly to the one farthest downstream, the first to go overboard. After picking up the first man, he reversed course, headed back toward the ship and, one by one, fished the four would-be rescuers out of the broiling water. Somewhat waterlogged, but otherwise unharmed, the five were deposited at the gangway.

For a short time following this incident, there were unconfirmed reports that more than five men had hit the water, but a muster accounted for every member of the crew. By the beginning of the midwatch, all hands had settled down to get what little sleep they could before reveille. The whole affair, from time of the first alarm to the time all were safe on board, was logged in ten minutes. No one could say whether the "Guayaquil Five" owed their lives to luck or the rigorous emergency drills which had been conducted since the day of commissioning. Anyway, the men of the *Emmons* had reacted swiftly and correctly in an emergency to avert what could easily have been a tragedy.

Another Guayaquil event parallels the story of the "swimming party." The following day, the *Emmons* was ordered to shift from her anchorage to a mooring buoy. During the process of leading a wire through the buoy ring, a sudden twist threw members of the mooring party into the river. This time, however, the men involved were under the supervision of a petty officer and properly attired in life jackets. They were promptly picked up and returned to the buoy. Compared to the happenings of the night before this was trivial. It does go to show that, regardless of the absence or presence of a human enemy, there is always plenty of danger in everyday shipboard operations.

The public markets of Guayaquil and the street vendors proved to be almost as fascinating to the *Emmons'* crew as the more orthodox sources of amusement. Barter was routine, and the men soon discovered that relatively common articles for sale in the ship's store, such as razor blades and tooth paste, were as acceptable as currency. Genuine Panama hats, which actually originated in Ecuador and were woven under water by the mountain Indians, were a popular item, as were the brightly woven belts and bands of cloth. By far the most plentiful, and among the cheapest items, were the sweet bananas, shipped throughout the world from Guayaquil. A whole stalk could be had for two tubes of tooth paste at a time when a single banana in the United States was going for about a nickel. No one on board went hungry for the luscious fruit as enterprising boatmen literally surrounded the ship hawking their wares. Many of the "bumboats" offered monkeys for sale. One of the headaches of the deck watch was to keep the vendors at a respectable distance without doing them physical harm and thereby destroying whatever goodwill the visit created. A good stream of water from the fire hoses proved to be the most effective means of keeping them clear of the sides. The boatmen responded good-naturedly, trying to win this new game.

Several people toyed with the idea of adopting one of the appealing monkeys as a ship's mascot. It remained for the gunnery officer to try to implement the idea. One evening he had accompanied the captain ashore to an official function. Following the affair, they decided to see some of the sights of the city unencumbered by protocol. Not knowing when they would be going back to the ship, they decided to send the gig's crew back in the liberty boat. In due time, they tired of sightseeing and manned the gig for the trip home, but not before the gunner bought a stalk of bananas and a small monkey from vendors on the dock.

Shortly after midnight, the gangway watch spotted the gig approaching the ship with the skipper at the tiller and the gunnery officer at the engine controls. Perched on the latter's shoulder was the monkey, apparently enjoying the proceedings. As usual, a strong current was running and it took several passes to bring the boat alongside the gangway. Once alongside, the skipper debarked and reported his return on board. In the meantime, two seamen had been sent down to help secure the boat. Before the lines were made fast, the current caught the bow and swept the boat out into the stream. The onetime engineer suddenly found himself promoted to coxswain. After several wild maneuvers, the boat was once again brought alongside. By this time all hands still topside had come to the quarterdeck to offer advice and encouragement. Needless to say, the "coxswain" received a hero's welcome when he reported his return aboard with a stalk of bananas clutched in one hand and a grinning monkey still perched on his shoulder.

With such an introduction, the simian might well have become a popular mascot. But the following morning he eliminated himself as a candidate for the job—and proved the wisdom of naval regulations against pets—by getting loose and tangling with some electrical equipment. From time to time thereafter other attempts were made to bring animals aboard. None lasted for any length of time. A parrot lasted for a few days, but was banned when the medical officer learned of its presence. A few stray dogs were adopted by members of the ship's company—or vice versa. However, none of them remained for long. Each of the successive commanding officers refused to allow dogs, or any other animals, to be kept on board, because of sanitation problems and fear that they might in some way interfere with battle readiness.

There was no need to try to influence the Ecuadorians in favor of the allied cause. They were already solidly committed. The press was enthusiastic about the visit of the destroyers. Every issue *of La Prensa* of Guayaquil interspersed items about the warships with the more somber war news. The current defeats of the Allies, including alarming claims by the Germans of destruction of merchant shipping, were depicted as "gloomy," but by no means hopeless. The Ecuadorians were well aware of the possibilities of lend-lease. One issue of La Prensa dwelt at length on the large amount of equipment being channeled to Brazil under the program. The day before the destroyers took their departure, *La Prensa* gave a detailed account of a "sumptuous luncheon for the authorities and officials of the city and editors of the local newspapers" given by the commanders of the destroyers *Hambleton* and *Emmons* "in appreciation of the courtesies received in this state and in this port." Two large pictures of the hosts and their Ecuadorian guests, spanning three columns, accompanied the story. The day following the farewell luncheon, the two ships slipped their cables and headed downstream to the relative safety of the open sea. They had been welcomed with genuine warmth and were assured of Ecuador's cooperation. Nonetheless, there was little regret when the destroyers shaped course to the north and the Canal Zone.

6.

After a one night stand in Balboa, the *Emmons* and *Hambleton* slipped into the stream of ships headed for the Caribbean. The sense of urgency with which the canal employees, from line handlers to pilots, tried to keep the ships moving at maximum speed, served as a reminder that America was at war. The strict security measures and the large number of armed guards along the way were ample evidence of the importance of the Canal to the war effort. News accounts of submarine sinkings in the Caribbean confirmed that the destroyers were nearing a combat zone.

They had yet, however, one more protocol calls to make on another friendly power, Colombia. Once clear of the Canal, the destroyers wasted no time in setting course for Cartagena, one of the oldest and most picturesque ports on the Caribbean. Once it had been one of the official ports-of-call for the Spanish trading fleets. For three days the shake downers enjoyed the historic sights of Cartagena and the warm hospitality of the Colombian Navy. It was the ending of carefree times for the ships and their crews.

The Colombians were as committed to the support of the United States as the Peruvians and Ecuadorians, but their press, while friendly, could not gloss over the disasters facing the Allies. The Japanese had all but eliminated the last of allied naval ships in the Java Sea. While the *Hambleton* and *Emmons* were at Cartagena, *El Siglo,* a leading daily of the capital city, Bogota, reported the fall of Rangoon and Batavia. Java was cut in two, and the newspaper speculated that the Japanese would soon be able to land on Australia. By far the greatest interest of the Colombian press was in the German submarine offensive off the United States East Coast and in the Caribbean. In reporting the "courtesy" visit of the destroyers to Cartegena, *El Siglo* admitted that it was puzzled as to why they were there. Implied, but unstated, was the thought that with so much damage being done elsewhere by German subs, the two new ships might well be put to better use.

This thinking was echoed aboard the ships. Most men aboard the *Emmons* realized from the news accounts that the Allies were losing the war at sea. There was a vague and unexpressed feeling that they should be taking a more active role—almost a sense of shame that they had not been in a combat zone.

Notwithstanding the submerged feelings of guilt, the officers and men had thoroughly enjoyed the shakedown cruise and cherished its memories for years afterward. And a lot had been accomplished. Once awkward gun crews could now work together smoothly. The engines required less manhandling to keep them going. Promotions had been frequent. All apprentice seamen were now seamen second or firemen. Many of the older crewmen had been promoted one notch. A cargo of pollywogs had become salty shellbacks.

An extra bonus had been the chance for more than 200 young Americans to see cultures far different from their own. A past president of the Emmons Association, Jerry McAlevey, then a seaman second class, remembers the cruise as a highlight of his service on DD457. He emphasizes the difference in cultures in his description of the shakedown from the viewpoint of an enthusiastic young recruit of 1942:

"Here it was wartime and we were on a cruise to South America. No war, and wine and women and song. It was some experience for a bunch of young kids who had never been away from home. The Canal, Peru, Chile, Ecuador, and Colombia....

"I suppose, even in peacetime a shakedown cruise like we had would probably be envied. We were far from the war zones, had excellent weather, the people loved us and we loved them back. We were fortunate to see at first hand other cultures....

"Going up the river to Guayaquil, Ecuador, was just like going into the jungle with Frank Buck. It was amazing how many different kinds of lands we saw on that short cruise. The very advanced cities of Lima and Santiago, to the jungle atmosphere of Ecuador. The dry, arid land of Colombia, and the honky-tonk atmosphere of the Canal cities. The shakedown cruise on the Emmons was something to be remembered forever. It was what the posters used to feature before the war. Join the Navy and see the world. Of course, we were to see the world in another way from then on."

4

War Becomes Reality

o o o o o o o o o o o o o o o o o o o o o o o o o o o o o o o o

At 0208 sighted flare and flame of explosion bearing 266°, distant about nine miles. Changed course toward. At 0240 sighted torpedoed tanker.

—***Emmons*** *War Diary, April 6, 1942*

When the *Emmons* left Boston in January, there had been few indications of the war along the eastern seaboard. However, while she was preparing for the shakedown cruise, the Germans were assembling a formidable force of their largest submarines for an all out assault on our coastal shipping. Before the Japanese attack on Pearl Harbor, Hitler had carefully avoided a confrontation with the United States in its home waters, although in actuality an undeclared war between the Germans and Americans was being waged along the North Atlantic convoy routes throughout 1941. The German self-denial changed with Pearl Harbor. Hitler gave his approval to a plan presented by Admiral Doenitz to mount an attack in the Western Atlantic. Immediately after the open declaration of war by the United States, the brilliant U-boat commander began to shift his "long-legged" submarines from the Northern and Eastern Atlantic convoy lanes to the North American Coast. Doenitz called the operation *Paukenschlag,* or "Drumbeat."

Originally, twelve 740-ton U-boats were stationed in the Newfoundland-Nova Scotia area. An additional five were stationed off the United States east coast with orders to begin the "Drumbeat" on January 13, 1942. They were augmented by a second wave of five boats in late January. By February 10, fifteen were in action between Newfoundland and Cape Hatteras. In mid-February, five were dispatched to the Caribbean to prey on oil tankers in the Aruba-Venezuela-Trinidad production area. Some even shelled refinery installations on Aruba.

This was about the mid-point of the *Emmons'* shakedown cruise and it was the success of the U-boats in the Caribbean which aroused such great interest and concern in South America. Doenitz planned to keep twelve U-boats on station off the East Coast, relieving them about every two weeks. By that time they would be low on torpedoes, fuel, and provisions, and would need to withdraw to the east of Bermuda to resupply. Fortunately for the United States this rotation weakened their effectiveness, but larger supply submarines called "Milch Cows" were being rushed to completion and would later be used to keep the combat submarines on station for longer periods of time.

Paukenschlag had been designed to catch American coastal shipping before defense measures could be perfected. It succeeded in doing just that. Without adequate defense plans or sufficient trained antisubmarine forces, the results were very nearly catastrophic until the pitifully few ships and planes available could be assembled, trained, and deployed. At first, reliance was placed on area patrols by ships and aircraft to detect and destroy the enemy submarines. No attempt was made to organize convoys, and individual merchantmen were sailed independently. This proved ineffective, and shipping losses for the first half of 1942 exceeded the ability to replace them.[1]

Paukenschlag was in full swing when the *Emmons* and *Hambleton* left Cartagena for Boston. Losses for the Atlantic and Arctic Areas in March, 1942, amounted to eighty-eight ships of 507,502 tons, most of them off the east coast of the United States. Of these, nineteen alone were sunk in the waters of the Fifth Naval District, off the Virginia and North Carolina Capes.

Given this grave situation it was only natural that the two new homeward bound destroyers should be diverted to help. Before they got as far as the Windward Passage, the principal channel connecting the Atlantic and the Caribbean, they were ordered to set up a patrol line north of the Passage between Cape Masi, the eastern tip of Cuba, and Great Inagua Island.

If any German submarines were present, they kept a low profile. Perhaps the hunting was better for them off the East Coast. Many sound contacts were made, but none proved promising enough to warrant expending depth charges. Surface contacts caused as much concern as underwater contacts. During the daylight hours, merchant ships approaching the busy Passage could be challenged and readily identified, but at night it was a different matter. Many of the merchant-

1. British writers are highly critical of the American High Command's rejection of their offers of advice and help in the crisis. The mounting losses forced adoption of the convoy system.

men either did not know the recognition signals or were afraid to reply. Once when the *Hambleton* could not get a satisfactory reply from an unidentified ship, she fired a number of star shells to illuminate the suspect. The air was immediately filled with frantic SOSs. Finally, having identified the panicked vessel as a merchant type, the skipper of the *Hambleton* summarily closed the incident by announcing on the intership communication channel "Gunfire is friendly, Gunfire is friendly."

The Windward Passage patrol lasted a week, with time out for fueling at Guantanamo Bay. On one occasion, the *Emmons* had no sooner connected up the fuel hoses than an emergency alert forced breaking the fuel connection and rushing to sea for another fruitless search.

Another time, haste in fueling resulted in overfilling one of the tanks and flooding a living compartment. Several inches of fuel oil soaked the lower tiers of bunks and any clothing which was stored at deck level. It took hours of work and all the waste rags aboard to clean up the mess. New bedding and clothing had to be issued to replace the oil-soaked. Several days passed before the nauseating smell of Bunker "C" fuel oil could be eliminated. At this point, many crewmen would have gladly exchanged destroyer life for the muddy foxhole of an infantryman.

The tedium of patrol was broken by unexpected orders to join northbound Task Force 22 which consisted of the carrier *Ranger,* cruisers *Augusta* and *Savannah,* and their screening destroyers. This marked the beginning of the basic employment of the *Emmons* for the next two and a half years. She, as a unit of DesRon 10, became part of fast, powerful task groups organized for special missions. Usually, they were built around the *Ranger* and whatever stray cruisers and battleships were available. The flagship *Augusta* was frequently included. Sometimes, when a carrier was not available, these task groups were built around cruisers and battleships alone.

A major assignment for Task Force 22 and its subdivisions was to have ready and positioned a trained battle group to oppose the German High Seas Fleet if its heavy units, holed up in captured Norwegian and French ports, should try to break out into the North Atlantic. If that happened, the United States forces were to operate in conjunction with the British Home Fleet.

Most of the time was spent in training exercises out of Newport, Rhode Island, Casco Bay, Maine, or Argentia, Newfoundland. At times, these training phases were boring and repetitious. On the other hand, the *Emmons* was spared the monotony, and the dangers, of repeated slow convoy runs across the turbulent North Atlantic, which was the lot of many Atlantic destroyers.

After the main body of Task Force 22 was dropped at New York, the *Emmons* proceeded independently to Casco Bay via the Cape Cod Canal. In the next two years she would use the canal so often going between the Boston-Casco Bay area and the New York-New-port area that her bow number, 457, became familiar to the natives along the banks of the waterway. They would man the sea walls to greet her and wish her good luck. It became so commonplace that the family of one of the ensigns aboard, who had a summer home on the route, instructed their caretakers to let the parents know whenever the *Emmons* went through the canal and whether she was headed north or south.

The visit to Casco was unaccountably brief. After only one day the ship was ordered down to Boston for the overdue post-shakedown overhaul. Most of the work done during the eight-day period there was for correction of defects which had showed up during the training cruise. On the recommendation of Commander Destroyers Atlantic Fleet, a temporary Oerlikon machine gun was mounted opposite the 1.1" quadruple mount on one of the foundations reserved for a future twin mount Bofors. This brought the total of 20mm machine guns to five.

2.

Leaving the Boston yard on March 29, the *Emmons* reloaded her ammunition and headed south through the Cape Cod Canal for calibration of the degaussing apparatus at Newport. The following afternoon, having completed this task and the calibration and compensation of the magnetic compasses, she headed north via the canal for a scheduled training period with other destroyers of DesDiv 19 at Casco Bay. She had hardly left the canal and set-course for Casco when, at twenty-five minutes into the midwatch, an urgent dispatch from Commander Atlantic Fleet cancelled the training period and directed her to report to Commander Eastern Sea Frontier for antisubmarine duty.

Fifteen minutes after CincLant's dispatch, Commandant First Naval District issued an urgent message that a submarine had been reported on the surface one mile north of the Boston light vessel's position. With no further information or orders, Captain Ragan changed course and headed at 25 knots for the reported position. Twenty-five minutes later, Commander Destroyers Atlantic Fleet gave his stamp of approval by ordering the *Emmons* to report to ComOne for duty. An hour later the ship was in the reported position of the submarine. Speed was slowed to 15 knots and a methodical sound search started. No submarine was found.

In retrospect, it appears unlikely that an enemy submarine would surface so near a light vessel on a clear, moonlit night. The report was probably made by some imaginative fisherman or plane crewman under the influence of the flood of reports of submarine sinking farther south. Bright moonlight on restless seas does sometimes create images for minds conditioned to see them. A skipper soon learned that after announcements of a possible submarine in the vicinity of his ship, it would not be long before a periscope was reported by someone. Most were products of imagination. Nonetheless, every report had to be carefully checked out, just in case.

In this instance, the hunt was called off at noon and the *Emmons* was directed to carry out the orders received from CincLant twelve hours earlier. For the third time in three days she went through the Cape Cod Canal, this time headed south to New York, to report to the new commander of Destroyer Division 19, Captain Charles Wellborn, Jr., USN. The new Commodore was temporarily flying his broad command pennant aboard the *Emmons'* old shakedown companion, the *Hambleton.*

3.

After a briefing at the headquarters of Commander Eastern Sea Frontier, ComDesDiv 19, with the *Hambleton* and *Emmons,* was ordered to join a task force being assembled off the Virginia and Carolina Coasts. The assigned mission was to search for and destroy enemy submarines which were raising hell off the Capes. The patrol area given the destroyers covered the shipping lanes between Wimble Shoals and Cape Lookout, a distance of a little more than a hundred miles. Near the middle of the assigned beat, Cape Hatteras juts out into the Atlantic like a knuckle and serves as a turning point for all coastal traffic. Quite naturally, the area became one of the focal points for the German submarines off the coast. By day they would lie quietly on the ocean floor, well clear of traffic, and surface after dark to close in on the shipping lanes. Because of the distance between protected harbors, many of the slow-moving merchantmen were obliged to round Capes Hatteras and Lookout at night when the U-boats became active. Silhouetted against the lights on shore they were easy targets. The area became known as the "happy hunting ground" for the submarines of *Paukenschlag.* In fact, the Germans were so successful that they began to use shellfire to sink the merchantmen rather than expend their precious torpedoes. Sinkings reached a peak in late March and early April, but began to taper off as defense forces were augmented and became better organized and trained. Limited coastal convoys started in April. It was not, however, until midsummer, when a fully integrated convoy system was in operation, that losses were brought under acceptable control.

For eight days the *Emmons* and *Hambleton* doggedly patrolled the hundred mile area off Cape Hatteras. Their experience has been described by Samuel Eliot Morison in his account of the Battle of the Atlantic. His story illustrates the frustration of the hastily assembled anti-submarine forces off the East Coast during the first few months of 1942.

Some of the highlights of the patrol are illustrated by the following excerpts from the *Emmons'* war diary.

> **April 2, 1942....** At 1455 steamer bearing 175°T., distant 8 miles, was observed to open fire, apparently at object in water ahead of this Task Group. At 1503 received submarine contact from same vessel (SS DELSUD) on 500 kcs.... At 1510 changed speed to 25 knots in direction of the reported contact.... submarine report was cancelled.... At 1958 detailed by CDD 19 to investigate strange steamer.... At 2020 spoke Panamanian steamer LAMBALA (HPXR) bound North, Rio to Baltimore. Proceeded to rejoin.
>
> At 2115 sighted flare, apparently dropped by plane, 4 miles on my port bow. Proceeded to investigate. At about 2128 made sound contact. At 2130 dropped five depth charges...two of which failed to explode.... At 2155 set course to rejoin CDD in HAMBLETON.
>
> At 2230 was detailed to proceed to vicinity of Bodie Island Light to investigate submarine(s) report transmitted by SS ESSO AUGUSTA.... No suspicious vessels sighted.
>
> **April 4, 1942....** At 0322 increased speed to 25 knots...proceeding to vicinity of SS ARGON off Cape Lookout. SS ARGON reported submarine on surface.
>
> At 0500 fell in astern of HAMBLETON. At 0512 HAMBLETON fired several bursts of star shells....
>
> **April 5, 1942....** At 0336 went ahead 25 knots in direction of submarine contact reported by SS CHESTER SUN. Results negative.... Proceeding to search area off Hatteras Inlet.... Submarine reported by SS PHOENIX.
>
> **April 6, 1942....** At 0208 sighted flare and flame of explosion bearing 266°T., distant about nine miles. Changed course toward. At 0242 sighted torpedoed tanker. Began circling and echo ranging. Part of tanker crew in life boats, part remaining on board. At 0600 tanker (identified as SS BIDWELL) able to proceed under own power. Escorted tanker clear of immediate area. 0810 HAMBLETON stopped, investigating turbine trouble. Patrolled station about HAMBLETON.... At 0903 made a sound contact. Developed, and at 0914 laid a five-charge pattern, set for "medium barrage,".... Made several sweeps of area; results negative.

> **April 7, 1942....** At 1230 sighted apparently new wreck vicinity Diamond Shoals. Coast Guard engaged in taking survivors from life boats and rafts.

The *Hambleton's* war diary notes that when the *Delsud* fired ahead of the formation on April 2, she was actually firing at the destroyers under the mistaken belief that she had sighted submarines. Her shooting was so bad that observers on the *Emmons'* bridge did not realize they were the target! It was only when the destroyers closed the merchantman at flank speed that she realized these were friends and cancelled the submarine report.

Nor does the official report explain that the depth charge attack made that evening was the first time the *Emmons* had ever made an attack against a possible enemy. The two charges that failed to detonate were probably set too deep for the shallow water. The three which did go off shook the slow-moving ship so severely that the power breakers tripped out, causing a series of casualties. Steam pressure dropped, and for a few minutes the ship was helpless. Many of the engineers and others with general quarters stations below deck thought the ship had been hit. Those who were not busy trying to restore power braced themselves for another "torpedo." Fortunately, it did not take long to get the ship moving again.

Neither does the war diary give the complete story of the torpedoed tanker *Bidwell.* When the *Emmons* and *Hambleton* arrived at the scene, the fires had subsided and there appeared to be no immediate danger of its sinking. This was confirmed by the tanker's chief engineer who was battling to control the damage with the men left on board. Hence, the commodore's decision to start a search for the attacking U-boat rather than stopping to give assistance. The *Bidwell's* captain, first and third mates, radioman, and a wounded seaman had been cut off from the rest of the crew by fire and smoke. Believing the vessel was sinking, they had abandoned ship in a forward lifeboat. The second mate, the only fatality, had jumped overboard in flames and was lost. When the men in the lifeboat realized that the destroyers were not going to stop at once to pick them up, they were furious and shook their fists in anger at the warships as they took up the submarine search. Left on their own, they later returned to their ship and helped to get her underway again.

The chief engineer of the tanker emerges as the true hero of the *Bidwell* torpedoing, but the destroyers must be credited with an assist. There is no way of knowing whether the attacking submarine would have, or could have, finished off the tanker. Chances are that it hightailed to seaward when the patrol ships came up. At any rate, the Bidwell's crew was given time to make repairs and get underway for the safety of Norfolk under the protection of the *Emmons.*

Curiously, at the Fifth Naval District Intelligence debriefing at Norfolk, the *Bidwell's* captain made no mention of the arrival of the destroyers, while the chief engineer was careful to do so. The Naval District Intelligence Report was very critical of the captain. Among other things, it noted that the engineer initiated a letter of complaint to the tanker's owners about the captain's haste in abandoning ship without a real effort to determine the extent of damage.

The *Emmons* had hardly rejoined the patrol after seeing the *Bidwell* safely on her way to Norfolk when the *Hambleton* had to stop and lie to, to investigate possible turbine trouble. The *Emmons* ran a protective screen around her while she diagnosed the trouble. The problem having been located and corrected, the two resumed their search, this time heading northeast toward Diamond Shoals off Hatteras. Shortly afterward, at 0908, the *Emmons* picked up an underwater sound contact. The position was some forty-five miles northeast of the scene of the *Bidwell* torpedoing, and well within range of possible positions of a submarine sneaking away from that point. Therefore, the contact was given a five charge depth charge salute. The *Hambleton* followed up with another drop. Results of the two attacks were negative and the contact was lost thereafter. It is possible that the contact was one of the numerous submerged wrecks in the vicinity.

As grim as the situation was, the patrol vessels slowed the tempo of the enemy attacks by their very presence. By their own accounts, the German submarine commanders kept a wary eye on the antisubmarine vessels from a distance. During the patrol, the reports of sightings and attacks were usually from the opposite end of the patrol area. Although numerous underwater contacts were made, only a few were considered positive enough to expend depth charges. Many were evaluated as submerged wrecks. The stormy Atlantic off the North Carolina coast has long been famous for its shipwrecks. In April, 1942, only those considered menaces to navigation were featured on the nautical charts. The latest successes of the German submarines added to the clutter. As the war progressed, the wrecks were more or less accurately charted to help sonar operators and officers evaluate their contacts.

Nearly every day empty lifeboats and life rafts were sighted, silent testimony to the effectiveness of the German offensive. Only two days before their time on the patrol line was up, the destroyers came upon a new wreck in the vicinity of Diamond Shoals. Coast Guard vessels were already on the scene and were picking up survivors when they arrived. Since there was nothing they could do to assist, the destroyers continued their search on the southwesterly leg of their patrol line. The submarines continued to stay out of their way, much to the disgust of the destroyer crews.

After eight frustrating days of running from one end to the other of the patrol area off Hatteras, the two destroyers were relieved of temporary duty under Commander Eastern Sea Frontier and ordered to report to CTF 22 at Hampton Roads. Their immediate assignment was to escort the *Ranger*, then undergoing overhaul at Portsmouth Navy Yard, from Norfolk to Newport.

4.

For the men of the *Emmons,* the experiences on the patrol line were both humbling and reassuring. Humbling, in that any adolescent ideas of the romance of war were soon abandoned in the face of reality. Reassuring, is that the ship had operated for eight days under less than ideal conditions against a competent and confident enemy without serious problems. True, they had bagged no submarines, but there was no reason for any member of the crew to look back with regret at his performance.

The Emmonites gained a healthy respect for the enemy. It could not be called fear—few would have admitted to fear—at least the craven kind. But there was a new understanding of what the war was all about. A haunting fear of many was that in an emergency they as individuals might not measure up, that through some oversight or mistake on their part the ship and their shipmates might suffer. Young men, not yet out of their teens, found a new sense of personal responsibility. In later years, many said they "grew up" on the *Emmons.* This sense of personal responsibility to the group was common to all ranks and ratings.

In a few instances, the fears engendered by a high sense of personal responsibility resulted in physical and mental disturbances. A case in point was the chief water tender in charge of one of the fire rooms. He became so obsessed with the smooth operation of his boilers that he practically lived in the fire room. One day after return to port, his subordinates found him on top of one of the boilers, naked, single-handedly trying to adjust the safety valves. It took the combined efforts of several men and sedation administered by the chief pharmacist's mate to calm him down. He was sent ashore for medical observation and rest. Presumably, he was transferred to less stressful duty. At least, he was never reassigned to the *Emmons.*

The visible signs of stress popped up in the older members of the crew, those with the greatest responsibility. Before specialists in upkeep of the new radar equipment were available, it was assigned to a chief radioman for maintenance. The equipment was new to him, very temperamental, and frequently out of adjustment. Somehow, he always restored it to operation, but the responsibility was more than he could take. He, too, was sent ashore for rest. These were unusual cases. For the most part, the crew took responsibility for their assignments in stride. Undoubtedly, there were hidden pressures which did not immediately surface.

Much of the time was spent at general quarters. Common sense demanded that battle stations be manned at each of the frequent alerts. This was in addition to the obligatory general quarters at sunrise and sunset every day. Between alerts, condition watches were maintained. Given the many calls to GQ, it is not surprising that the most popular off-watch pastime was catching up on lost sack time whenever other duties would allow it. Because of the additional crew members aboard, living conditions suffered. For one thing, there weren't enough bunks to go around. As a result, the latest drafts of recruits were issued hammocks. Many preferred sleeping on the decks or on their work stations to swinging in hammocks. A few staked out claims in such unlikely places as the sail locker. The "Guinea Pullman" forward was a favorite place. It was warm and out of the weather. Some of the specialists managed cots which they put up in their work shops. All hands acquired the knack of grabbing a quick nap between alerts in some sheltered spot clear of the traffic pattern.

Eating was another serious activity. Besides the regular meals served in the mess halls, a number of unofficial messes sprang up. Since the days of steam, black gangs have prided themselves on the ability to produce mouth watering mulligan stew in the fire rooms. Aboard the *Emmons,* the engineers prepared the traditional stew in aluminum pots over electric hot plates, instead of in the outmoded polished coal shovels. The after fire room crew departed from tradition even further to specialize in potato soup and hot chocolate. Most of the repair and work shops had their own specialties. The sail locker crew prided themselves on their grilled spam. The food fanciers claimed that spam served up in the sail locker was far superior to that served from the galley, although there is no doubt that it all came from the same source. Keeping the "messes" supplied required a great deal of ingenuity, including midnight requisitions. Canned goods were prized because there was no way for the unofficial messes to keep meat and produce refrigerated. Potatoes were no problem as the potato bin on the main deck was accessible to anyone. In fact, after several days at sea in all sorts of weather, it could be easily located, even under darkened ship conditions, by the odor peculiar to decaying spuds.

There was usually a group of hangers-on around the galley angling for a handout. On cold days a favorite place to keep warm was in the vicinity of the galley exhaust ducts—unless, of course, one was subject to sea sickness. Some expert scroungers made a practice of stopping by the galley to pick up whatever could be scooped up on the way to general quarters. The wardroom mess galley also became a favorite detour on the way to general quarter's stations. One third class steward's mate is alleged to have always reported to his GQ station with one or more chicken drumsticks stashed about his person.

One of the greatest problems was old-fashioned sea sickness. Not only was this hell for the unfortunate ones, but it created unpleasant conditions for their shipmates if the victims were overcome in the living compartments. By the time of the antisubmarine patrol, most of the crew had gained their sea legs. A few, however, were never able to overcome this particular torment. Fortunately, the weather off Hatteras did not live up to its unsavory reputation, and there were only a few days of moderately rough weather. Those days were enough to lay low those with more or less chronic *mal de mer.* Be it said that they tried valiantly to stand their watches and perform their duties, often at the cost of excruciating discomfort. Contrary to what might be expected, those who were not affected by the malady were compassionate rather than censorious. Frequently, they undertook the duties of the afflicted ones to allow them a little rest. As time went on, the hopeless cases were weeded out and sent ashore for treatment and what usually became permanent shore duty. Most were too proud to take this avenue of escape from the sea.

Some of the wags claimed that the commissary department always scheduled spaghetti with greasy meat balls or fried pork chops for days when rough weather was forecast. The hardier souls claimed that this was an advantage to them. As the ship rolled, all they had to do was to recite the menu as they stood in the chow line. If the weather was really bad, the squeamish would hurriedly head for the side rails, leaving them that much closer to the head of the line—and that many more pork chops.

5.

Not all the time was spent in the sack, eating, or at general quarters. After the routine ship's chores were done there was still time for recreation. On fair days, some filled the idle minutes by fishing off the fantail whenever the ship's speed would permit it. Others read from well-stocked supplies of paperbacks—a few from the better books of the ship's official library. Comic books were popular. A number of unofficial, but well-thumbed, girlie magazines passed from hand to hand. Compared to today's uncensored pornography they were singularly innocent.

Card games of all descriptions were widely used to pass away idle times. Solitaire and cribbage were always in vogue. Occasionally, a crap game or a poker game could be found. The stakes were not usually high, but even so, some of the luckier players amassed enough winnings that keeping them safe in the crowded living compartments posed a problem. Some trusted their shipmates and kept their winnings in their wallets or lockers. Others parceled out their winnings among non-gambling friends for safe keeping. Still others turned their money over to the ship's mailman for the same purpose. Some of the latter lost their winnings when it developed that the mailman was himself a gambler who used their winnings to finance his own games. At a later date he was investigated for alleged shortages in postal funds and removed from the ship.

Actually, there was not much money in circulation aboard ship, and very little legitimate need for it at sea. About the only items for sale in the ship's store besides clothing were tobacco, toilet articles and "pogie bait," that is, candy. In spite of the excellent pastries produced by the baker there seemed to be a never-ending craving for sweets.

Most people saved what little money they drew on paydays for liberties. It then was at a premium. There were a few "bankers" aboard who extorted usurious interest to finance a few nights of high living in the liberty ports. It may be said, however, that the "two for one" boys were never as active aboard the *Emmons* as they were reputed to be aboard other ships. Most people depended on friends to tide them over without the need of paying interest. Early in the *Emmons*'s career a War Savings Bonds drive was made. The crew responded generously and patriotically. The bonds were bought on the installment plan by deducting a small sum each pay period from the amounts due. Although the pay of a seaman was as low as $21 a month, very few missed the money deducted. Some even forgot it and amassed sizeable sums in bonds before they were discharged. Water Tender Second Class Joel Lindley, the "oil king," registered an allotment for bonds and promptly forgot it until years later. In 1950, when asked by the Navy Finance Center what he wanted done with his bonds, he remembered and used the accumulated savings to help pay for a new home he was building for his young family.

Among the seamen a popular pastime was discussing the idiosyncrasies of the officers and petty officers under whom they served. Some of the comments were far from complimentary, but, in general, they reflected respect and admiration for those to whom they were immediately responsible. They were also well aware that their personal safety and well-being was in the hands of those about whom they gossiped. Inevitably, a great amount of imagination was used in thinking up appropriate nicknames. Some, such as "Blackie" and "Groucho" were more or less freely used by everyone about the ship. Understandably, the more descriptive ones, such as "Puffy," "Puss Gut," and "Tobacco Juice," were rarely used near the person so honored.

The favorite places for exchanging gossip were around the scuttlebutts, in the mess halls, and in the relaxed atmosphere of the coffee messes. Much of it concerned the present patrol, how long it would last, and the chances of bagging a sub. Considerable enthusiasm was expressed at the idea of catching a sub, but little at the thought of continuing for any length of time beating back and forth between Wimble Shoals and Cape Lookout on the antisubmarine patrol.

There was little regret when the *Hambleton* and *Emmons* were ordered to rejoin Task Force 22 at Norfolk. Besides, both fuel and provisions were running low. Beans and rice had become far too prominent on the bill of fare.

6.

The stay at Norfolk was prolonged for four days because the *Ranger* was delayed in the shipyard. The time was not spent idly. Besides provisioning and fueling, the days were spent underway in Chesapeake Bay. One day was spent on the Wolf Trap Magnetic Survey Range. Radio direction finders were calibrated, compasses checked, and other equipment adjusted. Nights were spent snug alongside the pier at the Naval Operating Base. Liberty was granted each night.

Pent up energy was released in the bars and dives of Granby Street and on the river front where sailors with money in their pockets were welcome. Norfolk had come a long way from the prewar days when homeowners were reputed to have posted signs warning "sailors and dogs" to keep off their property. But the fact remained that the small city had little to offer a sailor on liberty beyond the amusement parks along the ocean front, several movie houses, and a wide assortment of bars and sleazy nightclubs. Human companionship without a price tag was not readily available to sailor's home ported elsewhere.

Many of the older men preferred to stay aboard ship and save their money for the anticipated return to New England ports where they had families and friends. Some, however, went ashore simply to feel land under their feet. Others, tired of the food served in the mess halls, wanted a change of chow. Some, in the words of Robert Service, "had a hunger not of the belly kind." Usually the liberty parties went ashore in groups of three or four shipboard cronies. After five months of commissioned service, they had learned to look out for each other on liberty as well as aboard ship. Somehow or other, they kept their friends out of serious trouble and saw that they got back to the ship on time. Even those who became belligerent after a few drinks had friends who tried to keep them out of harm's way or, when trouble couldn't be avoided, pitched in to give whatever support was necessary. From post-liberty accounts they got along very well with men from other destroyers. For some reason or other, at least in Norfolk, they became allergic to marines and "airdales." The latter was a term applied to anyone connected with aviation units, afloat or ashore. In following months, as the destroyer worked with aircraft carriers, and saw the "airdales" in action, the antipathy changed to admiration.

Not all the crew traveled in groups. There were a few loners. One of the leading boatswain's mates fell afoul of the shore patrol. After spending the night under arrest, he was discharged in the morning without a cent on his person. His story was that the shore patrol confiscated his wallet. Be that as it may, he found himself several miles from the base with only a few minutes before liberty was up. Not wishing to foul up his record and possibly be reduced in rating, he hailed a cab trusting that his shipmates would pay the bill when he arrived alongside the gangway. His faith in his shipmates was justified. He reported on time, the cab bill was paid, and the only loss he suffered was whatever sum had disappeared during the night.

Only one serious disciplinary case came up during the Norfolk layover. The exception involved one of the steward's mates who was restricted to the ship for some minor infraction of discipline. One of the rooms assigned to him for cleaning was that of the wardroom mess treasurer. The first night in port, the mess treasurer returned to his room after dinner to find the safe wide open. It had either been left open inadvertently or someone had obtained the combination and opened it. Nearly $300 of mess funds was missing. About the same time, a muster of restricted men revealed that the mess treasurer's steward was missing. The implication was plain. The general opinion was that the officer had opened the safe enough times in the presence of the mess man for the latter to memorize the combination. The shore patrol was notified and a few hours later the missing mess man was apprehended in a downtown bar with $269 on his person. When arrested, the mess man claimed that the money found on his person had been given to him for safekeeping by an unnamed sailor aboard ship. The following day at captain's mast he was awarded a summary court martial which was duly convened with three officers as judges.

The accused either was very astute or had good unofficial coaching in naval legal procedures. He refused to have a counsel of his own choosing or allow one to be appointed. At the trial he stood mute, refusing to plead either guilty or not guilty, to take the stand, or to make a statement. Although the court recorder, equivalent to the prosecutor in civilian courts, fancied himself as an amateur legal light, he found himself stymied in the face of the naval regulation which required that the recorder protect the interests of the accused as well as to prosecute, when the latter was without counsel. The only evidence he could present was that the mess money was missing, that the accused could have had access to it, had gone AWOL, and had been picked up with money on his person which only approximated the amount missing.

The mess man was acquitted on the offense as charged. The question then arose as to the ownership of the money found on his person. No one came forward to claim it and the acquitted mess man made no claim for it. It was eventually, probably extra legally, "returned" to the mess. A rough sort of justice was done when the steward's mate was assigned non-judicial punishment for the more easily proven offense of going absent without leave.

The *Ranger* was finally ready for sea on the 13th. Escorted by the *Emmons* and *Hambleton* she arrived at Narragansett Bay on the 14th and went about her own business while the destroyers engaged in training exercises in and out of Newport Harbor.

For the first time the five ships of Destroyer Division 19 were assembled as a unit at Newport. Commodore Wellborn shifted his broad command pennant to the designated flagship, *Ellyson,* and, at long last, was able to take his division to sea for exercises. The four destroyers of the other division of Destroyer Squadron 10, DesDiv 20, were still scattered around the Atlantic. Only occasionally throughout the entire war did the two divisions operate together.

For a week, Division 19 conducted training exercises off Block Island. Besides routine antisubmarine drills with a tame submarine and antiaircraft gunnery exercises, the destroyers engaged in high speed tactical maneuvers with the *Augusta.* They also practiced at the exacting maneuver of fueling at sea. Obviously, something was afoot.

Notably absent from the offshore exercises was the *Ranger.* While the Augusta and the destroyers were honing up their fast task force techniques, the carrier, alongside the dock at Quonset Point was engaged in taking aboard a group of sixty-eight Army P-40 pursuit planes and their combat crews under the command of Lieutenant Colonel John E. Barr. The army pilots had had no opportunity to qualify for carrier operations.

After a week, Task Force 36 composed of the *Ranger, Augusta,* and DesDiv 19, was formed. The task force left Newport April 22, 1942, headed for a mysterious Point "X" which in due time was identified as a point in the Gulf of

Guinea, off the coast of Africa. The mission was to launch the army fighters within easy flight distance of the field at Accra, capital of the British Crown Colony of the Gold Coast, now part of the Republic of Ghana. From there, they were to proceed overland via friendly air fields across Africa and the Middle East to Karachi, India. From India they were to be used to help stop the Japanese advance in Southeast Asia.

8.

When Task Force 36 took departure from Newport the position of the Allies was at its lowest point since the United States had become directly involved in the war. While the German submarines were having a field day off the Atlantic Coast of North America, the Axis had taken the offensive in all theaters.

The Germans had firm control of the land mass of Western Europe. Their submarines were threatening the supply lines to Great Britain. In Russia they had renewed the offensive in Caucasians and were slowly advancing on the Russian oil fields. The Middle East would be next. Italio-German forces virtually controlled the Mediterranean. In North Africa, Rommel, the Desert Fox, was building up his Afrika Korps for a successful attack on Tobruk. Beyond laid Egypt.

In the Pacific, the Japanese were near the peak of their conquests, and were trying to consolidate their gains before going on to Australia and India. They controlled most of the Western Pacific. A few places, such as Burma, still put up a strong defense, but continued resistance was largely dependent on maintaining the supply lines of vital equipment, including aircraft.

By April, 1942, the United States had truly become "the arsenal of democracy" as promised by President Roosevelt in his fireside chat of December, 1940. But it was one thing to produce massive amounts of guns, ammunition, tanks and planes, and another to get them into action on the battlefronts throughout the world. Essential strategic supplies were being delivered to England at great cost and great loss by way of the North Atlantic shipping lanes. Similarly, some material to Russia was pushed through the Barents Sea against formidable opposition from German submarines and aircraft based in Norway. German heavy ships were an additional menace to both Russian and North Atlantic convoys. A trickle of supplies was delivered to Egypt, the Middle East, and the Far East by way of the long, slow route around the Cape of Good Hope. Both the Mediterranean and Western Pacific were virtually closed to the Allies.

The delivery of badly needed aircraft was most difficult. In many cases long-range bombers and cargo planes could be flown overseas utilizing intervening bases. However, the long stretches over the Atlantic and the Pacific were effective barriers to the short-range fighter planes. Axis control of land masses adjacent to the normal sea routes was another hazard. Thus, in early 1942, there was a desperate need to somehow get the fighter planes across the yawning ocean spaces and around enemy-held territory to the various theaters of war.

In the spring of 1942, plans had been made to fly planes, men and material from the United States to the British Isles via airfields to be constructed on Labrador, Greenland and Iceland. This plan, designated OPERATION BOLERO by the Combined Chiefs of Staff, was designed to provide a relatively safe supply route to build up American forces for the eventual assault on Europe. However, it did not become operational until the summer of 1942, and only after a shaky beginning did it begin to relieve some of the pressure on the North Atlantic convoy routes.

There were no such convenient stepping stones leading to Russia, Egypt, the Middle East, and the Far East. Other means of getting the fighters to both Egypt and the Far East was imperative. A plan was devised to ferry them by aircraft carrier across the Atlantic and then overland to their final destination. This explains the formation of Task Force 36, built around the *Ranger* and her cargo of vital army fighters.

The *Ranger* was not the only fleet carrier to participate in joint Army-Navy air operations that spring. While Task Force 36 was working up and on its way to the Gulf of Guinea, two other important joint Army-Navy air operations were going on in widely separated combat zones. On April 18, sixteen B-25 bombers took off from the decks of the *Hornet* for the famous Doolittle raid on Tokyo. On April 20, in the Mediterranean, the carrier *Wasp,* borrowed from Task Force 99, operating with the British Home Fleet flew off forty-seven British Spitfires bound for beleaguered Malta. In early May, she repeated the performance, prompting Winston Churchill to quip, "Who says a WASP can't sting twice?" The *Ranger* subsequently made another ferry trip to the Gulf of Guinea to deliver fighter planes to the Egyptian front, but with another supporting cast. After the African invasion she carried several loads of Army fighters to Morocco.

9.

Thus it was that the *Emmons* found herself crossing the Middle Atlantic with Task Force 36 in the spring of 1942, far from the highly publicized war zones. The mission nonetheless was vital to the overall war effort. A carrier, a cruiser, a fleet tanker, and five destroyers were responsible for the safe delivery of sixty-eight

P-40 pursuit planes to an airfield in Africa from which they could be flown overland to the Far East. Considering the importance of the mission, the thirty-one day trip from Newport to Point "X" and back was remarkably easy. It was a vacation after the hectic antisubmarine patrol off Cape Hatteras. After adjusting to the exacting requirements of formation cruising, the ship settled down to a comfortable routine of sunrise and sunset general quarters, improvised gunnery exercises, and tactical drills.

From Newport the group headed almost due south, well off the coast to avoid the German submarines which were still operating close-in along the East Coast. After a week, the task force put in to Port-of-Spain, Trinidad, to take on fuel and provisions. In less than twenty hours they were underway again to angle across the Atlantic to the Gulf of Guinea. The route followed across the Atlantic was close to the famous Middle Passage used by slave ships of the eighteenth and nineteenth centuries bound from Africa to the West Indies.

Out of Trinidad, the formation was augmented by the tanker *Merrimac.* Her addition was necessary because the task force was scheduled to return directly to Trinidad as soon as the Army planes were launched. By having the destroyers' fuel from the big ships, the round trip could have been made without a tanker, but all ships would have been unacceptably low at the end of the line. The destroyers were especially sensitive. They had to be fueled about every six days to keep them in a satisfactory state of readiness for any action which might come up. Although the five destroyers had gone through training drills for fueling at sea, they got their first real experience with Task Force 36. The same was true of the *Merrimac.* The destroyers were actually fueled three times during the transatlantic crossing and return. Thanks to good weather all fueling went smoothly, but the first was slow by any standards. By the third fueling, the total time had been cut to nearly half for only a little less oil. According to the report of Commander Task Force 36, the saving in time was almost entirely achieved by faster approaches, connecting up, and casting off. The pumping time remained about the same. CTF 36 considered it "a very commendable performance." For the rest of the war, fueling at sea under any and all conditions became routine for the *Emmons.*

Very few underwater contacts were reported during the voyage. Just as the slave ships of earlier days sought to avoid cruising warships by staying out of the normal traffic lanes, the ships of Task Force 36 tried to keep clear of marauding submarines known to be dogging the shipping lanes off Africa and the approaches to the Caribbean. Periodic intelligence reports gave estimates of possible submarines along the track. For the most part these were not close enough to cause concern. A message of 7 May from the British Naval Command of West Africa to Commander Task Force 36 advised of an unconfirmed report of a large concentration of submarines off Grand Bassam along the Ivory Coast as of 5 May. Since Grand Bassam was only about 175 miles from Point "X," this might have been cause for changes in the plans, but as there was no later confirmation of the report the original plans were carried out.

Only eight underwater contacts were reported during the entire voyage. Most of these were near land and most were evaluated as no submarine. Nevertheless, each had to be treated as a possible enemy. Standard procedure was to turn the formation away from the point of contact at high speed, while the destroyer making the original contact, backed by one other, and proceeded to investigate. Unless the contact was quickly evaluated as harmless, the first destroyer usually dropped what was called an "embarrassing" depth charge barrage designed to discourage the possible submarine from getting any closer to the formation, and, hopefully, to kill or damage it. The second destroyer stood by to pick up the scent as the first turned away. Both then began a methodical, coordinated search and, if necessary, attack, until the contact was evaluated as non-submarine or they were directed to rejoin the screen. By then the hunters would be far astern of the main body and had to scramble to catch up at high speed.

The *Emmons* was involved in three of the hunts. Once was in the Gulf of Guinea when she picked up an unidentified contact and dropped an embarrassing depth charge pattern as a precautionary measure. On two other occasions she was designated to support other destroyers in following up contacts. Two days before reaching Point "X" another "embarrassing" charge was dropped—embarrassing for the *Emmons* because it was fired from Number 2 depth charge projector by accident while firing circuits were being tested. So far as was known, there was no submarine within miles. The depth charge arched gracefully over the side and exploded normally at 100 feet without doing any damage except scaring the daylights out of the engineers and others below decks. As a precautionary measure, several men in the vicinity of the projector when the impulse charge was fired were placed under observation for a few days for possible ear damage from the concussion.

The Task Force arrived at Point "X," off the Gold Coast, early on the morning of the 10th of May and preparations were made to launch aircraft from the *Ranger*. The winds and seas were moderate and the sky overcast. A touch of excitement was added when the *Ellyson* announced a sound contact which, fortunately, was soon evaluated as non-sub. Throughout the day the Task Force maneuvered some thirty to forty miles off shore to launch planes. It was not until the first group of twelve planes was airborne and headed north that the aircraft recognition experts aboard the *Emmons* realized that these were not the Navy planes they were accustomed to seeing fly on and off the *Ranger.* It was also noted that none of the fighters returned.

From time to time, flight operations were suspended because of tropical rain squalls which came and went throughout the morning and afternoon. By late afternoon the last of the sixty-eight P-40s left the deck of the *Ranger* and headed for land. Although a few took alarming dips as they left the carrier's deck, not one splashed, in spite of the fact that the army pilots had never before taken off from a moving runway.

As soon as the last plane was airborne, the Task Force resumed cruising formation and set a course which would take it out of the Gulf of Guinea on the long trip back across the Atlantic to Trinidad. Twenty minutes later, it was announced that all the Army craft had landed safely at Accra. From there they took off on their long journey across Africa and the Middle East to India and the Far Eastern battle front.

The voyage back across the Atlantic was as uneventful as the outward leg, with the exception that on the night of 17 May, the *Hambleton* and *Ellyson* collided during a heavy thundershower which had reduced the visibility to several hundred yards. The damage was not great, but the *Hambleton* was unable to safely maintain the formation speed because of a damaged bow.

The Task Force, less the crippled *Hambleton* and her escort, the *Macomb,* arrived back at Port-of-Spain the morning of May 21. The two destroyers pulled into port the following day. Emergency repairs were made to the *Hambleton*'s bow by the Naval Operating Base and technicians from the *Ranger.* She parted company with the rest of the force and proceeded to San Juan, Puerto Rico, where permanent repairs were completed.

After twenty-two days at sea, the task force had arrived at Port-of-Spain with storerooms practically empty. The destroyers were completely out of fresh provisions. The original plan was that all ships replenish from the supply ship *Pastores* which had been ordered to meet them. However, because of some staff snafu, the reefer did not have on board the anticipated fresh provisions, except for a limited supply of potatoes, onions and carrots—wonderful ingredients for a hearty stew, but not very satisfying for sailors hungry for fresh fruit and vegetables. Since there was not enough fresh produce available at short notice on the local market, the ships had to wait another week to make up the deficiencies.

Considering the *Ellyson*'s collision damage and the need for 100% mobility, Commodore Wellborn decided to shift his broad command pennant to the

Emmons for the voyage from Trinidad to the United States. He and his staff remained aboard until the division was reassembled at Boston Shipyard nearly two weeks later. The temporary shift was mutually beneficial. The officers and crew of the *Emmons* had an opportunity to get acquainted with the commodore and his staff, while they in turn gained first hand knowledge of, and confidence in, the abilities of their temporary flagship.

From Trinidad, Task Force 36, without the *Hambleton,* headed straight for Narragansett Bay. Enroute, the *Rodman* picked up a sound contact about 300 miles east of Cape Hatteras and made two depth charge attacks while the *Emmons* stood by. The contact was lost on the second attack and never regained before the two destroyers were ordered to rejoin the formation at flank speed.

Task Force 36 was dissolved when the *Ranger* and the four remaining destroyers entered Narragansett Bay, May 28th. They had been gone thirty-six days. On the way up from Trinidad, the *Augusta* and *Merrimac* had been diverted to other duty. The voyage had, for the most part, been in waters far from the highly publicized combat zones, although there always had been the possibility of an attack from enemy submarines lurking along the shipping lanes off Africa and South America. As usual, the dangers of day-to-day cruising at sea proved to be as great as or greater than threats from the enemy. The only damage suffered by the task force had occurred when the *Hambleton* and the *Ellyson* collided in a blinding rain squall. Sixty-eight badly needed fighters had been delivered across the Atlantic in flying condition. To have crated, shipped them across the ocean, and then reassembled them would have taken months. The mission had been accomplished without any permanent loss.

After an overnight stay in Newport, the *Emmons,* followed by the *Rodman* and *Macomb,* was underway early the next morning. They were bound, via the Cape Cod Canal, for Boston and a three day period of upkeep and repair at the Navy Yard in preparation for their next assignment.

John P. Mcarthy, a plank owner (one of the commissioning crew) who came aboard as an Apprentice Seaman. He earned the rate of Gunner's Mate, Third Class. "J.P" had collected shipmates autographs on the photo below, and sent it home to await his return. John was missing after the April 6, 1945 action and declared KIA in June, 1945.

McCarthy Family Collection

This official Navy photo shows the *Emmons* in her measure 12 camoflage during early duty in the Atlantic Theater. Later she took on measure 22 appearance (Haze gray above Navy blue hull), and ultimately the serriform Pacific camouflage scheme. This picture now hangs in his sister's home.

5

With the British Home Fleet at Scapa Flow

o o o o o o o o o o o o o o o o o o o o o o o o o o o o o o o

At 1130 got underway with Desdiv 19 consisting *of Hambleton* (CDD-19), *Emmons, Rodman, Macomb* enroute to Scapa Flow to operate with Destroyers of the Home Fleet. This Division now a part of TF-99.

—***Emmons*** *War Diary, July 14, 1942.*

After the three-day overhaul at Boston, the *Emmons* and *Macomb* reported for duty to Commander Task Force 22 at Newport. With the *Ranger* and *Augusta* they proceeded to the new operating base at Argentia, Newfoundland, where they arrived 5 June. One has only to look at a chart of the North Atlantic to understand its strategic location in relation to the convoy routes between America and the British Isles, as well as the passages around Iceland from German-held Norway to the open reaches of the Atlantic.

A motley collection of convoy escort vessels flying the flags of Britain, Canada, Free France, and Poland, as well as the United States, gave emphasis to the importance of the base to convoy activities. Most of the service force vessels, tankers, repair ships and tugs, belonged to the United States Navy. A seemingly permanent fixture was the destroyer tender *Prairie,* which had occupied the same moorings for so long that she was called the "Capital of Newfoundland" by the crews of visiting ships.

Task Force 22 spent the greater part of June at Argentia conducting training exercises in the Atlantic, to the south and southeast of Newfoundland. Ships of the force were not directly concerned with the many convoys passing between the States and Europe, although they were available if needed in an emergency. It is significant that many of the training exercises made use of British formations and tactical signals. For some of the ships, including the *Emmons,* it was a new situation. For others, it was the logical continuation of events dating back to the fall of 1940. For a fuller understanding of what the *Emmons,* as a part of Task Force 22, was doing at Argentia, it is desirable to review the progress of the war in the Northeast Atlantic and the changes in U.S. commitments which occurred in 1940 and 1941.

2.

In September, 1940, a deal was struck with England whereby she would supply bases in exchange for American destroyers. Prior to the destroyers deal it had been assumed in United States military plans that the British Fleet would control the Atlantic while the American Fleet concentrated in the Pacific. As the British situation deteriorated, there was a growing realization that the greatest threat to the security of the Americas might be from Europe rather than Asia. It was also recognized that Britain might not be able to maintain control of the Atlantic without massive assistance from the United States. Under the prodding of President Roosevelt, contingency plans were revised providing for the major effort to be expended in the Atlantic should the United States get into war with the Axis. A "holding action" was to be the order in the Pacific until such time as sufficient forces were readied to fight an all out war in both oceans.

The President was determined to do more to help Britain than revise war plans. His "Arsenal of Democracy" speech of December, 1940, was designed to prepare the American people for new efforts to help the British. It was a forerunner of the Lend-Lease Act of March, 1941. Staff talks between British, United States, and Canadian military leaders were inaugurated to ensure maximum efficiency in allocation of tasks and the means for accomplishing them, if and when the United States entered the war.

As a result of the British-American-Canadian staff conferences, summarized in war plans known as ABC-1, the Navy Department began to realign and reorganize the scant forces available to conform to the new responsibilities it would be shouldering in the Atlantic. In February, to cover the three major areas of likely naval action, three separate fleets were created, the Atlantic, Pacific, and Asiatic, each under the command of a full admiral. The old Atlantic Squadron became the Atlantic Fleet under the command of Admiral Ernest J. King, who was fleeted up from two-star rank. Shortly after the passage of the Lend-Lease Act in March, the President directed that the Atlantic Fleet be put on a wartime basis. Accordingly, the Chief of Naval Operations issued instructions for the Atlantic Fleet to "PREPARE FOR WAR." Preliminary plans were drawn up assigning areas of responsibility in the Atlantic and creating major task forces, numbered One to Ten. The first four involved surface ships assigned, or to be assigned, to the Atlantic Fleet. They were: Task Force One, Ocean Escort Force, based at Narragansett Bay and Boston; Task Force Two, Striking Force, based at Bermuda and Hampton Roads; Task Force Three, Scouting Force, based at San Juan and Guantanamo; Task Force Four, Support Force, based originally at Narragansett Bay, but later moved to Argentia, Newfoundland. The remaining task forces were: Submarines, Coastal Frontiers, a Bermuda Force, Patrol Wings, Service Force, and the First Marine Division. It was envisaged that forces in the Atlantic would be augmented at the expense of the Pacific to meet the new responsibilities and take some of the load off the British.

Throughout 1941 the fleet was kept busy by the demands of the undeclared war. United States forces gradually took over protection of convoys in the Western Atlantic. Protection of Greenland was assumed in April. American marines relieved the British garrison occupying Iceland in July. The base at Hvalfjordur was shared with the British Navy by units assigned to the defense of Iceland. The Scouting Force, responsible for the Caribbean and Middle Atlantic, gradually extended its activities to the South Atlantic and began to stake out bases at Recife and Bahia. The task force organization established early in the year continued to work very well, although there never were enough ships to meet all the commitments at any given time. Of necessity, there was constant shifting of ships from one task force to another to meet the most urgent tactical situation of the moment. This was particularly true of the capital ships and their assigned destroyers. Because the United States was not officially at war, the assignment of ships and their operations had to be made in the deepest secrecy.

One of the best kept secrets of the undeclared war was the organization and operations of the Support Force, under the command of Rear Admiral Arthur L. Bristol. Originally called the "British Isles Detachment," it was established as of 1 March 1941, to meet commitments dating back to December, 1940, and reaffirmed by joint staff talks. Originally designed to train and deploy support forces in British waters, its most important function became to provide support for shipping in the Atlantic. Not only was it responsible for operation of ships assigned, but also for planning and construction of bases from which they were to operate in Canada, Iceland, and the United Kingdom. Perhaps its most important base was the operating base at Argentia, Newfoundland. The staff of the

Support Force directed its many activities from the flagship, *Prairie,* which, as previously mentioned, became a semi-permanent fixture in Placentia Bay.

The beleagured British were quick to take advantage of the United States' willingness to shoulder heavier loads in the Atlantic, thus enabling them to shift some of their ships to other threatened areas of the Empire. At their request, the transatlantic mid-ocean meeting point, (MOMP), was moved closer to the United Kingdom in order to relieve some of the British escort vessels for service on convoy routes around Spain and Africa. In September, when the Home Fleet was seriously weakened by transfers to the Mediterranean, the First Sea Lord, Admiral Sir Dudley Pound, suggested that the Atlantic Fleet help guard the passages from the Norwegian and North Seas to the Atlantic. The Admiralty was afraid that the Germans, noting the depletion of the Home Fleet, would try to shake loose some of their battleships and cruisers from Baltic and Norwegian ports to raid the Atlantic convoy routes. Specifically, Admiral Pound suggested that Atlantic Fleet ships patrol the Denmark Strait between Iceland and Greenland for a few weeks, while the Home Fleet guarded the Iceland-Faroes passage. After approval by President Roosevelt, Admiral King directed that strong battle groups be maintained at Iceland and Argentia. The Iceland group was to cover the Denmark Strait and the Argentia group the Argentia-Azores line. Carriers, cruisers, and destroyers were ordered from the Striking Force at Bermuda to augment the ships already stationed at Iceland and Argentia. The Denmark Straits patrol was maintained well into 1942.

The Germans did not choose to risk their heavies at this time, but their very existence was a continuing threat. The British remembered all too well the tense days of May, 1941, when the *Bismarck* and *Prinz Eugen* broke out through the Denmark Strait into the North Atlantic, and were determined that it would not happen again. Their concern was justified and was shared by the United States. The German "fleet in being" kept a major force of the allied capital ships tied up for more than two years. After Pearl Harbor, major units of the Atlantic Fleet were kept at Iceland, Argentia, and Casco Bay to back up the British Home Fleet should the Germans move out of their bases in Norway and the Baltic. At times, when German aggressive action seemed most likely, United States ships were sent to operate directly with the British out of Scapa Flow. The pressure from this source was relieved somewhat in late 1943 when the *Tirpitz* was disabled by midget submarines and the *Scharnhorst* was cornered by the British and sunk off Norway's North Cape. The threat of German capital ships was eliminated altogether when Hitler, disgusted with the lack of success of the big ships, his "showboats," ordered them dismantled and their crews retrained for service in the more profitable submarines. Late in the war, some German sailors were even ordered to fight with the retreating Army.

Pearl Harbor brought little change in the tasks required of the Atlantic Fleet. Operations now were covered by the mantle of legal belligerency, but secrecy was maintained as a matter of prudence. The fictitious limits set for Western Hemisphere defense disappeared. The basic strategy adopted in 1940-41, to concentrate on defeat of the Axis in Europe while holding in the Pacific, remained in effect, but even "holding actions" require vast numbers of ships. Besides, it would have been foolish to permit Japan to digest her gains unmolested.

Consequently, the desperate situation in the Pacific drained the Atlantic Fleet of most of the newest and best ships, as well as many of the older ones, which had been assigned to augment the Atlantic Fleet during the undeclared war. All fleet carriers except the *Ranger* and *Wasp* went to the Pacific, and the *Wasp* was transferred in June, 1942. The old battleships of Battleship Division 5 *(New York, Texas, Arkansas)* remained in the Atlantic for most of the war. They had the help of the powerful new ships of Battleship Division 6 *(Washington, North Carolina)* for nine months, until they too were shipped west. Cruiser Division 7 *(Wichita, Tuscaloosa, Augusta)* were left in the North Atlantic while Cruiser Division 2 *(Memphis, Milwaukee, Cincinnati, Omaha)* took care of the South Atlantic. These ships formed the backbone of the Atlantic Fleet until near the end of the war.

Each of the major task forces had its quota of destroyers, the greatest number being assigned to the Support Force. Most destroyers permanently assigned to the Atlantic Fleet were of the *Benson* class, or older, and, like the *Emmons,* had been earmarked and equipped for Atlantic duty. The pattern developed of keeping new ships constructed on the East Coast in the Atlantic for their shakedown. Toward the end of their training period they would frequently be assigned to operating task forces to piece out the hard-working ships permanently assigned. Sometimes they were retained for several months for special operations such as the invasion of Africa, or to operate with the British Home Fleet to ensure containment of the German Battle Fleet.

With Pearl Harbor came a major restructuring of the high command and changes in the task force organization. Admiral King was named Commander in Chief United States Fleet (Cominch) and Chief of Naval Operations. Thus he became supreme commander of all United States naval forces. Admiral Stark was assigned to London as Commander United States Naval Forces in European Waters (ComNavEu). Admiral Royal E. Ingersoll became Commander in Chief Atlantic Fleet (CinCLant).

Early in 1942, Admiral Ingersoll issued a new Operation Plan renumbering and renaming the Atlantic Fleet's major task forces. The changes were more cosmetic than substantive and were made primarily to prevent confusion in task organization which had arisen from the old numbering system. Task Forces 1 to 10 became Task Forces 21 through 30. The old Ocean Escort Force became Task Force 21, the Striking Force, built around the battleships. The former Striking Force became Task Force 22, the Scouting Force, consisting of carriers and cruisers, while the old Scouting Force was redesignated Task Force 23, South Atlantic Force, to acknowledge its expanded area of responsibility. The Support Force was renamed Task Force 24, Escort Force, to more precisely describe its major function. Regardless of designations, task organizations continued to be formed from whatever ships were available, at any given time, to get the job of the moment done. An important new task force was Task Force 30, the Amphibious Force, built around transports and related vessels. The protection of troop transports of this force became one of the important jobs of all the other task forces of the fleet.

Another sizable group of Atlantic Fleet ships operated as Task Force 99, directly under the command of the British Home Fleet out of Scapa Flow during much of 1942. In January British intelligence had reported the new German battleship *Tirpitz* at Trondheim. Early in February the battleships *Scharnhorst* and *Gneisenau* with the battle cruiser *Prinz Eugen* made the now famous dash from Brest, up the Channel, to German ports. Although the *Scharnhorst* and *Gneisenau* were damaged by mines during the move, all reached safety in Germany. The *Scharnhorst* and *Greisenau* had to remain in Germany for repairs, but the *Prinz Eugen* soon joined the *Tirpitz* at Trondheim, as did the battleship *Admiral Scheer.* The *Hipper* joined a few weeks later. The British, already preoccupied with the containment of the German ships, were convinced more than ever that the Germans were concentrating their heavies in Norway for an all out effort in the Atlantic. What the Germans may have done had they been able to assemble their fleet intact at any one time is moot. It is interesting that while the British were convinced the Germans were preparing for major forays into the Atlantic, Hitler was equally convinced that the British were planning an invasion of Norway and insisted that his battle fleet be disposed to repel such an attempt. He also directed that submarines intended for action against allied shipping in the Atlantic be stationed to help in the defense of Norway. A direct result of the concentration on Norway was that the Germans not only had a strategic position for hit-and-and run raids in the Atlantic but also were in a position to inflict heavy damage to convoys bound for Russia around Northern Norway. Indeed, for a while in 1942, they very nearly stopped those convoys.

In March, 1942, in response to British appeals for backup against the German battleships, a powerful United States task force consisting of the brand new battleship *Washington,* the carrier *Wasp,* the heavy cruisers *Wichita* and *Tuscaloosa,* and six destroyers, was hastily assembled at Casco Bay. As Task Force 39, under the command of Rear Admiral John W. Wilcox, Commander Battleship Division 6, the force left Casco for the United Kingdom late in March. One day out of Casco the task force encountered a typical North Atlantic gale during which Admiral Wilcox was lost overboard from his flagship, the *Washington.* Command of the task force devolved on Rear Admiral Robert C. Giffen, Commander Cruiser Division Seven, known throughout the service as "Ike." Task Force 39 reported to the Home Fleet at Scapa Flow on 5 April and was redesignated Task Force 99 by Cominch to emphasize that it was independent of the Atlantic Fleet.

The addition of the American task force gave the Home Fleet awesome power, especially in battleships, for the British had assigned their newest and best battleships, the *King George V, Duke of York, Anson,* and *Howe,* not to mention the carriers and cruisers. The fleet was now far superior to any combination the Germans could send out of Norway. But the fact remains that the Germans, whether they moved or not, were effectively preventing badly needed allied ships from being deployed to other areas.

This point was quickly noted by Vice Admiral Jonas Ingram, in command of the South Atlantic Task Force. In a salty letter to Admiral Ingersoll, he cogently stated the strategic effects of the German "fleet in being." He wrote:

> I note by the press that Ike over in Scapa Flow says he commands the fighting part of the American Navy. All the Huns have to do is to tie the TIRPITZ up to a tree in Norway and allow all her crew to go on extended leave; she will still contain most all the British Navy and likewise Ike's force.

While the original ships of Task Force 99 were getting first hand training in British operations at Scapa Flow, strong elements of Task Force 22 were based at Argentia to oppose any German raiders in the Western Atlantic. After the return of Task Force 36 from the plane ferry trip to Africa, Task Force 22 had been reassembled at Narragansett Bay around the *Augusta* and *Ranger* and sent to Argentia. While standing by to repel German raiders, the ships of the force were under training for operations with the British. Thus, the *Emmons* found herself in June, 1942, at Argentia, in training for future assignment to the British Home Fleet.

3.

It was the threshold of summer when the *Emmons,* with Task Force 22, moored for the first time at the Argentia Naval Base in Placentia Bay. It was the farthest north she had been in her short career. To the stateside construction crews whipping the new base into shape the June weather seemed benign. Similarly, to the tired crews of the escort ships, coming and going to and from the stormy convoy routes off shore, the sheltered bay was a welcome haven. But to the crew of the *Emmons* and her sister ships, it seemed more like the North Pole after the warm waters of the South American Pacific and the middle Atlantic. Blues and foul weather gear replaced the tropical whites of the last few months.

The base had been underway as a major project almost from the signing of the destroyers for bases agreement in 1940. It had achieved increased importance with the creation of the ultra-secret Support Force in 1941. In August of that year it had been the site of the secret meeting between President Roosevelt and Prime Minister Churchill, which produced the agreement on war aims announced to the world in the Atlantic Charter. As the United States assumed more and more responsibility in the Atlantic, it became one of the key points in the Battle of the Atlantic. From there, Commander Support Force, later the Escort Force, supervised the protection of convoys in the Western Atlantic.

In June, 1942, construction of a modern base was going ahead at a rapid pace, but the facilities were still quite primitive. Some essential storage buildings and some barracks were completed. Secure berthing docks were still represented by jagged rows of pilings. Streets had been laid out but were not yet paved. The combination of the spring thaw and churning of construction machinery made them a quagmire of mud which seemed to have an insatiable appetite for overshoes and sea boots. The fueling facilities were not yet completed. Ships coming in from sea low in fuel oil had to go alongside a tanker moored to a centrally located buoy. The few recreational facilities were Spartan. For the crews there was a bowling alley, snack bar and beer hall, and there was a movie house, but most men preferred to watch the movies aboard their own ships. The officers had access to a dingy "club" which offered meals and a bar. The bar was by far the best feature of the club.

All in all, Argentia was not very inviting in 1942, but few aboard the *Emmons* cared. There was little time for liberty, or even for speculating on what the next move would be. Obviously, there was an important reason for the task force's presence at the Newfoundland base, but the concept of watchful waiting is hard for active young Americans to appreciate and most of the men looked forward to moving on to more exciting activity, whatever it might be.

Task Force 22 was far from idle. Nearly every day some of the ships put to sea for exercises. Each time one of the large ships would sortie she took with her a protective antisubmarine screen of destroyers. In the case of the *Ranger* the destroyers had dual duty. During flight operations one had to act as plane guard to fish out of the water those surviving flyers that were unfortunate enough to crash on take-off or landing. Part of the time was devoted to tactical exercises. When they did not have to screen the big ships the destroyers would conduct training of their own. One day it would be antiaircraft and surface gunnery exercises, another, simulated torpedo attacks. One day was spent making repeated mock attacks on a "tame" British submarine. Advantage was taken of lulls in scheduled exercises to take care of routine chores which could be done only at sea, such as compensation of compasses and calibration of direction finders. More often than not, scheduled exercises would be disrupted by the heavy fogs generated by the mingling of the warm air brought north with the Gulf Stream and the cold air accompanying the Labrador Current off Newfoundland.

On the positive side, the frequent fogs helped to smooth out the usually rough seas and to block off the cold, biting winds. Even so, temperatures remained low and the clammy mist had a sting of its own. Much unscheduled training in "blind" maneuvering was another result of the weather changes. The new radar proved invaluable and allowed the maintenance of formations and speeds which would have been impossible without it. Regardless of the new techniques, old fashioned precautions were taken whenever a fog closed in. Additional lookouts were posted and the fog signals started. Perhaps the loneliest men on the ship were the bow lookouts who at times felt they had a separate existence from the rest of their shipmates. In really bad fogs their only contact with a disembodied bridge, back there somewhere, was by telephone. Many a former *Emmons* lookout remembers climbing into foul weather gear and reporting to the forecastle for a two-hour stint of peering into the soupy mist for whatever might, or might not, be there. The unknown is always more scary than the known, and it was always comforting to the lookouts to be able to keep in sight the spray and white foam of another ship of the formation ahead or on a parallel course. Because of the concentration required and exposure to the weather, lookouts were relieved after two hours for two hours of less stressful duty, usually in the relatively cozy pilot house.

The destroyers got little rest even when no exercises were scheduled. One or more were kept on picket duty to seaward of the antisubmarine net gates. Others were designated as "ready duty" ships, required to be able to get underway on short notice. These were routine duties expected of destroyers wherever they happened to be. But the relatively primitive facilities of the Argentia base at this time were responsible for more unorthodox tasks. All ships of the task force, big and small, were required to be ready for extended duty on a few hours notice. This of course meant that they had to be topped off with fuel oil at all times. Since the dockside fueling facilities were not completed, a tanker, the *Winooski,* more or less permanently secured to one of the buoys in the bay, was the source for all ships. It was routine for the destroyers to go alongside the *Winooski* each time they came in from sea, before securing to their assigned mooring buoy. But the approaches to the *Winooski* were difficult and hazardous for the large ships and if there was a small YO, yard oilier, at Argentia at the time it was not in evidence. Keeping the big ships topped off posed a problem for the task force commander. In a variation of the "man bites dog" theme, the traditional roles were reversed and the destroyers were used as yard oilers to fuel the big ships. Twice during the waiting period at Argentia, the *Emmons* had to top off the *Ranger* before she could take care of her own needs.

Acting as fuel oil barge was not too bad and was certainly in keeping with Cominch's admonition to "Do more than your best with what you've got." But the final ignominy was being pressed into service as garbage scows for the big ships. There were no garbage barges, so the versatile destroyers were once more pressed into service to haul the garbage of the large ships out to sea whenever the latter had several days in port. On one occasion the *Emmons* was ordered to relieve the *Juneau* of her accumulated refuse. With the fantail piled high with the malodorous cargo, the *Emmons* preceded through the harbor "gates" to the dumping grounds before proceeding on the duty assigned. It was a great relief to get the decks hosed down and report for duty more in keeping with her mission—and her dignity. For once the cold weather was a blessing.

There was little to do on liberty but go to the bowling alley or walk around the base. A few did get to the small village outside the base where they were cordially received by the "Newfies" and enjoyed the excellent Canadian beer which sold at ten cans for a dollar. Some enjoyed fishing in the cold streams, but were not able to go very far because there was always the possibility of having to get underway in a hurry.

For one member of the crew it was like a homecoming. Seaman James F. Donovan, one of the famous "D" groups out of Newport Training Center, had left Newfoundland with his family when he was only eight years old. Donovan seemed to find friends or relatives wherever he went. He recognized some of the civilian base construction workers from around his home town of Medford, Massachusetts, and renewed acquaintance with them. From them he learned that there was a controversy going on over the wages to be paid to the skilled Newfoundland workmen who were employed on the base projects. The Massachusetts contractors proposed to pay the Newfoundlanders the same wages as workmen with comparable skills from the states, but the British government objected because they believed the workmen would be unwilling to go back to their regular wages after the war, thus introducing a disruptive factor into the shaky Newfoundland economy.

One *Emmons* crewman, Seaman William E. Dolasky, a member of the "D" group, and an ardent baseball fan, remembers Argentia as the place where he met, quite by accident, one of his heroes, Bob Feller, star of the Cleveland Indians. The ball player had stopped a small party *of Emmons* liberty men to ask where he could go on the base for a physical workout. The best Dolasky could do was direct him to the bowling alley, which at that time represented the only covered athletic facility available.

It would be an error to assume that the destroyers of Task Force 22 did nothing at Argentia but conduct training exercises and service the big ships. There was ample evidence in the coming and going of ships of the Escort Force that a deadly war was going on along the convoy routes to the south and east. Several times destroyers of Destroyer Division 19 were diverted from their routine tasks to go to the scene of reported submarine sightings by aircraft working out of the base at Argentia. On one occasion the *Rodman* was ordered out to investigate a "suspicious" steamer which proved to be a Norwegian freighter with perfectly proper papers. She had hardly completed her examination of the Norseman when she was ordered to proceed to the eastward of the Grand Banks to assist the escorts of a convoy engaged in a running battle with a submarine "wolf pack."

The *Emmons* got her share of emergency orders. The third day after arrival at Argentia she was ordered to the east of Newfoundland to assist in the search for a missing patrol plane. She left harbor in a dense fog and much of the two-day search was hampered by the prevailing low visibility. There were, however, occasional spells when the weather would clear. During one of the clear periods she had the thrill of exchanging recognition signals with a lone patrol plane which was also looking for the missing aircraft.

Under the direction of Commander Escort Force in Argentia she was gradually ordered to search in areas farther and farther to the north. The last search area assigned was centered at 50°20' N., 52° 00' W., and northeast of Gander. This was the farthest north the *Emmons* had been to date. Another first was registered off the Newfoundland coast. On the second day an isolated iceberg was sighted during one of the periods of good visibility. The captain seized the opportunity to test the radar and sonar against this unusual target. Both worked most satisfactorily.

The search was called off on the third day and the *Emmons* started back to harbor. But she was diverted twice enroute. The first time was when she received information that a patrol plane from Argentia was attacking a submarine to the east of Cape Race. Since the *Emmons* was only 125 miles from the reported position the Commodore ordered her to procede at best speed to the scene to pick up the hunt. On arrival at the reported position of the attack shortly before midnight, June 11, there was no evidence of either attacking plane or submarine. Nonetheless, an eighteen-hour search of a 20 by 30 mile area was conducted before the ship was once more headed for Argentia. Throughout the hunt the fog cleared, but, as often happens in the North Atlantic, the improvement in visibility was gained at the expense of increased winds and stormy seas.

The destroyer had hardly changed course toward Argentia when a four-masted schooner, wallowing in the heavy seas, was sighted. From her colors and rigging, the vessel appeared to be one of the many hardy Portuguese fishermen which were common on the Grand Banks. As a neutral fisherman she had every right to fish in international waters. Further, unlike her neighbor, Spain, Portugal was known to be sympathetic to the Allies—indeed, the following year she ceded rights to bases in the Azores. Normally, the Portuguese fishermen were quick to identify themselves. But, in this instance, repeated attempts at visual communications were ignored by the schooner. Since submarines were known to be in the area, and it was suspected that they were being resupplied from some mobile source, there was no choice but to call away the boarding party to check the schooner's papers and cargo. It would have been easy for the Germans to plant a supply and communication ship among the *bona fide* fishermen.

In view of the rough seas, the boarding call was made at considerable peril to the boat, its crew, and the members of the boarding party. Two members of the boarding party, who manned the gig for the investigation, William M. Hayes, the coxswain, and Anthony Salvatore Esposito, the bow hook, recall the incident vividly as one of the highlights of their introduction to the stormy weather of the North Atlantic. They attribute the safe launching and recovery of the gig to superb seamanship aboard the *Emmons.* Needless to say, they, too, did an outstanding job under tough conditions. The fisherman proved to be the *Santa Maria Manuela,* four months out of Lisbon, with proper Portuguese papers. No evidence of clandestine cargo or unusual radio gear was noted.

With nothing else to divert her, the *Emmons* rejoined the other destroyers of DesDiv 19 at Argentia. Her time at the northern outpost was nearing its end.

4.

On Saturday, June 20, the *Emmons* was underway before noon to conduct exercises off Argentia, but had to return to her moorings because of fog. Late that same day orders were received for Task Force 22 to get underway and proceed immediately to Newport. In spite of the fog all of the ships of the task force cleared the harbor before midnight and set course for Newport in compliance with the order. The fog persisted throughout the passage, but did not prevent arrival at the Rhode Island base in less than two days.

On arrival the destroyers were granted short availabilities at Boston Navy Yard beginning on June 23. The *Emmons* in company with the *Forrest, Corry,* and *Hobson* made the short trip to Boston via the Cape Cod Canal. After her two-day overhaul she returned alone by the same route. It was almost like homecoming for DD457 as she moved through the protected waters of the canal at an unaccustomed sedate pace. The ship's company responded enthusiastically to the warm greetings and encouraging cheers of the friendly Cape Codders.

In the meantime, Destroyer Division 19 had been alerted to fill to capacity with service ammunition, stores and fuel, and to "prepare for distant service." The four days at Newport following return from Boston were spent in feverish preparations for deployment to some unspecified "distant" area. Somehow or other the long-delayed annual inspection was conducted amid the preparations for a new assignment.

The precise definition of "distant service" remained a mystery, even to those entitled to know by their position. The orders for the division, now under the direct control of CinCLant, were changed nearly every day. As preparations for a move became obvious, there was considerable speculation as to what the next job would be. The preponderance of opinion was that the division would head for the Pacific. This proved to be very far from accurate. The first dispatch orders directed the division to report to the Commander Striking Force, CTF21, on June 30. This directive was modified directing the division, "when ready," to proceed to Base Cast, to escort the battleship *Washington* back to the United States. The last day of June that order was cancelled and the destroyers were directed to join Commander Task Force 37, at a rendezvous to be designated by the latter. CTF 37, in turn, set the rendezvous for the earliest time possible after 0830, July 1, off New York.

The Task Force 37 order proved to be the last and meant that the destroyers were to screen a troop convoy and its supporting battleships and cruisers. When the task force assembled off New York it was composed of the battleship *Texas,* the cruiser *Philadelphia,* Destroyer Squadron 13, and the destroyers of Division 19, minus the *Macomb,* all assigned to protect seven troop ships headed for Iceland and the United Kingdom. It was an exciting assignment for a destroyer, far preferable to escorting slow-moving cargo ships. Troop convoys moved and maneuvered at high speeds in contrast to the sluggish merchantmen.

The *Emmons* did not remain with the main body of Task Force 37 long. During the sortie from Newport on the midwatch, her starboard propeller had struck some submerged object causing a small crack at the tip of one of the blades. The damage was not severe and she had made the rendezvous off New York with the rest of the division. But when speeds approaching 25 knots were ordered there was a marked vibration in the starboard engine which boded no good for a long voyage. Further, any abnormality in a propeller increases ease of detection by underwater listening devices. The *Emmons* was ordered to Boston for emergency dry-docking and replacement of the propeller.

The dry-docking and propeller change took only 12 hours, but when she left the dry-dock during the small hours of July 3, new orders directed the *Emmons* to proceed to Halifax to wait for further orders. July 4 saw her entering Halifax, where she celebrated Independence Day with the other warships present by "dressing ship" with her signal flags. Also at Halifax she found a sister ship, the *Macomb,* and the troop ships *Siboney* and *Aorangi,* which for some reason had been separated from Task Force 37. The *Emmons* and *Macomb* were directed to escort the two transports, now designated as Convoy AT17B, across the Atlantic.

The splinter group was underway on the 5th. Captain Ragan was the escort commander until the *Buck,* with Commander Destroyer Squadron 13 on board, joined up the second day out of Halifax. Most of the passage was covered by fog, which at least kept the seas smoothed, a blessing for the crowded transports. Several drastic course changes were made to avoid enemy submarines reported along the assigned track. The *Emmons* picked up one sonar contact which was quickly evaluated as a large fish. On another occasion the *Emmons* took station six miles to starboard of the formation to take direction finder bearings on radio signals. As they were apparently enemy transmissions, course was changed to give the area from which that area a wide berth. The formation was kept "closed up."

As prearranged, on July 11, six days out of Halifax, rendezvous was made with a small British convoy. At this point the transatlantic convoy split up. The *Siboney* joined the northbound British convoy to Iceland. The *Aorangi* with the three American destroyers headed southeast for Greenock, Scotland. The following day, before entering the Firth of Clyde, the *Buck* shoved off for other duty, leaving the *Emmons* and *Macomb* to deliver the transport with its precious cargo to the port authorities at Greenock. Present at Greenock were the *Texas* and *Philadelphia* with the *Hambleton* and *Rodman.* The destroyers of Squadron 13 had already been detached for other duty, probably for duty with the Escort Force out of the United States base at Londonderry, Ireland.

5.

The meaning of the June directive to Destroyer Division 19 to "prepare for distant service" was soon clarified. At Greenock the four destroyers of the division were detached from Task Force 37 to replace the destroyers of Division 16 operating with the British Home Fleet at Scapa Flow. The latter were ordered to escort the *Washington* back to the United States. By the time Des Div 19 arrived at Scapa Flow, Admiral Giffin's command consisted of the cruisers *Wichita* and *Tuscaloosa* and the destroyers of that division under Commander Wellborn, the *Hambleton, Emmons, Rodman* and *Macomb.* The decrease in Task Force 99 was occasioned not so much by a lessening of the German threat as by demands of the Pacific Fleet. Although damage to some of the German heavy ships had temporarily taken some of the pressure off the Home Fleet, there was still a formidable German force in Norway, and the United States agreed to keep the remainder of Task Force 99 under British command until mid-August when it was anticipated that additional Royal Navy units from other theaters would be available to join the Home Fleet.

The first inkling most people on board the *Emmons* had that they would remain in European waters came shortly after arrival in Greenock. The ship had hardly gone alongside a tanker to fuel when six Royal Navy radio and signal ratings reported aboard for duty, complete with sea bags and personal belongings. They were to remain on board during the tour of duty with the Home Fleet to assist with communications and maneuvers during tactical evolutions. They were very efficient and proved invaluable in indoctrinating the American crew in British terminology, especially in the interpretation and execution of tactical signals. The *Emmons* signalmen and bridge watch had to learn an entirely new tactical language starting with a new alphabet—from "apple" to "zebra."

The English sailors were a source of great interest, sometimes of amazement, to the American sailors. It took the latter some time to learn that the Englishmen had been at war for more than two years longer than they, and had been on short rations that much longer. The Americans were always amused to see the English line up for liberty with their ditty bags crammed with cigarettes, candy and toilet articles from the ship's store. They were somewhat envious at the ease with which the Britons could shift from working to liberty uniforms simply by turning their collars "inside out." There were some Anglophobes who didn't like being under the tutelage of a "limey." A few resented what they took for their imagined superiority in war experience, although it had to be admitted that they had been under the gun for a much longer time than their American cousins. One of the not so unimportant differences arose over the question of personal hygiene. The English sailors, used to draconic water rationing, were reluctant to use the water available for showers. One had to be dunked under the shower to convince him that it was indeed O.K. One of the strangest customs, and a source of envy to the Americans, was the daily ration of grog. Somehow or other, the visitors semiofficially retained the right to their daily ration which was issued by the senior petty officer, who duly recorded it in his "log."

All the irritants were minor, and the English ratings were acknowledged to be superb seamen. They did an excellent job in keeping the *Emmons* abreast of the Royal Navy way of doing things. When they left the ship at the end of August any resentment at the "differences" had disappeared. Indeed, all hands appreciated the hard work and efficiency of the "limeys" and were sorry to see them go.

For all practical purposes, the *Emmons* became a part of the "King's Navy." Before proceeding to Scapa two days were spent at Greenock taking on supplies and drawing Royal Navy tactical publications.

Liberty was granted every day. Most of the liberty party headed straight for Glasgow and such entertainment as wartime restrictions permitted. The pubs were a novelty but a big disappointment to the crew—who liked their beer cold. Other liquor was rationed and virtually unobtainable in public places. Another thing which required getting used to be, were the strict closing laws. The custom of the bartender to proclaim "Time, gentlemen, please," at the official closing hour, then to proceed to gather up all glasses, empty or full, caused some arguments until the newcomers got used to such abrupt termination of their evening's activities.

The streets of Glasgow were teeming with people, most of who were in uniform. All were busy, and each one seemed intent on doing his or her bit to win the war. The first disgruntlement among the *Emmons* personnel at the rationing and the strict closing laws very quickly turned to admiration at the cheerfulness and obvious determination of the Scots to get on with the job at hand with whatever resources they could muster up.

Nearly every church and club maintained an open house for members of the armed forces. True, their hospitality was the "tea and cookie" sort of thing, but the warmth of the welcome was unmistakable. Most of the hospitality centers were run by volunteer auxiliaries, more often than not elderly women. Some of them maintained sales rooms where family belongings were sold at modest prices to raise funds for their activities. The Americans were warmly welcomed at the hospitality centers and were usually greeted as a much-appreciated ally. However, the volunteer hostesses were sometimes unaware of their identity, in spite of the fact that uniforms were required for shore leave and liberty. At one of the tea parties the engineer officer was chagrined to be introduced by one of the good ladies as an officer of "His majesty's Indian Navy." It is possible that to her, no real navy existed outside the Empire.

Women in uniform far outnumbered men in uniform on the streets of Glasgow, because men were manning the frontlines and ships in the battle zones. The women of the auxiliary corps were young, pert, and exuded confidence. So far as the Royal Navy was concerned most of the noncombatant jobs in the Glasgow area had been taken over by the WRNS. They kept records, maintained and issued stores, manned communication centers, maintained and issued publications. Among their many duties they acted as messengers and chauffeurs, usually by means of motorcycles as automobiles were reserved for the highest brass. They seemed to enjoy dashing around at all hours of the day and night with the greatest abandon. The executive officer recalls picking up some confidential charts at the Royal Navy issuing office, and being chauffeured back to the ship as passenger in the sidecar of a Wren-driven motorcycle. According to him the young woman must have thought she was at the controls of an airborne vehicle—only rarely did the sidecar wheel make contact with the cobblestones. He was happy to get back to the safety of the ship with his person and the charts intact.

The crewmen of the *Emmons* were quick to note the preponderance of women and were delighted by the fact. More than one sailor had the joy of "Roamin' in the gloaming' on the bonnie banks of Clyde," with a lassie by his side. Because of the high latitude of Glasgow there was practically no twilight or night in the early summer, so any romancing permitted had to take place in the light of day. The great parks of Glasgow were also made for roaming, but the prime target for men on liberty was a huge dance hall, so large that it was able to have a band at either end and one could dance to the music of his choice without being distracted by the band at the opposite end. Other favorites were the old-fashioned music halls of Glasgow, which featured vaudeville skits and imitators of the great Sir Harry Lauder.

When it did get dark, the streets of Glasgow were downright dangerous in the strictly enforced blackout. There was reason to take every precaution. The shipyards and industry along the Clyde were tempting targets for the German air force based across the North Sea. Although the bomb damage was not great, the old streets were in constant need of repair. Open ditches had few barriers and no lights to protect unwary drivers or pedestrians. Taxis managed to get along without lights, but at considerable risk to their passengers. Pedestrians had to literally feel their way around. One night, during the brief period of darkness several of the young *Emmons* officers, having closed up a club, wandered into an open ditch. They returned to the ship without serious injury but in considerable disarray.

The bustling business of the Clyde shipyards and the loading docks at Greenock were a never-ending source of interest to the Americans. The British still used cargo handling methods which depended on manpower and horsepower. No doubt their trucks and other motorized equipment were committed to the armed forces. Using methods which would have been a matter for labor dispute in the United States, the dockworkers kept the cargoes moving day and night. The Americans soon came to appreciate why the British had not been knocked out of the war by German technology long before the United States was drawn in. One of the outstanding memories of the Greenock docks was of long lines of heavily loaded vans and wagons pulled by teams of magnificent Clyde draft horses, patiently waiting their turn.

There had been no signs of enemy activity during the brief stay at Greenock, but few doubted that this situation would change when Division 19 arrived at the major base of the Home Fleet, in the Orkney Islands, just north of Scotland's mainland.

The four destroyers arrived there on July 15.

6.

Scapa Flow was the major base of the British Fleet in both World Wars. It was here, after World War I, that the Germans scuttled their fleet before disposition of the ships could be made by the victorious Allies. At the onset of World War II it again became the principal operating base for the British Navy. Surrounded by six of the Orkneys between which antisubmarine nets were stretched, it had been considered impregnable. But the torpedoing of the *Royal Oak* in October, 1939, while supposedly safe at anchor, by the U-47, had caused the Home Fleet to seek more secure harbors on the mainland. It was not until the Churchill Barrier, consisting of 250,000 tons of rock, was sunk across the eastern entrances, that the fleet returned in 1940. Thereafter, Scapa Flow functioned effectively as the number one base for the Royal Navy. Needless to say, elaborate precautions were maintained to prevent a recurrence of the U-47 incident.

The approach to Scapa Flow had been made through a cold mist which threatened at any moment to turn into a full rain. Ahead loomed the bleak, rocky crags of the islets guarding the Orkneys. To the south the black cliffs of the mainland seemed to deny any human warmth. The higher pinnacles of the islands and the mainlands were hidden in wreaths of cloud. Altogether, the shoreline conveyed a sense of menacing desolation.

As a welcoming British destroyer led the newcomers through the antisubmarine gates, the sense of depressing gloom gave way to one of warm security. Behind the shelter of the islands, the threat of rain lessened, although the skies remained overcast—indeed, that was the normal condition in Scapa Flow. The winds died down and the choppy seas smoothed out. It was warmer in the sheltered anchorage than it had been in the menacing approaches from the cold Atlantic. There was more than a change in physical conditions. Inside the harbor, as far as the eye could see, warships and auxiliaries rode quietly to their anchors or mooring buoys in the eight by twenty-mile anchorage. Ships boats darted from vessel to vessel on the business of the fleet. Slow-moving tugs shepherded covered barges, loaded with the thousand and one items needed to keep the warships ready for action. A division of destroyers was headed for the entrance, outward bound on some mysterious assignment. There was an overall air of vitality, an impression of purposeful power. The crew members of the American destroyers got a psychological lift at being part of this great armada at the cutting edge of allied naval power. The warships at Scapa represented virtually every type and nationality within the navies of the Allies. Most flew the White Ensign of the Royal Navy, but some, mostly destroyers, flew the colors of members of the British Commonwealth nations or of governments-in-exile whose homelands were occupied by Hitler's army. Among the battleships and carriers were three with which the *Emmons* exercised frequently during her period of duty with the Home Fleet. The battleships were HMS *Duke of York,* and HMS *Anson.* The *Duke of York* flew the personal flag of Admiral Sir John Tovey, C-in-C, Home Fleet. The carrier was HMS *Victorious.* Among the cruisers were the American heavy cruisers *Wichita* and *Tuscaloosa.* The great variety of destroyers intrigued the American destroyer men. They were a polyglot outfit. The famous pre-World War II "Tribal" class was represented, some of them manned by crewmen from the nations of the Commonwealth: Canada, India, Africa, and Australia. Other destroyers flying the White Ensign were manned by crews from governments-in-exile whose homelands were occupied by the Germans, such as Poland and Norway. A few were entirely manned by exiled crewmen and wore the ensigns of their native country. By far the greatest numbers of destroyers with the Home Fleet were the latest out and featured significant antiaircraft capability in addition to their antisubmarine weapons. Some were still "working up," to use the British phrase. The British still placed heavy reliance on torpedo weaponry. One looked in vain for any of the fifty World War I vintage "four pipers" transferred from the United States to Britain under the destroyers for bases deal. If any of them were with the Home Fleet they were not in evidence. Many of them had already been liquidated, others were on escort duty.

The ships present at Scapa Flow changed almost hourly as they moved in and out on different assignments. Although it was one of the tasks of the deck watches to keep account of the comings and goings, there was so much movement and the anchorage was so large that it was virtually impossible to keep an accurate account. It became routine to start the daily log with the all encompassing phrase, "Ships Present: U.S.S. *Wichita, Tuscaloosa,* Desdiv 19, and various units of British Home Fleet."

7.

Since the primary mission of the Home Fleet was to meet the German fleet head on if and when the opportunity occurred, much of its time was spent in training exercises and preparation for the hoped for event. From time to time it would put to sea in response to intelligence reports of German activity, or as support for Russia-bound convoys. At other times it would attempt to bait the Germans into coming out of their bases.

There was little of this activity during the *Emmons'* tour at Scapa Flow in the summer of 1942, although, with the *Tuscaloosa, Rodman,* and three British destroyers, she did make a dangerous run to Murmansk and back before her tour ended. Intensive training with British units was the order of the day. In this respect, operations out of Scapa Flow were not much different for the *Emmons* than operating out of Casco Bay or Argentia with Task Force 22. The *Victorious* replaced the *Ranger,* while the British battleships *Anson* and *Duke of York* replaced the Atlantic Fleet heavy units. Instead of using British signals and tactical formations part time for contingency purposes, all operations were now conducted under British rules.

A major difference between working out of Scapa Flow and United States bases in the Western Atlantic was the relaxed attitude toward possible air raids. Less than 300 miles from major airfields in Norway, the British depended on shore based batteries and aircraft for protection. Once within the sanctuary of the base, condition watches were secured and normal in-port watches were set. This was in marked contrast to the up-tight stance prevailing in United States bases several thousand miles away from enemy bases. At Boston Navy Yard, for instance, ships undergoing overhaul had to keep a third of their antiaircraft batteries manned and operational. This did not mean that the British were careless; they simply saw no reason to wear out their crews until there was a clear possibility of action. The Germans routinely sent high-flying reconnaissance aircraft over the Orkneys. At such times the air raid warnings were sounded and all ships were to "close up" for action. Actually, the reconnaissance flights were considered more of a nuisance than a threat. There was as much or more concern over a sneak underwater attack than an air attack, a hangover from the torpedoing of the *Royal Oak.* Constant antisubmarine patrols were maintained both inside the harbor and to seaward.

Another major difference between duty at Scapa and United States ports was the amount and quality of liberty. The Orkneys were sparsely populated and the few settlements had little to offer in the way of entertainment. Very little liberty was granted for the simple reason that there was little for the liberty parties to do except walk through the countryside and visit the meager official recreational facilities operated by the British auxiliary services. The latter were overcrowded. The beer was cheap but warm and often ran out before the liberty hours ended. Usually, the Americans and the British got along well together, but occasionally Anglophobia or anti-Americanism surfaced, and this may well have been one of the reasons for keeping liberty at a minimum. Difference in pay was sometimes a source of contention, as was the previously mentioned tendency of the British sailors to be condescending toward the Americans as "Johnnies-come-lately" in the war. The underlying tensions can be best illustrated by an incident related by Robert R. Reid, then MM2C. He and some other American petty officers had been invited by some English ratings to visit their petty officers club. While the group was enjoying their beer a local fisherman came in with a box of cooked lobsters which he offered for sale around the room with no takers. The Americans then bought his entire offering to share with their hosts. A short time later an English rating came in looking for the lobsterman. When he learned that none were left and that all had been bought by the Americans he became enraged and accused the Yanks of "buying up everything" because they were "so rich." A fight was averted by the other petty officers present.

For the most part, the crew stuck close to the ship, although a few later admitted they visited some of the farms "unofficially," in British boats, but found no reason for staying AWOL. Some recreation parties went ashore for Softball games, well supplied with beer from the ship's store, kept under lock and key for just such parties. Every effort was made to keep this beer cold. Shipboard movies remained the most popular recreation aboard ship, but toward the end of the tour, repeats of the available films took away some of the attraction. The crew enjoyed acting as hosts to small parties from nearby British ships. They regretted not being able to offer their guests any beverages stronger than coffee or lemonade.

Another form of recreation was known as "spyglass" liberty. After the day's work was done, those on good terms with the signalmen or fire controlmen would drift up to the bridge or fire control tower to scan the heather-covered hills around the anchorage for signs of life. For the most part, there was little activity, but for a few shepherds and their flocks of sheep. Occasionally, the romantic doings of unwitting, or uncaring, Royal Navy couples from the base barracks could be followed along the meandering paths through the heather.

Fishing and gambling had their devotees. Fishing inside the harbor was not what it was reputed to be in Scottish waters, but the fishermen never seemed to mind. The usual card games continued, with penny ante poker the most popular. Sometimes, after paydays, more than pennies were at stake. A redheaded seaman second, from one of the western states, emerged as the big winner. Appropriately named Diamond, and naturally nicknamed "Red," he came aboard ship at Newport just before the shakedown cruise with the big draft of "D"s. Red Diamond's luck, or skill, with cards became legendary aboard ship. Reportedly, he never lost, whether at poker or any other card game. One of his most lucrative games was solitaire, where he would sell one or more decks to shipmates for play at a dollar a card. He is reputed to have been able to keep up with the play of four or five decks at one time. He left the ship in September, after its return to the States, somewhat richer for the lack of liberty in Scapa Flow.

The *Emmons,* as with most destroyers, never had a chaplain, but every effort was made to meet the religious needs of the crew. On Sundays at sea, weather and condition of readiness permitting, one of the officers or volunteers from the crew would read brief services from the prayer books carried aboard. It must be admitted that attendance was not large. In port, church parties were sent to a chapel ashore or to larger ships in the harbor, whose complements supported a chaplain.

Usually, the SOPA, senior officer present afloat, sent out a signal on Saturdays indicating the ships where protestant and catholic services would be held. Invariably, chaplains could be found on board hospital ships, but destroyer duty usually kept the "cans" out of ports where ships displaying the Red Cross were found. At Scapa Flow, Sunday services were regularly held on the tender or one of the supply ships in the destroyer area. On the few Sundays the *Emmons* was in port, arrangements were always made to send church parties to the nearest ship flying the church pennant. The few men who were willing to change uniforms to attend church enjoyed the experience, but were perplexed by the English padres who, unlike the chaplains in the American service, remained civilians and were considered as such even aboard the naval ships they served. For the most part they adhered to the formal Church of England ritual.

8.

When it came to recreational activities in port, the officers fared much better than the crew partly because there was less restriction on their visits to the beach, but mainly because of the hospitality of the wardroom officers of the English ships, particularly on the destroyers. The officers were welcomed in the clubs and messes ashore whenever the operational schedule permitted. But such facilities were severely overtaxed. Liquor was strictly rationed. Each afternoon, as the bar opened, a long line of allied officers would queue up, hoping for a dram of Scotch whiskey. Apparently, rationing was not nearly as severe aboard ship as it was ashore, at least when the Americans were entertained. Almost every evening after the ships returned to anchorage from the day's exercises, a signal would be sent from one of the nearby British ships inviting two or more of the *Emmons'* officers over for dinner. At these affairs there was no scarcity of spirits or spirit. Following dinner, the English introduced their guests to a series of wardroom games, more often than not involving consumption of spirits either as reward for the winners or as a penalty for the losers. The games ranged from the intellectual to the suicidal. Sometimes toward the end of the evening the wardroom took on the aspects of a battleground. The *Emmons'* officers tried to reciprocate, but as they were confined to offering only tea or coffee after dinner, it was unusual for their guests to prolong their visit after the evening movies.

Close relations were established with several of His Majesty's ships. One of them was H.M.S. *Gleaner,* a veteran of the mine warfare in the North Sea and along the Norwegian coast. One of the *Gleaner's* favorite wardroom games simulated the sudden sighting of an enemy target. The officer designated as the officer of the deck would be blindfolded, hoisted in a chair and rocked back and forth by as many officers as could get hold of the chair. Theoretically, the rocking motion duplicated the roll and pitch of a small ship in a heavy sea. Usually, it was worse than the rhythm of nature. At some juncture in the rocking motion, a "lookout" would announce a target bearing anywhere from dead ahead to either quarter of the pitching "ship." The "OOD" could then snatch the bandage from his eyes and try to locate the target, an ordinary dart board on one of the bulkheads. He was then to let fly with darts in the general direction of the target while still being hoisted about. Hits on the target were few, but anything near was rewarded with a stiff drink. The officers of the *Emmons* felt a great loss when the *Gleaner* put to sea for duty in parts unknown.

Many of the English wardroom games involved play on words. A popular one involved the intonation of a repetitious bit of doggerel concerning a "Cardinal Puff Puff," which became more and more complicated as it progressed. Only the most nimble tongued could repeat it without error. The penalty for faltering or committing an error was downing of another drink while the next person attempted to mumble his way through the maze of words.

Not all of the affairs were so free and easy. From time to time the senior officers of the fleet would give formal dinner parties complete with the traditional port and toasts to The King and The President. Usually, the commanding officer and one or more officers of the American ships in port were invited to such affairs. There were no raucous games at these dinners, but after they were over the commanding officers of the British destroyers made a practice of inviting the American destroyer officers to stop by their ships for a nightcap. On one such occasion, following a very formal dinner aboard the flagship, *Duke of York,* the *Emmons* officers at that affair accepted the hospitality of the commanding officer of a British ship in their area. On going aboard the British destroyer they were a little bit shocked to hear their host greeted by his officers with cheers and several rousing choruses of "For He's a Jolly Good Fellow," which on this occasion promoted him to "a jolly good bastard."

The Americans were introduced to a new version of the children's game, "Follow the Leader." In this maniacal game, the leader led the players through the wardroom country, alternately crawling under tables, leaping over chairs, swinging from overhead pipes, running up ladders, then tumbling down them, all the while cheerfully chanting, "Here we go gathering nuts in May." Each successive leader tried to outdo the former in innovating new moves. Casualties amounted to only a few minor bruises and sprains. Any misgivings the Americans may have had concerning discipline aboard Royal Navy ships after such high jinks, were dissipated after a few weeks of operations at sea.

9.

There were relatively few disciplinary problems during the period in Scapa Flow. There wasn't much interchange with the beach except for stores handling parties and work on the excellent British mockups for training in antiaircraft firing, antisubmarine warfare, and sonar and radar operations. The training facilities were excellent and were more realistic and exciting than anything the crew had been exposed to before. A whole building was devoted to the antiaircraft exercise, and an attempt was made to have every member of the crew take part. Some few specialists, the sonar and radar operators, were sent ashore for longer and more intensive training than the ordinary gunners and depth charge operators. The sonar operators were enthusiastic about the British recording system of dropping on a simulated enemy sub, and regarded it as better than the U.S. system in use at the time.

Aside from the training exercise and store handling parties and a few short liberty parties, the only other contacts with the beach were supervised athletic and beer parties. On one occasion, a few men were invited to a tea dance at the Wrens' quarters which turned out to be a very nice, proper affair. It actually was a *tea* dance, strictly chaperoned. When the dance ended, the men were mustered on the dock and returned to the ship, much to their disgust.

With such restricted activities ashore, it is little wonder that most men stuck to the ship. The hardworking boat crews were usually exposed to temptation far more than the rest of the crew by the very nature of their duties. The whaleboat and the captain's gig, a whaleboat with fancier fixings, were the links between the ship, the shore, and other ships in the harbor. Frequently, they had to wait for considerable lengths of time alongside the docks ashore while the business at hand was being completed. The old navy game of waiting is very boring, and in most ports the crews would begin to look around for something to relieve the tedium. After a few trips to the boat landing at Scapa Flow, the crews learned there was little to entice them away from their responsibility and they found it easier to stand by their boat than to look for excitement.

Waiting at a British man-of-war was an entirely different matter. The boats' crews enjoyed the visits, official and otherwise, to Royal Navy ships, about as much as their officer passengers. If the distance between the *Emmons'* mooring and the Englishman was short, the boats would be sent home to return at a specified time. If the distance was great, the boat would normally be secured alongside or at one of the boat booms until called alongside for the return trip. The watch aboard the British ship would usually invite the boat's crew aboard for a cup of tea or coffee. It sometimes happened that more than tea or coffee was served. On one occasion, after a visit aboard a British destroyer, the executive officer and the first lieutenant found it advisable to take over the boat for the return trip while the crew enjoyed a sleep in the forward cockpit. After a short delay, the boat got back to the ship without mishap and the whole thing was chalked off to British-American amity.

10.

All hands were proud to be part of the powerful fleet assembled at Scapa Flow and enjoyed the relaxed atmosphere of confident competence prevailing there. The base was strategically located in relation to German bases on the European mainland, to the North Sea, Iceland, and the convoy routes to the west and north. The periodic air raid alarms kicked off by intruding reconnaissance planes over the Orkneys served to emphasize the nearness of enemy airfields to the eastward. Everyone knew that a direct confrontation with German air or naval forces was possible at any time.

The ideas as to the time, place, and nature of any possible confrontations with the Germans were necessarily vague. No one on board was privy to the constant flow of intelligence information on the disposition of enemy forces which dictated the activities of the Home Fleet. In fact, few were conscious of the strength of German ships along the Norwegian coast. On the other hand, nearly everyone knew of the precarious situation along the convoy routes and had some ideas as to the threat of German raiders patterned on the *Bismarck, Prinz Eugen* sortie of 1941. Most assumed that the next significant assignment would involve the *Emmons* in support of a major convoy in one way or another. Whatever it could be the men were ready for it.

There was nothing vague about the training schedule at Scapa. The American destroyers quickly settled down to a routine of almost daily exercises with British battleships and the aircraft carrier *Victorious* in the exercise areas to the west of the Orkneys. From time to time, the American cruisers *Wichita* and *Tuscaloosa* would join in. Usually, the ships would return to the protection of the anchorage for a night's rest before returning to sea the following day for a new set of drills with a different training group. Every week or ten days the schedule allowed a few days in harbor for recreation and upkeep. As at Argentia, the exercises frequently had to be postponed or terminated when the perpetual mist thickened into a fog. When the mists turned to rain it had little effect on activities except for the antiaircraft exercises. Considering the prevailing weather around the Orkneys most of the year, the Americans were lucky to have their tour there in the middle of summer. Aside from some moderately brisk winds and the nearly constant threat of either rain or fog, the weather remained tolerable. Adjusting to the nearly constant daylight of the summer months proved difficult for some.

The routine of upkeep and training was broken only twice before the scheduled time for return to the States in mid-August. The first came when the *Emmons* and *Rodman* escorted the *Wichita* and *Tuscaloosa* to Rosyth for an overhaul period. As soon as the cruisers were safe inside the antisubmarine nets, the destroyers turned around and proceeded back to Scapa. The next break came when the same two destroyers were detailed to escort the *Duke of York* to Hvalfjordur, Iceland, on some mysterious mission best known to the fleet commander.

6

Murmansk

o o o o o o o o o o o o o o o o o o o o o o o o o o o o o o

At 0919 sighted enemy reconnaissance plane bearing 200°. Formation shadowed throughout the morning................At 1425 shadowing plane closed to about 9,000 yards. Opened fire with guns #1 and #2. Shrapnel bursts were close and plane fled and shortly abandoned the shadowing.

—***Emmons*** *War Diary, August 26, 1942*

The excursion to Hvalfjordur provided a brief, but welcome, change of pace from the monotonous routine at Scapa, where the in-and-out exercises had started to be boring. When the *Duke of York* and the destroyers sortied on the 26th of July, it had been assumed that they were headed for more of the same. As the group left the exercise areas behind and set course to the north, there was much speculation as to the destination and no little excitement at the prospect of some action. After a day at sea the excitement waned as it became apparent that they were headed for Iceland. Even so, the change was welcome.

The ships arrived off Hvalfjordur late in the afternoon of the 28th and proceeded down the channel to the makeshift operating base. If the approaches to Scapa Flow had seemed dark and threatening, the passage from sea between the precipitous, rocky sides of the fiord to the base was awesome. The ships were dwarfed by the towering walls on either side. The volcanic rocks were pockmarked with yellowish-green summer vegetation which presented shifting patterns of light and shade as the rays of the late afternoon sun struggled to penetrate to the bottom of the canyon. There were no indications of human life, but an occasional waterfall tumbling over the edges of the chasm hinted at a more habitable land behind the summit. To observers on deck, looking up and astern, it seemed as if the sides of the fiord were closing in, shutting them off from the rational world they had left behind to enter an unreal, supernatural world.

The eerie sense of the supernatural was only partially dispelled when the ships anchored at the base, but the presence of other ships at least gave assurance that the new arrivals were not alone in a world still at war. Here nature seemed more menacing than man. The base itself was an important, if unpublicized, part of the war effort. It had originally been established to support ships guarding the avenues through which the Germans could gain entry to the North Atlantic, particularly the Denmark Straits between Iceland and Greenland. When the United States assumed responsibility for Iceland it took over the base. It never received the recognition other bases were given and its growth was more haphazard than planned. Nevertheless, it did a remarkable job of providing the necessary logistic services for ships operating in and out of Iceland waters.

To the newcomers, the base appeared forlorn and neglected. The working parts consisted of a few tankers, repair ships, stores ships, and a floating dry-dock. A few austere communication buildings and warehouses on the barren strip of land at the base of the cliff completed the installation. No one was really unhappy when, only twelve hours after anchoring, the destroyers received priority orders directing them to depart immediately for Scapa Flow. The reason for the orders was never explained.

The only real disappointment at the hurried departure from Hvalfjordur was that badly-needed fresh and frozen provisions had to be left piled on the deck of a supply ship when the order came. The supplies had been requisitioned as soon as the ships came within visual communication range of the base, and a working party had been awakened and sent over before reveille to help break the food out of the reefers and storerooms. That part of the task was almost finished when the working party was recalled. The only fresh provisions to reach the *Emmons* that day was a single bunch of red radishes which Ensign Joe Behan, the commissary officer, managed to grab from a broken crate as he left the deck of the supply ship.

One of the continuing problems at Scapa Flow had centered on the deterioration of the food, especially fresh and frozen provisions. When the United States first committed ships to augment the Home Fleet, every effort had been made to keep their presence unknown to the Germans. No one was fooled. Lord Haw Haw of Berlin radio fame, described the make up of the American force with the fleet shortly after it arrived at Scapa Flow, and the cover was publicly blown when the official visit of King George VI on board the *Washington* was highly publicized. However, part of the original agreement and plan for concealment had been that the American ships would depend on the British for fuel, and only one American supply ship would come to Scapa approximately every six weeks with general stores and fresh and frozen provisions. In the meantime, the American ships were to draw their stores from British sources. The British generously shared what they had, but after three years of war there wasn't much choice. What was available was strictly rationed. Some items simply were not to be had by either the British housewives or their fighting men.

At Scapa Flow, as larders were depleted, provisions were requisitioned from the Royal Navy Depot Ship, responsible for supply as well as administration of the base. Substitutions were frequent and quality was sometimes dubious. Harold Heming, the executive officer, recalls that there were complaints from both the crew and the cooks and bakers who were responsible for preparing the food. The latter were particularly vehement. On one occasion, a requisition for two crates of eggs was cut down to half a crate. On another, the bakers complained that flour provided was discolored and contained many substitutes, some of which were more animal than vegetable. Their biggest gripe was that they could not get it to rise. As the same flour was issued to all ships, there was nothing the harried exec could do but suggest that the bakers consult with their British counterparts on use of the stuff.

The difficulties of the commissary department were reflected in a dramatic increase of sales of candy bars in the ship's store, to such an extent that they had to be rationed. The dwindling supply of American candy was augmented by the highly prized English "issue" candy bars. These were large, 2 1/2" x 4" x 1/2", and of outstanding quality. The allowance of four per man, per month, was enough to keep the ship's store open for business until the regular stock could be renewed.

2

The destroyers arrived back at Scapa Flow on July 31, and slipped easily into the old routine. There were few tears at the return. Twelve hours at anchor in the bleak Iceland fiord had made the British base attractive by comparison. While the thought of the lovely fresh provisions left in Hvalfjordur lingered, there were not so many complaints about the food. For one thing, there was growing appreciation of the hardships the English had endured since 1939, and more understanding of the need for rationing. For another, there was a general feeling that the ship would return to the States very soon.

Actually, the *Wichita,* escorted by the *Hambleton* and *Macomb,* left Scapa Flow for the States in mid-August as scheduled. The *Tuscaloosa, Emmons* and *Rodman* should have gone home at the same time, but events were afoot which kept them under the Home Fleet for three more weeks and sent them on a wild dash across the Barents Sea to Murmansk, Russia, on a mission which provided enough excitement to satisfy even the most action-hungry for several months to come.

To understand this latest development, it is necessary to review the importance of the Arctic supply line to Russia and particularly the fate of Russia-bound convoy PQ17, which was virtually wiped out by the Germans in early July, 1942, about the time Task Force 37, including the *Emmons,* was starting out for Europe from Halifax.

The background for the dash to Murmansk is a somber one. Even before the United States was drawn into the war, the United States and Great Britain had agreed to supply Russia with war goods to the best of their ability. Most of the material was made in the United States but transported to Russia in allied merchantmen via the Arctic route, under the protection of the Royal Navy. The major terminals for the convoys were Archangel, on the White Sea, and Murmansk, on the Kola Inlet, a short distance from the Finnish border.

The convoys sent out during the fall and winter of 1941-1942, at an average interval of fifteen days, got through with relatively little interference from the enemy. This in spite of the freezing weather, frequent gales and blizzards and the southern advance of the winter ice pack. The latter cut off the sea room north of Bear Island and forced the convoys to go between the Island and the north coast of Norway, a distance of approximately 200 miles. Several factors contributed to the success of the winter convoys. For one thing, contrary to what might be expected, the endless nights proved to be a blessing to the convoys. While the darkness made station keeping difficult and the convoys tended to spread out, it made reconnaissance for the German aircraft based in northern Norway virtually impossible. It did allow submarines to stalk their prey on the surface, but they too had their problems in rough weather. The storms aloft also affected the performance of the radar less aircraft of the Luftwaffe. Another factor was the fact that the Germans had not yet moved either submarines or aircraft to the Norwegian theater in great numbers. Nor had they completed the move of their major ships into that area. Perhaps the main reason was that the Germans had not yet awakened fully to the importance of the Arctic convoys and their extreme vulnerability.

Throughout the winter, the execrable weather remained neutral, hampering movement on both sides. In January, the *Tirpitz* was spotted in the fiord near Trondheim, prompting Churchill to warn the Chiefs of Staff Committee that, "The destruction or even the crippling of this ship is the greatest event at sea at the present time.... the naval situation throughout the world would be altered, and the naval command in the Pacific would be regained.... The whole strategy of the war turns at this period on this ship, which is holding four times the number of British capital ships paralyzed, to say nothing of the two new American battleships retained in the Atlantic." In March, the *Tirpitz* made a foray into the Barents Sea which missed by only three hours intercepting eastbound convoy PQ12 and westbound convoy QP8 at the point where their tracks passed. Mercifully, a snowstorm kept the two convoys hidden from the raider. She did spot and sink a Russian straggler from the westbound convoy before returning to Norway. This was the *Tirpitz'* only success during the war, except, as Churchill noted, for keeping a whole fleet "paralyzed."

As the days lengthened, the balance began to favor the Nazis. By early May there was continuous daylight above the Arctic Circle. The longer days made it easier to spot and track the convoys. Those sailed in March, April, and May suffered increasing losses from air, submarine and destroyer attacks. The weather too took its toll. Convoy PQ14, sailed in early April from Iceland, suffered more from the elements than the enemy when it blundered into the ice pack in a storm. Fifteen out of twenty-three cargo ships and two escorts were so badly damaged by the ice that they had to return to Iceland for repairs. Only one of the remaining eight merchantmen was sunk by a submarine torpedo.

Almost by trial and error the Germans began to realize the vulnerability of the convoys. As action was renewed on the Eastern Front in the spring there was a growing awareness of the importance of the Arctic supply route to the Russian defenses. Hitler determined that the supplies had to be stopped. In April, he called Admiral Raeder to a conference during which he directed that the navy was to concentrate on the convoys around northern Norway. Further, he instructed Raeder to perfect plans for an all-out combined air-sea attack against the supply route in June. Hence, the buildup of naval and air forces in and around northern Norway and the worsening situation for the convoys pushing through to Russia in the spring of 1942.

For their part, senior British officers were well aware of the German buildup and the prospects of crippling losses if the convoys were continued throughout the summer. After the losses from convoy PQ15 in early May, especially among escort and support ships, recommendations were made to suspend the convoys until the airfields in Norway were neutralized or the passage of summer brought some darkness to provide cover. Churchill, under strong pressure from both Stalin and Roosevelt, would not go along with the recommendation. In fact, the two allied leaders were calling for an increase in the effort to push supplies through to Russia via the Arctic. In April, Roosevelt had written strongly urging Churchill to increase the size of the convoys, "so that the stuff now banked up in Iceland can get through." He frankly stated that he feared "political repercussions in Russia, but even more the fact that the supplies will not reach them promptly" if the size of the convoys were not beefed up. In short, political considerations overrode the professional judgment of the men responsible for the safe delivery of the supplies.

Accordingly, PQ16, with the best protection yet provided, was sailed from Iceland on May 21. Although it was subjected to heavy air attack and dogged by submarines during its passage through the Barents Sea, it managed to reach Murmansk and Archangel with the loss of only seven out of thirty-five merchantmen. The fear that the German heavies stationed along the Norway coast would attack the convoy did not materialize, but the Germans were preparing to throw everything they had at the next Russia-bound convoy.

By June, they had prepared plans and positioned forces for the all-out combined air-sea attack which had been directed by Hitler back in April. It was designated *Rosselsprung,* or "Knight's Gambit." All the elements were in place by the middle of June. The *Tirpitz* was at Trondheim with the cruiser *Hipper* and four destroyers. The pocket battleships *Scheer* and *Lutzow* were at Narvik with six destroyers. When it was certain that the convoy was approaching the Barents Sea, the two groups were to move north to Altenfiord and Vestfiord near North Cape. Stationed on the airfields of northern Norway were 264 aircraft of the *Luftwaffe,* predominately bombers and torpedo planes, but including long-range reconnaissance planes. Approximately twenty submarines were available in the area.

The British learned the broad outline of the German plan from Swedish sources and began to plan as best they could to defend against it. The target of "Knight's Gambit" proved to be Russia-bound convoy PQ17, which, after some delay, was sailed from Iceland with thirty-six merchantmen on June 27.

The *Tirpitz* and her companions played an important part in the British plans, which of necessity had to be a compromise. The Home Fleet was to provide distant cover, but if it advanced too far east with the convoy, the "door" to the North Atlantic would be left open behind it giving the German heavy units easy access to the vital convoys enroute to the United Kingdom from the United States. As a compromise, the Home Fleet was to cruise northeast of Jan Mayan Island until the whereabouts of the *Tirpitz, et al,* was definitely known. From that position it could move south to cut off any move into the Atlantic or southeast to intercept the *Tirpitz* if she attacked the convoy. It was hoped that luck in the form of favorable weather would help keep it hidden. If not, British submarines would intervene to slow down the Germans until the Home Fleet could arrive for a showdown.

The fleet commanders of both sides were hampered by restrictions imposed from above. A support force of cruisers and destroyers, including the American cruisers, *Wichita* and *Tuscaloosa,* and destroyers *Wainwright* and *Rowan,* was to accompany the convoy part way to provide protection from air raids and light enemy forces. However, the cruisers were not considered strong enough to stand up to the German battleships and were to withdraw before entering the Barent's sea and shift their support to homeward bound convoy QP13. As for the Germans, Hitler was paranoid about losing his battleships, and had issued orders that they were not to be used until it was positively known that they could not be attacked by aircraft from British carriers.

The first five days at sea passed in relative quiet for PQ17. Intelligence organizations for both sides kept their forces informed of the others' movements and dispositions. The British were most anxious about movements of the German heavies. No movement was reported until the 3rd of July, when British Intelligence reported that the *Scheer* had left Narvik for the north, presumably for Altenfiord, while the *Tirpitz* and *Hipper* had left Trondheim headed north. The *Lutzow* and three destroyers had run aground near Narvik and were out of action.

On the 4th of July, convoy PQ17 came under heavy air attacks. They were beaten off with some losses, and the convoy remained intact. Throughout the day the whereabouts of the *Tirpitz* was crucial. Unfortunately, through a combination of slowdown in decyphering German codes and temporary interruption of air reconnaissance around North Cape because of an accident, British Intelligence lost track of the *Tirpitz* until late in the afternoon of the 4th when the latest German codes were solved. The Admiralty and the Fleet were advised that the *Tirpitz* with her destroyers had joined the *Scheer* at Altenfiord at 0900 that morning and the destroyers had been ordered to fuel immediately. The question then became whether or not the *Tirpitz* had sailed from Altenfiord that afternoon. Naval intelligence officers deduced that she was still at Altenfiord and so informed the First Sea Lord, but could produce no concrete evidence to support their opinion. In the absence of such evidence, the latter assumed the worst, which she had sailed from Altenfiord during the afternoon and could be in position to intercept the convoy by 0200 the morning of the 5th. There was little chance that the Home Fleet could reach the convoy in time to save it. Late in the evening the Admiralty ordered the cruiser support force to withdraw to the west and the convoy to scatter and seek port as best they could on their own. It was hoped that by scattering, more of the ships could elude discovery and destruction than would be the case if they remained concentrated. As it turned out, the single, unprotected ships proved to be sitting ducks for aircraft and submarines which tracked them down.

Actually, the *Tirpitz* and *Hipper,* with their destroyers, had joined the *Scheer* at Altenfiord on the 4th as reported by British Intelligence. The group waited all day in vain for the go ahead orders. It was not until just before noon on the 5th that they received orders to proceed to the attack as planned. They were recalled after ten hours at sea because the *Luftwaffe* and submarines were doing as well or better than they could have done in tracking down and destroying the scattered ships of PQ17—and without the risk of a confrontation with the Home Fleet. Out of the thirty-six merchantmen which had left Iceland only eleven reached the precarious safety of Russian ports.

The rest of the tragic story of convoy PQ17 has been told and debated too often to be repeated in detail here. The account given thus far has been made because the aftermath has a direct bearing on the next important assignment of the *Emmons.*

3

After the disaster of PQ17 the Arctic convoys were suspended for the rest of the summer. But there were several problems which required action before the fall. For one thing, several hundred survivors from the convoy were stranded in Russian ports. For another, essential supplies and ammunition intended for Royal Navy ships based on Russian ports had gone down with ships of the convoy. In addition to replacing these, it was necessary to get advance personnel and equipment to Murmansk for two squadrons of Hampden torpedo-bombers which were being set up in North Russia. The British also planned to establish a medical unit with modern equipment at the port to augment the rather primitive facilities available to care for convoy casualties. Personnel and supplies had to be transported by sea.

As for the Russians, they were clamoring for more and more supplies. In fact, when informed that the convoys had been temporarily suspended, Stalin wrote an insulting letter to the Prime Minister in which he accused the British of bad faith on two counts: refusing to continue sending supplies via the northern route, and failure to create a second front in 1942. He further implied cowardice on the part of the British in regard to convoy PQ17. The political aspects of suspension of the convoys could not be ignored. Apparently, both Churchill and Roosevelt felt that some gesture should be made to placate Stalin. In a letter concurring with the Prime Minister's proposal to ignore the Russian's intemperate blast, the President wrote: "While I think that you should not raise any false hopes in Stalin relative to the northern convoy, nevertheless I agree with you that we should run one if there is any possibility of success, in spite of the great risk involved."

Although no regular convoy was sent along the northern route until September, the decision was made to send the most urgent supplies and equipment around Norway in warships. The naval vessels could also carry in needed personnel and bring out the survivors of PQ17. Among the latter were U.S. Navy men from the armed guards of the sunken American merchantmen. Of major importance, on the political side, the naval relief expedition would provide some tangible evidence to the Russians that their allies had not completely abandoned them. In this connection, it is interesting that while the expedition was being readied, Prime Minister Churchill and Averill Harriman, President Roosevelt's personal emissary, were in Moscow to break the unwelcome news to "Uncle Joe" that an assault against North Africa was to be substituted for any cross-channel attack against the Germans in 1942. They also discussed future military cooperation with the Russians, including the question of supply routes. Whether or not there was any direct connection between the supply trip and the talks going on in Moscow, the risks were nonetheless great and the stakes high.

The *Tuscaloosa, Emmons* and *Rodman* were given the job, which was designated Operation Easy-Unit. Enroute to Russia they were joined at various points along the way by the Royal Navy destroyers *Onslaught, Martin,* and *Marne,* all veterans of the battle along the Arctic convoy routes.

While the *Wichita, Hambleton,* and *Macomb* were preparing to return to the United States, the ships of Operation Easy-Unit began to load ammunition and naval stores which were available at Scapa Flow. Aboard the *Emmons* every available space in the magazines was filled with four-inch projectiles consigned to the Senior British Naval Officer, North Russia. After loading ammunition, the ships dropped down to Greenock where they loaded general stores and provisions, again consigned to the Senior British Officer, North Russia. The *Tuscaloosa* took on torpedoes, radar equipment, supplies and personnel for the projected British torpedo-bomber squadrons, as well as medical supplies and personnel for the proposed hospital unit.

The *Emmons* loaded about 35 tons of mixed stores of all descriptions, but mostly canned meats and vegetables, cheese, and sacked staples, such as beans and flour. Five Royal Navy ratings were taken aboard as passengers to Murmansk. Every unoccupied space, above and below decks, was utilized to stow the provisions. Even spaces under bunks and around the boilers were used. Some canned goods were stowed over the boilers. This proved to be a mistake as the high temperatures between the boilers and the overhead caused some of the cans to swell and explode, causing a considerable mess which had to be cleaned up. The frugal engineers, rather than see the ham and other salvageable items go to waste, used the remnants to augment their own fire room repasts.

American ships were responsible for the provisions, most of which were products of the United States, but the working parties responsible for stowing them on board wryly noted that the crates and cartons were neatly stenciled with the slogan, "BRITAIN DELIVERS THE GOODS."

4

Easy-Unit got underway August 13 for Seydisfjordur, a barren outpost on the northeast coast of Iceland, which served as a protected fueling stop for ships headed for and returning from the Arctic. However, two days out of Greenock, the group had to alter course for Scapa Flow because of an outbreak of spinal meningitis aboard the *Tuscaloosa.* After a day and a half at Scapa, during which twelve of her men were sent to Royal Naval Sick Quarters, the mission was resumed. The voyage to Iceland was uneventful except for the usual submarine alarms and investigations. The three ships reached Seydisfjordur on the 19th and began to fuel at once. The fueling operation was interrupted by a report from the shore signal station that enemy aircraft were headed for the area. When they failed to show, the fueling was resumed. Augmented by HMS *Onslaught,* the group set out for Russia at 1925. Although by now it was two months into summer and the days were getting a little shorter, it was still broad daylight.

Getting from Iceland to Murmansk, between the ice pack to the north and German forces to the south, was somewhat like running a gauntlet. At the Russian end of the 1500-mile route where the ships entered Kola Inlet, the gauntlet funneled down to within 50 miles of German-occupied Finland. When the ships of Easy-Unit made their dash across the Barents, German forces were poised to clobber the next convoy coming after PQ17. In anticipation of another easy victory there had been little change in their disposition. The *Tirpitz, Scheer* and *Hipper* had moved back down to Narvik, but in mid-August the *Scheer* left for Operation *Wunderland* in which she and submarines were to cooperate in attacking Siberian convoys heading west through the Kara Sea. She cruised to the north and northwest of Novaya Zembla while waiting for information on the convoys during the entire span of Operation Easy-Unit. Thus, German battle units were within easy striking distance on either side of the *Tuscaloosa* group while it was crossing the Barents Sea, going and coming. No one aboard the *Emmons* had the slightest inkling of the whereabouts of the German battle units, but everyone was acutely aware of the possibilities of air and submarine attack. The airfields around North Cape were loaded with Heinkels and Junkers with a few Blohm and Voss reconnaissance planes. Submarines still roamed the Norwegian and Barents seas in anticipation of picking off another eastbound convoy.

All but the first few miles of the track for Easy-Unit lay north of the Arctic Circle. Theoretically, the weather was far better in the summer than in the winter, but it was at best unpredictable. Being summer, the ice pack had retreated to the north, leaving the area between Bear Island and Spitzbergen clear. Thus, there was 120 miles more sea room for evasive maneuvering. The group took advantage of the fact to take a route north of Bear Island. The weather during most of the voyage was marked by overcast skies, mist, rain and fog. On the whole, this was good as it made the task for shadowing aircraft difficult. There was nearly always a stiff wind which sometimes reached gale strength.

Few aboard the *Emmons* will forget the bitter cold in the middle of summer. The mean atmospheric temperature along the route in July, the warmest month of the year, is between 40° and 50° F, which takes no account of the effect of wind on body comfort. It varies with the distance from the ice pack and whether the wind is blowing on or off the ice. The sea temperature hovered around freezing. In 1942, the practice of using chill factor to equate the effects of wind on temperature had not come into use, but the lookouts, bridge crews, and exposed guns' crews of the *Emmons* can testify to the piercing effect the combination of temperature, wind, and wet spray can have on the body. Sometimes, when steaming into a head wind, a near freezing spray would reach as high as the bridge and director tower. Because of the threat of air attack, most of the voyage was made in condition II, with watch on and watch off. The uniform of the day was foul weather gear, and many of the crew did not change clothes during the entire trip. Even the boiler room watches found it comfortable to wear foul weather jackets in front of the boilers. This was one time when the engineers did not accuse the "deck apes" of being soft.

The only really decent weather experienced by the relief group was the half day spent at anchor at Murmansk. At that time the skies were clear and the seas calm, although foul weather clothing was still comfortable. This spell of fair weather was brief. The very day the ships set out on the return voyage to Iceland, one of the sudden changes characteristic of the Arctic brought on a gale with winds to Force 8. Fortunately, the ships had fueled before leaving Kola Inlet and were in no danger of foundering, although to many aboard the *Emmons* it seemed the ship could not take such pitching and rolling for long. The commanding officer of the *Tuscaloosa* wisely slowed the formation speed from 20 to 10 knots until the winds eased. By far the worst storm the *Emmons* had experienced up to that time, it left an indelible impression on those who went through it. Anyone who has been through a storm on a destroyer is never likely to forget it. The ship, normally dependable and protective, seems to be possessed of demons. If the seas are ahead, the hull seems intent on pounding itself to pieces as it rises on the crest then plunges into the trough of the successive waves. If the seas are on the beam, there is the interminable roll to one side or the other. Then comes the pause while the hull hangs suspended as if debating which way to go. Finally, after a seeming eternity of indecision, it begins to return to the upright—only to repeat the cycle in a few minutes on the opposite side. Jerry McAlevey who went through the Arctic storm and others as bad or worse aboard the *Emmons,* sums up the physical and mental beating in these words, "You can't stand, you can't sit, you can't sleep, you can't eat. The body takes a beating—and the brain takes a beating."

In spite of the hardships imposed by rough weather, all hands kept their posts, sometimes at the expense of acute discomfort, sometimes by the use of unusual ingenuity. The experience of Fireman Julius Grieco is an example of both. During one of the storms on the Murmansk run, he reported to his watch station as smoke lookout abaft the pilot house wearing a brand new pair of shoes. There were no friction cleats on the deck in that area and the combination of a wet, slippery deck and the slick leather soles of the new shoes made it hard for Grieco to keep his feet. Much of the first hour of his watch was spent scrambling around on hands and knees trying to keep on his station. Just as a wisp of smoke came from one of the stacks, the executive officer emerged from the pilot house yelling to "knock off that damn smoke." Then, spotting the lookout on his knees, he asked what the trouble was. Managing to get to his feet, Grieco dutifully replied "Nothing, Sir." He then began trying to figure out how he could stay on his feet for three more hours without killing himself. Spotting a hook on the bulkhead behind him, he jammed the collar of his foul weather jacket over it. In his own words, he spent the next three hours "swinging like a pendulum" facing aft where he could keep an eye out for tell-tale smoke from the fire rooms.

No one aboard ship took a worse beating than the lookouts stationed in the bow. Normally, bow lookouts were not posted except during fog and periods of reduced visibility. However, both sides had planted extensive minefields off the Russian and Norwegian coasts. Many of the old-fashioned moored mines had come adrift in stormy weather and were now scattered throughout the Norway and Barents Seas. Regardless of their origin, they constituted a lethal menace to surface ships. So many drifting mines had been reported along the route of Easy-Unit that mine lookouts were stationed in the bow for the entire trip. Mine sightings were frequent, but nothing could be done about them except change course if they were dead ahead. Time was too precious to slow or stop to sink them by gunfire. James Donovan, one of the seamen assigned to the exacting mine lookout job, recalls counting as many as eleven mines in a two-hour watch. He also recalls that he didn't get a chance to change clothes the entire trip and was so groggy when the ship came back to Seydisfjordur that the boatswain's mate in charge of his watch section sent him below to get some sleep instead of to his fueling station.

Navigation above the Arctic Circle was tricky and uncertain. At that time of year star sights were not practicable because of the light. They would have been obscured most of the time anyway because of the prevailing overcast. The magnetic compass was of little use because much of the route was close to the latitude of the magnetic pole. And the gyro compass developed an eight degree error. The executive officer, who doubled as navigator, had to depend largely on dead reckoning, backed by an occasional position line from the sun whenever it could be seen at all. The exec-navigator spent much of his time plotting changes in course and speed and looking for a hole in the clouds or fog through which he could get a shot of the sun. Radar was a big help when close enough to a land mass and was especially useful in making the approach to the Kola Inlet. Soundings were of some help in checking positions. Tricky as navigation was, the group managed to reach their destination without any significant deviation from their track or loss of time because of bad navigation conditions. In spite of lack of positive fixes there was surprisingly little difference between the 0800, 1200, and 2000 positions reported in the *Emmons'* war diary and those reported in the diary of the *Tuscaloosa.*

5

A few hours after leaving Seydisfjordur, Easy-Unit crossed the Arctic Circle and all hands automatically became "blue noses," an honor reserved for those who have sailed in the Arctic, similar to the title of "shellback" for those who cross the equator. There was no horseplay as the *Emmons* entered the Arctic—there was a vast difference between near-freezing weather in waters known to be infested with U-boats and the balmy breezes of the tropics in the peaceful waters of the Pacific of six months before.

The Germans still believed convoy PQ18 would attempt the passage from Iceland to Russia and had intensified air reconnaissance out of Norway to augment observations of picket submarines already stationed in the Arctic Sea. The air raid warning, which had interrupted the fueling operation at Seydisfjordur, may well have been triggered by a German aircraft on a search for the convoy. Some time before the *Tuscaloosa* and her escorts had reached the Iceland fueling station, an enemy submarine, U-405, had mistakenly reported sighting convoy PQ18. After careful analysis, the German high command correctly concluded that the report was too vague and had been made under such adverse conditions of visibility it could not be accepted as proof that the convoy had sailed. However, they remained alert to detect any signs that PQ18 was on the move. It was not until August 20 that the Operations Division of the German Naval Staff came to the conclusion that PQ18 had been postponed and began to turn its attention elsewhere.

In the meantime, surveillance of the Iceland-Russia convoy route was continued as before. It was inevitable that sooner or later the ships of Easy-Unit would be sighted and reported, in spite of the poor search conditions. The first sighting came on the second dog watch of the 20th, almost exactly twenty-four hours after the group left Seydisfjordur. The formation was east of Jan Mayen Island steaming on a northeasterly course, at a speed of nineteen and a half knots, when a Blohm and Voss-138 reconnaissance plane came lumbering out of the mist to port.

Lookouts of the *Emmons,* on antisubmarine screen station on the port bow of the *Tuscaloosa,* were the first to spot the unwieldy plane abaft the port beam as it emerged from the mist about five miles away. There had been no previous warning of its presence. It is possible that the pilot was as startled to see the ships as the lookouts were to see him, as he was flying "slow and low" and turned to parallel the formation about the same time he was spotted. After tracking him for a minute or so the *Emmons,* followed shortly by the *Rodman,* opened fire on the intruder, whereupon he turned back into the mist, only to reappear almost at once on the same bearing. Fire was resumed. Twenty-three rounds were fired without visible effect as he pulled out of range, circling ahead of the formation, down its starboard side, and out of sight. The radio direction finder of the *Tuscaloosa* picked up a transmission from the plane which was assumed to be a report of the location of the force.

The short engagement created much excitement aboard the ships of Easy-Unit. Nowhere was it greater than aboard the *Emmons.* There was great elation that she had spotted and fired on a visible enemy—positively identified as such—as opposed to previous brushes with unseen and unidentified submarines. On the other hand, no one doubted that the Blohm and Voss was the forerunner of a major attack by bomber and torpedo planes whose job was to destroy rather than to hunt and report. Preparations were made to repel the attack when it came. Short of staying at general quarters, there really wasn't much to be done except recheck the guns and watch and wait. Luckily, the mist turned into a genuine fog which provided cover until the following day and even then the sky remained overcast.

The engineer officer tells a story which illustrates the tension aboard ship. The next day after the Blohm and Voss had been driven off, he had the watch on the bridge as officer of the deck. Most of the fog had dissipated, but the sky was overcast and the usual mist cut off the horizon. Toward the end of the watch one of the lookouts reported sighting something to starboard. When the officer of the deck looked out to that side he saw what appeared to be a perfect formation of low-flying torpedo planes headed directly for the ship. He shouted "there they come" and ordered the general quarters alarm sounded. As the "torpedo planes" closed in, sharper eyes identified the attackers as a flight of harmless water fowl skimming above the water.

Thanks to the almost continuous cloud cover, which frequently turned into rain or fog, there were no further aerial contacts, or, for that matter, any other contact with the enemy before the group reached Kola inlet, except one radar contact picked up by the *Tuscaloosa* in the low lying clouds. The contact was evaluated as an enemy plane, but it was never sighted and there is no reason to believe that it sighted the warships.

Among the crew of the *Emmons* there was a curious mixture of relief and disappointment at the failure of the Luftwaffe to show up in force after the sighting. There was no thought of the surface ships, although they could have easily outgunned the ships of Easy-Unit. As for the submarines, they were considered routine. The simplest explanation for the Germans' neglect was that they lost sight of the formation in the bad weather and were never able to pick it up again. The speed at which the Easy-Unit formation traveled was an advantage.

There are other factors which may have kept the enemy from attacking. Among other things, the sighting reports were vague and confusing. The War Diary of the Operations Division of the German Naval Staff for 20 August, 1942, records that air reconnaissance "sighted at 2020 1 heavy and 1 light cruiser

130 miles east of Jan Mayen." The time and location jibe closely with entries in both the *Emmons'* and the *Tuscaloosa's* war diaries. Obviously, the pilot thought the *Emmons* was a cruiser. Perhaps he was so busy dodging the *Emmons'* and *Rodman's* fire that he did not see the other ships of the formation in the mist. About midnight the same day, a German submarine in the area reported sound contact with a "steamer" on course 060° which the Naval Staff associated with the "cruisers east of Jan Mayen." Having already concluded that convoy PQ18 had not sailed, the staff officers were puzzled as to what the "cruisers" could be up to. Their tentative conclusion was that "It is possible that these vessels are being sent into action against the expected breakthrough of our ships into the Atlantic Ocean." Apparently, it never occurred to them that the "cruisers" might be bound for Russia.

Yet another event affected the Naval Staffs' thinking. On the night of the 19th the British had made a commando raid in force on Dieppe. The attack had been easily contained, but the Germans were still trying to evaluate its significance when the ships of Easy-Unit were discovered. The experts considered the raid on the French port a diversion to cover up some more important allied move. Until they were certain of what was going on they could not afford to scatter their forces. As for committing their heavy ships, the German command was ever mindful of Hitler's orders which forbade risking a surface action under any but favorable conditions.

Whatever the reasons, the ships of Easy-Unit were not spotted again before the return journey to Iceland.

6

The British destroyers *Martin* and *Marne* were sent out of Kola Bay to join the ships of Easy-Unit some three hundred miles to the north for the approach to the Russian coast. The rendezvous was delayed for nearly twelve hours by thick weather while the formation maneuvered at twenty knots about the designated meeting point. Finally, a radar contact was picked up barely two miles astern of the formation. Taking no chances, the OTC ordered the *Emmons* to investigate while all ships went to general quarters. As anticipated, the contact proved to be the two British destroyers which were directed to their places in the screen by the *Emmons.* Course was set to the south and the Russian coast.

The British-American expedition arrived off the entrance to Kola entrance late in the afternoon, August 23. Throughout the day the weather had cleared, a welcome change for the crews, but it vastly increased the chances of discovery by

German aircraft based in Norway and Finland or one of their submarines which lurked off the entrance to the inlet. The ships were met by the Russian destroyer *Gremiastchi* which led the formation up the channel to Vaenga Bay, the anchorage on the east side of the inlet reserved for foreign warships and merchantmen waiting to be unloaded at Murmansk. The port city, which gave its name to the convoy run, was several miles away at the head of the inlet and not visible from the anchorage. It had been largely built of wood and in August, 1942, was reported to be no more than a mass of burned-out rubble from repeated German incendiary bomb attacks with only a few concrete buildings left standing. There was a small naval base across the inlet, but in 1942 only the few British submarines operating in North Russia were welcome to use its facilities.

As the newly arrived American and British ships followed the *Grimaistchi* to their anchorage, they were passed by several Russian patrol craft which punctiliously rendered passing honors. The smartness and stiff discipline of their crews paraded at quarters were impressive by any standards, especially for small ships. Even so, there was evident curiosity about the first American men-of-war to visit their harbor. A few who were not in ranks even ventured to wave in friendly greeting. Except for a naval boarding officer at the anchorage, they were the only Russian military personnel seen by the crew of the *Emmons,* for there was no liberty or contact of any sort with the beach during the short visit.

The *Emmons* anchored at Vaenga Bay shortly after ten o'clock in the evening. As soon as the hook was down, HMS *Hazard* came alongside to port and a small Russian civilian vessel to starboard. Within ten minutes the ammunition and provisions were being offloaded. Speed was of the essence because of the constant threat of air raids from Petsamo airfield barely 60 miles away across the Finnish border, and a few miles beyond that was another German base at Kirkenes in Norway. The arrival of the ships of Easy-Unit had been timed to take advantage of the brief twilight and the early morning hours when the aircraft at Petsamos and Kirkenes were less active than during the rest of the day. The plan was to get the ships in and out before Jerry woke up and discovered what was going on.

The Russian craft which took off the provisions was manned entirely by women. They did everything from working the lines to handling the cargo, stolidly and unsmilingly. There was no indication that they were from the forced labor gangs which reportedly were used to work the cargo handling facilities at Murmansk; they were competent workers and appeared dedicated to their jobs. When word got around the *Emmons* that women were handling the cargo brought from Great Britain, practically every man aboard found some excuse for going topside to see for himself. The muscular, "two-ton" women, as some of the sailors called them, were not what they were expecting, but the destroyer men were awed by the ease with which they tossed around sacks of beans and flour. A few sailors tried to strike up an acquaintance with the Amazons, but found it slow going because of the language problem and the distrust which the Russians had for foreigners, allies or not. Some of the more persistent managed to barter candy bars for red star pins and hammer and sickle emblems which they all wore. One of the engineers haggling for a hammer and sickle with a woman he swore was twice his size had to take a bite out of his candy bar before she would agree to a swap.

A minor crisis, caused by lack of communication, arose with the woman who appeared to be in charge of loading stores in the Russian vessel. She kept angrily pointing to the destroyer's torpedo tubes and repeating her version of the word "torpedo," as if demanding that the ship's torpedoes be delivered to her gang. Finally, two seamen who knew a smattering of Russian were found, William E. Dolasky, of Polish extraction, and Joseph Terensky, part Russian. They reported to the bridge and between them found out that the agitated woman expected to get some torpedoes and other ammunition from the *Emmons.* She wanted the munitions loaded before the food because they expected an attack that morning and were short of ammunition. She made it clear that the Russians were far more interested in ammunition than food. Since there were no spare torpedoes on board and the ammunition carried as cargo was consigned to the British, possibly for further delivery to the Russians, it was necessary to get the message across that what she sought was aboard the *Tuscaloosa* rather than the *Emmons.* It took some time to convince her, but she finally took off in a boat for the *Tuscaloosa.* Off-loading of the provisions continued. She must have gotten satisfaction aboard the cruiser as she did not return to the *Emmons.*

The chief engineer of the Russian fuel oil barge, which came alongside after the cargo vessel left, was far easier to get along with. Apart from her coarse, threadbare clothing, she could easily have filled in as the grandmother of any of the *Emmons'* crew. She gladly accepted an invitation to visit the galley and obviously relished a ham sandwich washed down with several cups of black coffee. To show her appreciation, several lead alloy lapel buttons stamped with Stalin's face were distributed to her hosts. A short, solemn speech, which no one understood, went with the presentation.

The unloading of stores and ammunition was completed during the midwatch and both the *Hazard* and the Russian oilier cast off, but the *Hazard* returned within an hour with fifty-six survivors of PQ17 who were to be taken back to England aboard the *Emmons.* Fifty-three of them were navy men from the armed guards of some of the sunken ships. Three of them were merchant marine officers. There was a marked contrast in the morale of the youngsters of the armed guard crews and the older merchant seamen. Most of the former were in their late teens or early twenties and in the seven weeks since PQ17 had been attacked, seemed to have shaken off the trauma of their experience. They were all happy to be getting out of Russia and exhibited a lively interest in the destroyer's modern equipment which was so far advanced over the old-fashioned, hand-operated guns they had had to face the Germans with. On the other hand, the older merchant mariners were almost physical wrecks. They lighted and discarded one cigarette after another and drank cup after cup of coffee. The hands of one of them shook so badly he could hardly lift a cup of coffee without spilling it. Needless to say, they too were happy to get out of Murmansk aboard a warship.

The ship was fueled and ready for sea long before the breakfast hour, but it took longer to unload the *Tuscaloosa.* Most of the crew attempted to catch up on some sleep, but that was soon interrupted. Shortly before breakfast the *Emmons'* radar watch picked up an unidentified plane, assumed to be an enemy, several miles to the west, toward the Finnish border. It did not approach the anchorage and soon disappeared from the radar screen. Nonetheless, antiaircraft defenses were set, spoiling any chance for sleep that morning.

Finally, the *Tuscaloosa* completed offloading all of the cargo and personnel she had brought from England and received the passengers she was to carry back. Part of the delay was caused by the Russians' balking at allowing the medical unit to land. Apparently they were willing to take the supplies but not the personnel. The question had to be resolved in Moscow before they were landed. At 0949 the *Tuscaloosa* was ready to leave and signaled her group to get underway and put to sea.

7

The ships of Easy-Unit had been very lucky to get in and out of Vaenga Bay in less than twelve hours. The delivery of supplies had gone smoothly except for some difficulties with the Russians which were resolved. The weather stayed fair. The expected attack by the Luftwaffe had failed to develop either because the Germans were unaware of what was going on or had other plans. All hands were glad to feel the increasing swell as they left Kola Inlet and headed north on the first leg of the return journey to Iceland. They anticipated a "down hill" run, notwithstanding the German airplanes and submarines which could materialize at any time along the homeward route.

The fair weather did not hold. During the first night the wind shifted fromoff the Russian mainland from the southeast to off the ice pack from the northwest. During the morning watch course was changed to the westward to make the passage between Bear Island to the south and the ice pack to the north. A track close to the ice fields was maintained in order to keep as far away as possible from the German airfields in Norway. There was no way to get beyond the limits of their air strikes without running northwest. During the morning watch, course was changed to the westward to make the passage between Bear Island to the south and the ice pack to the north. A track close to the ice fields was maintained in order to keep as far away as possible from the German airfields in Norway. There was no way to get beyond the limits of their air strikes without running into ice.

Throughout the morning of the 25th the winds and the seas picked up with such intensity that by noon the group was experiencing the previously mentioned gale. On westerly courses the ships were heading into the wind and sea. They took such a pounding that the formation had to slow to prevent structural damage to the destroyers.

At the height of the gale, the *Onslaught, Martin,* and *Marne* left the formation on dispatch orders from C-in-C Home Fleet, and disappeared to the southwest in the general direction of the Norway coast. Their mysterious disappearance was not explained until they rejoined the formation twenty-four hours later. When they reappeared they reported that they had intercepted and destroyed the German minelayer *Ulm* off the Norwegian coast. She was on her way to plant minefields off Novaya Zemlya and the entrance to the White Sea when the destroyers caught her. The Royal Navy ships had on board forty-two prisoners taken from the sunken minelayer. Later, when the *Onslaught* moored alongside the *Emmons* at Seydisfjordur, her captain explained the operation as a triumph for British Intelligence. According to him, "the *Ulm* was exactly where Intelligence said she would be."

While the *Onslaught* was alongside, the *Emmons'* crew had a chance to see some of the fourteen prisoners she had on board. To the "Old Men" of the *Emmons* they appeared to be extremely young, "just kids." Before the American ships left Seydisfjordur three wounded prisoners were sent from the *Martin* to the *Tuscaloosa* for medical care and transfer to Scotland.

After the British destroyers had left the formation the gale began to lose its punch. Speed was gradually increased and by 1921 the ships were moving along at twenty knots. It was just as well, for two hours later the *Tuscaloosa* sighted a submarine periscope on her port quarter. As she executed a sharp turn away she fired a single 5" projectile to designate the spot. The *Rodman,* being nearest, was ordered to investigate while the *Emmons* did her best to screen ahead of the cruiser in the heavy seas. If, indeed, it was a submarine it was soon left behind at twenty knots. Because of the speed and weather conditions, the *Rodman* was called back to her screen position without having made contact. This sighting was one of four reported by the *Tuscaloosa* between Bear Island and Seydisfjordur.

On the 26th both a submarine and a hostile plane were sighted. Because there was still a moderate gale blowing the submarine sighting was not confirmed, but there can be no doubt about the Blohm and Voss 138 which was sighted at 0921. Unlike the snooper encountered six days before, this one was persistent. He made himself an unwelcome part of the formation and for four hours circled around and around the group, just outside the range of the 5" guns. The *Rodman* opened fire on him when he first appeared but with no apparent effect. He merely moved out a few hundred yards more. All ships continued to track him, hoping he would come within range, but he was too cautious to oblige. All the while he was sending out radio signals.

At 1330 a fresh BV-138 relieved the morning shadower. This one was less careful then the first. At 1415, on one of his turns he cut in a little bit too close on the *Emmons'* starboard bow. As he came into range the *Emmons* opened fire, whereupon he increased speed and turned sharply away emitting smoke. As he pulled out of range eighteen rounds were fired. The first salvoes were very close as observed from both the *Tuscaloosa* and the *Emmons* and noted in their war diaries. The gunnery officer of the *Emmons* believed the plane took some damage from the close explosions although it could not be confirmed. His subsequent actions tended to confirm this as he made a half circle around the formation and then disappeared, not to return. The ships of Easy-Unit reached Seydisfjordur unmolested except for two more unconfirmed submarine "sightings."

Apparently the first reconnaissance plane had sighted the three British destroyers somewhere to the southeast only a few minutes before stumbling onto the *Tuscaloosa* group. The three destroyers were sighted as of 0945 followed by sighting of the American ships at 1025. The sighting of the British ships was confirmed by a German submarine in the vicinity, but its estimate of course was more confusing than helpful to the German Naval Staff. A paragraph from the Arctic Ocean section of their War Diary for August 26 is quoted below.

> At 0945 air reconnaissance sighted 3 British destroyers in quadrant AB 3855 proceeding at 15 knots on a 270° course. Submarine U "88" reported the same destroyers in quadrant AB 3945 on an easterly course disappearing from

> sight. An inquiry resulted in the statement that the enemy's last reliably established course was southwesterly and that the reported easterly course was based on assumption. At 1025 air reconnaissance reported 1 cruiser and 2 destroyers on a westerly course in quadrant AB 3736. It is not clear whether these reports refer to a single or to 2 different forces.

The above may explain why the Germans made no follow-up on the group. They had not yet learned of the sinking of the *Ulm.*

An hour after the second Blohm and Voss decided to quit, the three British destroyers came up from the southeast and took their stations in the screen about the *Tuscaloosa.* Their arrival was most welcome as the group was still within the range of German air strikes out of Norway. By midnight the six ships were beyond the outer limits of such a strike, although still within easy range of long-legged reconnaissance planes. One threat was out of the way, but the tired crews still had to keep alert for submarines and the many mines floating around the Norwegian Sea.

The ships arrived at Seydisfjordur early in the morning, August 28. For all practical purposes the mission of Easy-Unit was completed when the ships reached the safety of the advance base. They had earned a little rest after nine days of stress from foul weather and the threat of enemy attacks. Vital supplies had been delivered to North Russia and the survivors of PQ17 had been brought out without further loss. Samuel Eliot Morison in his account of Easy-Unit's Murmansk run sums up their success in five words: "A neat mission well executed."

8

The three American ships left Seydisfjordur after fueling and drawing stores from the *Uranus,* which was waiting in the tiny port to service them. When they put to sea the three British destroyers were left behind to carry out whatever orders might be forthcoming from the Home Fleet.

The two nights and one day voyage from Iceland to the Clyde was most pleasant in contrast to the last nine days above the Arctic Circle in waters dominated by enemy forces. It was good to be back among friends—recognition signals were exchanged with several allied ships en route and the route was covered by friendly air out of Iceland and Scotland. Best of all, the weather was fair, with moderate winds and seas from astern. Although submarines usually hunted in that area, none dared to show its periscope.

At Greenock the survivors of PQ17 were transferred to the *Tuscaloosa,* and preparations were made for the belated return to the United States. Royal Navy charts and signal books were returned and, the last day before sailing, the six British signal ratings were sent back to their regular commands. They were given a rousing send-off when they left the ship. During the past two months they had been an invaluable addition to the ship's own communication gang, operating in a new situation under a strange command.

On September 1, Task Force 99 was officially dissolved by dispatch from Commander Naval Forces Europe. At that time, the last remaining ships of TF99 operating in European waters were the *Tuscaloosa, Emmons,* and *Rodman.* It would be the next year before United States ships were again assigned for operations with the British Home Fleet.

On the same day the task force was dissolved, the three ships dropped down the Clyde headed for the open sea and home. Although they didn't know it at the time, they were being recalled to take part in the greatest sea-to-land assault ever mounted up to that time: the Anglo-American invasion of North Africa, Operation TORCH.

7

Invasion of North Africa

o o o o o o o o o o o o o o o o o o o o o o o o o o o o o o o o o o

....0820 Commenced steaming various courses at various speeds, screening USS Santee during flying operations. 0950 Plane crashed off bow of USS Santee. Commenced steering various courses at various speeds, maneuvering to rescue crew. 0956 Stopped all engines. Lowered crash boat; boat proceeding to pick up plane crew. 1010 Crash boat returned to ship and was picked up...all treated for shock. None of rescued personnel injured. 1015 All engines ahead full, 20 knots. Maneuvering to regain position "A" on port bow of USS Santee. 1034 On station....

—***Emmons*** *Log, October 15, 1942*

After dropping in at Hvalfjordur for fuel, the three ships headed across the Atlantic for home. The usually turbulent Atlantic seemed tame after the Arctic. A few days out, a message from CinCLant assigned the *Emmons* and *Rodman* ten-day availability at Boston Navy Yard. There was much elation at the prospect of getting several days leave to visit families and friends during the overhaul period. Beyond the pleasant prospect of leave there was the question—where do we go next? Few looked forward to the prospect of assignment to the Escort Force. Many aboard were convinced that another month would see the *Emmons* out of the Atlantic on the way to the Western Pacific. No one suspected that in two months they would be off the coast of North Africa.

The destroyers were not to go directly to Boston. Since the *Tuscaloosa* was headed for the Brooklyn Navy Yard for overhaul, they had to escort her to New York. Sunset, September 9, found them secured to the 25th Street Pier of the Brooklyn Navy Yard awaiting fuel. As they were to get underway for Boston at daybreak the next day one section was given liberty to expire at 0200. In spite of the short liberty there was heavy bartering by the Brooklyn and Queens crewmen for the few precious hours on their home turf. Most were able to make some sort of swap with their Boston and New England mates.

Only two cases of over leave were serious enough to warrant disciplinary action and not a single man was absent when the ship got underway with the *Rodman* at daybreak. For some reason or other the short route to Boston via the familiar Cape Cod Canal was bypassed for the longer route to seaward of Nantucket Shoals and the Cape. As the ships passed Nantucket Shoals light, a fog hovering off shore lowered the visibility to 400 yards, threatening to delay their arrival at Boston. But as they cleared the shoals and steadied down on a northerly course, the fog lifted and they were able to arrive off Boston the next day at daybreak. A few hours later they were bedded down at the Navy Yard with engines and boilers secured, ready to begin overhaul.

2

The ten days at the navy yard passed quickly. No major changes were made in the armament, but many small alterations based on the operational experiences of other ships of the class were completed. One, not so small, was the building of an elaborate pipe guard around the 1.1 machine gun to provide a positive stop in case of failure of the automatic stops. With machinery secured and no readiness requirements other than antiaircraft defense, the crew was able to undertake routine upkeep and accumulated repairs which could not be done while the ship was in a ready condition. The leading petty officers soon discovered that a little coffee worked wonders getting unofficial help from the navy yard shops. It seems the shop crews were as addicted to the brew as the ship's crew but were usually in short supply because of rationing.

The fact that the *Emmons* was no longer a neophyte in the eyes of the navy was signaled by the massive personnel changes which started as soon as the ship reached the yard. The navy was expanding rapidly and it became routine for a fifth to a quarter of the ship's crew to be replaced every time it returned to the States from extended overseas duty. This turnover of personnel continued throughout the next two years and was halted only when the *Emmons* reported to the Pacific as a high speed minesweeper in 1945.

From the time of reporting to the yard to the end of December, over a fourth of the old crew was transferred to other ships or stations. Many of the transferees were senior petty officers who had helped put the ship in commission and were now called on to repeat the performance for newer, greener ships. Among the sixty-eight who left the ship were twenty-four petty officers, seven of them chiefs. Two of them left the ship as warrant officers. Eight were seamen especially selected to attend service schools and were expected to return.

The skimming of talent from the top was compensated for by an infusion of fresh young blood at the bottom. Of 105 men received on board during the period September-December, the greatest number, seventy-one, were apprentice seamen and seamen second class, most of them fresh out of the training centers with little more than a month in the navy. Unlike the earlier drafts, most of them were reservists who had signed up for the duration of the war. A large draft which reported aboard two days after the ship secured to the dock at the navy yard was dominated by men whose names began with T. The M's and P's dominated later drafts.

Only twelve of the newcomers were petty officers, but thanks to the training program started by the captain and the executive officer at Bath, gaps created by the wholesale transfer of petty officers were easily filled from below. Another phase of the training program paid off well: among the 105 men received were eighteen former crewmen who had been sent to service school before the ship left for Europe. Nine of these wore the "crow" of a petty officer which they had earned at the schools. Four of them sported the insignia of the newly created rating of sonar man. The rating of radar man would come along in a few months.

Advancement in ratings kept pace with the shifts of personnel. Practically everyone from seaman up advanced a notch. In the last quarter of 1942 alone, 105 men, nearly half of the crew, were promoted. Advancement from apprentice to seaman second was automatic, but above that the promotions were based on evaluation, recommendation, and the completion of specialized courses. Among the seamen there was much scheming and scrambling to get assigned as strikers to a division where advancement was considered to be most rapid. The ratings of signalman, quartermaster, radioman, sonar-man, and later, radar man were most sought after. Two seamen second class, William M. Hayes and Owen B. Butler, assigned to the bridge gang, tossed a coin to decide which would become a quartermaster striker and which would go to the signal gang. Both were advanced in rating and transferred from the ship after Operation TORCH. After the war, Hayes made the navy a career and retired as a chief quartermaster. Butler left the ship as a signalman third class, one of several petty officers selected for officer training. After going through the V-12 program at Dartmouth he was commissioned, but following the war he chose business as a career and ended up as Chairman of the Board and Chief Executive Officer of Procter & Gamble.

After the rigors of the Arctic there was increased interest in getting out of work and watch stations exposed to the weather into jobs sheltered from the elements. The crews of the open machine guns were particularly exposed to cold, wet weather. Anthony "Tony" Siragusa, then a seaman second class, was one who determined to change jobs. From his station as first loader on the 1.1" machine gun, he could look down whenever the engine room hatch was open and see the engineers drinking coffee in comfort and apparently enjoying life while he was stuck cold and shivering above. He decided to join the engineers. A chit requesting a change in rating forwarded through the chain of command was bounced back several times, but perseverance and the support of helpful petty officers finally got him a change in rating to fireman third class. An added incentive to get off the 1.1 mount was its tendency to override its stops—this was before the pipe stops were installed at the yard. He also claimed that every time No.3 five-inch gun trained forward of the beam and cut loose, the machine gun crew had to pick wadding out of their necks and ears.

Comparable changes occurred among the *Emmons'* officers. The policy of promoting upward and out and of filling billet assignments from within continued. By the end of 1942, only seven of the officers who put the ship in commission were left on board. All of them had been upped at least one rank since the commissioning and two of the ensigns at that event were full lieutenants a year later. There were now fifteen officers aboard. All of the new officers except one were newly commissioned ensigns, all were reservists. The exception was Lieutenant (jg) J. A. Sill, MC, USNR, who was ordered to fill the medical officer billet now allowed for destroyers.

Except for the transfer of Lieutenant George E. Pierce, the first gunnery officer, to lighter-than-air training, the Bureau of Navigation left the original slate of senior officers intact until October, when Commander Ragan was ordered to command another destroyer.

3

After the yard period the *Emmons* and the *Rodman* reported to Task Force 22 and proceeded to Casco Bay where they joined the new battleship *Massachusetts* for several days of "in and out" exercises off shore. The training routine at Casco was terminated rather abruptly when the two destroyers were ordered to escort the battleship to Norfolk. There they joined the other destroyers of DesRon 10, now under the command of Captain James L. Holloway, Jr.

It was soon apparent that something out of the ordinary was in the making. The always busy Norfolk base was bustling with preparations for Operation TORCH. Although detailed operation plans for the North African invasion had not yet been issued, the American forces committed to it had been designated and were being assembled at the Virginia base just a month before the D-day date of October 8.

The British and American combined staffs had agreed on the African venture in July, when it became apparent that the original plan for a cross-channel attack on Europe would have to be postponed because it involved too great a risk in 1942. A large number of troops and a vast amount of material had been assembled in the British Isles and it was highly desirable that they be put to some effective use rather than remain idle until everything was in place for the frontal assault. Further, the Allies were still on the losing end of the war, a point reiterated in September by Under-Secretary of the Navy Ralph Bard in a speech castigating self-delusion and complacency throughout the country. He bluntly stated, "How about for a change, just say we are still losing a war and realize that we damn well mean it." Clearly, it was time to move from defense to offense.

After reviewing the possible alternatives to a direct assault on Nazi-held Europe, the combined staffs decided that an amphibious landing in French Morocco and Algiers offered the greatest strategic return with the least risk of failure. Many factors influenced the decision. There was a very real danger that Rommel and his Desert Corps would overrun Egypt and push on to the oil-rich Middle East. In the game of intelligence and counter intelligence it became known that the Germans were fearful the Allies might take over the French African colonies and were themselves toying with the idea of occupying Dakar and other strategic points simply to prevent the Allies from doing so. In a sense, there was a race between the Allies and the Germans for control of the French colonies. Russia was clamoring for a second front to relieve the pressure on its army. It was desirable to take positive action to convince the wavering neutrals, Portugal and Turkey, that they should not join the Germans.

Throughout the summer high level planning went ahead for the invasion. In August, General Dwight D. Eisenhower was appointed Commander-in-Chief of the Allied Expeditionary Force, and British Admiral Sir Andrew Cunningham was named Allied Naval Commander. The first broad plan for TORCH was issued on September 20. It was simple in outline but complex in execution. Basically, the plan called for three separate task forces to make coordinated landings along the Mediterranean shores of Algiers and the Atlantic coast of Morocco. In the Mediterranean, an Eastern Task Force was to land in the Algiers area and a

Center Task Force in the vicinity of Oran. These two task forces were assembled and staged in Great Britain. The troops assigned were preponderantly American, but most of the naval ships were British. The Western Task Force, consisting entirely of American troops and ships, was to land along the Atlantic coast near Casablanca.

It was by far the largest amphibious assault so far attempted. Success of the African venture was imperative if the Allies were to shift to the offensive before the following year and depended on the meshing of many diverse elements, plus a "little bit of luck." Not all the factors involved were under the control of the operational commanders. Many new techniques and much specialized equipment had been developed for the tricky ship to shore movement, and most had never been tested in combat. Ideas which got their first combat trials along the African coasts would become commonplace for future operations. Although many changes in techniques and material had to be made as a result of experience gained during TORCH, the basic plan would remain the model for the remainder of the war.

Some elements beyond the control of the military commanders were political, such as questions raised by an Allied attack on the territories of nominally neutral France. The reaction of French authorities in Africa was unpredictable. President Roosevelt believed that our long standing friendship with France insured a friendly reception. At one time he had proposed that the land forces involved be entirely American to capitalize on that friendship. General Eisenhower was not so sure and was reported to have felt we were "sailing a dangerous political sea...one in which military skills and ability can do little in charting a safe course." Another political question was the effect of the landings on Spain. If she abandoned her facade of neutrality and openly joined Germany, they might together close off the Strait of Gibraltar. Regardless of the difficult questions involved, the three-pronged attack had been approved. It was hoped that the French authorities in Africa would receive the allied troops as liberators rather than aggressors. If not, the task forces were to attack anyway, hoping for such swift success at the key landing points that general opposition would collapse.

As previously mentioned, most of the troops and ships which would comprise the Western Task Force of TORCH were assembled at Norfolk. Rear Admiral H. Kent Hewitt, head of the Amphibious Force Atlantic Fleet, was chosen to command the naval phase of the assault as Commander Western Naval Task Force. The naval ships under his command were organized as Task Force 34. For all practical purposes, the Western Naval Task Force and Task Force 34 were the same until the assault forces were established on shore. Then General G. S. Patton, jr., commanding Western Task Force United States Army, would take over. Because the master plan had been slow to trickle down, Task Force 34 had to be organized and trained to the extent time permitted during October, after the *Emmons* and her companions had arrived at Norfolk.

The operation plan for Task Force 34 was issued in early October and provided for four task groups, based more or less on the functions to be performed. They were: the Covering Group, consisting of a new battleship, the *Massachusetts,* with accompanying cruisers and destroyers; the Attack Group, consisting of the combat loaded transports and cargo vessels with their screening destroyers and related ships; the Air Group, consisting of the fleet carrier *Ranger,* four escort carriers, and destroyers; and the Fire Support Group, consisting of old battleships, cruisers, and destroyers.

The final attack plan, which underwent revision almost to the day of the landings, assigned the ships, except for the Covering Force, to three attack groups, each of which was to land its accompanying troops on the Moroccan coast. The Northern Attack Group's target was Port Lyautey, the Center Attack Group was responsible for taking Casablanca, and the Southern Attack Group for landing troops and heavy tanks at Safi, some 120 miles south of Casablanca. Each of the attack groups had attached to it a miscellaneous collection of tankers, tugs and mine craft. Each had one or more beacon submarines attached. Essential training exercises for TORCH started in October, less than a month before D-day. Most of the badly needed exercises were conducted in Chesapeake Bay because of the danger of submarines offshore. Literally every available ship in the Atlantic, and some from the Pacific, had been pressed into service for the African gamble, sometimes at the expense of on-going operations such as the North Atlantic convoys. Some ships which had been expected from the Pacific could not be spared because the battle for possession of Guadalcanal was reaching a crucial stage as preparations for the African invasion were in progress.

Many of the 106 ships assigned to Task Force 34 were former merchantmen newly converted to naval vessels. Of twenty-six transports and eleven attack cargo ships available to the Amphibious Force in early October, eleven had been hurriedly converted in August and September and five had been transferred from the Pacific. Some were not fully operable for one reason or another, others had not received their allotted landing craft, and when they did arrive many of the crews had had no practical training in actual landing exercises. By "making do" with what was available, Task Force 34 was able to sail for Africa with twenty-eight transports and cargo ships in reasonably good shape.

The Air Group also had problems with recently converted merchantmen. Four of the five carriers assigned were tanker hulls converted to light escort carriers, or "jeep" carriers as they were popularly known. At least two of them were so new that they had no chance for significant training before they left Norfolk for Bermuda where they had several weeks of flight operation before taking off for Africa. In his report of the TORCH operations the captain of the escort carrier *Sangamon* commented:

> The departure from Norfolk was attended with great interest by all hands because approximately fifty percent of the ship's company was men who had never previously been to sea in any capacity and in addition almost the same percentage had been in the Navy only a few months.

Similarly, the skipper of the *Santee* reported:

> Completion of the ship had continued while the fitting out and shakedown were proceeding. By 13 October the air group had operated aboard only 1 1/2 days and guns had been fired only for structural tests. With only five experienced aviators in the air group and a bare handful of officers and men who had previously seen salt water, the training began from scratch.

4

Compared to the newly-converted transports and escorts, the destroyers and other combatant ships earmarked for TORCH were well off so far as readiness for combat was concerned. For instance, the *Emmons,* now in her tenth month of commissioned service, had already operated in three oceans under conditions ranging from excellent to terrible. Of her original crew, 115, or slightly more than half, were still serving on board. Most of the time since commissioning had been devoted to training, even when she was on operations which could easily have resulted in battle, as at Scapa Flow. It is not surprising that her officers and crew considered her ready to carry out almost any assignment handed her.

There was, however, one gap in her combat training. Fleet landing exercises, including shore bombardment and gunfire support for assault troops, had been conducted at Culebra Island, off the eastern end of Puerto Rico, since 1934, but the *Emmons* had never had the benefit of live training in such exercises. The same was true of other ships of the division. Since in any type of operation, but especially during amphibious landings, destroyers are likely to be indiscriminately shifted from one job to another, it was necessary to check them out in shore bombardment under simulated battle conditions. Accordingly, the ships of Division 19 were scheduled for a five-day training stint in Chesapeake Bay, which was to end October 3rd with the ships firing at shore targets on Bloodsworth Island. The first four days of exercises went off without a hitch, as did the first few runs on the targets at the island. But then, as the *Emmons* came out of a sharp turn and began a "blind" run, none of the first salvo landed anywhere near the designated target. Instead, the shells fell near a group of fishing vessels tending their nets in an area well clear of the target range. Fortunately, none of the innocent fishermen were hit and ceasefire was ordered immediately.

There was probably more concern aboard DD457 than in the fishing fleet. To say that the captain was annoyed would be putting it mildly. The gunnery officer was ordered down from the fire control tower to render an explanation. Since he had not had time to determine the cause before reporting to the bridge, he was unable to give a satisfactory explanation until after the stormy session with the skipper. Then it was determined that a momentary power failure, just as the ship came out of its turn, stopped the fire control equipment for a few seconds before the order to fire was given. It had not had time to get back "on target" before the first salvo left the ship.

After everything was checked and rechecked the exercise was resumed. This time the shells landed close to the target and were brought on by spotters. The rest of the practice went well to everyone's relief and the division headed for Norfolk and the Naval Operating Base. Everyone except the gunnery officer and a few of his fire control men were glad to get back to the base. The gunnery officer later confided that for several days he wasn't sure whether he would be officially reprimanded, relieved of duty, court martialed, or drawn and quartered. There really wasn't much time to go into involved investigations and disciplinary action and, in the long run, none of the actions were taken. And the gunner remained on the job until his detachment a half year later. As for the fishermen, they didn't appear upset and graciously accepted apologies for the wild shots, even wishing the *Emmons* good luck in their reply. It could have been a bit of irony but everything indicated that they meant it.

The remaining ten days at Norfolk were divided between the naval base and the navy yard at Portsmouth. The yard period was devoted to bringing the communications gear and electronics equipment up to date. It seems that every availability brought new equipment. Quite naturally, advantage was taken of the time to fine tune other equipment and correct the defects which naturally accumulate between yard periods. After the shoot at Bloodsworth Island the fire control and gunnery equipment received double attention.

Liberty in Norfolk had changed little since the last visit. The city was simply too small to provide for the recreational needs of the thousands of sailors who left their ships every night to go out on the town. A few well organized official and semi-official recreational facilities took some of the pressure off Granby Street and the waterfront dives, but these were still the focal points of activity. The goals of most liberty parties remained wine, women and chow. The proprietors of the bars and restaurants were still intent on getting all they could from the sailors, and the military police were still trying to protect each side from the other.

A few of the *Emmons* crew were netted by the lawmen, but thanks to her buddy system none of the offenses were major. Most of the crew stayed out of trouble. Sometimes arrests, even those deserved, were avoided by the timely action of shipmates. One such incident occurred when a group off the ship spotted a sign in the window of a Granby Street restaurant offering sirloin dinners for less than a dollar. Being very hungry and appreciating a bargain, they went in and ordered dinner. They never finished what may or may not have been their sirloins, because one of the group, a meat cutter in civilian life, cast a practiced eye at his steak and announced that it was no sirloin. Further, he proposed to teach the proprietor and anyone else connected with the fraud a physical lesson in honesty. Afraid he would tear the joint apart, and not thinking the cut of their meat that important, his shipmates rushed him out before the MPs arrived on the scene.

All in all, the time in Norfolk passed pleasantly enough. Meanwhile, Rear Admiral Ernest D. McWhorter, Commander of the Air Group, and also Commander of Task Force 22, divided his five carriers and the nine destroyers of DesRon 10 into three separate task groups and sent each group off to Bermuda for intensive training as soon as they were ready for sea, with stores, ammunition, and air groups all on board. The *Santee, Emmons,* and *Rodman* comprised Task Group 22.3. Since the *Santee* was the last carrier to receive its air group, TG22.3 was the last to leave Norfolk, sailing on the 13th.

When the *Emmons* left Norfolk with TG 22.3 she sailed under a new skipper, for on the 10th, out of a clear sky, a dispatch from the Bureau of Naval Personnel ordered Tommy Ragan to command of another destroyer. The same dispatch named the executive officer, Harold Heming, as the new commanding officer and ordered Baxter Billingsley up from the bowels of the ship to be the new executive officer. Lieutenant Orville O. Liebschner assumed the duties of engineer officer. Except for some reassignment of officer billets these changes had little effect on the overall operations of the ship as the organization and policies established even before commissioning had been the responsibility of Hal Heming as executive officer.

5

Task Group 22.3 arrived at Port Royal, Bermuda, on October 15. For the next ten days the *Santee,* along with the other carriers, engaged in intensive flight training to whip the new pilots and crews into shape for the upcoming operation—not that anyone knew at this point what that would be. The *Emmons* usually worked out with the *Santee.* One day she accompanied the *Ranger,* another day, she joined the other destroyers of DesRon 10 in antisubmarine exercises.

Conditions off Bermuda were nearly ideal for exercises, far superior to those found off Argentia or Casco Bay. In spite of nearly ideal weather conditions, an occasional plane was lost because of the inexperience of the pilots and the smaller decks of the converted carriers. Most of the planes' crews were rescued intact, thanks to the quick action of the destroyers which had double duty as antisubmarine screen and plane guards. The *Emmons* did her share. She was responsible for rescuing the crew of a Grumman torpedo bomber which went in off the *Santee's* port bow during flight operations preparatory to entering port the day of arrival at Bermuda. The pilot and his two crewmen were picked up uninjured, given treatment for shock, and delivered to the *Santee* after the group secured in Port Royal.

There was little liberty in Bermuda because of the tight training schedule and the difficulty of getting in and out of Port Royal. Most of the nights were spent at sea with the carriers, but once or twice the ships came through the rocky harbor entrance of Hamilton to bed down for the night at Murray's Anchorage. At daybreak they would put to sea again to take up the monotonous training routine. The calm, balmy nights riding to anchor in the protected waters of the anchorage were most welcome. With the problems of the day behind there was time for relaxation. Some men tried fishing from the fantail, others enjoyed the evening movie, many turned in early to get what sleep they could before getting underway at daybreak the next morning, but most just shot the breeze with their shipmates.

Much of the gossip centered around rumors of what the carrier force was up to. It had been apparent at Norfolk that something out of the ordinary was in the wind and the activities off Bermuda confirmed the suspicions. Even a blind man could see that the concentration of so many carriers and the intensive training at this strategic base pointed to something big, but what? Only the top commanders had known at Norfolk. Commanding officers and others who "needed to know" learned the details of the forthcoming operation when the attack plan was distributed at Bermuda, but it was not until the carrier group was safely at sea and well on the way to Africa that all hands were cut in on the secret.

It must be admitted that there was some apprehension mixed in with the speculation—the unknown is always bothersome. Toward the end of the training period several events added to the tension aboard. Two days before the group left Bermuda, the ships gathered at Murray's Anchorage and Port Royal to make final preparations for the Atlantic crossing. One of the evolutions was to "strip ship" for action. The "strip ship" bills required all excess gear, not needed to keep the ship in operation, and which might become a fire or missile hazard in case of a hit, to be landed. In the olden days such material was jettisoned at sea before battle. In more modern times it is landed before a dangerous operation, or, better yet, never allowed on board. But there has always been a difference between the requirements for reasonably comfortable living conditions during day to day operations and the demands of actual battle. The *Emmons,* having been outfitted after the war started, had had most nonessential flammable material such as paint and linoleum carpeting eliminated. However, there was a considerable amount of excess bedding, clothing and small stores, wardroom linens, spare lines and cordage which had to be sent ashore. Going through the outdated files and records on board, and determining which should be retained and which should go was a major task. Even library books had to be weeded out. It took the better part of a day to get all the stuff together and cart it away to a shed which had been allocated to the *Emmons* for its storage. In theory it was to be picked up if and when she returned to Bermuda.

Naturally, all hands were aware that stripping ship was not routine. Their curiosity was further piqued when a priest came on board to hear confessions. The hearing of confessions on board was not entirely unprecedented, but it was unusual enough to keep the rumors rolling.

The tension gave way to the more immediate demands of the sea when, on October 25, the carrier task group, screened by the destroyers of DesRon 10, left Bermuda for the Moroccan coast. This time they were sailing officially as Task Group 34.2 of the Western Naval Task Force. The *Emmons* and *Rodman* with the *Santee* were no longer designated Task Group 22.3, but were now Task Group 34.2.3, the Air Group of the Southern Attack Group which was to capture the port of Safi.

6

When the carriers left Bermuda the main body of Task Force 34 had already left Norfolk for the long haul across the Atlantic. In an elaborate ruse designed to give enemy observers the impression that two separate forces bound for widely separated areas were involved, the attack groups were sailed on succeeding days. On October 24 the ships of the Northern and Southern Attack Groups cleared the Virginia Capes on a southeasterly course as if headed for the Caribbean. The ships of the Center Attack Group sailed the next day and took a northeasterly course as if headed for the British Isles. When well clear of land the first segment made an abrupt change of course to join the second on the 26th, both then maintaining a course toward the British Isles. Meanwhile, the Covering Group sailed from Casco Bay to join the main body on the 27th. The last major group to join was the Air Group, which took its place in the formation on the 28th. Task Force 34 was then complete and changed course to the southeast in the general direction of Dakar, still intent on concealing its true destination from any chance observation by submarines or neutral merchantmen.

The men of the *Emmons* had been impressed by the formidable carrier group when it formed up off Bermuda. The size and power of Task Force 34 when all of its components came together was awesome. The *Emmons* remained with the carrier group which was stationed toward the rear of the formation so that the flattops would have plenty of sea room in which to maneuver while launching and recovering aircraft. Even from this position ships could be seen as far as the eye could reach in all directions. The hundred ships covered an expanse of ocean twenty-five miles square. At the core of the formation were twenty-seven transports and attack cargo ships carrying more than 34,000 combat troops and the arms and equipment for the initial landings. These were to be protected at all costs. With the transports were the tankers and other auxiliary craft. In the van was the covering force. Surrounding the formation were two concentric rings of battleships, cruisers, carriers and destroyers. The destroyers were the most numerous. Totaling thirty-eight, they formed the outer screen and were scattered throughout the formation. It goes without saying that the people of the *Emmons* were proud to be part of such a mighty armada.

The formation slogged along at fourteen knots to accommodate the slower ships and conserve fuel. By day the fleet zigzagged to confuse any subs which might be lurking in its path. From time to time it deviated from the projected track to avoid areas where submarines were reported. During the night of November 2-3 a major change of course was made to the northeast to give the impression the armada was bound for the Strait of Gibraltar. It was not until the 7th, D-l, that the ships headed directly to their target areas.

The weather for the first week was splendid, but on the 3rd began to deteriorate. By the 4th, northwest winds had reached gale forces and the seas were rough, so rough, in fact, that some of the smaller ships had to leave the formation to find a course where they could ride more comfortably without danger of rolling over. Even the battleships feared damage to their boats and forecastle machine guns. The destroyers, more used to being knocked about, took the gale in stride. There was concern at this point that by D-day the surf on the landing beaches would be so high that landing would be impossible. Alternate plans would have required the Task Force to continue on through the Strait and land the troops on the Mediterranean coast of French Morocco. A decision had to be made before the 7th when the Task Force was to split up into its separate attack groups. Admiral Hewitt, on the prediction of the meteorologist that the storm would pass in time for the landing beaches to calm down, made the tough decision to stick to the original plan. He proved to be right.

As the fleet plodded along, each ship held daily briefings and mock exercises to indoctrinate the crews and troops in the roles they were to play in the real thing. The hastily prepared plans were under constant revision. The revisions were distributed to all ships by destroyer guard mail. Many of the changes were triggered by the constant flow of intelligence reports on French forces in the target area, their numbers and disposition, as well as changing political and psychological considerations. The probable reaction of the French toward the attack remained an unanswered question as the task force neared the Moroccan coast. Secret intelligence was augmented by public broadcasts from enemy and neutral capitals which together gave little cause for optimism. Admiral Darlan, commander of all military forces for Vichy France, was reported in Casablanca and supposedly had predicted an allied invasion there as well as at Dakar. On the other hand, Berlin broadcasts claimed there was so much tension between the major allies, Great Britain, the United States and Russia, that a second front in 1942 was improbable. Vichy reported the evacuation of women and children from Dakar had begun. As D-day approached, Madrid reported with surprising accuracy the make-up and passage of the Eastern and Center Task Forces through the Strait of Gibraltar. Another broadcast from Vichy announced the determination of the French leaders in Africa to defend the colonies against any attack. All in all, the reports gave little promise of surprising the French.

There was no indication on the public broadcasts that the Western Task Force was detected before it arrived off the Atlantic beaches. The expected submarine attacks did not develop. As for the *Emmons,* this was the only one of the many transatlantic crossings she made when no suspicious underwater sound contacts were made. Because of a desire to save the carrier planes for combat duty, most of the scouting flights were made by aircraft from the cruisers and battleships. As a consequence the destroyers of the air group had little to do except patrol their screen stations. The *Emmons* and *Rodman* were assigned stations astern of the carriers.

Because they were near the rear of the formation the *Emmons* and *Rodman* were detailed on at least two occasions to provide antisubmarine protection for ships which suffered engine breakdowns and could not keep up with the Task Force. One time it was the transport *Hugh L. Scott,* loaded with troops; the other time it was one of their own group, the newly converted carrier *Suwanee.* Repairs in each case were made quickly and the stragglers were able to catch up with the formation before it disappeared over the horizon. Of the two charges, responsibility for the *Scott* caused the most concern because of the hundreds of troops aboard. The anxiety of one seaman aboard the *Emmons,* Anthony Esposito, would have been even greater had he known at the time that his brother was among the troops on the disabled *Scott.*

The gale toward the end of the crossing caused some inconvenience aboard. Most of the crew by now was over seasickness, but even so it was hard to sleep with the rolling and pitching. Regular meals were suspended and extra care had to be taken getting about the ship. No one ventured on the forecastle or main deck unless he had to. On one of the dark, rainy nights two of the crew, one headed aft, the other hurrying forward, collided in the middle of the catwalk between the after machine guns and the amidships superstructure. They managed to stay on the catwalk and in the darkness thought only how lucky they were to keep their balance. But by morning one of them found that his nose was no longer on center. It took the skill of the medics, working in the unstable sick bay to restore his broken nose to its proper place in his face.

By the 6th the gale subsided enough to permit fueling the destroyers from the carriers. The winds and seas were still high enough to make the operation hazardous, but with D-day less than two days away there was little choice, and the fueling went ahead as scheduled. It took the *Emmons* better than two hours to fill up while carefully maneuvering alongside the *Santee,* but she pulled away at the end without damage. None of the destroyers of Squadron 10 suffered damage except the *Forrest* which banged up her superstructure maneuvering alongside the *Suwannee.* Her armament and capacity for operations were not impaired.

Early the next morning, the 7th, the task force began to break up into separate attack groups to permit reaching the target areas in the small hours of D-day. The Southern Attack Group, Task Group 34.10, having to go the greater distance, was the first to be detached. An hour before sunrise the *Santee, Emmons* and *Rodman* left the formation to join up with that group, headed almost due south for Safi. During the afternoon, the commanding officer of the *Santee* issued an order releasing all prisoners from confinement and remitting all uncompleted sentences adjudged by him. There was no reason for such action aboard the *Emmons*—there was no one in the brig.

7

At dusk Task Group 34.2.3, plus the minelayer *Monadnock,* pulled away from the main body of the Southern Attack Group to take station some sixty miles off Safi where the *Santee* and her escorts had the dual role of preventing surprise surface attacks from seaward and providing air support for the landings. Midnight found the four on station and the *Santee* preparing to launch aircraft at daybreak.

Meanwhile, the troop carriers and cargo ships had anchored eight miles to seaward of Safi, while the *New York* and *Philadelphia* moved quietly to their fire support stations. The destroyers *Mervine, Knight* and *Beatty* prepared to act as control ships for the first waves of landing craft, after which they were to take up fire support stations close inshore. The *Cowie, Quick* and *Doran* formed a screen for the transport area. The old four-pipers *Bernadou* and *Cole,* especially altered as assault ships by cutting down masts, stacks and superstructure to reduce draft and lower their profiles, prepared to sneak, or if necessary, force their way into the small Safi harbor. The stage was set.

The ancient fishing and phosphate settlement had been carefully selected as one of the three points of attack for several reasons. In case serious opposition developed farther north at Casablanca and Port Lyautey, medium and heavy tanks would be needed to support the attacking troops. At that time the Navy had no landing craft capable of landing such tanks ashore. Safi had adequate dock and cargo handling facilities for unloading the tanks and was lightly defended. Once the Sherman tanks on the *Lakehurst* were put ashore they could be driven overland in a matter of hours in case of resistance up the coast. Possession of the port would also block interference from the major garrison and airport of Marrakech eighty miles to the southeast if the French commander at that strong point, General Henry-Martin, put up a fight. He was supposed to be favorable to the Allies and was expected to welcome the Americans, but there was no guarantee. In retrospect the soundness of the choice of Safi is evident. The port was indeed lightly defended—after it capitulated it was learned that there were only 450 French troops stationed there, including the crews of three shore defense batteries ranging from 75mm. to 155mm.

The transports began launching landing craft before midnight. Disembarkation of the troops and the thousand and one things needed ttem them moving—food,medicalsupplies,jeeps, trucks, ambulances, artillery, ammunition, tanks, fuel, walkie-talkies—followed shortly after. The weather was fair and clear. A moderate ground swell caused some rolling during the disembarkation period, but was by no means bad. A gentle offshore breeze helped to carry the noises of the off-loading away from the beach.

The Safi landings were off to an auspicious start. But no amphibious operation ever went exactly as planned, and it must be remembered that the African invasion was a bellwether. There, landing attack techniques and equipment were for the first time being tested in combat. The officers and men of both services had had scant training, the landing craft and other equipment were not yet perfected. As a result TORCH had more than its share of "snafus," and the Safi group was no exception.

Due to the inexperience of all hands it took longer to off-load the troops and equipment than planned. Heavily burdened troops were naturally extremely cautious in lowering themselves down the cargo nets into the bobbing boats. So slow was the disembarkation that Admiral Lyal A. Davidson, in command of the Southern Attack Group, was obliged to postpone H-hour from 0400 to 0430.

The submarine *Barb* which had been reconnoitering the landing beaches for several days was to have surfaced at a given point and act as guide for the assault ships. After the transports anchored, a scout boat and the destroyer *Mervine* were to contact the submarine and carry back the latest information on beach conditions to General Harmon, commander of the troops, aboard his headquarters ship, the *Harris,* The submarine carried a group of army personnel who were to row in a rubber raft to a point off the breakwater and guide the destroyers *Bernadou* and *Cole* through the harbor entrance by infrared lights. The *Barb* surfaced as planned, but apparently in the wrong position as she could not be found by the scout boat. The army men in the rubber boat had to row so far that they did not arrive on station until after action had started. The officer in charge of the scout boat, Ensign J. J. Bell, volunteered to substitute the scout boat for the missing marker boat.

The *Bernadou* and *Cole* had been designated to spearhead the attack. Each carrying a specially trained company of infantrymen, they were to lead the first waves of landing craft through the harbor entrance, then land their infantrymen onto the docks to take over the cranes and other harbor installations before the French were alerted. Immediately after it was certain they had been spotted, the *Bernadou* was to shoot a skyrocket carrying an American flag. In theory, the flag would unfurl and float slowly down, illuminated by the rocket's light as a signal to the French that the invading forces were American. All went according to plan until the *Bernadou* was well inside the harbor, when it was met with a hail of machine gun fire from the docks and breakwater. A 75 mm. battery east of the town and a 130 mm. battery to the north joined in. The flag-rocket was fired and the rocket lighted up the harbor making the destroyer an excellent target for the French gunners. But the flag was not there in the rocket's glare. Fortunately, the French fire was wild and no one was injured. The gunfire support ships temporarily silenced the shore batteries.

As planned, the *Bernadou* broadcast the signal "Batter Up" when she was fired on. Back in the flagship *Philadelphia,* at 0435, five minutes after H-hour, Admiral Davidson gave the signal, "Play Ball," which meant that opposition had been met and that force was to be opposed with force. The fight for Safi was on.

The *Cole* was to have followed the *Bernadou* by eleven minutes, guided by an infra-red light from the latter's stern. Somehow she lost sight of the light and began to follow the *Beatty* which appeared out of nowhere. The *Beatty* in her turn changed course and disappeared into the darkness, leaving the *Cole* to find the harbor as best she could. In the meantime she had missed the entrance and was headed straight for the middle of the breakwater when Ensign Bell in the scout boat sighted her and alerted her by signal of the danger. By a series of emergency maneuvers the *Cole* avoided the breakwater, adjusted course and entered the harbor during a lull in the firing. Once inside she slipped into an unoccupied berth alongside the main pier where her special troops hit the dock unopposed.

There was no little confusion at the line of departure for the succeeding waves of landing craft. Two of the landing beaches, Red to the north of Safi, and Yellow to the south, were found to be unsuitable for landings, the first because steep bluffs prevented easy exit, and the second because of high surf. In the long run this caused no problems as the landing craft were directed to beaches in and near the harbor.

As the *Bernadou* found out, the French had not been caught napping. Nor could surprise have been expected under the circumstances. The broadcasts monitored on the way across the Atlantic indicated that the French anticipated an attack on Casablanca and Dakar at some unspecified time. H-hour at the Mediterranean ports of Algiers and Oran had been set for 0100 on the 8th, three hours before H-hour at the Atlantic ports. Even Washington seemed intent on giving ample warning to the defenders of French Morocco. The president's press secretary, Stephen Early, had been instructed to break the news at the exact time of the first landings which were, of course, in the Mediterranean. At 9 p.m., Saturday, the 7th, the assembled reporters in Washington were told United States troops were landing in North and West Africa at that very moment. They were given a mimeographed copy of President Roosevelt's statement announcing the landings and a translation of his appeal to the French which was to have been broadcast from the *Texas* off Casablanca three hours later. The news of the landing and the president's appeal were being broadcast around the world more than three hours before the touchdown on the West coast of Africa. Of course, the French might have thought the news applied only to North Africa, but the most elementary prudence demanded that all coastal defenses be alerted. An alarm from Casablanca was received by the French army forces in Safi at 0230 while off-loading operations were still underway eight miles offshore.

Before the first boat waves left the transport area for the line of departure, two fast, noisy air rescue boats, which were to act as assistant control vessels for the first waves, caught the attention of the gun crews of the *Lyon.* As they roared through the waiting boats looking for the transports which were to give them instructions, they were mistaken for enemy torpedo boats and the *Lyon's* nervous gunners opened fire. Happily, no one was hit.

An hour later, a gasoline tank strapped to the side of a half-ton truck being lowered from the *Dorothea Dix* banged against the transport's side and ruptured. The gasoline sprayed into the waiting LCV below and ignited when it hit the boat's hot engine. LCV, truck, and the ship's side were engulfed in flames. The boat's crew was blown clear and was picked up by other landing craft in the vicinity, while the blazing LCV was cast off and drifted astern, shooting off fireworks as ammunition aboard exploded. Danger to other ships and boats was over only when one of the explosions ruptured the LCV's hull and it sank. The burning truck was dropped into the sea.

The loss of the LCV and the truck was not the only result of the mishap. Aboard the *Dix* it was assumed that the original fire came from a torpedo and she announced that she had been hit. Hearing this, the destroyer *Knight* left the landing craft she was shepherding and went dashing back to hunt for the nonexistent submarine. The abandoned landing craft milled about for some time and eventually returned to the *Dix* to be reformed and dispatched to Yellow Beach. They arrived there, five hours behind schedule, only to find the surf too high for safely beaching landing craft. By that time the situation ashore was well enough in hand to divert the loaded craft to one of the other beaches.

These illustrations of the many things which went wrong during the Safi landings are detailed in the Atlantic Fleet volumes of "U.S. Naval Administration in World War II." That account bluntly states that "luck" saved the day for TORCH, but then goes on to recount how the dedication, bravery, and initiative of American fighting men overcame the potentially dangerous errors.

The operation at Safi was a success, the first on the Atlantic coast to secure its objective. By daybreak army troops were in control of the harbor although still subjected to desultory fire from the French batteries and snipers in the hills surrounding the town. Troops and supplies were pouring ashore without significant opposition. By 0710 naval gunfire silenced the last of the French big guns. By mid-afternoon of D-day transports, including the *Lakehurst,* carrying the precious tanks, were unloading over the docks.

Sure, luck played a part in the success, but it was more than luck which won Safi. Admiral Davidson summed it up when he wrote:

> That the Southern Attack Group was able to land at Safi with but two naval casualties (wounded) and no material damage other than the loss of eight landing craft stranded and one burned, and with comparatively light casualties among the Army Assault Troops (estimated ten killed and seventy-five wounded) is attributed to Divine Providence, good weather, surprise, retention of the initiative and accurate and overpowering gunpowder.

8

Sixty miles offshore the *Emmons* and the other ships of the carrier group had little information about what was going on ashore. What little news there was came from intercepted dispatches and, after restrictions were lifted, intership voice transmissions. The men aboard could only imagine the hectic activities in the transport area and off the beaches. Naturally, there was a great deal of anxiety and an itchy desire to do something to help things along, but given the assignment, there was nothing to be done but keep an eye on the *Santee,* the sky and the horizon. The air search radar and sonar were kept going continuously.

The first indication that action had started came at 0430, when the lookouts reported gunfire on the horizon. This possibly was the flash from the *New York*'s 14" guns or the French 130 mm. battery firing at the *Bernadou.* It could have been the latter's sky rocket, or French star shells. Again, it could have been the gasoline fire and explosions alongside the *Dix.* Whatever it was, it relieved some of the tension to know that for good or bad, the attack had begun. All hands were called to general quarters. A short time later orders were received to "take all possible offensive action against Vichy French forces," official confirmation of what was already known: the French would not surrender without a fight.

The crew stayed at general quarters stations all day. At dawn the first flight of fighters left the carrier's deck. Other flights were launched and recovered throughout the day, more planes taking off than returning. The tanker *Merrimac,* having completed unloading her deck cargo in the transport area, joined the formation early in the morning, presumably because the carrier group was thought to be out of harm's way. She tagged along for two days before returning to Safi to act as a fueling station inside the harbor. The weather remained clear with occasional rain squalls. Wind and sea were calm. Visibility was excellent. By midmorning it was clear from overheard voice transmissions that Safi was in American hands. Very satisfying, but readiness had to be maintained. The *Santee, Merrimac* and *Monadnock* had to be protected from predatory submarines and there was always the chance that the French fleet at Dakar might come up from the south to take part in the show. If it did, chances were its first contact would be the southern carrier group. Radar and sonar sweeps had to be maintained, guns manned and ready, spare boilers warmed up and ready to be cut in. Vigilance was the order of the day.

About dusk, the *Santee* recovered the last plane for the day and soon after the ships secured from general quarters. An hour or so later the lights of a steamer were sighted to the west. This caused a little excitement until it was learned that she had been checked out as a neutral. By now the whole world knew of the invading fleet off the African ports, but there seemed to be no reason to advertise the presence of the *Santee* group, so course was changed to pass well clear astern of the merchantman. She must have known she was entering troubled waters and no doubt was just as anxious to get past the attack area as the navy ships were to avoid detection.

D-day off Safi for the *Emmons* ended quietly. There was satisfaction in knowing that the invasion was going well and that she was a part of it. But there was also a sense of frustration that she was not playing a more active role—that she was so near, yet not a part of the action. There had been much the same feeling when she was enjoying the pleasures of the shakedown cruise while the German submarine offensive was raising hell along the East Coast. There was, however, a vast difference. During the shakedown cruise, the young crew had been inclined to look upon the war as a romantic interlude, soon to be over. Now, nine months later, a more realistic view had replaced that romanticism. Service at sea meant hours of work, continuous drills, endless watches, much physical and mental discomfort, and some danger. They were now fulfilling a major task in the invasion, protection of the carrier, but for the moment there was nothing exciting about it.

While it was all watchful waiting for the *Santee's* destroyer screen, it was hectic for the inexperienced crews of her aircraft. Their mission was to fly combat patrol over the landing beaches and maintain an antisubmarine patrol to seaward. In so doing twenty-one of thirty-one planes aboard were lost, only one of them from combat. Of the first flight of seven Wildcats sent up at daybreak on D-day, only one came back to the carrier. Five got lost returning to the carrier. Four of the five, running low on fuel, made emergency landings on the French field at Mazagan where they were captured; the other crashed at sea—its pilot picked up by the *Rodman* sixty hours later. The seventh was never seen again after reporting that his oil line had been cut. Two later flights ran out of gas and landed at Safi airfield but some were unable to take to the air again because of damage caused by the poor condition of the field.

In spite of the heavy losses, the *Santee's* air group rendered valuable service as observers for the Army during mopping up operations in the area around Safi. Sometimes they were called on to strafe the few opposing ground troops in the foothills. The French air base at Marrakech remained a cause for worry. Contrary to expectations, the French sent a bomber squadron to attack the transports and other ships in the captured harbor early in the morning of D+1. Apparently the bombers were not opposed in the air, but the transports were protected by a fog. Only one plane came through the overcast to drop its bombs on a fish house near the piers, setting it afire. The bomber was shot down by antiaircraft fire from the transports. In order to prevent repeat attacks, the *Santee's* planes were sent to bomb the French air base at Marrakech. On the way there planes of the squadron broke up a column of trucks carrying French troops toward Safi. Another column of trucks was attacked on the way back. At Marrakech they claimed the destruction of fifteen bombers on the ground. Another attack, November 11, destroyed twelve French bombers on the ground. This attack was made after an armistice was declared but before the news had filtered down to the attack level. After the cease fire was announced *Santee* planes dropped packs of cigarettes with notes announcing the fact over isolated groups of French troops.

Except for a more relaxed atmosphere, November 9 was not much different from D-day, including the pleasant weather, so far as the *Emmons* was concerned. The Army was in control ashore at Safi and there were no visible threats to the ships offshore. In the absence of any immediate threat it was not necessary to man battle stations except for the routine dawn and dusk call to general quarters.

It was a distinct relief to be able to get on with routine tasks instead of spending hours on battle stations wondering what would come next. In a "stand by" situation, long hours of waiting with nothing to do but wonder were more than boring—they were maddening. Men on stations which had to do with the minute to minute operation of the ship, such as the bridge crew and the engineers, were too busy to do much worrying, but men on stations which had nothing for them to do until action was actually joined, had too much time for thinking. For instance, the gun crews, once their guns were cast loose and prepared for battle, had little to do but imagine what might happen next. The farther away from visual contact with sea and sky the battle station was, the worse it was. No one was farther down in the ship than the lower handling room crews. Once the station was manned and the ammunition train filled there was nothing to do but wait. The effect of standing idly by for hours waiting and wondering what would come next is described by a former crewman whose battle station was in one of the lower handling rooms during Operation TORCH. He said:

> I don't remember much about the invasion. My general quarters station then was in the lower handling room of Gun 4. That was the lowest point in the ship unless you were a snipe. Maybe even lower than they were. That was really the only time in my entire life I was truly scared. The reason was that we were dogged in way below deck and our only communication was with the upper handling room. They also didn't know what was going on except what they heard from the gun mount. The not knowing and, worse, the not seeing were scary.

Another seaman, whose battle station was first loader in one of the gun mounts, also confesses to nervousness during the TORCH operation primarily because of the long hours of inactive waiting. His words echo the universal naval complaint at standing by, "Just waiting, that's always the game. They gave you the word to standby and standby again."

In contrast to the feelings of claustrophobia brought on by being "dogged in" in the bowels of the ship during general quarters, the sheer joy of being underway on the deck of a destroyer in fair weather is expressed in a later description by the first lower handling room crewman:

> One of the wonderful feelings in my life was when I was at sea in good weather. The peace and serenity while idly lazing in the sunlight. The tremendous wake when at flank speed. The phosphorus in the water at night.

9

When the plans for TORCH were drawn up it was anticipated that French opposition, if it came at all, would come from the sizeable French fleets at Casablanca and Dakar and the aircraft scattered among the airfields of Western Morocco, primarily at Port Lyautey and Marrakech. The fleet at Casablanca would have the support of the 14" guns and antiaircraft battery of the immobilized battleship *Jean Bart,* while the Dakar ships would be led by the battleship *Richelieu.* There were no significant naval ships at Safi. It was considered almost certain that German submarines operating off the Strait of Gibraltar and along the shipping routes would try to disrupt the landings.

Once again the planners proved to be right. The greatest resistance to the invading forces came at Port Lyautey and Casablanca where French Vice Admiral Michelier was in command of coastal defenses.

Landings at Mehedia, near Port Lyautey, and Fedhala, near Casablanca, were plagued by the same problems which had slowed the tempo at Safi. Nonetheless, in spite of foul-ups the troops were successfully landed on D-Day and began their push for the main objectives, Port Lyautey and Casablanca.

The troops driving toward Port Lyautey had the toughest time, primarily because of the slow progress in getting artillery and other material across the beaches and the stubborn resistance of a battery of six 138.6mm guns located in the Kasba, an old fort overlooking the landing beaches on either side of the mouth of Wadi Sebou, a river flowing down past the city of Port Lyautey. They also had to fight off attacks from aircraft and tanks, the latter coming up in force from Rabat, the capital of Morocco. Both aircraft and tanks were destroyed or driven off by aircraft from the American carriers offshore. The vital airport at Port Lyautey was finally captured the morning of the 10th by a combined attack of troops fighting inland from the beaches and a special combat team carried up the Wadi Sebou on the *Dallas.* The old four-piper, specially fitted for the job like her sisters the *Bernadou* and the *Cole,* had to force her way at ebb tide through the boom at the mouth of the river and upstream against enemy fire to disembark her troops opposite the target airport.

The landings at Fedhala also had their share of problems. Because Fedhala and Casablanca are only twelve miles apart by sea their defenses had to be considered as one from the viewpoint of ships offshore. As at Mehedia, the landings at Fedhala were harassed by shore batteries which refused to stay silenced. The beaches there were also strafed by French aircraft, while tanks offered resistance inland. The carrier planes took care of both threats. The town of Fedhala and its port were secured by noon on D-day and the troops were preparing for the march on Casablanca by nightfall. Carrier aircraft had undisputed control of the air by the 10th.

Aside from submarines, the major threat to the ships in the transport area and their protecting heavy ships and destroyers was the French fleet in Casablanca harbor. The fleet had the support of the *Jean Bart* and two coast defense batteries on either side of the harbor. One of them, an eight-gun battery of four 144mm and four 138mm on El Hank, the promontory west of the harbor, was especially troublesome. The *Jean Bart* was claimed to have been silenced several times during the invasion but somehow managed to get back into action. She was finally silenced by 1,000 pound bombs dropped by bombers from the *Ranger.* The battery on El Hank would also play "possum" only to resume firing when an American ship came within range. After the cease fire the battery was found to be fully operable.

D-day featured two separate battles between the French fleet and the American ships off Casablanca. The first lasted most of the morning of D-day when the French cruiser *Primauguet,* seven destroyers, and eight submarines came out of the harbor and tried to reach the vulnerable transport area while the Covering Group was off to the northwest. They succeeded in shooting up some landing craft and got to within four miles of the transports before they were stopped by the cruisers and destroyers of the Attack Group while the Covering Group came into the action at flank speed. During the action torpedo attacks by the French destroyers and submarines narrowly missed the *Massachusetts, Tuscaloosa, Wichita* and *Brooklyn.* The gallant but futile effort of the French was easily defeated by the superior firepower of the American ships. The attacking forces were driven back on Casablanca all but wiped out. Four of the destroyers were sunk, three reached the harbor severely damaged, and only one reached the haven unscathed. The *Primauguet* was a shambles but still afloat at the end of the battle.

The action of the French submarines after the melee is hard to understand. Apparently they made no further attempt to get into the transport area. Instead, they scattered after their surface ships were driven back on Casablanca. Perhaps it indicated reluctance on the part of the Frenchmen to fight Americans. Of the eight submarines, one, the *Meduse,* was bombed by carrier planes and beached herself near Mazagan; two made it to Dakar; one got as far as Cadiz, Spain, and was scuttled by its crew; one returned to Casablanca; and three were reported missing. Three other subs never made it out of the harbor and were sunk at their berths.

The afternoon of D-day, a lesser engagement took place when our ships drove an odd assortment of two destroyers, two minesweepers and a corvette back into the harbor, largely undamaged. The French ships were actually trying to rescue the survivors of some of their destroyers sunk or damaged during the morning battle, but their course in the direction of the landing beaches was too threatening to allow them to proceed unopposed.

Virtually all resistance in the original assault areas, along both the Mediterranean and Atlantic coasts, had stopped by the evening of the 10th. American troops were in firm control of Algiers and Oran and had started a drive toward Tunis. In the Western Task Force area, Safi, Port Lyautey and Fedhala had been captured and the French authorities in those places were co-operating with the invasion forces. Of the original D-day targets only Casablanca still held out and there General Patton's troops, to be joined by the Sherman tanks coming up from Safi, were massed for a frontal assault on the city. The attack was to start after daybreak on Armistice Day, November 11.

The attack never started. Fighter-bombers from *Ranger* were actually airborne and forming up to hit their assigned targets when Admiral Michelier requested a conference under a flag of truce at Fedhala. He had received an order from Admiral Jean Darlan in Algiers to cease resistance. Michelier felt obliged to honor the order; indeed, he was probably happy to have authority from the top to get out of a hopeless situation with his honor as naval officer and a Frenchman unsullied.

Darlan was in Algiers to visit a sick son when the invasion started, or so it was stated. Whatever his reason for being there, as top military commander for Vichy France he had to be reckoned with and negotiations to gain his support were begun as soon as the Americans entered Algiers. The admiral blew hot and cold on the question of cooperation with the Allies. He first issued a cease fire order to French forces in Algiers on the 8th, and then tried to rescind it when he failed to get the clear-cut backing of Marshal Petain in Vichy. Finally, shortly before midnight on the 10th, he issued a cease fire order to all French forces in North Africa. It was this order which stopped the fighting at Casablanca.

In the meantime, to complicate matters, General Mark Clark accompanied by General Henri Giraud had arrived in Algiers on the 9th. The French general was definitely pro-Allied and had made a daring escape from a German prison. He had been picked by Eisenhower to take charge in French Africa. Unfortunately, Darlan and Giraud were anything but friends and each wanted supreme authority over French activities in the area. Since Giraud apparently could exercise no real authority over the colonial French, the Americans had to continue negotiations with Darlan, who did have clout with the colonials and the French military, as witness the results of his cease fire order of the 10th. It was not until the 12th that Darlan and Giraud agreed to share authority under the prodding of General Clark and Robert A. Murphy, our consul general in Algiers.

Admiral Darlan's order was honored in Algiers and Morocco, but the intervention of German forces prevented compliance in Tunis, where a hastily assembled German army stepped in to prevent surrender of the French. Fighting in Tunis continued until the last troops, under General von Arnim, surrendered May 12, 1943. As noted above, Darlan's order reached Casablanca barely in time to prevent a bloody battle for that city. At the Fedhala conference requested by Admiral Michelier the French agreed to stop fighting but not to surrender. They retained control of their installations, arms and munitions. All prisoners were returned. The French agreed to co-operate with the invaders and eventually became full-fledged allies. Thus, on the anniversary of World War I's Armistice Day the old allies were brought together again in World War II.

10

In the long run it was the German U-boats which did the greatest damage to the ships of the Western Task Force.

The Germans were slow to react to the African invasion although they, as well as the French, had been well aware that something out of the ordinary was in the making. The buildup in England of forces destined for the Mediterranean had been detected and the staging ports kept under air surveillance. A report from an agent in Lisbon on the unusual concentration of ships in Gibraltar and their types was forwarded to the German Naval Staff. The agent had included the presence of 70,000 troops and suggested that they were to be used in Spanish Morocco and French North Africa, in conjunction with an assault on Casablanca and Dakar. By November 5, Berlin had received a report from the Italian Consul at Punta Delgada that an American convoy bound for Africa had passed the Azores. Two days before the landings Rear Admiral Luetzow of the German Naval Staff was quoted as saying "Casablanca, on French Morocco's west coast, is a danger spot far out shadowing Dakar."

If anything, the Germans had too much information. They knew the Allies were preparing for a major operation, but where? The Libyan campaign of the British Eighth Army had been carefully coordinated with the African invasion. Kicked off at El Alamein October 23, it had been a tremendous success. By November 8, D-day for TORCH, General Montgomery's troops had pushed Rommel's panzers back 104 miles to the west with heavy losses in tanks destroyed and prisoners taken. It was only natural for the German staff to consider that the gathering forces of the Allies might land behind Rommel to prevent his further retreat. Other considerations were an invasion of Italy or somewhere in the Aegean. The constant fear of an Allied move against Norway, Hitler's old phobia, could not be overruled. Nor could the widely debated cross-channel move be discounted. One theory, held as late as November 4, was that the buildup was for a convoy to relieve beleaguered Malta.

Most of the information available to the Germans pointed to the Mediterranean, and they began to build up their air force in that area, but could not afford to deploy other forces until they were certain where the blow would come. The reported move of the Algiers and Oran task forces through the Strait, on 5-6 November, confirmed the belief that action was coming in the Mediterranean; but the question still remained, where?

It was not until the landings were actually being made on the Mediterranean beaches in the early morning of November 8 that Berlin was certain of the target areas. The British Broadcasting Company had the news at 2 a.m., and the Berlin radio broadcast the news at 3:45 a.m. Even then they were slow to react. After the full scale of the invasion was known they continued to be preoccupied with the Mediterranean rather than the Atlantic coast. Not that they were indifferent to the later landings in Morocco. It was simply that they, as well as the Allies, had to set priorities for resources available, and the Mediterranean landings posed the greater threat, as witness Rommel's predicament in Libya. Of the fifty U-boats which Allied planners had estimated would be available for deployment against TORCH convoys, those with sufficient fuel, twenty-five, were ordered to proceed at top speed to the Moroccan coast and the approaches to Gibraltar. The nine ordered to concentrate off Morocco were named the *Schlagetot,* or "Death Blow" group.

Of the submarines ordered to Morocco, one arrived on the 9th and others began to gather until all nine were operating off the beaches by the 12th. They concentrated off Fedhala-Casablanca, but made passes at ships off Safi as well. The first notice of their presence came on the 10th when one of them fired a spread of four torpedoes at the *Ranger,* then in company with the *Cleveland* and guarded by the *Emmons'* sister ships, the *Ellyson, Corry,* and *Hobson.* While the rest of the group took evasive action at high speeds, the *Corry* made an emergency attack on the estimated position of the sub, dropping a full depth charge pattern, without visible results. An hour later, the *Ellyson,* on the *Ranger's* port bow, sighted a periscope 700 yards on her own port bow and made another harassing depth charge attack, again without verifiable results.

The submarine pack was more successful on the 1lth when one of them managed to get into the transport area off Fedhala around dusk and hit three ships at anchor. The first was the transport *Joseph Hewes* which was sunk with a large part of her cargo. Fortunately, all the troops and most of the vehicles had already been put ashore. The tanker *Winooski* and the *Emmons'* sister ship *Hambleton* were next to get it. The tanker was hit in a water-ballasted fuel tank and her damage was slight. She was in business fueling ships next day. The *Hambleton* was more severely damaged. Her forward engine room and after fire room were flooded. She lost twenty men, killed or missing. By outstanding damage control work she was kept afloat and towed into Casablanca where temporary repairs were made. Eventually, she returned to the United States under her own power for a thorough rebuilding.

The sub attacks off Casablanca reached a crescendo on November 12th. The Center Carrier Group far offshore fought off attacks for three hours during the morning. During the afternoon the *Rowan,* escorting the *Chenango,* picked up a contact. The *Tatania* and *Cole* heading into Fedhala were attacked but escaped unharmed. While all these actions were in progress, the U-130 cautiously sneaked between the protective minefield to the north of the anchored transports and the shore to reach the transport area undetected. Three sitting ducks, the transports *Edward Rutledge, Tasker H. Bliss,* and *Hugh L Scott* were torpedoed. All three eventually sank, but loss of life was minimal because of the large number of boats in the vicinity. No more losses in the Western Task Force were sustained after the 12th because of increased antisubmarine efforts and the fact that more and more ships could be unloaded in the protected ports, thus lessening the time they had to remain exposed in the transport area. The last ship to be hit, the cargo ship *Electra,* was sailing independently well off shore when a torpedo found her, but she managed to reach port. It is significant that of all the casualties off the Moroccan coasts she was the only one to be hit while underway.

The Southern Attack Group at Safi presented a far less attractive target to the U-boats than the Center Group. For one thing, there were fewer ships there and, thanks to the early capture of the port; the transports could unload in the safety of the harbor. For whatever reasons, the Germans did not bother the ships of the Attack Group at Safi. They did, however make several passes at the *Santee* group farther offshore. The first attacks were made just before noon on the 10th as the carrier was preparing to fuel the cruiser *Philadelphia,* one of the gunfire support ships sent out from the Attack Group.

It was the *Emmons* which picked up the first scent of submarines in the southern area. At 1158, as the *Philadelphia* was beginning her approach to the *Santee,* the *Emmons* picked up an underwater sound contact which was evaluated as a sub and immediately began to investigate as she alerted the other ships of the formation. A minute later the *Santee* sighted two torpedo wakes which passed under her stern as she executed an emergency turn. The *Emmons* lost contact but made three search sweeps without results before rejoining the formation to screen the big ships as the interrupted fueling operation was resumed.

The delayed fueling of the *Philadelphia* was completed by mid-afternoon and flight operations aboard the *Santee* were started as soon as she cleared the carrier's side. During the flight operations the *Emmons* made another sound contact which was lost almost immediately. Nevertheless she made three search runs through the area while the other ships cleared out.

There were no more alarms until the following midwatch when the *Rodman* heard a torpedo pass close aboard. She started a search for the attacking sub but came up with negative results. The *Emmons* took up station to screen ahead of the *Santee* and *Monadnock* as they maneuvered to clear the area where the fish had been fired.

The cease fire at Casablanca had little effect on the ships in the Safi sector. After the midwatch torpedo scare the *Emmons* and *Rodman* settled down to the comfortable routine of screening the *Santee* and *Monadnock* as the former conducted flight operations. Between flight operations the carrier fueled the *Monadnock* without incident. After five days of fairly vigorous steaming it was time to replenish the escorts. Normally they would have fueled from the tanker turned carrier, but to obviate the danger from submarine attack inherent in underway fueling operations, the pair of destroyers were ordered into the safety of Safi harbor to fuel from the *Merrimac.*

They were relieved of escort duty by two destroyers sent out from the Attack Group, the *Cowie* and *Knight,* and arrived off Safi late in the afternoon. It was their first chance to see Africa close up. As escorts they had caught occasional glimpses of lights and hilltops ashore, but never in significant detail. Not only was the tedium of escort and plane guard duty broken, there was now a chance to see for themselves what was going on inshore, to identify some of the points which had seemed so mysterious and menacing on the operation plans and to locate some of the places mentioned in scraps of voice radio conversations overheard during the sharp, short engagements of D-day.

When the destroyers entered port around 1700 those aboard were somewhat disappointed. A gentle offshore breeze carried the odors identified with seaports the world over. What could be seen of the town from the harbor appeared to be benignly placid. Except for the burned out fish house and a few heaps of rubble on the docks there were no signs of French resistance to the take-over of the harbor facilities.

The bustling activity on the docks was the only indication that a war was still going on. The troops and their vehicles had disappeared into the hinterland, leaving behind a few detachments to assist in moving the piles of equipment on the docks to their units, to stand guard around the docks, and to man the antiaircraft guns set up to protect the harbor. There was now little danger from Marrakech as General Henry-Martin had sent a delegation down that morning to negotiate the terms of a cease fire in response to Darlan's orders. There was, however, still a chance of interference from Dakar where the governor, Pierre Boisson, had not yet agreed to throw in the lot of French West Africa with the Allies. The naval ships kept a reduced part of their antiaircraft batteries manned, just in case.

The bulk of the cargo from the transports had already been put on the docks when the *Emmons* and *Rodman* came into harbor, but the unloading continued without letup not only to keep the troops inland supplied, but to empty the berths for additional ships which were on the way. Part of the burden was taken over from the tired sailors and soldiers by natives who were hired for one cigarette or a hunk of bread for every case handled and five Moroccan francs a day.

As fascinating as the activity on the docks was, some of the *Emmons* crew were more interested in watching the nurses on the decks of some of the nearby transports. Part of the original plan had been to have the transports double as hospital ships until more permanent facilities could be established. There wasn't much time for watching either the docks or the nurses as fueling was completed in less than an hour, far faster and far safer than it could have been done at sea. At dusk the *Emmons* was following the *Rodman* out of the harbor to rejoin the *Santee.* There had been no opportunity to replenish provisions.

11

The two destroyers reported to the *Santee* after daylight the following morning and took up their regular screening stations. The *Cowie* and *Knight* returned to the transport area off the port. Although the *Emmons* and *Rodman* did not know it, they had spent their last night off the Safi beaches. The wind-down for the Western Naval Task Force had begun.

After the cease fire there was no longer reason to keep such a formidable armada off the African coast. The escort and support ships which had been taken from their Atlantic convoy duty for the African venture were sorely missed, losses along the routes mounted during November, and in the strictly British area of responsibility the Arctic convoys had been temporarily suspended. The very success of TORCH created a need for more ships than ever to provide men and material for the new theater of operations.

Another potent reason for getting unneeded ships away from the Moroccan coast was to lessen the danger from submarines. There simply were not enough berths in the newly acquired ports to handle all of the original attack groups, much less the follow-up convoys approaching the coast. As a result many of the ships had to remain at anchor off the ports with the dire results which have already been mentioned. Admiral Hewitt early adopted a policy of returning emptied transports and cargo vessels back to the States under the protection of combatant ships as soon as enough were unloaded to make it worthwhile to form a convoy. As for the combatant ships, their job was finished except for the anti-submarine patrols provided by the destroyers and carrier aircraft. This chore was gradually taken over by aircraft flown in to the airfield at Port Lyautey and by patrol vessels assigned to the Sea Frontier Forces, Western Naval Task Force, under the command of Rear Admiral John L. Hall, Jr., who set up headquarters in Casablanca.

The wind-down came quickly off Safi, thanks to the speedy capture of the port. While the *Emmons* and *Rodman* were fueling in the port, the *Monadnock* had fueled from the *Santee,* taken aboard the carrier's excess .50 caliber ammunition for use of the Army ashore, and left to report to the inshore group. With the departure of the *Cowie* and *Knight,* Task Unit 34.2.3 was back down to the original three ships which had left Norfolk thirty days before for the big adventure. Now they were preparing to reverse the steps which had brought them to the Moroccan coast and the first important victory of the war in the Atlantic.

After a morning of routine flight operations, the *Santee* signaled a change of course in the direction of Safi. The change brought the ships within range of a submarine between the launching and recovery area and the shore, possibly the same one which had made the attacks on the 10th and 11th. The U-boat took the opportunity to make one last, futile effort to get at the *Santee.* About an hour after heading for the shore, the *Rodman* reported sighting the wake of a torpedo which passed close aboard, headed in the general direction of the carrier. While the *Rodman* made an emergency depth charge attack in the direction of the U-boat, the *Santee* and *Emmons* cleared the area by emergency turns, and then continued on toward the shore as the *Rodman* started a fruitless search for the attacker. This was to be the last significant event for Task Unit 34.2.3 off Morocco.

The reason for the move inshore was revealed an hour later when the ships were approached by a crash boat about five miles off the port. It was bringing out the crews of the planes which had been forced to land at Safi airfield and had been unable to take off. While the carrier stopped to welcome her prodigal sons the *Emmons* circled to prevent any submarine from breaking up the homecoming. She was soon joined by the *Rodman* which had abandoned its search at the scene of the attempted torpedoing. With the returned flyers safely aboard, the carrier picked up speed and signaled a course which would take the group to a rendezvous with Task Group 34.2 west of Casablanca.

At daybreak the next morning, November 13, about 400 miles from Casablanca, the *Santee* group joined homeward bound Task Group 34.2. When the group steadied down on course for Bermuda it included the *Ranger, Santee, Suwannee, Brooklyn, Cleveland, Fitch, Ellyson, Rodman, Emmons,* and three destroyers of DesRon 13, the *Woolsey, Ludlow,* and *Swanson.* The main body had been working westward all the previous day and like the southern group had had problems with submarines. During the day they had fought a running battle with a pack of U-boats from the *Schlagetot* group off Casablanca, but they had come through without any losses.

Unencumbered by merchantmen the task group was able to move along at its own pace toward Bermuda. After the juncture of the two groups there were no more submarine attacks. Several underwater sound contacts were made by the destroyers and investigated, but all were classified as no submarine. It is likely that there actually were no submarines along the track as Berlin had ordered all U-boats in the Eastern Atlantic to concentrate off the Strait of Gibraltar and the Moroccan coast.

By far the greatest hazard of the voyage was the turbulent weather. Apparently the invasion had been neatly sandwiched between two periods of foul weather. After five days of fair skies and moderate seas off the African coast, the weather once again turned nasty. On November 13 and 14 the winds approached gale force and the seas became so rough that fueling of the *Brooklyn* and the three destroyers of DesRon 13, scheduled for the 13th from the *Housatonic* and *Chemung,* which had joined the formation for that purpose, had to be postponed. Conditions had not improved the following day, so the *Brooklyn* and DesRon 13 destroyers were detached with the tankers to fuel when conditions were favorable, then to proceed to their destinations independently. Meanwhile, the carriers and four destroyers of DesRon 10 maintained course for Bermuda. By the 17th the weather had abated enough to permit the *Santee* and *Suwanee* to fuel the accompanying destroyers.

The *Emmons* had another problem apart from the foul weather. There had been no opportunity to fully provision ship since Task Group 34 had left Norfolk. Fresh provisions and flour had been used up and dry provisions were beginning to run low. One crew member who got some bread passed over on the highline while fueling from the *Santee* swore "it tastes like cake, not bread." It is just as well that Congress had changed the observation of Thanksgiving Day from Roosevelt's next to last Thursday in November back to the traditional last Thursday. For on Thursday, November 19, which would have been Thanksgiving under the Rooseveltian schedule, the carrier group was still at sea. On that date the Commissary Department was reduced to serving hot dogs and hard tack as the main meal for a hungry crew. The situation didn't improve until the ship reached Bermuda. While no one was actually near starvation, some augmented their meals with emergency rations secured to the life rafts. Most of them had to be replaced after inspection at Bermuda.

12

The storm had completely dissipated when the carrier group reached Bermuda on the 21st. The warm air and sparkling sunlight off the greenish-blue waters surrounding the islands was a most welcome change from the past few days. However, there was little time to enjoy the pleasant climate, within twenty-four hours the group would be underway for Norfolk.

Several items had to be taken care of during the stopover at Port Royal. As soon as the ship had docked at the Naval Air Station, working parties were sent to get provisions and to return the "strip ship" gear which had been put ashore the month before. There was no lack of volunteers for the provision detail and it paid off for them. One of the working parties had a friend in the shore station commissary department who sent out a roasted chicken for each of them which they ate immediately like a bunch of starving aborigines. The party was also given two large containers of ice cream, one for the *Emmons* and one for the *Rodman*. The container intended for the *Rodman* was partially devoured before it was delivered aboard that ship. It was reported that more crates than usual were dropped while being passed from the truck to the gangway. The apples, oranges, even tomatoes which spilled on the dock quickly disappeared under dungaree shirts on the way to their owners' lockers.

The working party sent to retrieve the "strip ship" items which had been sent ashore the month before did not fare nearly as well as the provision party. During the month someone at the Air Station decided to put the shed assigned to the

Emmons to other use and the material had been moved to several different storage places. The moves had been made none too carefully. Many of the items were never located and some had been exposed to rain. Many of the books and manuals were ruined. Fortunately, the files had been stored in heavy cardboard cartons and were legible if somewhat soggy. At the time, this was of no great concern to the ship's company. They were homeward bound.

13

The task group reached Norfolk November 24 and the individual ships reverted to their normal commands. For most of them this meant Task Force 22 and was simply a change in numerical designation—for all practical purposes Task Group 34.2 of TORCH and Task Force 22 had been the same. Of greater interest to the destroyers was the prospect of ten days availability at their home yard in Boston. The *Emmons* didn't tarry long in Norfolk. The following morning she and the *Rodman,* escorting the *Massachusetts* and *Tuscaloosa,* left for Boston. They were relieved of their escort duties along the way and continued on to Boston independently, arriving there on Thanksgiving afternoon. Because of the brief stay in Norfolk there was still a shortage of provisions so the traditional Thanksgiving meal aboard the DD457 was postponed until the turkeys and all the trimmings could be gotten together. Most who didn't have the duty that night enjoyed a belated Thanksgiving at home, or in the homes of their shipmates.

There is always a special sense of accomplishment on returning to home port after a period at sea, in peace or in war. This time there was an added thrill. All hands were surprised by the rousing welcome they received as the ship approached her berth at the navy yard. A band and a delegation of cheering workmen were on the pier to greet the returning destroyers. No one on board pictured himself as a hero, but they were all proud to have been a small part of such a massive and complex operation as TORCH. The warm welcome was gratefully accepted as a tribute for a job well done.

The entire invasion had been on such a vast scale that very few could yet fully appreciate its impact on the course of the war. But as time passed, they, as well as the rest of the world, realized that TORCH was one of the major turning points in the global conflict. President Roosevelt recognized this fact in a December interview carried in the nation's newspapers. In summing up the crucial events of 1942 the President said:

The war has entered a new phase. United Nations Forces attacking from Egypt and North Africa are contesting with the Axis for control of the African coastline of the Mediterranean. The Soviet Army, having held with stubborn bravery at Stalingrad, has now assumed the offensive. The Japanese have been recklessly expending ships and men in the Solomons, a battleground of our own choosing. The Axis powers have temporarily at least lost the initiative. We must do all we can to keep them from regaining it.

8

Second Tour with the Home Fleet

o o o o o o o o o o o o o o o o o o o o o o o o o o o o o o o o o o

0013 OBDURATE reported sound contact,...

0055 OPPORTUNE reported sound contact,...

0344 MILNE reported sound contact,...

1000 FURIOUS ordered to have planes on 5-10 minutes notice.

2043 RODMAN reported sound contact and dropped depth charges.

2127 EMMONS reported a sound contact and dropped depth charges.

2209 OBEDIENT reported a sound contact and dropped depth charges.

0018 MACOMB dropped depth charges.

0135 EMMONS reported sound contact, executed emergency turn to 150°(T).

—Extracts from CTG 92.4 War Diary, 11-12 June 1943

The ten day availability at Boston was over far too soon. The *Emmons* left the yard exactly one year after the Japanese attack on Pearl Harbor. Thanks to the receipt of new personnel on board all the old hands not under a disciplinary cloud had been able to take three or four days leave.

The yard period had been one of the most productive since the shakedown cruise. No less than forty-two alterations dictated by the war experience were completed. Some of them were minor, but all were designed to increase battle efficiency and chances for survival in case of damage. Among the latter was the addition of cutout valves in the fire main and extra fire plugs on the main deck. The bulky towing hawser was replaced with nonflammable wire rope. The pyrotechnic locker was relocated from the bridge structure to the weather deck where it would be less hazardous if ignited. Two lockers for chemical clothing for use of damage control parties were installed on the deck housing. Weight control remained a major concern, additions in the gunnery department or in communication equipment required changes in the hull not only to accommodate the new installation but also to compensate for the almost inevitable increase in weight. For instance, one of the two smoke generators had to be sacrificed to make up for weight added elsewhere. The biggest and most important alteration was the addition of three Oerlikon machine guns, two on the wings of the signal bridge and one on a raised centerline platform forward of the bridge structure.

One of the worst disasters ever recorded in Boston occurred while the *Emmons* was at the yard. The flash fire which took the lives of 491 patrons of the Cocoanut Grove night club came the night of November 28. None of the crew were in the club at the time, but several men on liberty were nearby and gave what help they could at the hellish scene.

2

Throughout the winter and part of the spring the ships of Destroyer Division 19 were scattered throughout the Atlantic and Caribbean on escort duty with high speed convoys or capital ships. Between convoy runs they engaged in training exercises wherever they happened to be. During the winter season, the *Emmons* had the good luck to be assigned duty with major naval ships or transports moving between the United States and the Canal Zone or North Africa. Thus she missed the foul weather and the continuing battle with U-boat wolf packs which fell to the lot of destroyers attached to the slow merchant ship convoys of the North Atlantic.

The day the *Emmons* and the *Rodman* left the navy yard they proceeded directly to Key West to await further orders. They had no idea what their task would be or how long they would be waiting, but the time was not spent idly. For two days they put to sea during daylight hours for exercises with a tame sub. At night they returned to port, and liberty was given to a third of the crews. The main attraction for both crews was a skating rink outside the base. There, for reasons never explained, the normally friendly crews got into a free-for-all which required several shore patrolmen to quell and resulted in a lot of bruises and some black eyes. Happily, the ships put to sea the next day to meet the *South Dakota,* coming up from the Canal Zone, so there was plenty of time to cool off before the two destroyer crews again went on liberty in the same port.

The whole purpose of the trip to Key West had been to escort the *South Dakota* from the Caribbean to New York. The battleship had played a leading role in the Second Battle of Guadalcanal, one of the few battles of World War II where battleships met head on, and had been mauled so badly that she was sent back to the East Coast for repairs. She was delivered to the Brooklyn Navy Yard a week before Christmas.

As the *Emmons* and *Rodman* had left the Boston yard only a few weeks before, they were in no urgent need of repairs. So they were sent to the exercise areas in Long Island Sound and off Montauk Point for antisubmarine and gunnery training pending the next job. Most of Christmas week was spent in the drill areas. Daylight hours were devoted to training, but toward sundown the destroyers would seek shelter in one of the many bays or coves along the shores of Long Island. The dawn to dusk training schedule did not allow general liberty, so only a few people were able to get ashore—the mailman and members of the commissary department, and a few who were able to convince the executive officer of some urgent telephone calls that had to be made. The rest had to be content to view the quiet suburban towns along the shore from the anchorage. At dawn and at dusk, the light reflected from patches of snow on the wooded hills served as a poignant reminder of the Christmas season. At night the lights of an occasional car or the cough of their engines accentuated the difference between life in suburbia and aboard the warship. Although only a few hundred yards separated the ship from the towns, they were worlds apart.

No exercises were scheduled for the day before Christmas and the destroyers were released early in the morning to return to New York. They made the passage through the treacherous cross currents of Hell Gate and down the East River, with its heavy traffic of tugs, barges, and ships and boats of every size, to the Brooklyn Shipyard Supply Depot, where they fueled and provisioned to be ready for the next move.

3

Liberty in New York was granted to a third of the crew for Christmas Eve and another section expected to go ashore for Christmas day. But it was not to be. After the traditional Christmas meal at noon, the *Emmons* and *Rodman* were underway for Norfolk, where they would join the other ships of DesDiv 19 to escort eight troop-laden transports bound for the Panama Canal Zone and the Pacific.

As Task Force 39, the transports and their escorts cleared the Virginia Capes the morning of December 27. The officer in tactical command was aboard the transport *Charles Carroll.* The escorts commanded by Commander Destroyer Division 19 consisted of the *Ellyson, Emmons, Rodman* and *Macomb* of DesDiv 19, plus the *Murphy* and *Strong.* The trip was humdrum. So far as the *Emmons* was concerned, the most exciting event occurred at midnight, December 31. The task force had gone through the Windward Passage during the day and was somewhere off Jamaica as midnight approached. All was quiet on the bridge as the oncoming midwatch settled down for the four-hour stint. The men on the darkened bridge were conscious that a new year was at hand but there was no thought of celebration on the bridge of the blacked out destroyer steaming silently through the Caribbean night as part of a top priority convoy. But one member of the watch, the junior man, saw that the New Year did not come in entirely unrecognized.

The captain was on the bridge checking out the oncoming watch before he turned in. He, too, was thinking of the New Year and, while chatting with the messenger of the watch, nineteen-year-old Apprentice Seaman William R. Patton, casually asked him how he would be celebrating the New Year if he were back home. Without hesitation, Patton reached up and gave the whistle cord a long pull. Thus, the *Emmons'* deep-throated whistle ushered in 1943 much to the surprise, and consternation, of the captain and the bridge watch. The other ships of the formation didn't respond to this unauthorized salute to the New Year, but chances are they would have liked to.

The second day of the New Year found the task force off the Canal Zone. While the *Ellyson* led the column of transports down the swept channel to Cristobal, the other destroyers of the screen patrolled to seaward. As the transports approached the harbor entrance an explosion astern of the *Carroll* jammed her rudder and did considerable damage to the propeller shaft and the after part of her hull. Two men were missing at a subsequent muster. She managed to make the harbor under her own power but had to anchor until tugs could push her into her berth. The *Emmons* was too far to seaward at the time of the explosion to know what was happening, but she became indirectly involved four days later when she was detailed to carry Rear Admiral Van Hook and Major General Oldfield, the senior U.S. officers of the Canal Zone, and members of their staffs, on an inspection survey of the swept channel. During the time Admiral Van Hook was aboard, his flag was flown at the main in place of the usual commission pennant. The destroyer was never told what caused the explosion, but it is likely that one of the mines of the protective fields planted offshore had drifted into the swept channel.

After the transports were all safely in the harbor the screening destroyers were released by CTF 39. In accordance with a secret dispatch from CinCLant, the *Emmons* and *Macomb* were singled out for separate orders which required them to stay around the Canal Zone for an additional seventeen days. At least temporarily, the *Macomb* replaced the *Rodman* in the *Emmons-Rodman* duo.

The long wait at the Canal Zone was divided between training exercises and upkeep periods alongside the docks. The *Emmons* was able to give liberty nearly every night, something of a record since the outfitting period at Boston. The sailors spent their time bargaining for souvenirs or visiting the bars and dives of the Panamanian cities. Even the most avid "liberty hounds" soon tired of it; the more so as a sailor's pay didn't last long in Panama.

The time was broken up by a trip through the canal with three days on the Pacific side. The high light of the seventeen days of "standing by to stand by" for the *Emmons* was the excursion through the canal and back. The purpose of the trip was to conduct two days of special exercises in the training areas of the Gulf of Panama. The first full day at Balboa was devoted to conferences and briefings, but liberty was granted in Panama City for those not concerned with planning and preparations for the exercises. Most of the crew was broke after Colon, but a few were able to scrape up enough cash to explore the capital. Although the return to the Atlantic was explicit in the movement orders, many on board thought this might be the first leg of a transfer to Pacific Ocean duty.

One liberty group was treated to unexpected and undeserved free drinks in one of the small, side street bars of Panama City as the result of a dispute between the owner and the bartender. The owner was trying to fire the bartender for reasons unknown to the sailors, but rather than accept dismissal, the burly bartender bodily lifted his small employer from the floor and forced him to sit on the counter next to the cash register while he generously dispensed drinks on the house. The source of this tale claims that the bartender first took the cash for a drink from a customer and carefully rang it up, but instead of dropping the money into the register, ceremoniously passed it over to the next customer who then tendered it in payment of a drink. The process was solemnly repeated for each customer in turn.

The second full day on the Pacific side was used for battle torpedo practice. For the first time since her torpedoes had been fired on acceptance at Newport, the *Emmons* launched two of her fish in two separate runs using the PT 156 as a target. It was a high point for the torpedo gang. They had the satisfaction of seeing their babies run straight and true after a year of loving care. The recovery of the torpedoes took far more time than the firing runs, but both torpedoes were brought back on board in good shape. Back on the Atlantic side, the working parts were turned over to the sub base at Coco Sola for a thorough cleaning and overhaul. They were returned to their tubes before the *Emmons* left Panama, not to leave them again, except for cleaning, until they were permanently removed in November, 1944.

The day following the battle torpedo practices, six Ecuadorian naval officers came aboard to observe the *Emmons* in action. To the old hands on board it was a reminder of events of nearly a year ago when the ship had hosted the young Peruvian officers on the shakedown cruise. The daylight demonstrations involved routine surface and antiaircraft gunnery practice using towed targets. Between runs, ship handling exercises were held for the benefit of the visitors. The most spectacular exercise came after dark and was as exciting for the ship's company as for the South American officers, because it came as close to real combat as possible without the exchange of live ammunition. The objective of the drill was to detect and repel a high speed torpedo boat before it could get close enough to the ship to launch a torpedo attack. Star shells were used to light up the PT boat as soon as it was picked up by radar. The target, once again the PT 156, made several runs from different points of the compass, attempting to sneak in undetected. The *Emmons* successfully picked up and illuminated the target each time. There was no way of telling whether it would have been destroyed by the 5" guns and machine guns before launching torpedoes or not, but the exercise provided valuable, realistic training for the destroyer and demonstrated the capabilities of a modern warship for our allies. All hands, including the Ecuadorians, had high praise for the Gunnery Department.

The practice was finished by midnight, but the ship remained underway the rest of the night. At daybreak she headed down the channel for the Miraflores locks, stopping only to disembark the guests. Late the same day she left the Gatun locks and proceeded to the sub base at Coco Solo to join the Macomb.

The waiting was almost over. Five days later, January 18, the two destroyers joined Task Unit 91.1.4, consisting of the *Chester* and the army transports *Florida, Clem* and *Yarmouth,* headed for the States.

Normally, ships coming up from the Canal Zone use the Windward and Crooked Island Passages. This time the destination of the transports was Miami, so the task unit went around the western end of Cuba through the Yucatan Channel and rode the Gulf Stream through the Straits of Florida. Off Miami, four sub chasers took charge of the transports while the warships continued up the coast to Norfolk, destination of the *Chester.* However, the destroyers' work was not finished at Norfolk. As the cruiser stood in to Hampton Roads the old battleship *Arkansas* stood out to be escorted to New York. An indication that the Battle of the Atlantic was beginning to tip in favor of the Allies was the fact that not one of the ships under the care of the *Emmons* and *Macomb* between the Canal Zone and New York was molested by a submarine. Many of the *Emmons'* crew who had taken part in the hectic antisubmarine patrol off Cape Hatteras nine months before, noted that the "happy hunting ground" of the U-boat skippers of the spring of 1942 had been significantly quiet as the *Chester* was herded around Hatteras in January, 1943.

4

Apparently there was no urgent job for the two destroyers after delivery of the *Arkansas* to New York on January 26th. The other ships of the squadron were with the *Ranger,* ferrying army planes to North Africa; so advantage was taken of the lull to ship them into the Brooklyn Navy Yard for eight day availability to catch up on the huge backlog of ship alterations which had continued to grow since the last yard period in Boston. It was the first time the *Emmons* had been assigned a yard period away from her home yard at Boston. The New Yorkers, New Jerseyites, and men from Philadelphia were delighted to have ten days in Brooklyn, but not so the New Englanders. As soon as the assignment to the New York yard was announced the telephone lines became busy. The convergence of families on the city was accompanied by the usual frantic search for affordable rooms on a short term basis.

By far the most important alteration accomplished at Brooklyn was the installation of two twin 40mm machine gun mounts on the foundations which had been prepared for them before the *Emmons* left Bath. It had taken better than a year for production of the efficient Bofors guns to catch up with demand. The availability of the guns and the ship at New York at the same time had been one reason for assigning the yard period. The 1.1" quadruple mounts and the light 20mm mount which had been placed in the spots intended for the 40mms, as an interim measure, were removed from the ship. No one was happier at the exchange than the crew responsible for maintaining and operating the recalcitrant 1.1" mount.

With the installation of the new Bofors twins, the *Emmons* finally had on board the "ultimate" armament which had been decreed for her as far back as July, 1941. Actually, she had three more 20mm Oerlikons clustered around the bridge than had been considered necessary before the war, and K-guns had been installed for throwing depth charges to either side. There were to be no more major changes in armament until she was converted to a high-speed minesweeper late in 1944.

At the Brooklyn yard the Emmonites were for the first time treated to the sight of American women working alongside the men at the building ways. Their reaction was mixed. At Murmansk they had been goggle-eyed watching the muscular Russian women doing the work of men. It hadn't occurred to them that the same thing might be necessary in their own country. But there it was, women operating cranes, handling material, riveting steel plates—and doing it well. There wasn't much difference between Rosie the Riveter and Olga the Roustabout, but Rosie was friendlier—at least one could talk to her, and she wasn't afraid to smile.

5

After the navy yard work was completed the *Emmons* went off to the Long Island exercise grounds to try out her new machine guns. Three days later, with the *Macomb,* she returned to Brooklyn to prepare for a Translantic crossing. Sunday, February 7, the two left New York as part of Task Force 35, escorting a convoy of slow ships headed for North Africa. However, their stay with the slow convoy was short. Barely twenty-four hours after leaving New York they were detached to report to Task Force 36, also bound for Africa.

Task Force 36 was a faster convoy, consisting of transports and cargo ships protected by the battleship *Arkansas,* the cruiser *Philadelphia,* and nine destroyers, including the *Emmons* and *Macomb.* Most of the twelve-day crossing was made at fifteen knots under good sea conditions. The formation slowed only for fueling operations or for unforeseen emergencies as when two of the merchantmen collided. On that occasion, after the damage was assessed, the crippled ships were sent to Bermuda with the *Macomb* and *Doran* in attendance. On another occasion the formation was slowed while one of the destroyers transferred a case of acute appendicitis to the *Philadelphia.* Test firing of weapons and impromptu gunnery exercises were conducted without changing speed. One benefit of the steady steaming and good sea conditions was that the destroyers had to fuel only once in the twelve-day period. The *Emmons* fueled at ten knots from the *Arkansas,* late in the afternoon of the fifth day. The task force arrived at Casablanca February 19, and the transports and heavy ships proceeded directly into the harbor, while the destroyers patrolled off the entrance. Since its capitulation in

November, Casablanca had become a major supply terminal for Allied forces in North Africa because of its accessibility and relative freedom from Axis air attacks. The Sea Frontier force established by the Navy had forced the German U-boats to keep a respectful distance from the coasts. Vast quantities of supplies and some troops crossed its docks headed for Algiers and Tunisia by railway and truck via the Taza Gap in the Atlas Mountains. The harbor had been largely cleared and the docks restored by navy salvage crews. There were actually more berths available for handling cargo in February, 1943, than there had been before the invasion. However, there still was not room to accommodate all the ships of a major convoy. As a consequence, the destroyers of Task Force 36 were rotated between Casablanca and Fedhala when they were not on picket duty offshore.

Normally, the escorts of a convoy arriving at a major port would be fueled, provisioned, and assigned to the next outgoing group. In the absence of a departing convoy, Task Force 36 was kept intact and returned to the States as a unit with the ships it had brought eastward, after the eight days it took to offload them. The *Emmons* spent the first three days at the satellite port of Fedhala, sandwiched between the *Knight* and *Davidson* alongside a pier at the U. S. Naval Section Base. After three days the trio was shifted to Casablanca for fuel and two days alongside the phosphate pier before going out for picket duty. The crews were granted curtailed liberty in both Fedhala and Casablanca. They had been paid for the first time that month by the supply officer at the Fedhala base, but flush as they were, few men went on liberty after their natural curiosity about the French colonial settlement was satisfied. There was little to see in the open parts of the cities—and the casbahs, the native sections, were off limits to U.S. military personnel. It was not the Humphrey Bogart-Lauren Bacall movie Casablanca for these Americans. The sailors found activities in the harbors far more interesting. The *Jean Bart* was the stellar attraction—the crippled French battleship showed the damage 16" shells and 1000 pound bombs could do to an immobile target. One of the *Emmons'* sightseers reported that the battleship looked as if a can opener had ripped her open "like a sardine can, on the starboard side from the bridge right down to the bow." Large craters inshore of the docks gaped where shells and bombs had fallen wide of their marks.

Three days before Task Force 36's sojourn at Casablanca ended, six of its destroyers, including the *Emmons,* were ordered to sea to set up antisubmarine protection for the anchorage outside the harbor. They alternately manned a moving patrol line between the defensive minefield and the anchorage, and provided antiaircraft protection at anchor. While they were anchored they were required to provide an armed picket boat to prevent unwelcome intruders, enemy or otherwise, from entering the anchorage area.

After all the ships had been emptied and the escorts topped off with fuel, the task force formed up outside the harbor for the return trip on February 27. Some time during the offloading period the *Macomb* and *Doran* had rejoined, having dropped the collision-damaged merchantmen at Bermuda. On its departure the task force's destroyer complement was back to the nine it had left United States waters with eighteen days before.

There were still twelve days of Atlantic weather to be faced and the strong possibility of running into some of the Nazi submarines known to be operating along the routes between the United States and Gibraltar and North Africa. The luck that seemed to sail with the *Emmons* held, and the task force had no problems with either the weather or the U-boats. The winter of 1942-1943 was one of the worst on record for the North Atlantic, but most of the really bad weather was concentrated on the northern routes between America and the United Kingdom.

The lack of enemy submarine action was more surprising because the Germans mounted their most intensive campaign against transatlantic shipping in the months of February to May. During January, allied shipping losses had decreased, but the respite was only temporary. At the end of January, Hitler, disappointed at the lack of success of his surface ships, had fired Admiral Raeder and named Admiral Doenitz as Commander in Chief of the Navy, with the rank of Grand Admiral. Quite naturally, Doenitz favored his U-boats over the other branches of the navy. Work on heavy ships was slowed or suspended, including the aircraft carrier, *Graf Zeppelin,* and Germany's diminishing shipbuilding capacity was applied to the production of submarines. His biggest problem, which in the long run proved insurmountable, was to provide trained, experienced crews for the new boats.

Doenitz considered the months of January through March, 1943, the peak of submarine achievement. During February and March he was able to keep an average of 116 operational U-boats in the Atlantic, sixty of them in the North Atlantic. For a while, according to British intelligence sources, the U-boat command kept more subs on the New York-Gibraltar route, substantially the same as the New York-Casablanca route, than on the more northern routes to the United Kingdom because the high command insisted that priority be given to stopping the Allies in Tunisia. In spite of the determination of the Axis to cut off supplies to Africa, they were far more successful along the northern routes to Europe than those farther to the south. It is not difficult to understand: convoys along the northern routes were more frequent, generally larger, and slower. Furthermore, there was less room for evasive action than in the middle latitudes. Even so, the southern convoys felt the sting of the stepped-up Axis offensive. In January, a small but important convoy of nine tankers bound from Trinidad to Tunisia lost seven out of the nine to a wolf pack. About the same time a fast convoy, GUS-3, returning from Casablanca to the U.S., fought off another pack without loss. Later the same month, UGS-4, a slow convoy heading eastward to Morocco, lost three stragglers to submarines near the Azores. While Task Force 36 was still at Casablanca, UC-1, a convoy of 33 ships, mostly tankers, en route to Curacao, was attacked midway between the Canaries and the Azores with the loss of three tankers in ballast. The day after Task Force 36 reached New York, UGS-6, a slow convoy, was spotted by one of a group of U-boats on patrol 500 miles southwest of the Azores and was subjected to attack for six days as the freighters plodded toward Casablanca. However, because of aggressive action by its escorts, only four of forty-five ships were lost.

It is significant that most of the losses along the United States-Gibraltar route occurred near the Azores in areas beyond the range of land-based air cover—this was long before an agreement had been made with the Portuguese government for the United States to establish air bases in the Azores. It is also significant that the losses were from slow convoys rather than fast ones. Despite their moderate success in the Middle Atlantic, the Germans decided to concentrate on the northern routes where they were having greater success. By April, only a few undersea craft were left in the Middle Atlantic, but the shift north came too late to stop the flow of supplies to the United Kingdom. In fact, for the Allies the crisis was over by the end of March, although they were not certain where they stood until May, when Doenitz temporarily withdrew his U-boats from the North Atlantic.

The German admiral correctly blamed the collapse of his U-boat offence in the North Atlantic on increased numbers of Allied escort ships, improved depth charges, more aircraft cover, including very long range land aircraft and escort carrier planes, plus the introduction of specially trained support groups. Most of all he blamed the newly installed short wave, 10cm radar on escort ships and search aircraft, which he complained enabled the searcher to detect the U-boats at long range without the latter being aware they had been spotted. In May, his U-boat losses exceeded the ability to replace them. It was a shock. In his memoirs he stated, "By May 22 we had already lost thirty-one U-boats since the first of the month, which came as a hard blow; for…an increase in U-boat losses had not until this moment been perceptible." He came to the conclusion that such losses were unacceptable and, in his own words, "I accordingly withdrew the boats from the North Atlantic. On May 24 I ordered them to proceed, using the utmost caution, to the area south-west of the Azores. We had lost the Battle of the Atlantic."

As for Task Force 36, it had crossed and recrossed the Atlantic during the height of the Battle of the Atlantic, returning to New York without mishap on March 12. The *Emmons* and the *Macomb* fully expected to be underway with another convoy after a day or so in New York to replenish supplies and make minor repairs needed after the thirty-two days with the fast task force. But they had only been on loan to the troop convoys because of overall shortages of escorts in the Atlantic. Now developments in Europe required that they be returned to their regular assignment, Task Force 22.

6

When Task Force 34.2 was dissolved after it returned from TORCH in December, Admiral McWhorter was directed to assemble, train, and maintain Task Force 22 in readiness for operations against German battleships and cruisers. When assembled, the task force was to comprise the battleships *Alabama* and *South Dakota,* the carrier *Ranger,* the cruisers *Tuscaloosa and Augusta,* and eight destroyers of DesRon 10. Only the two battleships were new to the group. Because of other commitments there was little chance to train the rejuvenated task force as a unit until March, when events in Europe made it imperative to assemble at Casco Bay and prepare for action. Under a new Organization Plan for the Atlantic Fleet issued that month, Task Force 22 was designated the Striking Force.

From October, 1942, to February, 1943, the German heavy ships in Norway were relatively quiet. The *Tirpitz* was undergoing repairs at Trondheim while the cruisers *Hipper* and *Koln* remained at Altenfiord or Narvik, ready to pounce on passing Russian convoys, which had been resumed in early December after their temporary suspension because of Operation TORCH.

Almost simultaneously with the resumption of the convoys, the pocket battleship *Lutzow* arrived in northern Norway to give added weight to the German fleet. She had left the Baltic with orders to break out into the Atlantic to attack the United States-Great Britain convoys. The raid never materialized because she, with the *Hipper* and six destroyers, attempted to intercept a Russian-bound convoy between Bear Island and Murmansk on New Years Eve of 1942. Instead, they themselves were intercepted by the British cruisers *Sheffield* and *Jamaica,* which, with the help of the escorts of the convoy, drove them back to their base. During the engagement, which was largely fought blind because of snow storms, the *Hipper was* damaged and subsequently sent back to the Baltic accompanied by the *Koln.* The *Lutzow*'s Atlantic raid was cancelled.

For a while the *Lutzow,* the light cruiser *Nurnberg,* and the *Tirpitz,* laid up for repairs at Trondheim, were the only large surface ships in Norway that the Allies had to worry about. But they were enough to keep a good part of the Home Fleet tied up. Moreover, the battleship *Scharnhorst* was known to be ready for sea and exercising at convoy attacks in the Baltic. The *Tirpitz* completed her repairs early in February, and British Intelligence reported she was preparing to leave Trondheim February 27. In the meantime, the *Scharnhorst* made several attempts to leave the Baltic without being detected and finally succeeded on March 10. The Admiralty was not certain whether she was headed for the Atlantic or northern Norway, until it was determined that she had arrived at Narvik on the 11th. The same day the *Tirpitz* left Trondheim. At the same time, cryptographic service picked up radio traffic between the *Tirpitz, Scharnhorst, Lutzow,* and the German naval command, in a cipher which they could not unscramble.

All this activity in Norway in early March caused shivers at the Admiralty. The concern was increased because of heavy losses then being sustained along the North Atlantic convoy routes; the Germans could be planning a breakout into the Atlantic or further blows at the Arctic convoys. The British Home Fleet was alerted to meet either threat. The flagship *Anson* was moved to Iceland. Special air-sea patrols to detect movement of the German battleships through either the Denmark Strait or the Iceland-Faroes passage were activated. The Arctic convoys were once again suspended.

It was at this juncture that Task Force 22 was reassembled at Casco Bay with an agreement that it would be placed under the command of the Home Fleet in case the Germans broke out into the Atlantic.

7

Before the *Emmons* and *Macomb* reported to Task Force 22 they spent nine days at the Brooklyn Navy Yard making voyage repairs and catching up on alterations. The biggest changes involved bringing the electronic equipment up to date. Some items were installed which had been hanging over from the outfitting period. The growing importance of radar was evidenced by changes made around the bridge structure to accommodate new components and improvements on the old. By far the most important change was the replacement of the old long-wave search radar with the latest out, the short-wave SG, which was proving its worth in the battle of the Atlantic.

The *Emmons* wasted no time in joining Task Force 22 when she was released from the yard. After two days for reloading ammunition and testing the new equipment put aboard at Brooklyn, she joined up with Task Group 22.2, which was made up of the battleships and cruisers assigned to the task force. This group, in turn, rendezvoused with Task Group 22.1, built around the *Ranger* and her aircraft, on March 25, off the New England coast. After a few days of air exercises and torpedo defense drills, the united task force put in to Casco Bay to prepare to move on to Argentia.

By this time some of the urgency to activate Task Force 22 had dissipated. The *Tirpitz, Scharnhorst,* and *Lutzow* had been located at Altenfiord on March 22, where they remained for several months. Intelligence sources indicated that they were more concerned with the Arctic convoys, which they did not yet know had once more been suspended, than breaking out into the Atlantic. Nonetheless, the concentration of three such powerful battleships in northern Norway could not be ignored. The possibilities kept both the British and the American high command apprehensive, the more so considering the precarious situation of the North Atlantic convoys at that time. The decision was made to keep Task Force 22 intact and to move it to Newfoundland where it would be that much closer to the probable area of action if the German fleet should move into the Atlantic.

8

When the task force arrived at Argentia on April 5, old timers aboard the *Emmons* could hardly believe it was the same place they had left ten months earlier. From the harbor the base had the appearance of a small city, as indeed it was. An air base, and an army installation nearby, made Argentia one of the most important points in the Northwest Atlantic. Streets were now paved—trucks, jeeps, and construction equipment hurried about their business without fear of miring down. The supply depot was stocked and manned to meet the myriad requirements of the fleet. Comfortable, but by no means luxurious barracks had been set up to house transients and the personnel of the base. Ample recreational facilities for use in any type of weather had been built. Some workshops were available, but most repair work for ships was still done aboard tenders. Best of all, from the viewpoint of the destroyers, were modern docks where the smaller ships could receive all needed services from the shore, including fuel. Even so, the ships of Task Force 22 were in and out of the harbor so often that they were assigned mooring buoys most of the time in port. And the destroyers fueled from the big ships as often as they did at the pier, although a YO, yard oiler, was now available.

Some things had not changed. The neatly rounded twin peaks jutting above the water near the harbor entrance still served as navigational markers, and were still called Mae West by the sailors. And the weather remained atrocious—more than one exercise had to be postponed or cancelled because of heavy fogs or stormy seas. Some of the storms were so severe that several men were lost overboard. Surprisingly, the big ships suffered more in this regard than the destroyers. April 15 was a particularly bad day. During the forenoon watch, the *Augusta* lost three men overboard. The *Rodman* and *Hobson* left the formation to search for them and the *Rodman* was able to find one of them. That evening, after dark, the *Alabama* reported a man overboard. The *Fitch* was detailed to search—a heart-rending task under any circumstances, but virtually hopeless at night in stormy weather.

Most of the exercises simulated surface action against major units of the German Battle Fleet. Sometimes it was the battleships and cruisers against the carrier group. Sometimes one of the destroyers would be designated the *Scharnhorst,* or one of the other German battleships, to try to make an attack on the formation and then, when detected, try to escape. Whenever the task force operated as a unit British tactical formations and signals were used. The destroyers had the rare opportunity to simulate torpedo attacks. When not engaged in task force exercises, the destroyers were sent out to conduct fundamental gunnery exercises and antisubmarine drills. A British submarine, whose crew was well versed in U-boat tactics, was used as a target for the latter. Routinely, the destroyers were required to stand picket duty off the harbor entrance. Yet another task, which seemed to be the special province of the *Emmons* and *Rodman,* was to act as escort and plane guard for the *Ranger* during flight operations in Placentia Bay.

The Germans were very conscious of the *Ranger* and her task force. While she was at Argentia they announced that the carrier had been sunk by a U-boat "while guarding a convoy lane across the Atlantic." The story, which appeared in the American press and was broadcast by radio, said that the victorious U-boat skipper was decorated by Hitler himself. The *Emmons* crewmen were greatly amused at the report—they could look across the harbor and see the old flattop gently riding to the tide at her mooring buoy.

Thanks to the heavy schedule, the month of April passed quickly. Given the type of exercises and the use of British tactical formations and signals, no one aboard the DD457 was really surprised when they found themselves crossing the Atlantic once more to become a part of the British Home Fleet.

9

It had been the intention to maintain Task Force 22 intact, but, as usual, demands for ships throughout the Atlantic, and stepped-up action in the Mediterranean, were putting a strain on both the American and British fleets. Preparations for the invasion of Sicily drew upon the strength of both navies, as did the support of operations in North Africa which were nearing a climax. The Battle of the Atlantic was also at its crucial point. The increased demands had their effect on Task Force 22. The *Augusta* and *Tuscaloosa,* with three destroyers of DesDiv 20, were detailed to escort the transport, HMS *Queen Mary,* bearing Winston Churchill across the Atlantic for another Washington conference.

In the meantime, the three German battleships concentrated in North Norway could not be disregarded. The decision was made to bolster the weakened Home Fleet with power from the Atlantic Fleet as had been done the year before. Accordingly, a task force composed of the *Alabama, South Dakota, Ellyson, Emmons, Rodman, Macomb,* and *Fitch* was carved out of Task Force 22 and temporarily designated Task Force 61. Admiral Ingersoll chose his own chief of staff, Rear Admiral Olaf M. Hustvedt, to command. The destroyers, all of which were from Destroyer Division 19 except the *Fitch,* were under the command of Captain Thomas L. Lewis, who had recently relieved Captain Holloway as ComDesRon 10. The *Fitch,* from DesDiv 20, was named to replace the *Hambleton,* which was still out of action at Casablanca. The *Ranger* was assigned new destroyers and remained at Argentia until her services were needed elsewhere.

Task Force 61 put to sea May 12 bound for Scapa Flow. The relatively high speed of seventeen knots was maintained throughout the crossing—a speed which put no strain on either the new battlewagons or the destroyers. The weather was by no means mild, but, on the other hand, produced none of the violent gales which had plagued the convoys along the route throughout the winter and early spring. British fleet cruising formations and antisubmarine screens were used throughout the passage. Two days out of Argentia, before entering the area of known submarine concentrations, the destroyers fueled from the battleships. Both the *Emmons* and the *Macomb* suffered slight damage to side plating above the waterline while coming alongside the *Alabama* and *South Dakota* respectively. In neither case was the damage sufficient to impair seaworthiness.

The greatest worry continued to be the U-boat wolf packs strung along the convoy routes; Doenitz had not yet issued the order to withdraw his boats from the North Atlantic, although he was already disturbed at their mounting losses. There was ample evidence for Task Force 61 that they were still present in force.

Ships guarding enemy radio frequencies picked up transmissions thought to be from U-boats. Twice the task force was diverted from its planned route because of reported submarine concentrations ahead. SG radar contacts were made from time to time. Those which did not disappear from the screen turned out to be friendly: one was a Portuguese fisherman near Newfoundland, another, which persisted, was identified as three Swedish merchantmen under safe conduct. Nearly every day one or more of the destroyers picked up underwater sound contacts, most of which were evaluated as submarine. About half of them resulted in depth charge attacks. No kills were recorded—the task force was moving too fast to permit prolonged follow-up. The *Emmons* dropped two depth charge patterns on a contact she definitely evaluated as a submarine, and made an embarrassing attack on another contact which was later adjudged non-sub, probably a large fish. The contacts were more frequent in the area south of Greenland, where there was less air cover than was available on both the western and eastern legs of the passage.

Regardless of the many submarine alarms and the route changes caused by the wolf packs' concentrations, the task force maintained its speed of advance and arrived at Scapa Flow as scheduled on 19 May 1943. The day before, several empty life rafts had to be checked out by destroyers of the screen. As the formation neared land the ships had to be alert to dodge floating mines. Off Cape Wrath they were met by H.M.S. *Scylla,* which piloted them through the minefields to the entrance to the huge naval base. Off the entrance, the destroyers were released to proceed through the well-remembered Switha Gate in the antisubmarine nets, to the familiar destroyer berthing area in Gutter Sound. The *Emmons* was once more a unit of the British Home Fleet.

No time was wasted in working the American ships in with the British units. Liaison personnel were sent aboard as soon as the ships were moored at their assigned berths. After a day of signal drills in port, the Americans put to sea for tactical exercises which were gradually worked up to full scale mock battle exercises. When not engaged in fleet exercises individual ships conducted gunnery and antisubmarine exercises. Quite naturally, the fleet exercises featured surface action and repulsion of air attacks, but antisubmarine exercises were a high priority for the destroyers.

Two days after arrival at Scapa, Task Force 61 became Task Group 92.4, under the administrative command of Admiral Stark, Commander of U.S. Naval Forces in Europe (ComNavEu), and under the operational command of Admiral Sir Bruce Fraser, the new Commander in Chief, Home Fleet.

10

When the *Emmons* moored to the assigned buoy in Gutter Sound, the destroyer anchorage area, it seemed as much like home as any place she had been on either side of the Atlantic. Unlike Argentia, there were few outward signs of change at the British base. There were fewer ships present than there had been the year before, and there were far fewer *Luftwaffe* reconnaissances over-flights. As time passed, less obvious changes could be detected. The determination which had been so noticeable in the summer of 1942 was still there, but the grimness had been replaced by cheerful optimism—there was now not the slightest doubt of ultimate victory.

Once inside the submarine nets, the British destroyers were as relaxed as ever, and the same ribald games were played with their wardroom guests. But visits between the British and American destroyers were not as frequent as before; neither had much time in port now because of increased operational demands. On one occasion, during the first period at Scapa, a Norwegian destroyer sent over a signal inviting the captain and some of the wardroom officers over for luncheon, but made the exact time dependent on return of their boat which was then out catching fish for the meal. The Americans arrived about the time the Norwegians returned with a fine catch of salmon. While the fish was being prepared the guests were introduced to "glug"—a potent appetizer to a delicious luncheon.

Whether by accident or design, the American ships were in port on Sunday, July 4, 1943. All ships in Scapa Flow observed the American Independence Day by flying the American Ensign at the mainmast. Admiral Fraser, the Commander in Chief, had the American skippers aboard his flagship for cocktails in honor of the occasion. Rear Admiral D, as the commander of destroyers of the Home Fleet was titled, had a reception for the destroyer officers, and if no mention other than in a toast was made of independence, much was made of Anglo-British cooperation in the fight to preserve liberty and democracy.

Life for the crew was somewhat better than it had been in 1942. Although the American destroyers were still dependent on the Royal Navy for everything but clothing and small stores after their supplies ran out, there were fewer complaints. Food was plentiful and there was a reasonable variety. The *South Dakota* and *Alabama* were a big help with scarce items as long as their own supplies lasted. Several visits to the U.S. base in Hvalfjordur, Iceland, provided a chance to replenish from fleet reefers.

More people were able to get ashore whenever the ships had a little time in port. The Americans enjoyed meeting their British opposites and they got along well together; joint organized recreational parties continued to be one of the most popular means of whiling away the time in the Orkneys. The Americans would furnish the beer while the British ratings were able to hold on to a part of their rum rations. Contrary to what might be expected, the combination apparently cemented relations between the two.

Besides the organized parties there wasn't much to do except walk through the countryside or visit the British service clubs, which may explain why the parties were so popular. A few men became acquainted with some of the Wrens, members of the Women's Royal Naval Service, but there was really not enough time ashore to form any lasting alliances.

One night, after a recreation party had returned to the ship and turned in, the duty officer had the unpleasant task of going through the living compartments with the chief master at arms and waking each man who had been ashore to inspect his right arm for cuts and blood. A Wren had been assaulted by a sailor whom she identified as an American; he had broken a glass in his hurry to get away from her and had cut his right arm. The sleuths gave a silent prayer of thanks when the inspection was completed without finding any bloody hands in the *Emmons* party. Later, the assailant was identified as a sailor from one of the battleships.

Many men preferred to stay on board ship in Scapa Flow. Usually, they were tired enough from standing condition watches at sea to welcome a few hours of uninterrupted sack time. Although the daily routine of drills, cleaning chores, and maintenance, had to go on in port as well as at sea, there was still time for some of their favored leisure activities. No one person had inherited the mantle of Red Diamond, but various games of chance, from penny ante poker, to crap games for fairly high stakes, attracted devotees to the more isolated compartments. More public games of gin rummy, cribbage, and checkers could be found on deck during the long twilight hours, or below decks whenever rain or fog set in.

The *Emmons* had its share of practical jokers too, who delighted in finding someone green enough to go hunting for a left-handed monkey wrench, or in salting pipes or cigars with a pinch of gun powder.

As with any group of youngsters with time on their hands and no place to go, there was a considerable amount of horseplay, usually friendly, but nearly always involving physical activity. On one occasion, the recipient of a bag of jelly beans from home was passing them around when someone made the interesting discovery that there was only one black bean left in the bag. There followed a friendly free-for-all for possession of the black prize, which ended up on the deck with the other beans and a bunch of sailors chasing it around like a fumbled football. This fracas ended with the biggest man of the lot nursing a black eye, while the smallest came up with the black bean.

The high point of any day was the delivery of mail from home. Deliveries were fairly regular at Scapa, every week or ten days—but slow in getting there. The record timer from the East Coast, based on postmark dates, was sixteen days. The first men sent ashore after entering port were usually the commissary steward and the mailman, and often, if a boat could be spared, before the ship was moored. Everyone knew when the mailman returned and whether or not he brought back mail. If he did, practically all work stopped until it was sorted and turned over to the division petty officers for distribution. Some men got a letter in the same envelope and addressed by the same hand for every day between deliveries, and some Lotharios received many letters in colorful, scented envelopes. They were the fortunate ones—some poor souls drew complete blanks. Usually the home folks were careful not to worry their sailors with problems at home, but sometimes they couldn't keep the sad news of a death or a misfortune out of the mail. Once in a while someone would receive a "Dear John" letter. Shipmates were sensitive to bad news and made every effort to help their buddies over whatever hurt the mail had brought. Occasionally, an anxious parent would write to the skipper if there was bad news and leave it up to him to pass it along as he saw fit and in whatever manner he thought best. For the most part, they underestimated the resiliency of their sons and the fact that they were no longer boys.

Almost every day while at Scapa, the American ships put to sea for training, usually with units of the British fleet. Dates tended to become blurred, but somehow the time passed quickly enough. The Americans continued to be amazed at the efficiency with which training events were conducted. Hardly any time was wasted from getting underway early in the morning 'til returning to port late in the afternoon.

Elementary exercises with British target submarines were held inside the Flow. Advanced training was moved to areas outside the protected area after a ship was checked out in fundamental procedures and safety precautions. Grenades were dropped to simulate depth charges. Usually, when heavy units with their escorting destroyers sortied, bound for either an operational mission or for training, a special series of exercises was more or less routine. While crossing designated areas outside the harbor the formation would be subjected to running attacks by one or more submarines. Then followed a series of very realistic mock attacks by Royal Air Force planes. The pilots seemed to vie with each other to see which could come closest to the destroyers without actually making contact. Once clear of the air attack areas, the ships would proceed on their mission, to designated training areas for gunnery exercises or for individual ship workouts. The heavy ships always kept their destroyer screen around, regardless of their activities. One of the rocky islets off the Orkneys was used for shore bombardment exercises.

Antiaircraft training ashore was given in a domed structure equipped with movie projectors and sound tracks which were capable of giving the trainees the terrifying impression of multiplane attacks from several directions at once. Emphasis was placed on fire discipline—firing in deliberate bursts so as to conserve ammunition and avoid having an empty gun as the target closed in. The sound tracks accompanying the attacks were deafening. The antisubmarine training mockup was no less ingenious, but considerably less nerve-racking, reflecting the inherent psychological difference between being the target or the hunter. Here emphasis was placed on careful analysis of all known elements, including use of the Doppler effect to determine the relative motion of the target. The sound target used tactics known to be in use by the U-boats.

11

In reality, far more time was spent in Icelandic waters and on special missions than in the Scapa Flow area. After eleven days of intensive training exercises, Task Group 94.2 left Scapa Flow for Hvalfjordur, Iceland, on the first leg of a complicated set of moves in the Norwegian and Barents seas, collectively called Operation "F.H." in the British directives governing the movements. One move involved a relief expedition of British destroyers to deliver supplies and mail to United Kingdom forces stationed in North Russia—almost identical with the one in which the *Emmons* had participated the previous August. While one expedition was headed for Russia, another, composed of cruisers and destroyers, was to carry relief personnel and stores to the small Norwegian garrison at Barentsburg on Spitsbergen. Simultaneously, two corvettes were to make the dash past northern Norway to return to home waters. Two old friends of the *Emmons* were listed in the operation plans, but had nothing to do directly with the Battle Fleet. HMS *Onslaught* was to accompany the destroyers of the Russian relief expedition past Bear Island, then reverse course and accompany the westbound corvettes past the meridian of Greenwich before returning to Seydisfjordur. HMS *Gleaner* was responsible for escorting the necessary tankers from the United Kingdom to Seydisfjordur.

Any one of the moves of Operation "F.H." could have been made without the backing of the Battle Fleet if carried out swiftly under favorable weather conditions. But, in the aggregate, they mounted up, and at least one might have attracted the unwelcome attention of the German Battle Fleet, consisting of the *Tirpitz, Scharnhorst,* and *Lutzow,* which the British Intelligence Service placed at Altenfiord. In addition, eight modern destroyers and about twenty submarines were based on Norwegian ports, most of which could be moved on short notice. The German Air Force in the area was considerably less than it had been before the invasion of Africa, but could still put up a formidable array of Junkers 87s and 88s, and maintain good surveillance of northern waters with B.V. 138s and F.W. 200s. Thus the operation plans called for the stationing of the Battle Fleet consisting of the battleships *Duke of York, South Dakota,* and *Alabama;* the aircraft carrier *Furious;* the cruisers *Berwick* and *Scylla;* and the destroyers *Milne, Orwell, Opportune, Obdurate, Obedient, Ellyson, Emmons, Rodman, Macomb,* and *Fitch,* 200 miles southwest of Bear Island in a position to support the other groups as necessary. More importantly, it would be in position to bring the German Battle Fleet to a decisive action if it ventured too far out of its lair in search of an easy prey.

The voyage to Iceland through waters dominated by Allied air and naval patrols produced little out of the ordinary. The C. in C. Home Fleet insured that every available moment was used for training. At Hvalfjordur the Battle Fleet was rounded out by the *Furious* and *Scylla.* Three days were spent at anchor in Hvalfjordur while the other elements of Operation "F.H." took their positions. The Commander of Task Group 92.4 took advantage of the delay to send liberty parties down to Reykjavik on two days, using destroyers as liberty boats. The *Rodman* got the nod one day, the *Emmons* the next. It was a mild sort of a break for the two ships—at least they could let more men go on liberty from the docks than they could have by sending them by other ships. The excitement of seeing a new capital city was marred somewhat by the anti-Americanism some of the men on liberty encountered. But that could not detract from the uniqueness of the city.

When the other units of the operation were in position to start their moves, the ponderous Battle Fleet moved, via the Denmark Strait, to Akureyri, Iceland's second largest city. It was located on the north coast, just under the Arctic Circle, at the head of a long winding fiord. By the time the ships had entered the fiord they had crossed and recrossed the Arctic Circle, thus entitling all hands to the dubious title of Blue Nose. For most of the men of Task Force 92.4 it was their first taste of Arctic weather, and most of them would end up in the Pacific in three or four months. But for over half the crew of the *Emmons* and most of the other destroyers there was no novelty in living with near freezing weather on the eve of summer and a sun that disappeared for only a few minutes at the end of the day.

Akureyri was the home of several thousand United States troops whose job was to stop any Axis attempt to take possession of Iceland, but there was little evidence of their presence along the streets of the small city. There was little to tempt the people who went on liberty except a few shops which specialized in excellent woolen goods and leather products, most of which were too heavy and bulky for temperate climates. A few people bought luxurious, long-haired sheepskins which came from the prize animals of the region—source of the fine yarn spun in the antiquated but productive mills of the area. After an hour or two, the few people who went ashore were glad to get back to the comfortable warmth of their ships.

The Battle Fleet got underway during the midwatch of June 9 for the covering area southwest of Bear Island and arrived there the afternoon of the 10th. For two days they zigzagged back and forth at sixteen to eighteen knots waiting for word from the relief expeditions—and hoping that the German Battle Fleet would move out of Altenfiord. In this they were disappointed, but there was plenty of evidence of enemy air and submarine activity. Numerous radar contacts of unidentified planes were made, and on two occasions the *Duke of York* reported visual contact during clear periods in the persistent fog. The night of 11-12 June was particularly dangerous as submarines were able to close in under the cover of fog. The *Emmons,* along with the *Ellyson, Rodman, Macomb,* and *Obedient,* made depth charge attacks on underwater sound contacts during a single four-hour period spanning the first watch and the midwatch. Most of the destroyers made more than one attack on their targets before they were obliged to return to their screening stations by fleet doctrine. The *Emmons* made an embarrassing attack and two deliberate attacks before she went back to her station on the starboard bow of the guide, but as she slipped into her old slot a signal was sent over from the flagship inviting attention to instructions for screening vessels to return to formation after first attack if the assumed submarine was far enough away to do no harm. She was never able to positively identify the sonar return as a sub, but a torpedo wake was sighted passing her. The *Macomb* reported sighting a conning tower and somewhat later a periscope. It is just as well that the destroyers were not allowed to stay with their contacts indefinitely; with so many coming so close together there was very real danger that the *Furious* and the battle-wagons would be left open to any submarines which might be ahead of the formation.

The need for the covering force ended a few hours after the concentration of submarine contacts. Word having been received that all units of Operation

"F.H."—not counting the Battle Fleet—were in safe positions, and there being no indication of movement by the German fleet, the Commander in Chief detached Task Group 92.4 and the *Berwick* to go back to Iceland while he took the remainder of his Battle Fleet to Scapa Flow.

The Germans were well aware that there was an unusual amount of activity above the Arctic Circle to the north and northeast of Iceland, but reports of sightings were so scattered and inconclusive that they were unable to connect them up into a comprehensive pattern. On June 9, German air reconnaissance reported three destroyers 240 miles northeast of Iceland on course 60°—possibly the Russian relief group before detachment of the *Onslaught.* On the 11th, a single destroyer was sighted west of Bear Island, at high speed on a westerly course—probably the *Onslaught* looking for the two eastbound corvettes. The first hint of the Battle Fleet was contained in the German Naval Staff War Diary of June 12, the day the fleet was broken up to head for Scapa and Hvalfjordur. In a summation of reported sightings on June 12, the War Diary stated that U-711 had definitely reported sighting a carrier plane west of Bear Island. The same date, air reconnaissance had spotted eight vessels, "the type and size of which could not be established," north of Iceland. This was likely Task Group 92.4 headed for Hvalfjordur. The sighting of the carrier based plane prompted an air search for "an enemy aircraft carrier suspected west of Bear Island" late on June 12 and again on June 13 and 14. Needless to say, results of the air search were negative, for, as we know, the Home Fleet had been split up and was heading for Scapa and Hvalfjordur by the time the search was started.

The German Staff records make no mention of alerting their Battle Fleet at Altenfiord, but presumably this was done. The German heavies made no move to put to sea and probably would not have done so as long as there was danger of meeting carrier aircraft.

While Operation "F.H." was in progress the German Naval Staff continued to receive and evaluate intelligence reports from all quarters indicating that another major allied landing was imminent. In fact, Churchill, in a speech to Commons on June 8, announced, "It is obvious that 'amphibious operations', with their particular complications and risks, are imminent on a large scale." As before the African invasion, the Germans were faced with a multitude of choices, ranging from Norway through the occupied countries to Spain and Portugal on into the Mediterranean as far as Greece. Some of the reports were obviously planted to keep the Axis forces guessing. One, for instance, told of the "largest convoy yet" being assembled in New England for an attack on Norway and Denmark in July, to serve as a relief for operations in the Mediterranean. The unusual number of naval vessels in North Africa, including large numbers of landing ships and transports, coupled with other reports, led the Germans to conclude that the first blow would come on the Italian islands of Sicily and Sardinia, with Corsica and Southern France as likely secondary targets. The surrender of Pantelleria, in the Strait of Sicily, on June 8, strengthened their conviction. The Nazis were disgusted with their Italian ally for turning over the island without putting up a fight "owing to a lack of water."

At Hvalfjordur there was little to do except be ready to move if one or more of the German heavies headed for the Atlantic via the Denmark Strait. As Admiral Hustvedt put it, he was "King of Denmark Strait" for a few days. Most of the ships remained at anchor for the six-day watch at Hvalfjordur, but the destroyers were pressed into service to carry liberty parties down to Reykjavik. The *Emmons,* of course, did her share. The interlude at Hvalfjordur was ended 19 June when the task force was ordered to rejoin the Home Fleet at Scapa Flow.

12

The *Emmons* had only one night at Scapa Flow. Less than twenty hours after mooring she was off again in response to orders from the Commander in Chief, Home Fleet, to precede to Invergordon, Scotland, to pick up a party of officials for transportation to Scapa Row. First reaction was that once more the DD457 was being pressed into ferry service. As it turned out she had been selected for a special honor, for the party of officials turned out to be Mr. A. V. Alexander, First Lord of the Admiralty, the equivalent of our Secretary of the Navy; Admiral H. R. Stark, Commander U. S. Naval Forces in Europe; Vice Admiral Sir Geoffrey Blake, R. N.; and Rear Admiral F. H. G. Dalrymple Hamilton, R. N. Accompanying them were numerous lesser staff officers and the First Lord's personal steward. Admiral Stark and the First Lord were piped aboard just before noon on the 24th and the ship got underway immediately.

The passage to Scapa, made at flank speed, took just a little over four hours. Royal Air Force planes rode shotgun at a discreet distance. It was obvious that the transportation was arranged more to give the British officials a first hand look at an American destroyer than to get them from Invergordon to Scapa Flow—they could easily have flown the few miles. It was also apparent that the guests enjoyed being at sea on a warship for a few hours, away from their desks in London. For the First Lord and some of the British officers it was their first visit aboard an American destroyer. Admiral Stark was in uniform and all hands knew who he was and were proud to have him aboard. The Royal Navy men also were in uniform, so everyone quickly recognized their ranks, if not their particular role in the command system. But many were mystified at the identity of the stout, pleasant figure in civilian clothes. Sonar man Louis Lakin, who was on watch in the sonar room abaft the pilot house, recalls that he thought the civilian was probably a clerk until he overheard one of the be medalled aides ask his lordship if be would like his cloak as the party was preparing to go below to inspect the main battery.

The First Lord and the admirals spent most of the passage on the bridge, observing and asking questions. They were interested in all phases of the ship's operations, from condition watches to damage control measures. Enroute, a regular show was held on the bridge to demonstrate different pieces of equipment, including the foul weather gear issued for use in the North Atlantic and Arctic. The British were particularly interested in the ship's organization by divisions and watches—who did what, and the extent of their responsibility. There was considerable discussion and some comparison of methods and materials in the two navies. In routine operations underway, the Americans placed far more reliance on the officer of the deck, whereas in the Royal Navy, either the captain or number one, the exec, was nearly always at the conn. Admiral Stark was especially interested in the merits of a closed bridge, such as the *Emmons*'s, as opposed to the open bridges widely used in the British Navy. Before he left the ship, the admiral asked Captain Heming to submit his opinion on the subject to the Navy Department—the question of open vs. closed bridges was being considered in connection with upcoming escort carriers.

Whatever else may have attracted the attention of the visitors, the focus of interest was the armament. Enroute, the ship exercised at general quarters, demonstrated a depth charge attack, and fired all batteries. In the absence of a moving target the burst from a 5" shell served for the machine guns. The gunnery department was complimented for its performance. Admiral Stark, an old ordnance expert, approved. "Nice shooting, son," was his judgment passed to Tony Esposito, who fired the 20mm machine gun on the wing of the bridge.

In one department, the British unabashedly claimed superiority over the American way. Toward the end of the voyage the Britons accepted an invitation to have tea in the wardroom, while Admiral Stark preferred a cup of coffee on the bridge. Mr. Alexander professed horror when he was served tea made with the usual tea bags. Chief Steward Ginn's comment was that what was needed was a cup of tea like his mum used to make. Finally, some bulk tea found in the pantry and brewed under the First Lord's personal supervision proved satisfactory.

The *Emmons* delivered the visitors to the *South Dakota* where Admiral Stark and the head of the admiralty were to be quartered during their stay in Scapa.

After they had left, the ship went alongside the oilier for fuel and then to her moorings in Gutter Sound. Once secured, Captain Heming thought his task was completed, but long after dinner he received a signal from the fleet flagship inviting him aboard to a party in progress for the visitors. Such an invitation being tantamount to a command, he donned his best uniform and went aboard the *Duke of York,* where he was warmly greeted by the First Lord and introduced as the CO of the only American ship that knew how to make a proper cup of tea—having been duly instructed.

13

After the visitors from London had gone back to their desk jobs, the Home Fleet settled down to a series of training exercises designed to prepare it for the next operation involving the entire fleet.

Several days were allowed for in-port upkeep, one of which was our Independence Day. Thus, Sunday, July 4, was celebrated at anchor. The Fourth of July also marked the second change of command for the *Emmons* since commissioning. During the morning, the holiday routine was broken by parading the crew at foul weather quarters to hear Lieutenant Commander Heming read dispatch orders detaching him from command. Once again the system of promotion from within was invoked. Lieutenant Commander Billingsley, the executive officer, read a dispatch directing him to assume command. Lieutenant Foss, the sonar officer, became the new executive officer. Lieutenant Liebschner took over Foss's duties, and Ensign Herbert K. Francis, USNR, succeeded Liebschner as engineer officer. With the departure of Hal Heming, the only officers of the commissioning group left on board were Billingsley, Foss, and Liebschner. Only three of the fourteen officers aboard at that time were career men—the rest were reserves. Of these, seven were recently commissioned ensigns. Whatever elation the new skipper may have felt at his advancement was cancelled out a few hours after the change of command when a second dispatch he received that day announced the death of his father back home.

Incredible as it may seem, the Fourth of July was also the first date that the Germans noted the presence of Task Force 92.4 with the Home Fleet. The Naval Staff War Diary noted on that date that "According to an intelligence report of 3 Jul, from an agent in England, the US cruisers ALABAMA, SOUTH DAKOTA and 5 destroyers have joined the Home Fleet and will probably leave with it for the north about 8 Jul."

The German spy was correct on both points. Task Group 92.4, except for the *Alabama,* left Scapa Flow on July 7 with the Battle Fleet as part of Operation CAMERA. The operation was timed to coincide with the preliminary movements for the Allied landing on Sicily. The plans called for four separate forces, including the Battle Fleet, to leave Scapa Flow and Iceland ports in time to converge off the South Norwegian coast on D+l, July 8. The whole idea was to give the enemy the impression that a large scale raiding force was about to hit the coast. One of the forces consisted often trawlers simulating a convoy with appropriate support forces. The Battle Fleet was to support all forces as they took positions for the demonstration. Reliance was placed on routine German reconnaissance to pick up the forces offshore and alert their command system to the impending "raid." In case enemy air failed to sight the Home Fleet forces they were to open up with their radios to give the shore direction finder stations something to work on.

The operation was carried out according to plan and did, indeed, attract the enemy's attention, but failed to persuade them that a major raid or landing was in progress. A group of two cruisers and their escorts heading southeast from Iceland was picked up and reported by a Blohm and Voss reconnaissance plane late on July 7. The same group was reported twice on the 8th. Another cruiser force out of Scapa Flow was reported the morning of July 8. A "probable" battleship and one destroyer were reported late on the 7th, but this combination does not fit the operation plans for CAMERA, unless the misty weather prevented the reporting plane from seeing the entire Battle Fleet formation. At 1550, on the 8th, the Battle Fleet, consisting of "a formation of 1 aircraft carrier, 3 cruisers, and 9 destroyers" was definitely reported. The simulated convoy was not detected unless a reported single merchantman escorted by one destroyer was part of that group. Apparently, the German pilots had difficulty distinguishing between battleships and cruisers—indeed, the Naval Staff frequently complained about the inexperienced *Luftwaffe* pilots' sighting reports.

If anything, the antiaircraft defenses of the Battle Fleet were too good for complete success of the plan. Throughout July 8, H.M.S. *Furious* kept patrol and fighter planes in the air. Shortly after the sighting report mentioned above, her Spitfires shot down the shadowing Blohm and Voss after a brief fight in the clouds. A replacement patrol plane sent out from Norway was unable to relocate the formation because of bad weather.

The main objective of Operation CAMERA was achieved. The attention of the German defense force was attracted by the unusual activity off the Norwegian coast, and the Admiral Commanding Group North Fleet ordered an alert of coastal defenses. His battle group was put on three-hour notice, coastal convoys were cancelled, and submarines were stationed off Vestfiord, Trondheim, and Beigen. He considered operations against the coast, mining operations or air attacks were possible, but reported: "The enemy's disregard for concealment may also indicate a planned diversion for the purpose of tying down our forces in the area."

By mid-morning of July 9, the various groups of Operation CAMERA had returned to Scapa Flow and Iceland. Later in the day, German photographic reconnaissance planes over Scapa Flow found the Battle Fleet serenely riding to their moorings. The German Naval Staff and the commander of Group North Fleet remained puzzled at the show of force, but the latter relaxed the alert measures he had ordered the previous day. His final conclusion was that the show of force was a reaction to the movement of the German Battle Fleet out of Altenfiord for exercises on July 4-6, "although the composition and undisguised movement of the enemy formation do not appear to indicate a definite intention to attack our forces." In Berlin, the Naval Staff was perturbed that the British-Americans could keep such a powerful force off Norway without opposition. The War Diary for July 9 noted: "In any case, it should be noted that the enemy remained close to the German-occupied coast for a long time, apparently without expecting serious counter-action, which is further evidence of his exact knowledge of the strength and disposition of our forces."

Meanwhile, the Allied amphibious forces of Operation HUSKY were approaching Sicily. British-American airborne troops started the successful invasion of the Italian island the night of July 9-10. The Axis partners had been preparing for an attack on Sicily for some time. As their intelligence service indicated, it was the most likely point of attack in the Mediterranean. Churchill himself had predicted heavy fighting in the Mediterranean—and elsewhere—"before the fall of the leaf," in a speech in the Guildhall on June 30. It was almost with relief that the German Naval Staff learned of the assault on Sicily and began preparations to repel it, or at least to keep the Allied forces tied up for several months. The Staff was confident that Sicily could be saved if the Italian troops and naval forces were used effectively in cooperation with the meager German forces in the area. Typically, the staff officers regretted that there were not more German naval ships in the area.

Unfortunately for them, there were not more Nazi ships available. And they still had to keep Churchill's hint at fighting "elsewhere" in mind. Although intelligence reports indicated Sicily was the most likely target in the Mediterranean, they continued to receive reports of projected landings in other areas. For instance, on July 4th a report from Portugal advised that a large convoy was ready to sail from Halifax in several sections, beginning July 8. Mountain artillery, motor sleighs, skis, snow shoes, and electrically-heated uniforms, presumed to be aboard, led to the suspicion that troops and material of the convoy were intended for operations in the Far North. Another intelligence report indicated a convoy carrying 35,000 men was to leave Halifax for England on July 5. So, regardless of what happened in Sicily, the Germans had to keep a wary eye on the North Atlantic convoys and the British-American forces in England and Iceland. Their War Diary for July 9, for events in Norway and Northern Waters, somewhat ruefully ends with the note that "even on the afternoon of 9 Jul., it is still uncertain what formations were—or still are—in the area between the Shetlands and Norway."

14

While the battle for Sicily was going on, the Home Fleet continued to keep an eye on the German Navy in Norway. If Nazi reconnaissance planes had been over Scapa Flow the afternoon of July 10, they would have found two battleships, one cruiser, and five destroyers missing from the Home Fleet lineup. Around noon that day, the *Alabama, Anson, Kent,* and DesDiv 19 got underway for Hvalfjordur, where they were to keep the Denmark Strait under surveillance to prevent any breakout into the Atlantic by the German heavies via that route. With the summer thaws, the Strait was approaching its greatest width between the ice packs to the north and northwest and the Icelandic coast.

On July 12, the Battle Group arrived at Hvalfjordur, where they were joined by several British cruisers already based in Iceland. The big ships spent most of the time at anchor, but, as usual, the destroyers were kept busy at the many duties expected of small ships, including patrol duty and ferrying liberty parties to Reykjavik. ComDesRon 10 took advantage of the lull to take his five destroyers to sea for routine training exercises, including mock torpedo attacks and full power runs. In port, he tried to catch up on the inspection schedule which had largely been abandoned under wartime cruising conditions. The *Emmons* was given a surprise military inspection on the 17th. Although she had just returned to port the day before, she passed the inspection with ease.

In the absence of any enemy attempt to force the Strait, the Commander of the Iceland Battle Group, who was also Second in Command of the Home Fleet, devised an exercise to test the readiness of his command if they should try it. The cruiser *London,* representing the *Tirpitz,* was to attempt to sneak through Denmark Strait from the east undetected, or, if spotted, to force her way through to the open waters of the Atlantic. Accordingly, fictitious intelligence briefs reported the *Tirpitz* as missing from Altenfiord, and the game was on. The *London,* alias *Tirpitz,* was spotted, by air and by Army observation stations at Langanes, heading west. Accordingly, the Battle Group put to sea on July 19 to intercept her in Denmark Strait. The cruisers *Norfolk* and *Kent* were sent ahead to make contact and shadow while the main body closed in. Once the *"Tirpitz"* was picked up there was little trouble in plotting her position. The weather was characterized by large patches of fog near the ice edge; otherwise it was clear.

As the Battle Group speeded up to twenty-five knots to intercept the target, it became clear that she was trying to reach the cover of the fog patches. The destroyers were ordered ahead to be in position to make a torpedo attack when contact was made. In the meantime, the Battle Group itself was running through intermittent fog. Shortly after the destroyers took position ahead, the fog lifted and a low-lying field of detached ice was sighted dead ahead. By prompt emergency maneuvers, all ships except the leading destroyer avoided the ice. The *Ellyson,* which was in the lead, ploughed into the ice, bow on. The damage was extensive, but not fatal, consisting of a clean deep cut at the waterline which curled the bow back like foil. Flooding was confined to the bow compartments and the *Ellyson* was able to return to Hvalfjordur where repairs were made in the floating dry-dock provided for just such emergencies. Once more, the forces of nature proved to be the more treacherous enemy.

The remainder of the Battle Group continued on and made contact with the simulated *Tirpitz.* After a running battle the latter would almost certainly have been destroyed by the combined power of the Hvalfjordur forces.

15

The *Emmons* was involved in one more operation off the coast of Norway before her tour with the Home Fleet was over. This was Operation GOVERNOR, conducted between July 26 and 29, and almost identical with Operation CAMERA, conducted earlier in the month. The objective, as with CAMERA, was to arouse enemy interest and focus attention on the South Norwegian Coast by a simultaneous converging movement in that area of a number of forces designed to simulate a large scale raid. The area of convergence was about a hundred miles off Bergen. Forces involved were slightly larger than those of CAMERA.

The major difference was that the Battle Fleet was now split into two groups: Force A, consisting of the Iceland Battle Squadron, moving to the southeast; and

Force B, the remainder of the Battle Fleet, coming north from Scapa Flow. The carrier *Illustrious* joined Force A at Hvalfjordur the day before departure and remained with it throughout the operation. The carrier *Unicorn* was attached to Force B coming up from Scapa Flow. The *South Dakota* was the only American ship with that force. The only real opposition to the demonstration was expected to come from submarines and German aircraft based in Norway, although there was always the wistful hope that the German Battle Fleet, then at Altenfiord, might come to the south to interfere.

The operation went off smoothly and achieved its objective of disturbing the defense forces of occupied Norway. Beginning at 0605 on July 28, a stream of sighting reports began to flood into German naval headquarters. Although, as before, they were inaccurate and confusing, there were enough coming from different points to convince the Naval Staff and the Admiral, North Group Fleet that formidable British-American naval forces were concentrating off Norway's coast for undetermined reasons—and indeed that was true. Possibilities were considered to be a carrier attack on Narvik or Alta, flank protection for a landing operation, or simply a demonstration "similar to the movements on 8 and 9 Jul." This time their reaction was quicker and stronger than it had been before. Their Battle Fleet was placed on one hour notice and the coastal defenses alerted. The 5th Air Force was requested to step up its reconnaissance flights and apparently did so "in spite of its expressed objections."

Throughout the day the Hvalfjordur Battle Group worked its way south to the convergence area off Bergen, where it was to rendezvous with the cruiser *Belfast* toward the end of the demonstration. The rendezvous was made on time and the light cruiser took up station as part of the screen. Shortly after, a dispatch from the Admiralty was received warning that the enemy air force at Stavanger had been ordered to attack. Actually, no attack in force ever developed, but enemy aircraft contacts were frequent in the ensuing hour. At 1803 enemy planes were reported at fifteen miles by radar. Shortly afterwards, both the *Alabama* and *Anson* began to fire at the reported planes. The *Emmons* had no targets, visual or radar, during the firing. But she did come out of the action with a slight scar when the heel from a spent 5" shell landed on her forecastle. It was never learned how many planes there were, or of what type. Half an hour later, fighters from the *Illustrious* reported shooting down a Blohm-Voss 138 reconnaissance plane. No further contacts were reported and the Battle Group began its withdrawal to Scapa Flow according to plan.

Operation GOVERNOR was the last significant move of Task Group 92.4 with the Home Fleet. In consideration of the global panorama of the war, it was only a small operation, but it must have been galling to the German Naval Staff that, twice in one month, major units of the Allied fleet could assemble off the coast of occupied Norway without significant opposition. Nor could they be certain where the next blow would come. In July of 1943, things were not going well for the Axis. Intelligence reports of an impending invasion of Norway were seemingly substantiated by movements of troops and air groups to the north of the British Isles. Massive air attacks on Hamburg had virtually destroyed that port and vital shipping was being shifted to Rotterdam. An air raid on Trondheim had destroyed or damaged the dockyards and naval depot, including the naval stores and workshops. Communications between command areas had been disrupted. The ships of the Battle Fleet were in poor condition and required extensive overhaul.

In their staff meetings, the Germans recognized that Sicily could not be held and were considering how to cut their losses in that area. On July 25, Mussolini had resigned and Marshal Badoglio had formed a provisional government. Although the Italians announced their intention to continue to fight, the Germans had little faith in them and were debating what to expect from the new regime. Their distrust of their ally was evidenced by a directive that no orders to German forces should be issued by telephone; such orders were to be distributed by courier, bypassing the Italians. They were aware of a swelling anti-German feeling in Italy. The same feeling, with more reason, was echoed in Denmark. On June 30, the Danish Armed Forces Day, unruly mobs in Copenhagen had openly attacked German military personnel. The only satisfaction the Naval Staff could find in the reports was that no German naval personnel had been involved.

Reports from the Pacific were no more comforting. The military attaché at Tokyo advised that the Japanese could take Chungking, but did not expect its fall would lead to Chiang Kai-shek's overthrow. The Japanese were bracing for attacks, which they expected to be costly in men and materiel, all along the periphery of their conquered empire. Japanese-Russian relations were a major cause for concern. The Germans noted that Japanese diplomats in Russia were treated almost with contempt. One of the foremost goals for the Nazis was to insure that Japanese-Russian relations did not deteriorate any further.

All in all, it was not a good period for the Axis, but the Germans were far from being defeated. They realized that the submarine offensive had bogged down, but optimistically hoped to reverse the slide in that area by new construction and new weapons. They hoped that improved antiaircraft guns would stop losses of their U-boats from air attack. They had a new torpedo under development called *zaunkoenig,* which would be acoustically activated and was designed for use against destroyers and other escort vessels. They had belatedly recognized that it would be necessary to eliminate the escorts before they could count on getting at the convoys.

16

Once back at Scapa Flow, Task Group 92.4 prepared to return to the States. It was back to its original composition when the *Ellyson* reported in on July 31, the repairs to her ice-damaged bow having been completed at Hvalfjordur. The following afternoon the task group left Scapa for Hampton Roads, its duty with the Home Fleet completed. As a farewell gesture, Admiral Sir Bruce Fraser, Commander in Chief of the Home Fleet, came out in his barge and took temporary command of the screen as the group formed up outside the harbor entrance at Switha Gate for the homeward voyage.

9

The Iowa and President Roosevelt

o o o o o o o o o o o o o o o o o o o o o o o o o o o o o o o

....At 1025 USS EMMONS left station and maneuvered to come close aboard to starboard. At 1025 all engines ahead two-thirds. At 1027 all engines stopped. At 1035 changed heading to 150° (T). At 1045 USS EMMONS motor whaleboat came alongside and transferred patient and at 1047 cast off. At 1047 all engines ahead one-third.... At 1150 USS EMMONS resumed station in anti-submarine screen.

—*USS* ***Iowa*** *War Diary, 24 November 1943*

The group arrived at Norfolk August 9, after a rough, but otherwise uneventful passage, from Scapa Flow. En route, Task Group 92.4 had been dissolved and, at Norfolk, the ships were released to proceed to their home yards for routine repairs. For the battleships, it was the end of their Atlantic duty. After their yard work was completed, the *Alabama* and *South Dakota* were organized as Battleship Division 9, and left to join the growing Pacific Fleet. They were two of a long line of capital ships, not to mention destroyers and smaller, which made the journey westward every few weeks. By now the massive construction program begun after the outbreak of World War II was at its peak. Most of the new ships were sent on to the Pacific as soon as their shakedowns were completed, but some were kept in the Atlantic for varying periods to help the hard-working Atlantic Fleet meet its growing commitments as the allied offensive closed the ring on Nazi-occupied Western Europe. Thus, when the *Alabama* and *South Dakota* headed west, the newest and fastest battleships, the *Iowa* and *New Jersey,* were held temporarily in the Atlantic to provide support for the widely scattered Atlantic forces.

The breakup of Task Group 92.4 caused major realignments of Task Force 22, the Striking Force of the Atlantic Fleet. To compensate the British for the withdrawal of the powerful battleships, a new task group, consisting of the carrier *Ranger,* cruisers *Augusta* and *Tuscaloosa,* and destroyers *Corry, Bell,* and *Isherwood,* was sent over as Task Group 121.1 to operate with the Home Fleet. The new task group designation conformed to the designation of U.S. naval forces in Europe as the Twelfth Fleet. It left Halifax for Europe August 11.

In the meantime, the destroyers of DesDiv 19 left Norfolk on August 10, for twelve-day availability at the Navy Yard, South Boston, where they arrived August 11. Admiral Hustvedt, wearing his hat as Commander Battleships, U.S. Atlantic Fleet, rode the *Rodman* from Norfolk to Boston, with his staff split up between the *Emmons* and the *Rodman.* On arrival at Boston, the admiral shifted his flag from the *Rodman* to the *Iowa,* then in dry dock at the South Annex, Boston Navy Yard. The nucleus for a fast, powerful task group was now assembled at South Boston.

With the departure of the *Ranger* group for Europe, the old Striking Force became a paper entity until August 21, when Admiral Hustvedt was designated to command a rejuvenated Task Force 22, consisting of the *Iowa, Ellyson, Emmons,* and *Rodman,* all of which were nearing completion of their yard overhauls. The new commander was ordered to take his ships to Argentia, where they were to be ready to counter any major enemy threat in the North Atlantic. The waiting period was to be utilized in combat training for air, surface, and underwater action. The *New Jersey* and the two other destroyers of DesDiv 19, the *Hambleton* and *Macomb,* were later added to the task force, but rarely operated with the *Iowa* group.

2

No major repairs or alterations were done on the *Emmons* during the twelve-day availability. A multitude of accumulated minor alterations and routine repair jobs which could not be undertaken while in a condition of readiness, such as removing and grinding steam valves, aligning batteries, and cleaning fuel oil tanks, kept the yard force and the ship's crew busy. A unique experience was being hauled up on a marine railway for completion of work on the ship's underwater body. She had actually been docked with other destroyers in one of the yard's dry docks for routine inspection, cleaning, and painting of her underwater hull and fittings, when it developed that the dock was needed for a larger ship. The dock was flooded and the destroyers parceled out to other facilities. The *Emmons* was towed to a privately operated marine railway in Chelsea for the completion of the underwater painting. The tricky maneuver was accomplished without any trouble, and she was eased back into the water in time to be ready for sea by August 24, her completion date. The biggest complaint stemming from the abrupt change from dry dock to marine railway was at the loss of upkeep time caused by the unscheduled move. Another was the confusion and inconvenience experienced by one section of the crew returning from leave while the move was in progress. They reported to the yard expecting to find their ship where they had left her, but instead spent half a day chasing around the harbor after her.

During the three months away from U.S. ports, the ship had enjoyed relative stability in personnel. As soon as she reached Boston, massive changes began. Once more, there was an infusion of new blood; a draft of fifty-nine men came aboard the first two days after she docked at the navy yard. Forty-six of them were seamen second class or firemen third class, just out of boot camp. The rest ranged from seamen first to chief petty officers, who were starting their second hitch in the Navy or were recent graduates of service schools. Six of the latter were former Emmonites who had been left behind when the ship left for Europe, or had been sent back to school from Scapa Flow.

The movement was not all one way; some of the more seasoned officers and petty officers were siphoned off to new construction. There was a brisk exchange of personnel throughout the yard period, and some scattered receipts and transfers throughout the rest of the quarter. On the whole, there was a gain in net numbers, but a loss in experience. By the end of the quarter eighty-seven men, including fifteen former Emmonites returning home, had reported aboard, while sixty-seven were transferred to other ships or stations, for a net gain of twenty. There were then 278 men aboard, well above the allowed complement, which was now established at 260. Promotions continued at a rapid pace. Seventy-seven men, approximately twenty-nine per cent, were advanced one rate during the quarter.

Turnover in the wardroom during the third quarter was about the same as among the crew. The quarter ended with the same number of officers on board that it started with, fifteen. Six of them were new: four of them reserve ensigns, and two of them newly-made warrant officers. The latter marked a new departure in the assignment of warrant officers promoted aboard destroyers. They were now being ordered to other destroyers where their specialized skills could be used to best advantage in the same type of ship. Of course, Commander Heming was the most senior loss to the *Emmons,* but two senior lieutenants were transferred as well. One was Lieutenant Liebschner, who had reported to the Commissioning and Fitting Out Detail in Bath, one year out of the Naval Academy. His loss left only the new skipper, Billingsley, and executive officer, Foss, out of the original commissioning detail. Liebschner had only to move his gear across the gangway at the navy yard pier to take up his new duties as executive officer of the *Ellyson.* The other lieutenant to be shipped out was the ship's medical officer, Lieutenant J. A. Sill, (MC). He was not replaced until November.

3

The destroyers were ready for sea on August 24, several days before the *Iowa* was ready. Earlier, ComDesRon 10 had been ordered to take the *Ellyson, Emmons,* and *Rodman* to New York, on completion of the yard availability, to escort the French battleship, *Richelieu,* to Hampton Roads. The orders had never been cancelled, so the three took off early in the morning for the big city via the Cape Cod Canal. Before they left the western end of the canal, the orders to New York were cancelled. Commodore Lewis decided to anchor his three ships in Buzzards Bay, off the western exit, to await clarifying orders.

New orders were not long in coming. In less than an hour, the three destroyers were underway and heading back through the canal in response to a priority dispatch directing them to proceed to Halifax, Nova Scotia, by August 29. Apparently someone had decided that DesRon 10 was an international unit; at Halifax the destroyers were to report for duty to the British battle cruiser *Renown.* As there were several days to kill before reporting to Halifax, the three destroyers were ordered back to Boston for three more days of upkeep at the navy yard.

They never did set out for Halifax. Task Force 22 had a prior claim on their services and the orders to report to the *Renown* were cancelled. When the *Iowa* was ready for sea, the task force, as previously constituted, got underway for Argentia; arriving there August 30.

Task Force 22 remained at Argentia for nearly two months. During that time the battleship and three destroyers operated as a close-knit unit, preparing for any attempt of the Germans to send their big ships against the Atlantic shipping lanes past the first line of defense of the Home Fleet at Scapa Flow. Thanks to the diminished submarine threat in the North Atlantic, and the up-to-date facilities of the booming naval base, the destroyers were not required to take on any other duties besides an occasional turn at picket duty outside the harbor entrance.

The destroyers thoroughly enjoyed working with the *Iowa.* For one thing, she was the first of the latest class of battleships which came into service in 1943—the *New Jersey, Missouri,* and *Wisconsin* were the others. The statistics of the *Iowa* class were awesome by any standards; from their nine 16" guns to their better than thirty-five knots speed, they outshone any previous battleships. The *Iowa*'s displacement of 45,000 tons was more than twenty-seven times the *Emmons'* 1,630 tons, and she mounted five times as many 5"/38 caliber double purpose guns, not to mention more than ten times as many 40mm machine guns. But it was speed which the destroyers admired the most—and which gave them the most trouble. They were used to running around the big ships with ease—not so with the *Iowa.* On full power trials there was such a small differential in speed that the destroyers had trouble keeping on their screening stations. When a major course change was made at high speeds the outside flank destroyers had a hard time getting into their proper stations on the new course.

Another reason for enjoying work with the *Iowa* was the mutual respect which existed between the *Iowa*'s skipper, Captain John L. McCrea, and the destroyers' skippers. He had a keen understanding of the needs and problems of the "small boys" who were responsible for his own ship's antisubmarine protection.

As pleasant as the interlude in Argentia was, by the middle of October most of the crew of the *Emmons* were beginning to get restless from the long period of training exercises without any hint of enemy action. Besides, the weather was beginning to deteriorate. Fully half of the scheduled exercises had to be cancelled or postponed because of foul weather. But they were soon to escape the boredom, as events far beyond their power to influence were taking place in Washington, London, Moscow, and Chungking, which would bring a drastic change of scenery to the ships of the task force then at Argentia.

4

As the noose around Nazi-held Europe tightened, it became imperative that the big three, Roosevelt, Churchill, and Stalin, meet to coordinate plans for hastening Germany's defeat and to iron out awkward questions which were sure to arise on her surrender. The foremost consideration was to advise Stalin of Anglo-American plans for opening a second front in France in 1944 and to insure cooperation of Russian forces with the move. Russia had refused to accept the invasion of Italy as fulfillment of the promise of a second front. Indeed, the Soviet Army's official organ, *Red Star,* had stated that actions in Africa and the Mediterranean had failed to divert a single German division from the Eastern Front. Agreement would have to be reached on the occupation and treatment of Germany after her surrender. Another question for resolution was the participation of Russia in the war against Japan when her western flank was secure.

The diplomatic resolution of questions concerning the Far East also demanded attention. Militarily, the situation in the Pacific had improved to the point where victory was almost a certainly. Thus, the eventual disposition of Japan's empire, most of it acquired by conquest, but some as a result of mandates from World War I, needed resolution before it became a cause of contention among the victors. The United States was anxious to see the status quo restored but also was concerned that democracy should have a chance for survival in the region. She hoped to see China replace Japan as the major power in the Western Pacific.

A series of high-level conferences, led off by a meeting at Moscow between Secretary of State Hull, British Foreign Secretary Anthony Eden and Russian Foreign Minister Vyacheslav M. Molotov was arranged to discuss allied cooperation in prosecuting the war and securing the peace after it was over. The get-together of foreign ministers in Moscow was followed by a meeting of Roosevelt, Churchill and Stalin in Teheran which lasted from November 28 to December 1, 1943. Before going to the Teheran conference, Roosevelt and Churchill met with Chiang Kai-shek in Cairo to discuss the problems of the Far East, during the war and afterward. A second meeting was held with the Chinese in Cairo after the Teheran conference adjourned. As the Russians were officially at peace with the Japanese, they had no official representatives at the Cairo conferences.

The trip to Teheran was a greater undertaking for the lame Roosevelt than it was for either Churchill or Stalin. Teheran had been agreed to only because the Russian refused to go farther from the crucial fighting on his western front. The President could have made the long, tiresome journey entirely by air, but chose instead to cross the Atlantic in the relative safety and comfort of the *Iowa.* The battleship offered several advantages over air, and the President's attachment to the Navy and the sea was well known.

For whatever reasons, the decision was made to use the *Iowa* for the ocean part of the President's lengthy journey. Thus it was that in late October the ships of Task Force 22 found themselves en route from Argentia to Norfolk, where they arrived October 24. On arrival at Norfolk, the *Iowa's* commanding officer was directed to report to the Commander in Chief, U.S. Fleet, for duty in connection with giving passage to the President and his party and the Joint Chiefs of Staff to an undisclosed North African port. Naturally, the mission was not revealed to anyone else in the task force.

Captain McCrea had been Roosevelt's naval aide until, at his own request, the President had released him to take a command at sea. When he went to Washington to be briefed on the forthcoming trip he saw not only Admiral King, but was summoned to the White House to discuss the voyage. At his suggestion one major change in the proposed plans was made. Under the original setup the President would have gone to Norfolk by special train to board the *Iowa.* Such a trip would have been hard to keep secret. After studying the charts Captain McCrea proposed that the *Iowa* be brought up to the mouth of the Potomac as far as her draft would permit and the President board her from the presidential yacht *Potomac* on what was ostensibly a short cruise for relaxation in the Potomac and upper Chesapeake. The plan was adopted and served as a good ruse to mask the President's departure from the capital.

Preparations for the voyage were elaborate and conducted in great secrecy. The *Iowa* and her destroyers were given availability at the Norfolk Navy Yard. As far as the destroyers were concerned, nothing out of the ordinary was involved; it consisted of fine tuning antisubmarine and radar installations and updating communications equipment. The *Emmons* was dry-docked to inspect and make minor repairs to her underwater sonar dome. Because of the President's physical handicap much more was involved aboard the *Iowa.* Several alterations in his living accommodations had to be made, which, if they became known to a foreign agent, would certainly have identified the prospective passenger. The most spectacular of these was the installation of a passenger elevator—a device not usually found in a battleship. As much of the work as could be considered normal was done at the shipyard, but material necessary for its completion was put aboard in crates. The ship then moved to an anchorage in Chesapeake Bay, where the installations were completed by the ship's force and selected workmen from the navy yard.

When the installation of the elevator was completed, the *Iowa* proceeded to an anchorage, as far up the Potomac as her draft would permit, to receive her passengers. The Joint Chiefs of Staff and their staffs came aboard from the USS *Dauntless* on November 11. The President and his party came aboard from the USS *Potomac* the following morning. Included in the President's party of twenty-three were Harry Hopkins, Admiral Leahy, Major General Watson, Rear Admiral Ross T. McIntire, his personal physician, and four secret service agents. As soon as the *Potomac* cleared the side, the battleship got underway for a deep water anchorage in Hampton Roads, where she spent the night taking on over a million gallons of fuel oil which had been left off before the trip up the shallow Potomac. Shortly after midnight, November 13, she weighed anchor and stood out of Hampton Roads, en route to Oran, where the President was scheduled to take to the air for the remainder of the trip to Cairo and Teheran.

5

The protection of the President and the accompanying brass aboard the *Iowa* was a matter of greatest concern. The ships directly connected with the operation were designated as Task Group 27.5, under command of Captain McCrea. In the Atlantic zone, practically the only danger was from the many German submarines still deployed throughout the ocean. It was known that some wolf packs were operating near the *Iowa's* projected track. Some were equipped with the new acoustic torpedo. Nearer to Gibraltar and the Mediterranean, the possibility of air attacks had to be reckoned with. The recent establishment of allied air bases in the Azores, and the presence of escort earner hunter-killer groups, helped out on air coverage, but the main standby defense against submarine attack remained the destroyers. Speed was another defense. The crossing was to be made at twenty-five knots, not only to save valuable time for the President, but to lessen the chances of detection. The drawback was that at twenty-five knots the destroyers could not make it across the Atlantic without refueling. To maintain speed, three relays of three destroyers each were set up. The first relay, Task Unit 27.5.1, composed of the *Campbell, W.D. Porter,* and *Young,* was to accompany the *Iowa* for two days out of Norfolk and was to be relieved by Task Unit 27.5.2, composed of the *Hall, Pullin,* and *Halligan* from Bermuda. That trio would stay with the battleship to a point south of the Azores where Task Unit 27.5.3, the *Ellyson, Emmons,* and *Rodman,* was to take over for the critical run in to the Strait of Gibraltar, there to be relieved by Task Force 86, a mixture of British and American ships from the Mediterranean, which would see the *Iowa* safely through the Strait and the western end of the Mediterranean to Oran.

6

Task Group 27.5 was not formally activated until November 12, the day the President embarked. Until then and, indeed, throughout the operation, the *Iowa, Ellyson, Emmons,* and *Rodman* were listed as Task Force 22 in the weekly Composition of Task Forces. The destroyers of Task Unit 27.5.3 completed their yard repairs long before the battleship and were ordered to the Azores via Port Royal, Bermuda, there to wait until time to join the *Iowa* south of the islands. At that time the orders to wait for the *Iowa* were known only to Commodore Lewis and his staff and they had no knowledge of the *Iowa's* connection with the President.

The *Emmons* and her companions arrived at Horta, Fayal Island, Azores, on November 11. The passage from Norfolk had been lie-surely and pleasant; the destroyers had been able to conduct a number of training exercises which could not have been held with a big ship to worry about. Of most interest was the testing of new FXR noise-maker gear—dubbed the Foxer—a device designed to be towed astern, which, by its high noise level, would attract the now widely used German acoustic torpedoes away from their intended target, the ship's propellers.

At Horta they spent the first night alongside a British oilier, HMS *Imperial Garden.* Because of a scarcity of regular fuel oil, the ships were forced to accept fifty per cent diesel—a big headache for the engineer gangs when they joined the *Iowa.* Another problem for the *Emmons'* black gang, which showed up after joining the battleship, was a slight increase in the normal fuel oil consumption at twenty-five knots and above. This was later attributed to a small piece missing from the tip of one of the blades of the starboard propeller, which was discovered at the next dry docking. At the time of inspection, there was no way of determining when the damage had occurred, but it is probable that it happened when the ship was berthed alongside the *Ellyson* in the inner harbor at Horta, after fueling. The Portuguese pilot assigned to move the *Emmons* apparently had never handled a ship as powerful and lively as a destroyer. In going alongside the *Ellyson* he used too much power in backing down, and then overreacted, setting up a surge which threatened either to back the ship into a breakwater astern, or take her charging out of the harbor with the *Ellyson* attached. The captain had to countermand the pilot's orders, and after a few judicious changes in the engine orders the ship was snugged in alongside the *Ellyson,* with no indication of harm to either until the damaged propeller was discovered weeks later.

There was no regular liberty in Horta, but nearly everyone who wanted to get ashore was able to do so on one of the organized sightseeing and recreation parties. There wasn't much to see on the tours except the waterfront, a few churches, and a few small factories—the usual attractions for sailors were not included. One of the stops was an old church which had been built by the Jesuits. The priest who acted as guide to the church took gleeful pleasure in relating how his group had taken the church from the Jesuits when Portugal banished that order in the eighteenth century.

Horta, with its narrow streets and old buildings, which had an old-world quality about them, was in the process of changing from a colonial outpost to a more modern settlement. Its economy was still based on the sea and its strategic location. It had long been dependent on seafaring men and their ships for its existence; one of the main attractions was an old section of the waterfront used for processing whale carcasses. The coming of transatlantic air transportation had added a new dimension to the town's strategic importance. Pan American Airways had an important base there, and at the time of the *Emmons*'s visit the British were in the process of establishing a military air base.

Not all the products of the island came from the sea; the women were famous for their handmade linens and lace. Many men on the tours were able to pick up beautiful tablecloths and scarves to take back to their own women at home.

Other products of the island were good wines and a mild, cheap brandy. No provision had been made for purchasing these items on either the rubberneck tours or the athletic parties. But where there is a will.... One group left the *Emmons* under the charge of one of the new ensigns to play softball against men from another destroyer on a field provided by Pan Am. On the way they had to stop in a narrow street while the officer sought directions to the field. Unknown to him, the party had been followed by several street vendors offering various products for sale. One of the items was the native brandy, which went for the fantastically low price of a dollar, U.S. currency. While the ensign was not looking, several of the athletes substituted brandy for the water in their canteens. That day the *Emmons'* players enjoyed the game far more than their opponents, although the "home" team was unusually short of hits and committed many errors. Other than the miraculous changing of water to brandy there were no breaches of discipline. Nothing but happy talk prevailed and the party returned to the ship a little bit tired, but overall quite content in defeat.

Several men who wanted to see more of Horta than was visible from tours or athletic fields decided to do a little unofficial sightseeing. They stowed away in the whaleboat going in to the beach on a late night trip, sneaked ashore, and started out in search of adventure. In an attempt to hide their identity, they tucked their hats inside their pants and turned their blouses inside out. This feeble attempt at disguise would have fooled no one under normal circumstances, but their luck held. There was no shore patrol present and they found their way to a lively tavern, complete with wine, women, and a juke box. It was frequented by Pan Am pilots and ground crews who took the wayward sailors under their wing and became their unofficial hosts. When the time came to return to the ship, the Pan Am people obligingly provided a boat to save the sailors from the long tiresome trip through the uncharted streets and along the quays of the harbor. The luck of the unofficial liberty party held and they sneaked back aboard undetected over the stern. They had a few minutes of anxiety the following morning when some of their Pan Am friends of the previous evening came aboard for a visit. They thought surely the flyers would mention the night before, but their friends were discreet. The culprits breathed a lot easier when the visitors' boat pulled away from the ships.

7

The second day in Horta, Commodore Lewis received a dispatch setting D-day as November 13, and H-hour as 0001. His group now became Task Unit 27.5.3, with orders to rendezvous with the *Iowa* about 430 miles to the south, at 1300 on D+4, the 17th. In order to conserve fuel, the destroyers left the Azores on the 15th, in ample time to proceed at a leisurely pace to the designated meeting point. Even at full capacity, they had barely enough fuel to reach Gibraltar at the projected speed of the *Iowa,* so it would be necessary to observe strict economy.

Early on the morning of the 17th, friendly planes were sighted. They proved to be from an old friend of the *Emmons* and *Rodman*—the *Santee.* The latter was sighted a few hours later, and confirmed the plotted position of the *Iowa* to the west. The *Iowa* and her screening destroyers were picked up on radar shortly after noon, as the commodore maneuvered his ships to take up their screening stations on the base course at twenty-five knots. The exchange of escorts was made without a hitch, in a maneuver similar to the passing of the baton between runners in a relay race. As the destroyers of the new relay drew close to their stations they picked up speed as the off-going team slowed and peeled off to head for Bermuda. The new escorts had power available for flank speed in case they had to make a stern chase or a long side approach to get on station, but it was not needed and they were able to secure the extra boilers shortly after joining. Nevertheless, fuel consumption became a major problem for all of them, and particularly for the *Emmons,* before they reached Gibraltar.

Everyone, even the few people who knew the mission of Task Group 27.5, was mystified by the first signal sent from the *Iowa:* "Under no circumstances is this ship to be used as a point of aim target." It was standard practice for destroyers to use a convenient heavy ship of a formation as a point of aim to train gun and torpedo crews in getting on and tracking a moving target The *Iowa* had been a favorite target of the destroyers of Task Force 22 for the last three months; now it was forbidden. The order raised a few eyebrows aboard the *Emmons.* Although some had already begun to suspect the purpose of the *Iowa's* high speed run across the Atlantic, it was months before the reasons for the order against using her as a practice target was learned through the navy grapevine. It was not made public until long after the war when official accounts were declassified. The *Iowa's* "Action Report," narrating the events of the President's trip, gives the details.

The *W. D. Porter,* one of the first groups of destroyers out of Norfolk, accidentally fired a live torpedo at the *Iowa,* during tracking drill, from her station on the battleship's starboard bow. The *Porter* immediately alerted the *Iowa* by voice radio that a torpedo was headed in her direction, and added that it had been launched from her by accident. Not knowing where the torpedo was, Captain McCrea immediately ordered full speed and turned his ship toward the *Porter* to present the narrowest possible target along its presumed track. The loose fish passed about 1,000 yards off the starboard quarter and exploded in the hard wake kicked up by the battleship's twenty-nine knots.

At the time, the President and his party were assembled on the port side of the first superstructure deck to watch a demonstration firing of the 40mm battery. When the alarm for battle stations was sounded, bellowed by "This is not, repeat not, a drill," and "Torpedo on the starboard beam," the President directed his valet, Steward First Class Arthur Prettyman, to push his wheelchair around to the starboard side, not, as was to be expected to take the elevator up to his emergency station, the conning tower, but to look for the torpedo. The President recorded the incident and stated that the torpedo missed by 1000 feet. In a later, typed and corrected version of the diary he noted that Admiral King was much upset and he feared would take drastic disciplinary action.

The incident was investigated by just about everyone, including the FBI. It seems that when the *Porter* received orders to prepare for distant duty when the voyage was organized, her torpedo gang had inserted live primers in the firing mechanisms of each torpedo. Somehow one had been left in place. As the story made its way around the fleet, many a destroyer skipper must have muttered to himself—"There but for the grace of God..."

The *Emmons* had no problems with errant torpedoes, but, soon after joining the *Iowa,* the question of fuel oil consumption became a nightmare for all hands. Because of the damaged propeller, the fuel oil consumption took a jump above that normally used at twenty-five knots. To make matters worse, wind and sea conditions made it necessary to increase the formation speed by a knot and a half in order to make the next rendezvous point, some 300 miles southwest of the Strait of Gibraltar. The fuel situation became so grim that it began to look as if the *Emmons* might have to face the humiliation of abandoning her screening station to limp into Gibraltar at an economical speed. Indeed, the commodore threatened to abandon her if she couldn't keep up. Keep up she did, thanks to Draconian measures involving all hands and all departments. For two days every effort was concentrated on preserving fuel oil. Unnecessary power was shut down; guns, directors, and other equipment were operated only enough to insure that they were in ready condition; fresh water for showers and shaving was cut off; drinking water and water for cooking and coffee making was rationed; the galley served cold cuts and sandwiches whenever possible; lights and heat in living quarters were reduced to a minimum. It wasn't comfortable, but it worked.

Rendezvous with the mixed British-American task force responsible for seeing the *Iowa* safely through the Strait was made on time. It brought no respite for the *Emmons* and *Rodman,* which became part of the force. The *Ellyson* was detached to proceed fifty miles off the track of the formation to transmit important dispatches, so as not to compromise the position of the presidential formation to listening enemy direction finders. The *Emmons* and *Rodman* stayed with the *Iowa* force for another twelve hours until they were released opposite Gibraltar to ease into the British base for much needed fuel and provisions. Thanks to the cooperation of all hands, the *Emmons* anchored with enough fuel left in her service tanks to get alongside the tanker's hulk by morning light.

In the meantime, under the protection of Task Force 86, the *Iowa* scooted through the Strait at twenty-seven knots. The passage was made during the night in order to minimize the chance of detection by German observation stations, which were staked out on either side of the Strait on Spanish soil with the acquiescence of the Franco government. In spite of all the precautions, the *Iowa* was picked up and silhouetted for more than half an hour by Spanish spotlights. There is no reason to believe that the searchlight operators had any knowledge of the *Iowa*'s passenger list, and they were within their rights as neutrals to illuminate any ships off their shores. No hostile action was taken, nor was any expected from a nation publicly professing neutrality. Nevertheless, as a precaution, the destroyers between the battleship and the shore were ordered to lay down a smokescreen to protect her from prying eyes. By far the greatest danger was that submarines operating in the area might be alerted and attempts to intercept the group farther along.

The *Iowa* arrived off Oran by first light on the 20th. As soon as she anchored at the adjacent naval base of Mers-el-Kebir, the President and the Chiefs of Staff, with their parties, disembarked to continue the journey to Cairo by air. The *Iowa* spent the rest of the day fueling, but got underway before dusk in order to return through the Strait of Gibraltar under cover of darkness. She hastened her departure from Mers-el-Kebir at the suggestion of British Admiral J. H. D. Cunningham, Commander in Chief Mediterranean, who confided to the captain that the presence of the *Iowa* would be known to the Germans within a few hours after her entry into the Mediterranean, and that he considered her a "profitable target" for the glider bombs the Germans were then using. On the westward passage, the *Iowa* was again protected by Task Force 86, until well clear of the western approaches to the Strait. The task force was augmented by Admiral Cunningham's flagship, HMS *Sheffield,* until the open sea was reached west of the Strait.

8

While the *Iowa* was fueling at Mers-el-Kebir, the destroyers of Task Unit 27.5.3 completed fueling and provisioning at Gibraltar. Shortly after midnight they were underway again to rejoin the battleship about 150 miles to the southwest, well clear of the approaches to the Strait of Gibraltar, where they relieved the Mediterranean task force of escort duties. Once the reassembled Task Group 27.5 had steadied down, course was shaped for Bahia, Brazil, where the *Iowa* was to await the President's arrival by air after the conferences ended.

The eight-day passage between Gibraltar and Bahia was very dull after the great expectations caused by the dash to Gibraltar and the prospects of going on into the Mediterranean to become part of the action there. The destroyer men were not yet aware of the meaning of the sudden changes of the past few days. Many aboard the *Emmons* were disappointed at the reversal of direction after the fueling stop at Gibraltar, but they had high hopes that the erratic actions of the *Iowa* foreshadowed some important confrontation with the enemy. They had no way of knowing that the abrupt changes were designed to avoid trouble rather than to ask for it. Off the African coast several merchant ships flying neutral colors had to be investigated. They all proved to be Spanish and were allowed to go on their way unmolested.

Several events unrelated to war activities served to break the monotony. During a moderate storm in the vicinity of the Cape Verde Islands, Signalman Third Class Richard K. Mutzabaugh developed a case of acute appendicitis aboard the *Emmons.* The ship's new medical officer, Lieutenant (jg) Charles R. Williamson, was of the opinion that he should be operated on at once. He had reservations about performing the operation in the destroyer's small sick bay under the prevailing sea conditions, but to delay until the seas calmed down might be too late. An exchange of signals with the *Iowa* settled the dilemma; the patient was ordered to the battleship, where conditions for operating were far more favorable. When all was ready, the formation was brought to a favorable course; the *Emmons* closed to a position on the lee quarter of the battleship, and the formation was stopped while the patient was transferred from the destroyer's whaleboat. In spite of the prevailing seas, the transfer was completed in sixteen minutes from the time the formation was stopped until speed was resumed.

Mutzabaugh was taken immediately to the battleship's sick bay, where the operation was shortly performed by her surgeon. The *Emmons*'s signalman had the highest praise for the treatment he received aboard the *Iowa* and credited her medical personnel with saving his life. During his stay he learned the President and most of the brass of Washington had been aboard. There was no secrecy about the matter and no one warned him to keep quiet about it, but he thought it best to keep his own counsel when he returned to the *Emmons* over a week later. He was the first person aboard the *Emmons* to have any positive knowledge of the causes for the strange movements of the past two weeks.

The day after Mutzabaugh's transfer, advantage was taken of improved weather conditions to slow and fuel each of the escort destroyers from the *Iowa.* At the relatively slow speed of twenty knots, there was no danger of sucking their fuel tanks dry before reaching their destination. Nonetheless, it was wise to keep them topped off so that they would be as ready to respond to emergencies at the end of the voyage as at the beginning. Besides, the task group could take advantage of air cover from nearby British bases on the African Coast before it started to move southwestward across the Atlantic toward Brazil.

During the midwatch, Thursday, November 27, the formation crossed the equator. It was the first time since her shakedown cruise that the *Emmons* had crossed the line. Because of the extraordinarily high rate of turnover among the crew since the shakedown, an overwhelming majority of those on board were polliwogs. In fact, only eighty-two of the original crew was left on board, but by now, most of these had established their authority as leading petty officers of their divisions and, with the help of a few shellbacks received from other ships or stations, they kept firm control of the initiation ceremonies. There was no talk of rebellion among the polliwogs as there had been off Ecuador in 1942. Once again the traditional ceremonies were restricted to daylight hours because of darkenship requirements in submarine waters. For all that, King Neptune and the Royal Party appeared in the morning and a day of festivities began. Under the watchful eyes of the hardened shellbacks of'42, the tender polliwogs of '43 earned their shellback certificates. Nothing, from kissing the bloated belly of the Royal Baby to wriggling through a garbage-filled canvas chute, was omitted. For several days some of the neophytes could not get near the ship's garbage without a queasy feeling or sit on their tender backsides without wincing.

9

Early in the morning of November 29, the task group began the approach to the swept channel leading to Bahia. At first light a friendly blimp on antisubmarine patrol was overhead to patrol the waters off the entrance. By 1:00 p.m. the ships had secured in their assigned berths. Because of her deep draft the *Iowa* had to anchor in Bahia Roads, but the escorts were nested at a berth in the inner harbor, not too far from the huge elevators which provided transportation between the old town at dock level and the newer city atop the steep bluffs facing the harbor. Commander, Fourth Fleet, Admiral Jonas Ingram, flying his flag from the cruiser *Memphis,* was SOPA, Senior Officer Present Afloat. Thanks to arrangements made by his staff, fueling and provisioning was expedited, and liberty for one section began as soon as the provisions were aboard.

The old-timers aboard the *Emmons,* remembering the welcome they received in the Spanish-American countries of the west coast during the shakedown cruise, anticipated a good liberty in the Brazilian port. Those who made it were not disappointed—but there were some differences. Nearly two years had passed; instead of visiting friendly, neutral countries as yet untouched by the war, they were now visiting an allied nation very much at war with the Axis. Until recently, Brazil had had every reason to fear invasion from across the Atlantic. Now that danger was past, but German submarines were still active in the South Atlantic and were preying on Brazilian ships. Furthermore, Brazil had a sizeable army fighting alongside the Americans and British in Italy, and several important American bases were now in operation on her territory. The war's impact on Brazil was reflected in wartime restrictions on the population, which in turn curtailed some of the activities of the liberty parties after dark. However, there was no diminution of friendliness toward the Americans.

Those fortunate enough to draw a few hours of liberty in Bahia did enjoy it. For one thing, the city was large enough to provide something of interest for all tastes. One of the oldest European settlements in the western hemisphere, and for years the capital of Portuguese Brazil, the city abounded in ornate churches and picturesque ruins from the colonial period—which delighted the sightseers and history buffs. Vestiges of the heyday of the sugar industry, and the concomitant slave trade with Africa, still were in evidence in the dock area. For those who merely wanted to stretch their legs, there were many well-kept parks to explore. There wasn't much to buy in the markets—the people who traded there were far more interesting than the stuff they bought and sold.

The *Bahianos* were a delightful mixture of Portuguese, African, and Indian, stemming from the early colonial days. They were deeply religious, but the formal Catholicism to which most adhered was mingled freely with the spirits of the African cults and the superstition of the native Indian tribes. With such a background, there was little room for the racial discrimination and puritanical intolerance found in some other parts of the world. It is small wonder that the American liberty parties enjoyed Bahia and its people. Thanks to its size, there were enough bars and restaurants that the liberty parties could scatter out without having to compete for one or two popular spots. However, because of wartime restrictions, the regular establishments were closed before the end of liberty hours, forcing the men to wander about the town or return to their ships. Many men returned to their ships—better off for the early closing. But some found their way to one of the many bordellos which were apparently immune to the closing regulations and which provided bar and restaurant services in addition to their primary reason for existence. Many who wanted nothing to do with the women ended up there. Two innocents from the *Emmons'* liberty group, walking toward the elevators and home, were passed by two paddy wagons loaded with sailors. They concluded there had been a riot back of them somewhere. It was not until they reached the ship and were recounting how there had been some sort of trouble ashore, that they learned the friendly Brazilians had provided free transportation for their guests between the houses and the official prophylaxis station.

The sailors who got ashore the first night were the only ones able to explore the charms of the picturesque old city. Before liberty hours were up, the shore patrol was busy rounding up all men from Task Group 27.5 and sending them back to their ships. Captain McCrea had received a priority dispatch from Cominch changing the plans. Originally, the *Iowa* and her escorts were to have remained in Bahia until the President flew in from the conferences to begin the sea-leg part of his homeward journey. Now, instead of boarding the *Iowa* in Brazil, the President would go aboard at Freetown, Sierra Leone, or Dakar, French West Africa. In the meantime, the *Iowa* group was to proceed to Freetown to await further orders.

Accordingly, the group left Bahia the morning of November 30, en route to Freetown.

10

By any yardstick, the four-day voyage to Freetown was unexciting—not even an underwater sound contact. No notice was taken of the second crossing of the equator in five days. Evidently Neptune was pleased with his new shellbacks—the weather remained fine and those who were not inclined to question what was going on were content to soak up the warmth of the tropical sun. The most important thing to nearly everyone aboard the *Emmons* was that they were now headed northeast again after a one-night stand in Bahia, the third crossing of the Atlantic within a month. By now the rumor was going around the ship that the erratic moves was connected with some mysterious errand of President Roosevelt. The thought helped to hold down wild conjectures and did a lot to alleviate some of the resentment over the apparently aimless crisscrossing of the Atlantic.

One day out of Freetown, the three destroyers of Task Unit 27.5.2 appeared from nowhere and joined the formation. They went into the British port as part of the group on December 4, but got underway the following day to go to Dakar, there to fuel to capacity and then proceed to the west at an economical speed to relieve the *Emmons* group of destroyers when the *Iowa* started her homeward dash. The battleship and her normal retinue of destroyers remained at anchor in the Sierra Leone River another day before leaving for Dakar, where they were to pick up the President on December 9.

Liberty in Freetown, limited to daylight hours, was as unexciting as the passage from Bahia. One positive aspect for the *Emmons*'s liberty party was the opportunity to broaden their cultural experience. One of the days was Sunday, so some men made a point of visiting the Freetown churches. They were startled to see pictures and images of the Virgin and Child and the familiar saints portrayed as blacks. It didn't seem so strange, however, when they took a closer look at the worshipers. English spoken with a British accent by blacks was also something new for the newcomers aboard. Late one afternoon, several sailors witnessed a fight between two natives in which one was practically disemboweled by a rough-edged knife before anyone could intervene. A more pleasant prospect for the sightseers was a bridge overlooking a shallow stream where the Sierra Leonese women congregated to pound the family wash on the smooth stones.

11

The arrival of the *Iowa* at Dakar was timed for late the morning of December 9, early enough to have time to top off the destroyers, and yet not leave her exposed for too long at anchor in the roadstead, which did not have adequate antisubmarine protection. Because of her draft she could not get behind the nets which were available for smaller ships. Before he left Freetown, Captain McCrea had made arrangements with the British Flag Officer Commanding West Africa to place two British destroyers under his control to augment the patrol of the *Ellyson, Rodman,* and *Emmons* while his ship was at anchor in the roadstead. The three U. S. destroyers were fueled one at a time, the *Rodman* at the Naval Base, Dakar, and the *Ellyson* and *Emmons* from the *Iowa.* Because of her slightly higher fuel consumption, the *Emmons* went alongside the *Iowa* last, and left from alongside to take up her patrol station just two hours before the President arrived. The rumors making the rounds of the *Emmons* received unofficial confirmation while she was alongside the *Iowa.* Although Mutzabaugh, the appendicitis patient, knew the truth, he had kept it to himself when he returned aboard in Freetown. Nevertheless, the rumors that Roosevelt was aboard the battleship persisted, founded largely on the knowledge that she had been fitted with an elevator. During the fueling operation, one of the *Emmons*'s seamen spotted a buddy from his home town on the *Iowa*'s fantail. While they were shouting across from ship to ship, the *Iowa* sailor confirmed that the President had indeed been a passenger on the first eastward crossing of the Atlantic. Starting from there, it didn't take much imagination to figure out what the *Iowa* and her escorts were doing poking around the West Coast of Africa.

Meanwhile, the President and his party were on their way by air from Tunis to Dakar, a long, tiresome 12 1/2-hour flight. While waiting for the second and third planes bearing his entourage, the President sat in his plane looking over and signing official mail which was delivered by courier from Washington. When all planes had landed, the party went by motorcade from the airfield to the French Naval Station at the port, where they boarded the French destroyer *La Gazelle* for transportation to the *Iowa* in the outer harbor.

Once alongside the *Iowa,* the President was hoisted aboard the battleship in a special boatswain's chair rigged from the starboard whale-boat davit. The other members of his party had to get aboard as best they could up the steep gangway leading from the destroyer to the battleship. As soon as all the President's party was safely on board and the *Gazelle* had cleared the side, the *Iowa* began to get underway. Shortly before her anchor broke ground the *Emmons,* patrolling several miles to the southwest, picked up a sound contact which was believed to be no sub, but which was too good to disregard—probably an old wreck, as it showed no motion. As a precaution, one 600-pound depth charge was dropped over the spot. If it had been a U-boat, it would have escaped unscathed from that particular attack; the depth charge failed to go off because the depth setting was too deep for the shallow water. A few gingerly passes at a respectful distance from the unexploded charge showed no movement in the target. In the meantime, the *Iowa* was underway and left the anchorage, heading west at twenty knots. Had there been a live contact, it would have been left for the British destroyers to hunt down, for the *Emmons* had to close in and join the screen around the battleship as she emerged from the harbor.

Once the screen was in place, the *Iowa* signaled a speed of twenty-five knots, a speed she held most of the way across the Atlantic to the Virginia Capes. At this speed it was again necessary to use three relays of escorts as had been done on the eastward journey. Except for the last group, which saw the *Iowa* past the Capes, the composition of the escort units was the same as it had been on the eastward trip, but in reverse order. Thus, two days out of Dakar, the *Emmons* unit was relieved by Task Unit 27.5.2, which was responsible for the safety of the *Iowa* across the middle reaches of the ocean.

For the *Emmons,* the homeward voyage was a lark compared to the run in to Gibraltar. Humming along at twenty-five knots in a moderate sea with the wind astern, the homeward voyage was more like a pleasure cruise than a wartime assignment, although the watches and drills still came around with monotonous regularity. From all accounts, the President and his party took advantage of the balmy weather to enjoy the complete relaxation the sea voyage afforded after three weeks of concentration on the Teheran and Cairo conferences.

Under the favorable cruising conditions there was no threat of running out of fuel oil as there had been going east. When the destroyers of DesRon 10 were released by the *Iowa,* they were directed by CinCLant to proceed to San Juan or, if possible, Bermuda. Since all the ships, including the black sheep, *Emmons,* had ample fuel to reach Bermuda comfortably, Commodore Lewis opted for the latter destination. Although it was considerably farther than San Juan, it shortened the overall distance to Norfolk, where his three ships were scheduled for a navy yard period.

After five days of easy steaming, they arrived at Port Royal, Bermuda, and December 16. That same day the *Iowa* anchored at the mouth of the Potomac to disembark the President, and the task units connected with his historic trip were dissolved. The following day the three destroyers at Bermuda were underway again, but not for Norfolk as originally planned. Good luck continued to follow the *Emmons* and her companions. Instead of Norfolk, the three were headed for their home port, Boston. Someone had thoughtfully changed their scheduled yard overhaul to the Navy Yard, South Boston. When they arrived back home on December 19, they had crossed the Atlantic four times in the span of forty-five days and had visited ports in three continents, not to mention stops at Bermuda and the Azores.

10

Antisubmarine Duty in the Mediterranean

o o o o o o o o o o o o o o o o o o o o o o o o o o o o o o o o

....0809 sighted enemy submarine bearing 042° (t) distance 14000 yards. 0812 Opened fire on submarine with main battery. Went to general quarters. 0813 Ceased firing. 2 rounds 5"/38 cal expended. 0818 Submarine was sunk in position 37°48', 00°16'E. Commenced maneuvering in a circular screen around USS ELLYSON and USS RODMAN while these vessels rescued enemy survivors.

—***Emmons** Log, 17 May 1944*

The timing and location for the yard availability could not have been better for the *Emmons.* The sixteen-day period at the South Boston annex was the longest since the fitting-out period at the old navy yard. The crew enjoyed being in the home port for both the Christmas and New Year holidays. Many of them had families in the area, but the old New England-New York commissioning crew was pretty well thinned out after two years of constant change.

The longer overhaul period was necessary to complete several major alterations dictated by wartime operations. The most important of these was installation of a Combat Information Center (CIC), to receive, evaluate, and then pass along to the bridge and gun control stations the many pieces of information coming into the ship, from whatever source, on enemy and unidentified contacts. Designed primarily to sift out and disseminate combat information, it served equally well for normal activities such as navigation, maintaining station in tactical formations, or the tracking and control of friendly aircraft. Before, information from the sophisticated equipment scattered throughout the ship, or from other ships in company, had reached the bridge and fire control directors in a more or less helter-skelter fashion. All the information generated by radar, sonar, radio, navigational equipment—what have you—was channeled into one central location for correlation. As part of the installation, new model search radar, SG-A, replaced an older model.

Alterations were made to the bow to strengthen it for ramming. The bilge keel was also strengthened. To make the steel deck of the wardroom, stripped of its linoleum, less hazardous to negotiate in rough seas, fire retardant deck treads were put down. During this process the highly flammable adhesive caught fire. An alert fire watch with the help of other sailors put out the fire with portable extinguishers, long before the yard fire department arrived on the scene and before it could spread. Even so, most of the furniture was damaged. The greatest loss, however, and most keenly missed, was a prized collection of popular and classic phonograph records, which were so warped by the heat as to make them useless.

To replace the sonar dome, the ship was docked in a floating dry dock—another first for the *Emmons.* The mystery of the excess fuel oil consumption at high speeds during the *Iowa* operation was now cleared up. During routine inspection of the underwater hull and fixings, the damage to the starboard propeller was discovered, and it had to be replaced.

The *Emmons* continued to lose petty officers and experienced seamen from the top of her roster to other ships and stations, but there was some slowdown of the wholesale turnover of personnel experienced in former home visits. Losses of petty officers were replaced for the most part by seamen and firemen from the receiving stations. There were no large drafts from the training centers during the yard overhaul period. Of the fourteen men received on board at the navy yard before New Year's Eve, all but four were seamen first class, who, for one reason or another, had not been advanced to petty officer, although at least one had been designated a radio striker by virtue of having been sent for extensive training to radio school. During the last quarter of 1943, the ship lost more men than she received, by sixty-four to thirty-nine. She ended the quarter with 249 attached, the lowest count for the last year and a half.

Among those detached was John P. Kreckel, who left to receive an ensign's commission. During his two years on board he had advanced from coxswain to chief boatswain's mate and became chief master at arms. He was more than a petty officer to the young seamen under his care, because he had always considered it his responsibility to look out for their welfare as well as for their conduct. He instilled in them a sense of responsibility for their shipmates and their ship.

He was fond of reminding the youngsters that the *Emmons* was not just a ship—it was home.

One of the few petty officers among the newcomers was Donald L. Yecke, who reported aboard as a baker third class while the *Emmons* was still at Argentia. Having served an apprenticeship in his family's bakery and attended the Navy's school for cooks and bakers, he was a master at whipping up tasty breads and pastries, and he took pride in providing a great variety of desserts. Yecke did a lot to keep the hungry men of the DD457 content with their temporary home. He very quickly gained the affection of his shipmates and his confections became their boast among the crews of the other ships of the division. His former shipmates still speak of his cakes and pastries as one of the pleasant memories of their wartime duty: he was one of those killed by the kamikazes off Okinawa.

2

The same day the *Emmons,* with the other ships of Task Group 27.5, arrived at Freetown, the *Ranger* and her group, which had been operating at Scapa Flow as Task Group 112.1, arrived back in the United States, their duty with the Home Fleet completed. On that date, December 4, 1943, Task Force 22 was reconstituted under the command of Admiral Hustvedt. It was to consist of the *Ranger,* Battleship Division 7 *(Iowa, New Jersey),* Cruiser Division 7 *(Tuscaloosa* and *Augusta),* and the nine destroyers of Destroyer Squadron 10. The organizations remained a paper force throughout December, because all the ships were either undergoing navy yard overhaul, or were on detached duty, as was the case with the *Iowa* and her three destroyers. The mission was much the same as before, to train for and repel any major threat by the German fleet in the Atlantic.

It was not until early January that the reconstituted task force assembled at Narragansett Bay and Casco Bay for a period of rigorous training. By that time it had been whittled down to the *Ranger,* the two cruisers, and the five destroyers of Division 19, the *Ellyson, Emmons, Hambleton, Macomb,* and *Rodman.* The battleships were Pacific bound and the four destroyers of Division 20 had been ordered to other duty.

After the task force was in full operation, two of the destroyers would work with the carrier out of Quonset Point while two others worked with the cruisers, or independently, out of Casco Bay. The *Emmons* and *Rodman* worked as one team, while the *Ellyson* and *Macomb* were the other. About every two weeks the two teams swapped jobs. The fifth ship of the division, the *Hambleton,* was undergoing an intensive schedule of individual ship exercises to help her catch up after her long period of inactivity. Occasionally, the entire task force met at sea to train as a unit. Antisubmarine exercises received the most attention for the destroyer training, but much time at Casco Bay was devoted to gunnery, night spotting, and night battle exercises. Besides the ordinary gunnery exercises, time was devoted to shore bombardment and drills which sharpened the capabilities of the new combat information centers. Among the drills were fighter direction exercises in which the destroyers directed friendly aircraft in intercepting simulated enemy aircraft attempting to attack the formation.

The three months spent operating in and out of Casco Bay, Quonset Point and Newport, was the longest period the *Emmons* had ever spent in home waters since the start of the war. The weather, especially at Casco Bay, was lousy most of the time, but there were few complaints—it was no worse than the Arctic or Argentia. Nearly every weekend was spent in port with one-third of the crew getting liberty, and it was easy for a few men at a time to get short leaves. From Quonset Point or Newport, the liberty parties were able to get to Boston or New York without too much hassle, although the incidence of over leaves took a jump because of the transportation problem. The story is that sailors in Newport who had no family or friends in either New York or Boston would go to the bus station and head for one or the other of the big cities, depending on which direction the first bus that pulled into the station was headed.

Casco Bay posed more of a problem for liberty parties. It seemed to the men aboard that the *Emmons* was always assigned a berth at the end of the line. After picking up the *Emmons'* party, the omnibus liberty boats would stop at every ship in the bay before heading for the city, and then reverse the procedure on the outward bound trip in the small hours of the morning. There had to be some unusual attraction in Portland to justify the long, cold ride into town and back. Although sheer boredom with shipboard routine or romantic interests in the city got some to brave the trip, for most it was easier to go ashore to the recreation centers around the anchorage, or to tramp through the snow-covered communities nearby. Whenever there was a reasonable chance for a few days in port and finances permitted, men would try to arrange for wives or girl friends to come up to Portland for a few hours together. There was never any certainty that the ship would be in port when they arrived, and it was always difficult to arrange for a place for them to stay on short notice. The venerable Eastland Hotel and a large, rambling wooden hotel were the most popular places, but they were usually booked up, as were the lesser hotels. A number of private homes and boarding houses sometimes had rooms available. Most trusted to luck and something was always worked out. There would be a cancellation, or a friend and his family, who had reservations, would share their room on a hot-bunk basis. There were always the restaurants and night clubs, and at the least, a few hours of conversation and holding hands in the hotel lobbies and the bus station. Many a sailor had to leave his wife or sweetheart in the crowded station before facing the early morning ride back to the ship.

Snow and fog were prevalent in Casco Bay but every once in a while it cleared, and then the beauty of the sparkling bay, surrounded by snow-covered woods, made up for some of the discomfort. Fog frequently caused cancellation or postponement of scheduled exercises. Navigation in and out of the bay was hazardous, but use of radar made it possible to sortie and return to port at times when it would otherwise have been impossible.

The ship came and went so often during this period that the special sea details began to look for something interesting to do when not busy handling lines or anchor gear. The men who manned the fantail now made a habit of singing as they came to anchor or to moor alongside another destroyer. They would never have been called to the concert stage and their repertoire was not extensive, but they enjoyed it, and it expressed the joy they felt at getting safely home after another period at sea. They avoided the stylized sea chanties so popular with professional choruses; rather, they favored those they had learned in school, the type favored by barbershop quartets, such as "My Gal Sal," "My Old Kentucky Home," and the "Battle Hymn of the Republic."

3

With the coming of spring, Task Force 22 was broken up. Its major reason for being, the threat of the German heavy ships in Norway, had all but disappeared. By December, 1943, the *Tirpitz* and *Scharnhorst* were the only large ships left and, as we know, the *Scharnhorst* was cornered between Bear Island and North Cape and sunk by the British Navy near the end of 1943. The *Tirpitz* remained a potential threat until April 3, 1944, when, at Alta, she was put out of action for at least three months by a massive air attack from Fleet Air Wings belonging to the Royal Navy carriers *Victorious* and *Furious.* Some of the more inefficient German big ships had been retired and their crews assigned to other duties, including submarines and ground forces. The others, among them the pocket battleships *Lutzow* and *Scheer,* were either undergoing overhaul or were on training duty in the Baltic. Clearly, the Nazi Battle Fleet was on the wane.

Indeed, the Axis forces were on the defensive in nearly all of the European area. The Italian government had capitulated, but at Monte Cassino, German armies were stubbornly resisting allied advances up the peninsula. Allied ships could once more move from one end of the Mediterranean to the other, although against significant submarine opposition and an occasional air attack. In Greece and Yugoslavia, the occupying troops had more than they could handle from partisan groups. The Russian counteroffensive, started in tandem with Operation TORCH in 1942, had continued throughout 1943 against desperate German efforts to regain the initiative. By the end of March, 1944, most of the territory taken by the Nazis in 1942 had been regained. In the north, the 872-day siege of Leningrad had been lifted. To the south, a large German-Rumanian army, isolated in the Crimea by the Russian advance, was preparing to evacuate the area. Russian troops were once more in that part of Poland they had annexed after the infamous treaty of 1939 with Hitler. To the south, they were poised on the borders of eastern Rumania.

In Western Europe the air was tense with expectancy. The United Kingdom was awash with troops and equipment preparing for the knockout blow to the Nazi war machine. The whole world, including the Germans, knew that a cross-channel invasion was imminent. What was not known, except to a few, was where and when the blow would fall. Consequently, the German high command was forced to prepare for any eventuality as best it could. In the meantime, allied aircraft flew over Germany and occupied Western Europe almost at will against Goering's deflated Luftwaffe.

By the end of March, in the Pacific area, the Japanese too, had been forced to the defensive. The Solomon's were cleared except for major units isolated on New Britain and New Ireland. The Japanese on New Guinea were penned up at Hollandia and on the Huom Peninsula. Amphibious forces under Admiral Nimitz's Pacific command had captured the Gilbert and Marshall Islands. Advanced bases were being set up at Kwajalein and Eniwetok preparatory to moving on to the Marianas and westward. In Burma and East India, British, American, and Chinese troops were locked in battle with the Japanese for control of the vital supply routes to China. The Japanese were still dominant there, but were unable to finish off the resilient Chinese.

There was no doubt that the Axis sun was setting. Partisans in occupied countries became bolder in their opposition to Axis occupation forces. Many nations, which for one reason or another had remained on friendly, even cozy, terms with the Axis, began to put as much distance as possible between themselves and the hitherto victorious powers by curtailing strategic supplies and withdrawing special favors. Some, such as Sweden, had had no choice but to cooperate with Germany. Others, such as Spain and Argentina, had been in ideological sympathy with the dictatorships. The latter had opposed a strong declaration of unanimity against the Axis at the Inter-American Conference at Rio in 1942, and had continued to favor the dictators long after the other American states, even Chile, had either declared war or broken relations. By January, 1944, the Argentine dictator saw the light and broke diplomatic relations with the Axis.

In spite of their setbacks, the Germans were far from surrender. Following the withdrawal of their submarines from the North Atlantic in May, 1943, there had been a brief lull in the attacks on Allied shipping. But the U-boats were merely being regrouped by Grand Admiral Doenitz to exploit weaker spots in the anti-submarine defenses and to await development of new weapons and techniques. Among the new devices being evaluated was the *Zaunkoenig,* an acoustic torpedo which homed in on the noise of a vessel's propellers. The snorkel breathing apparatus was another, as were various devices for fooling radar and sonar detectors. In spite of air raids on their building yards, production of submarines was maintained at an alarming pace. Indeed, the number of submarines completed in 1944 exceeded the numbers launched in 1942 or 1943. Improved boats, which could run faster submerged as well as on the surface, were underway. The acoustic torpedoes were developed specifically to attack convoy escorts. The Germans finally had come to realize that they had to eliminate the screening vessels before they could get at the heart of a convoy.

Fortunately, in the continuing battle for technical and productive ascendancy, the Allies were able to hold the edge. Although there were never enough ships and trained men to cover all points at all times, the alarming shortages which had existed in December, 1941, were a thing of the past by 1944. It was no longer necessary to throw untried ships into emergency situations as the *Emmons* and *Macomb* had been during the submarine blitz off the East Coast in 1942. There were now enough ships to assemble and train specialized groups such as Task Force 22 and the hunter-killer groups of 1943 without the necessity of breaking them up to meet unforeseen emergencies.

When Grand Admiral Doenitz was looking around for weak spots for employment of his submarines, he seized on the Mediterranean as one of the areas where they could be profitably employed. Accordingly, he attempted to build up his submarine fleet there. Between September, 1943, and May, 1944, twenty-seven attempted to sneak through the Strait of Gibraltar. Only fourteen succeeded, but those, combined with the U-boats already operating out of Toulon, and armed with acoustic torpedoes, created havoc with the numerous convoys supporting the Italian operation. By February, 1944, a maximum of eighteen German subs were operating in the Mediterranean, along the coasts and in the restricted passages between the islands and the mainland. In February, allied shipping losses in the inland sea were three times the losses to enemy subs in the Atlantic and Arctic combined, second only to losses sustained in Doenitz's other newly developed hunting ground, the Indian Ocean. The German losses were great, but so were the losses to Allied escort vessels. The Nazis were now using their acoustic torpedoes to pick off the convoy escorts before getting at the convoy itself. The Mediterranean subs were not yet equipped with the snorkel.

To counter the revived U-boat threat in the Med, the Allies adopted a new tactic called Operation SWAMP. This required some of the escorts of a convoy to stay on the scene of an attack, or confirmed contact, until the sub was either sunk or made good its escape. Shore-based aircraft were sent out to help in the holding-down tactics. The objective was to hold the submarine down until it was forced to surface to recharge batteries. SWAMP was admirably suited to the restricted waters of the Mediterranean and its nearby airfields. The combination of search aircraft and surface ships was most effective. Several submarines were bagged after extensive hunts lasting a day or more. However, it obviously required more convoy escorts than were normally available. In the course of a protracted hunt a convoy might be so weakened by loss of escorts engaged in holding-down operations that it would be vulnerable to attacks farther along the route. Additional destroyers were needed to take up the scent in cooperation with the shore-based aircraft. Thus, the original escorts could resume their screening duties with the convoy while the hunt continued.

The need for additional antisubmarine ships in the Mediterranean only partially explains the *Emmons'* next assignment, temporary duty with the Eighth Fleet. A more compelling reason was the buildup of ships for the projected invasion of Southern France over the beaches of the Cote d'Azur. At that time the landings in the south, Operation ANVIL, later changed to DRAGOON, were scheduled to be made simultaneously with the cross-Channel invasion, OVERLORD, as a pincers movement on German forces in France from both the Mediterranean and the Atlantic. In March, the Commander in Chief, U.S. Fleet, had directed the Commander in Chief, Atlantic Fleet, to transfer forty destroyers along with an assortment of old battleships, old and new cruisers, destroyer escorts, patrol craft and minesweepers to the Eighth Fleet by early May for temporary duty in connection with the invasion. The breakup of Task Force 22 made the destroyers of Division 19 available for this assignment.

4

The *Emmons* did not know of the above developments until after mid-April when Task Force 22 was dissolved. She and *the Rodman* left Quonset Point with the *Ranger* on the 26th of March for two days of escort and plane guard duty during flight operations off Cape Cod. The second day the group was joined by the *Augusta,* escorted by the other three destroyers of the division, for an additional day of exercises for the entire task force. At the end of the combined exercises the ships of the task force were detached to proceed to Quonset Point, Casco Bay, or Boston. It was the last time Task Force 22, as then constituted, would work together as a unit.

The *Emmons* was detailed to accompany the *Augusta* to Boston and was unexpectedly assigned a week's upkeep at the South Boston Navy Yard annex. The other ships of the division were also assigned yard periods during the next two weeks. They didn't know it, but they were being prepared for extended overseas duty which would include a few weeks of submarine chasing in the Mediterranean and the invasion of Normandy, to be followed by the invasion of Southern France. Much of the work done on the *Emmons* had to do with the installation of new equipment in preparation for the forthcoming assignments and improvements in the new Combat Information Center. The old SC radar was replaced with a modern SA-2 set, and radio equipment for communication with shore fire control parties and friendly aircraft was brought up-to-date. At this stage of the war, the guns and machinery installation of the *Benson* class destroyers were pretty well set, but nearly every visit to a navy yard saw major changes in fire control installations, radar search sets, and communication equipment.

Following the period at the navy yard the *Emmons* returned to Casco Bay, where she continued the regimen of escort duty for heavy ships, and individual destroyer exercises. She still had no inkling of what her next job would be. However, the wheels were moving at fleet level. On April 11, Captain Converse, the new commander of Destroyer Squadron 10, received top secret orders from Cinclant to proceed to the Mediterranean with the five destroyers of Division 19, and six additional destroyers from Divisions 13 and 25. There they were to report to Commander Eighth Fleet for temporary duty. At the same time the four destroyers of Squadron 10's other division, 20, were ordered to the United Kingdom to report to Commander Twelfth Fleet for temporary duty.

Task Force 22 was dissolved on April 15. One by one, the eleven destroyers which were to proceed to the Med under Captain Converse were assembled at Casco Bay, where they completed preparations for the Atlantic crossing. The eleven were the *Ellyson, Emmons, Hambleton, Macomb,* and *Rodman* of DesDiv 19; the *Niblack, Gleaves* and *Benson* of DesDiv 13; and the *Woolsey, Ludlow* and *Edison* of DesDiv 25. As Task Group 27.4 they took departure from Casco Bay on April 20.

5

The Atlantic crossing was noteworthy for several reasons. For one thing, the task group was composed entirely of destroyers—no carriers, battleships, cruisers, or transports demanding protection and attention. Commodore Converse was able to dispose his ships on a scouting line covering more than sixty miles across in the hope that any stray submarines still haunting the middle Atlantic would fall into the net. There was no such luck. Weather conditions during some of the crossing were anything but favorable for radar and sonar search.

On the third day out of Casco Bay the group encountered a storm which caused considerable damage. While it was not statistically as great as some of the gales encountered in the Arctic and North Atlantic, it was just as destructive. Coming from the northeast it created unusually heavy seas across the path of the formation. Some of the destroyers found the going so rough that the commodore decreased speed to eleven knots and gave permission to maneuver to lessen the danger from excessive rolls. At the height of the storm, about mid-afternoon, an unusually deep roll to starboard swamped the *Emmons*' starboard whaleboat, smashing it so badly that it had to be jettisoned. One section stubbornly refused to go under and had to be sunk with machine gun fire. For the remainder of the war the *Emmons* carried only one whaleboat, not because the jettisoned one was irreplaceable, but because of the weight factor.

During the storm all topside traffic was stopped except for emergencies such as cutting away the whaleboat. There was no thought of serving food or coffee until conditions improved. After the storm there was considerable debate as to the extent of the greatest roll. Some of the old salts nonchalantly estimated the maximum at a moderate 30°. The higher above the main deck the observer, the greater the estimate. Some members of the gun director crew, who experienced the wildest motion, made the most exaggerated claims, up to an impossible 90°. To them, arcing from one side to the other, high above the center of gravity, it seemed they were looking straight down into the hungry seas as the ship paused to right itself at the end of the deepest rolls. Members of the bridge watch, who had the benefit of the clinometers, estimated the maximum roll at an alarming 45°.

During the worst of the storm most people not on watch stayed in their bunks, struggling to hang on. One ingenious seaman, who had a middle bunk, got hold of a piece of line and laced it to the outer frames of his own bunk and the one above, forming a netting on the outboard side. He had to crawl into his cubicle from the end, like entering a low tunnel. The net didn't give him any more sleep, but at least he didn't have to remount after every few rolls.

Fortunately, no one aboard the *Emmons* suffered anything worse than cuts and bruises. Other ships were not so lucky. Shortly after 2230 the *Macomb* reported that her executive officer was missing, having last been seen at 1530. In view of the elapsed time, the many changes in course and the still nasty condition of the sea, the commodore made the difficult decision not to try to back track to search for the lost officer. The loss of the *Macomb's* exec had a direct effect on the *Emmons.* When the task group reached Mers-el-Kebir, her gunnery officer, Lieutenant (jg) Joseph N. Behan, Jr., USN, was ordered to report to the *Macomb* as executive officer. His billet aboard the *Emmons* was filled by Lieutenant (jg) John J. Griffin, USNR.

After the severe storm of the 23rd there were no other unusual occurrences. Drills and watches occupied the time, and the new men who had reported aboard before leaving the states began to adjust to the routine of a protracted period at sea. That is, all but one young seaman who simply could not stand the humdrum routine. He had come aboard as a recruit at Casco Bay full of patriotism and a desire to fight our enemies. In this he was no different from the rest of the crew. But he became depressed by the endless rounds of sunrise and sunset general quarters, sweeping details, watches and drills. Worse, there was no enemy in sight, and he saw little chance of meeting one. Before leaving the States he had gained some attention when one of the members of the censor board felt obliged to report to the captain a letter written by the youngster to a friend in which he bragged that he was safe from the prying eyes of the FBI—he was now a member of the U.S. Navy and serving on the USS *Emmons,* a true fighting ship. Naturally, the matter was referred to staff intelligence officers, who in due time came back with the reassuring news that any trouble the young sailor might have had with the FBI was brought about by his desire to serve in the Army without the formality of going through the enlistment process. He had somehow obtained an army uniform, gone to Fort Hamilton in Brooklyn, mixed in with a new unit being formed, and drilled with it for several days before someone spotted him as a stranger. After going through investigation he once more found himself degraded to civvies and looking for a place where he could get into the fight. The Navy was his answer—only this time he legitimatized his ambitions by enlisting. After training he was assigned to the DD457.

The long trip across the ocean without any signs of an enemy, except an occasional false submarine attack, was more than he could bear. The *Emmons* hadn't been anywhere near an enemy for months and no one knew what they would be doing when they arrived wherever they were going—more drills, probably. If he couldn't take part in a *bona fide* battle his imagination supplied the deficiency. Another letter was written describing what would have been one of the sharpest actions in the war. Shells screamed through the air but none touched the *Emmons.* In the end she emerged victorious over a savage enemy. This, in spite of the fact that he had observed all the officers huddled under the wardroom table at the height of the battle. The harsh contrast between fantasy as reported in his letter and mundane fact must have been too much for the young hero. If he couldn't get at the Germans his everyday shipmates were not so elusive. After a series of one-on-one scraps he ended up at captain's mast charged with threatening a fellow mess cook with a butcher knife. The last the captain heard from him was a plaintive letter demanding to know why he had been sent ashore for medical observation instead of being given a court martial—the right of any fighting man.

The young seaman was not the only one to wonder what was in store for the *Emmons* at the end of this particular voyage, the more so as there were no big ships along. For many of the old-timers aboard this was their eighth eastbound crossing of the Atlantic since reporting aboard. They were used to churning up a lot of water with no apparent purpose, but, by now, they knew that they would find out what it was all about in good time, and that it would make sense. They did not have long to wait before the first part of their current mission was made clear.

After stopping at Horta for a few hours for fuel, the destroyers transited the Strait of Gibraltar on April 30. Following the storm of the 23rd, the weather had been moderately good. There were no signs of submarines along their way until they had formed up by divisions in columns of open order on the western approaches for the passage through the Strait. The *Ellyson,* at the head of Division 19, picked up a sound contact and made a nine-charge depth charge attack. As the *Emmons* and *Rodman* were last and next-to-last in column, they were ordered to follow up. The *Emmons* did pick up a contact and dropped five depth charges, although not absolutely certain that it was a U-boat. Thereafter, she and the *Rodman* searched the area for an hour without positive results before rejoining the formation for transit of the Strait. The contact was subsequently evaluated as probably non-sub.

Once past the Rock of Gibraltar, the destroyers again formed a scouting line and reduced speed to search the area between Gibraltar and Oran, an area which had been a profitable hunting ground for U-boats, especially the area around Spanish-owned Alboran, an island in the narrow western end of the Mediterranean, about 140 miles east of the Strait and midway between the African and Spanish coasts. All ships entering or leaving the Med via the Strait of Gibraltar were obliged to pass within a few miles of the island to either the north or south. If any subs were skulking along the route of Task Group 27.4, they kept their distance.

6

Early in the morning of May 1, the eleven destroyers arrived in Oran and proceeded directly to the old French naval base of Mers-el-Kebir, west of the commercial harbor. On arrival at Oran the task group was dissolved and the units began operating as part of Destroyers, Eighth Fleet, under the Commander, Naval Forces Northwest African Waters, Vice Admiral H. Kent Hewett, USN. Their primary tasks were to train for the invasion of Southern France and augment the antisubmarine forces in the Mediterranean.

For Destroyer Division 19 this particular phase of their duty in the Eighth Fleet proved to be truly temporary. In less than three weeks the *Emmons, Ellyson, Hambleton,* and *Rodman* were on their way to England to participate in the Normandy Invasion. As time for the twin assaults on France came closer, it became apparent that the ships, primarily British, originally earmarked for Overlord, the naval phase of the cross-channel move, would be insufficient For one thing, the scope of the northern invasion had been enlarged by the addition of a five-mile stretch of landing beaches in the American sector between Pointe du Hoe and the Cotentin Peninsula, which were designated Utah Beach. Over these beaches two additional divisions of American troops were to be landed in the assault phase. The widened front and support of the extra divisions required more ships than the original allocation.

In addition, aerial reconnaissance revealed that the Germans' boast about their Atlantic Wall was not idle talk. Almost daily new defense installations were reported. The Germans bragged that coastal defenses from the northern tip of Norway to the Franco-Spanish border consumed 10,000,000 tons of concrete—enough to fill a line of trucks half way around the earth. Heavy casemates and pillboxes with elaborate interconnecting trenches and tunnels took the bulk of it. In addition, elaborate sets of obstacles, backed by mines, were strewn along the possible landing beaches. The defense preparations in France, from the Pas de Calais area to Cherbourg, were especially formidable, and were growing stronger every day under the energetic direction of Field Marshal Rommel. The expanded plans for the Normandy assault, plus the formidable German defenses at the chosen landing sites, necessitated a reappraisal of the forces required for the assault. A ready source for additional naval strength at Normandy was the gathering armada for the invasion of southern France. Decision was made to postpone the Mediterranean operation in order to make some of its ships available in the north. Among those shifted from the Mediterranean to England in late May was Destroyer Division 19.

The three weeks of temporary duty in the Mediterranean were anything but leisurely. A stiff schedule of training exercises in preparation for Operation ANVIL was drawn up. In actual practice, very little of it was completed, as training events took second place to antisubmarine activities. It seemed that every time an exercise, such as shore bombardment in the area set up at Arzeu, east of Oran, was ready to go, it would be interrupted by an emergency call to rush to the scene of a torpedoing or a reported U-boat contact. There were almost daily reports of sinkings in the convoys plodding along the North African coast. Not all of the casualties were merchantmen; the number of escort vessels lying immobilized along the quays of Mers-el-Kebir was ample evidence of the efficacy of the acoustic torpedo—most of them were missing their sterns.

Captain Converse made antisubmarine work his top priority. To that end he made a special trip to the Royal Air Force base at La Sienia, near Oran, to meet the commanders of the air squadrons his ships would be working with, and to work out communications to be used during a hunt. It is well that he did so, as the third day after arrival at Mers-el-Kebir, he was ordered, late in the afternoon, to take the *Ellyson, Emmons, Hambleton,* and *Rodman* to sea to join a submarine hunt north of Bougie, where the U-371 had attacked westbound convoy GUS-38 and torpedoed one of the escorts, the USS *Menges.*

Near the seaward end of the Oran swept channel, the *Emmons's* sonar operator reported hearing the sound of a torpedo passing close aboard. The *Emmons* and *Rodman* conducted a box search for twenty minutes, but did not pick up a contact before they were ordered to rejoin the division heading toward the scene of the *Menges* torpedoing at twenty-four knots. There the original American convoy escorts had been joined by a mixed group of British, French, and American ships pulled out of the Gulf of Bougie. One of these, the American-built French destroyer escort *Senegalais,* caught the U-371 just as it surfaced and sank it by gunfire. Not, however, in time to prevent the U-boat from getting off a final acoustic torpedo which hit and damaged it.

The *U-371* had been disposed of during the midwatch of the 4th, while Captain Converse's group was still speeding eastward along the African coast. When news of the sinking was received, the group headed back to Oran. During the afternoon, the *Hambleton* and *Rodman* were ordered to Djidelli to pick up the survivors of the *Menges,* while the *Ellyson* and *Emmons* continued to home base at a modest speed.

The leisurely pace of the two was interrupted early in the morning watch on May 5, when an urgent dispatch reporting the torpedoing of the destroyer escort *Fechteler to* the west of Oran was received. The *Fechteler* was one of the escorts which had remained with GUS-38 after the torpedoing of the *Menges.* The convoy had reached the narrow waters between the Spanish coast and Alboran Island when it ran across the *U-967.* As soon as the report was received the *Ellyson* and *Emmons* headed for the scene of *Fechteler's* sinking at best speed. Arriving on the scene by 1045, they joined the destroyer escorts *Lowe, Moseley,* and *Steady* in a box search for the U-boat. About noon the *Nields* and *Niblack* joined the hunt, relieving the *Lowe* and *Moseley* to rejoin the convoy, and the *Steady* to return to Oran.

The remaining destroyers continued the search to the north and northeast of Alboran Island throughout the rest of the day and night with negative results. There was no better luck when the *Hambleton* and *Rodman* joined up the following morning, although the *Hambleton* dropped depth charges on a contact she evaluated as doubtful. The addition did allow expansion of the search area, but, given the proximity of the Spanish coast, the guilty U-boat no doubt was resting comfortably on the bottom in neutral waters during most of the search. The search was called off by Commander in Chief, Mediterranean, at noon on the 7th, and the group returned to Mers-el-Kebir empty handed.

To the old-timers aboard the *Emmons* and *Hambleton,* the dashing from one emergency to another during the last four days was reminiscent of the frustrating antisubmarine patrol off Cape Hatteras in April, 1942. There were, however, some marked differences. For one thing, here in the Western Mediterranean they were not alone; there was ample back-up of ships and aircraft. For another, although their own group had not bagged a submarine, one by one the submarines in the Med were being eliminated. While still able to cause serious damage, the U-boats were no longer capable of stopping the movement of men and material to the fighting fronts in the Mediterranean, or anywhere else for that matter.

7

When the four DesDiv 19 ships engaged in the sub hunts arrived at Mers-el-Kebir they were berthed alongside the tender *Vulcan* for five days of repair and upkeep. It was the first real opportunity since reporting to the Eighth Fleet to take care of the many repair items which had accumulated after leaving the States. The *Macomb,* which had not been sent out on the submarine alarms, was temporarily assigned to DesDiv 21 for antisubmarine duty.

The five days for upkeep gave the men a chance to see something of Oran. Under French influence the city was surprisingly modern and had suffered little damage in the TORCH invasion. Nonetheless, war had taken its toll; there was a severe shortage of consumer goods and not much for those on liberty to do except to visit the markets and a few so-called cabarets. The casbahs had the appeal of the unknown, but as usual, the native quarter had been declared off limits to army and navy personnel. A few who tried to penetrate its mysteries ended up in trouble with the military police. Some of the men were arrested for simply walking down the wrong side of the street separating the casbahs from the rest of the city. Their excuse was they couldn't read the French signs warning that the area was off limits—they had somehow overlooked the English translations posted alongside for the benefit of American and British personnel.

The food displayed by street vendors had little appeal, and the wines produced in the region had disappeared from the markets. There was some cheap, but strong, *eau de vie* available for those who didn't mind a splitting headache the next day. About the only attractive goods offered for sale or barter were handmade leather articles. There was some trafficking in the black market; cigarettes, as usual, were a good item in the unofficial market. However, in Oran the hot item was white mattress covers, highly prized for conversion to the long flowing garments worn by the natives. A shortage of mattress covers and sheets developed aboard the *Emmons* which was not corrected until she reached England.

By far the most popular spots for liberty for both officers and men were the excellent beaches near Mers-el-Kebir. There, good food and drinks were served in the clubs and recreation centers which had been set up precisely to keep the military personnel away from the city. Many of the employees of the facilities were former Italian prisoners of war who had not yet been repatriated. The Italians thoroughly enjoyed their new status, and proved to be outstanding cooks and bar tenders.

8

The tender overhaul period for the four ships of DesDiv 19 was rushed to completion so that they could join a submarine hunt near Alboran Island being conducted under the direction of Commander Destroyer Division 21. The four were ready for sea early the morning of the 14th. However, before they got underway their orders were changed. Captain Converse was directed to take charge of an entirely new hunt about 125 miles northeast of Oran where a submarine, later identified as the *U-616,* had torpedoed two merchantmen of westbound convoy GUS-39. In the meantime, Commander in Chief, Mediterranean, activated Operation SWAMP and Royal Air Force planes from near Oran took off to join the latest hunt. ComDesDiv 21 was ordered to break off the hunt near Alboran and proceed to the scene of the latest torpedoing with the *Nields, Gleaves* and *Macomb.*

The four destroyers out of Oran arrived on the scene shortly after noon to find the *Hilary P. Jones,* one of the escorts of GUS-39, in the process of dropping depth charges on a promising contact. However, she could not pick up the contact after the attack and ComDes 10 took charge of the search. The escorts of GUS-39 were released to rejoin their convoy. About mid-afternoon ComDesDiv 21, with the three ships from Alboran, reported and joined the search. Shortly after their arrival one of the Wellingtons participating in the air search reported a disappearing radar contact thirty-seven miles to the northwest of the area where the destroyers were searching. Captain Converse sent the newly-arrived destroyers to cover the area of the new contact while his four ships continued a box search about the point of the *Jones'* last contact.

There were no further contacts until after dark when the submarine surfaced to recharge batteries about thirty miles north of the point where it had attacked convoy GUS-39. It was spotted by one of the patrolling Wellingtons, which alerted the destroyers and dropped two flares to mark the position. When the destroyers reached the sighting point twenty-three minutes later the sub had submerged, but the *Ellyson* picked up a good sound contact and made an eleven-charge drop. There were no immediate visible results and contact was lost after the attack. A box search was started using the *Ellyson's* last contact as a reference point. The following morning a prominent oil slick, about ten miles long, tending from northwest to southeast, was observed a few miles north of the preceding night's attack, leading to the belief that the U-boat had suffered some damage. It was probably trying to escape to the north to the French coast—or, even nearer, the Balearic Islands, less than a hundred miles away.

No further contacts were made until early in the morning of May 16, when another aircraft reported a disappearing radar contact. The position was considerably to the west of previous reports, indicating that the U-boat might be attempting to make the shoal waters of the Spanish coast or to lose itself among the many fishing vessels offshore. In order to prevent the sub from reaching the sanctuary of neutral waters, the search area was moved closer to the coast with DesDiv 21 operating to the north of DesDiv 19.

By nightfall of the 16th, after running submerged for more than two days and nights, the *U-616* was getting desperate. Once more she came to the surface, and once more was spotted by aircraft. The reported position was somewhat to the east of the early morning report, but still placed the prey within forty miles of the Spanish mainland and seventy-five miles of the southernmost of the Balearic Islands. The two groups of destroyers converged on the spot at best speed. Both groups made radar contact about the same time, in spite of the radar decoys put up to confuse the searchers. Just before midnight, the *Macomb,* coming from the north, caught the surfaced submarine in her searchlight beam and opened fire with her 5-inch battery. The sub, at first thinking the light came from a low-flying airplane, opened fire with her 20 mms, but soon realized her mistake and crash dived. The *Macomb* and *Gleaves,* being the nearest, were teamed up to make several coordinated attacks, while the rest of the destroyers patrolled around them to prevent the target from sneaking away. The attacks had no apparent effects, and contact was lost at 0307. A new expanding search was started around the last point of contact.

This tactic prevented the U-boat from getting clear of the area. After three hours of negative results, the *Hambleton* made positive contact and dropped a full depth charge pattern. The *Ellyson* was then sent in to make a creeping attack under the *Hambleton's* direction. Contact was lost after the *Ellyson's* attack and it looked as if the search process would have to be started all over. But the *U-616* had had enough. At 0808 she broke surface about a mile off the *Ellyson's* port quarter and her crew began to abandon ship. Surrounded by seven destroyers, all of which opened fire, she had no chance. The gunfire may have hastened her sinking but sea valves had been left opened and she sank stern first within five minutes of surfacing. Apparently, most of her crew escaped. The *Ellyson* and *Rodman,* detailed to pick up survivors, reported rescuing seven officers, including the captain, and forty-six crewmen.

Throughout the three-day chase the *Emmons* had no unusual opportunities to play a stellar role. She maintained her position in the complicated search formations and stood ready to back up her sister ships which were in position to make depth charge attacks. When the U-boat surfaced, she was on the outer support circle some 14,000 yards away. In spite of the distance she got off two shots from the ready gun before ceasefire was ordered by ComDesRon 10, as it became apparent that the enemy was finished. It was her second time to have a positively identified enemy in her sights. And the results were most satisfying, far more so than the first time when she had chased away the Blohm and Voss shadower in the Arctic nearly two years ago.

9

Well pleased with themselves, the seven destroyers formed a scouting line, with 2,000 yards between ships, and headed back to Mers-el-Kebir under a cloudless Mediterranean sky. Earlier in the morning, ComDesRon 10 had received a dispatch ordering him to take four of the destroyers of Division 19 to the United Kingdom for temporary duty with the Twelfth Fleet and the invasion of France. Anxious to get his ships back to port, fueled, and ready to start for England as early as possible the next morning, he gradually increased the speed of the scouting line to twenty-seven knots.

The increased speed may well have saved the *Gleaves* and *Macomb,* on the extreme left of the line, from taking torpedoes in their sterns. During the lunch hour, the lookouts of the *Emmons,* on the right side of the scouting line, reported two explosions in the wakes of the left flank destroyers. Ships in the center and on the left not only saw the geysers, but heard and felt the detonations. Instinctively, eyes began searching the heavens for signs of a bomber, but the blue skies were clear. About the same time the *Gleaves* reported momentarily sighting what appeared to be a periscope. It didn't take long to deduce that the explosions came from acoustic torpedoes which had gone off prematurely in the hard wake thrown up by the destroyers at twenty-seven knots. The submarine which launched the torpedo was later identified as the *U-960,* which had just recently wormed its way through the Straits of Gibraltar and had been lurking about the shipping lanes north of Oran.

Without hesitation, Captain Converse organized a box search about the point of attack. At the same time, he alerted Commander in Chief, Mediterranean, and Royal Air Force Squadron 500, at La Sienia, of the fresh attack. A new SWAMP operation was underway.

The four ships of DesDiv 19 destined for England did not stay with the hunt very long. Commander Destroyer Division 25 had left Oran early that morning with the *Madison, Niblack,* and *Benson* to relieve Captain Converse's group in the hunt for *U-616*, before that sub had been finished off. They had not yet returned to Oran and were ordered to relieve DesDiv 19 in the new operation. They reached the scene in a little better than an hour. When the fresh ships reported, Captain Converse left them to continue the operation with the ships of DesDiv 21 and the *Macomb,* under the direction of their division commander, Captain R. B. Ellis. For the second time that day Converse headed his four ships to Mers-el-Kebir to begin preparations for the move north.

After a night at Mers-el-Kebir devoted to fueling, provisioning, and taking on ammunition, largely depth charges expended during the hunt for *U-616,* DesDiv 19, minus the *Macomb,* got underway for England and the big show the morning of May 18. That same day, the *U-453* scored what proved to be the last German submarine success of the war in the Mediterranean, when it torpedoed a small freighter east of Sicily. It paid dearly for this feat when it, in turn, was sunk by a mixed group of British and Italian escort vessels on May 21.

Meanwhile, Destroyer Divisions 21 and 25, backed by the Royal Air Force, was closing in on *U-960.* Division 19 cleared the Straits of Gibraltar during the midwatch of May 19. As they steadied down on a northerly course at the end of the approach channel, the bridge watch of the *Emmons* heard ComDesDiv 25 announce the finish of the *U-960.* The Mediterranean had become anything but a happy hunting ground for Der Fuehrer's *Unterseeboote.*

11

Normandy

o o o o o o o o o o o o o o o o o o o o o o o o o o o o o o o

0 to 4 Tuesday, 6 June 1944

...in company with USS Doyle as escorts to Mine Sweeper Squadron 31, of H.M.C.N. Ship in condition of readiness "one." All hands at battle stations.... 0359 Stopped all engines, lying to off French Coast in Bay of Seine, having completed assignment as escorts to mine sweeper squadron 31, awaiting "H"-hour in compliance with orders for Operation "Neptune."

—***Emmons*** *Log*

The only exciting event during the voyage occurred about 250 miles west of Land's End on the approach to the English coast. The *Emmons* picked up a promising sonar contact and delivered two depth charge attacks on a possible submarine. Then she directed the *Ellyson* in two creeping attacks. The *Hambleton* made two more attacks to the eastward of the original contact. After three and a half hours all contacts were lost. Since there was no positive proof of the nature of the contacts and any further investigation would delay scheduled arrival at Plymouth the hunt was discontinued.

The next day, May 22, the four destroyers arrived at Plymouth and reported for duty to Commander Task Force 122, the Western Naval Task Force, for OPERATION NEPTUNE, the naval phase of OPERATION OVERLORD, the Normandy Invasion. They were the last of thirty-one U.S. destroyers assigned for the assault to arrive in England and almost immediately were parceled out to various task groups. For all practical purposes DesDiv 19 was temporarily broken up and the individual ships came under control of the task group to which they were assigned. The *Emmons* was first assigned to duty with Task Group 122.4, the Assault Area Screen. Within a few days the orders were changed to the Bombardment Group, TG 124.9, Assault Force "0," for Omaha Beach, as a replacement for the *Endicott,* which had suffered damage in a collision.

Although the final decision on the exact date of D-day had not yet been made by Eisenhower at the Supreme Headquarters Allied Expeditionary Force, the dates had been narrowed down to two periods in June when the combination of tides and moonlight would be optimum. The weather would be the deciding factor. However, operation plans and orders for the various task organizations with their multitudinous annexes, charts and contingencies had been made and were distributed to the *Emmons* and other ships a few days after arrival. One of the major tasks of the waiting period for the invasion was keeping up with the merciless flood of paperwork and subsequent changes.

The first five days at Plymouth were spent making preparations for the invasion, broken only by a shore bombardment exercise at Slapton Sands, the principal training area for the assault troops and supporting naval vessels. Conditions there were similar to those expected at Normandy. Plymouth was the center of the American staging areas in the southwest of England and was overcrowded with all types of ships waiting for the big show. Anchorages and moorings were at a premium and were being constantly changed as ships were ordered alongside tankers for fueling or to docks for provisions and ammunition. In spite of the constant movement the Harbor Master seemed to have firm control of the comings and goings. The illusion of chaos was heightened by the great number of barrage balloons bobbing overhead from moorings ashore and on ships in the harbor. These were intended as defense from low flying aircraft and "buzz bombs," Germany's latest threat to the English mainland. No air raids were made while the *Emmons* was in the harbor although an occasional alert was sounded. From time to time the disconcerting roar of a rocket could be heard, but none landed near the port.

The *Emmons* was ordered to Milford Haven on the 28th of May to exchange some of her 5" antiaircraft shells with the *Endicott* for an equal number of rounds designed for use against land targets. The special ammunition had been issued to the *Endicott* when she was slated as one of the fire support ships at Omaha. The exchange was completed before dark and the following morning the *Emmons* got underway at first light for Weymouth Roads to await further orders.

While she was standing out of Milford Haven a wounded carrier pigeon made a forced landing on deck. There were no messages on the pigeon but it was in no condition to continue on its own. It so happened that one of the McConnell brothers, Tom, a sonar striker, was a bird fancier. He took charge of the frightened bird and carefully nursed it back to health. He, or she, remained on board throughout the uproar of Normandy and sailed with the ship when it returned to the Mediterranean more than two months later. This bird was the closest thing to a mascot the *Emmons* ever had. For reasons best known to it, the temporary mascot, fully recovered, went AWOL the day before D-day for OPERATION DRAGOON, the invasion of Southern France. Its disappearance just before that action was a disquieting omen for the more superstitious.

2

Back to NEPTUNE. At Weymouth Roads the *Emmons* remained at anchor waiting for the signal to start. D-day was set for June 5. H-hour at Omaha Beach was scheduled for 0630. A final briefing attended by all commanding officers was held ashore. The flow of orders and changes thereto came to a virtual standstill thanks to Admiral Ramsey, RN, the allied commander for all naval operations, who said "enough." The relative quiet was somewhat like the lull before a storm. A considerable amount of time and energy was spent tracking down several rounds of white phosphorus allocated to fire support destroyers. After a trip a day for four days to shore facilities the ammunition was located and received from a coaster anchored less than a mile away.

A final briefing conference for commanding officers was held ashore following which the ship's officers and key petty officers began to master the details of the NEPTUNE plans. Of course, gunnery and communication personnel had more to digest than other departments. The communication people were greatly amused by the code name assigned the ship, Easy Money, which could readily be translated into EM for *Emmons.* Restrictions on general information to the ships' crews were also lifted. Accordingly, the captain called all hands aft and gave them the news and a brief description of the *Emmons'* assigned tasks. The announcement was received with enthusiasm and a great deal of congratulatory back slapping. Actually, the feeling was one of relief that the operation was now out in the open. It is doubtful if anyone aboard failed to know what the activity of the past two weeks was up after all. Needless to say, no liberty was granted after the announcement.

All hands were keyed up. The gunners were particularly eager. Two days before the kick-off, Shore Fire Control Party No. 9 from the Army's First Division and six or seven captains and lieutenants from the Army units to be supported came aboard to go over communications and procedures for calling in and spotting naval gunfire. The meeting established mutual confidence. The shore fire control party personnel left the ship confident that the *Emmons* could deliver accurate fire within the range of her batteries.

Another brief conference was held the day before scheduled D-day between the Commanding Officers of the *Emmons, Doyle* and the 31st Minesweeping Flotilla of the Royal Canadian Navy. The 31st was scheduled to sweep approach channel No. 3 to the transport area for Omaha, the transport area itself, and finally, Omaha fire support Area 3, during the night of 4-5 June. The two destroyers were to provide defense for the flotilla during sweeping operations. According to plans, the minesweepers were to withdraw to seaward when their job was done while the destroyers remained in the fire support area until the shore bombardment phase began.

3

By June 3rd the weather over England and the Channel was deteriorating badly. Advance predictions of conditions in the assault area for D-day, 5 June, were far from favorable. Nevertheless, General Eisenhower gave the order to proceed as planned in order to get the slower and more distant convoys in assigned positions if a break in the weather should come. Ships began to move from staging ports along the English coast and from as far north as Belfast, Ireland. All were headed, at their own pace, for Point Zed, a point of departure south of the Isle of Wight, for the run across the Channel to the Bay of the Seine. Considering the differences in speed of the different convoys the times of arrival at Point Zed and departure there from were crucial for the success of the operation.

As the whole world now knows, General Eisenhower held a conference of his principal commanders at 0400, Sunday, the 4th, to evaluate the situation. At that time the weather had worsened. Winds as high as Force 6 on the Beaufort Scale, 22 to 27 miles per hour, were predicted over the Channel. Seas would be dangerous for the smaller landing craft. Further, overcast skies would hamper or prevent some of the scheduled air operations. The meteorologists did, however, hold out prospects for more favorable weather by the 6th. The General reluctantly decided to postpone the operation for one day. By 0500 on the 4th a signal was sent out from Supreme Headquarters Allied Expeditionary Force postponing OPERATION OVERLORD for one day. Units already at sea were directed to put in to designated ports along their routes.

As for the *Emmons,* when the message postponing D-day arrived, she was lying quietly at anchor in Weymouth Roads waiting her turn to get underway shortly after noon. All preparations for the invasion had been checked and rechecked. There was no great rush to get underway as the distance to the rendezvous with the minesweepers was less than ninety miles and could be covered at moderate speed in five or six hours. When the postponement order came some of the convoys closing in on Point Zed had already passed Portland Bill at the entrance to the anchorage at Weymouth.

The postponement had little effect on the ship or the crew except for a mild sense of disappointment at the delay. As one of the ready duty destroyers for Weymouth the engines were already warmed up, ready to go on short notice. The false start carried with it one small bonus. When the message came the galley was preparing the traditional pre-battle breakfast of steak and eggs, which was duly served.

Being the ready duty destroyer, the *Emmons* was not allowed the extra day at anchor most ships received as a result of the delay. Neither were some of the ships already at sea. Some of the slower convoys were turning the corner at Point Zed, and some of the minesweepers were preparing to start their sweeping operations when the postponement order was received. The high command was concerned that some units might have missed the postponement message, the more so as radio silence was imposed on ships already at sea. To make doubly certain they did not go plodding on to the French coast alone and unsupported, the ready duty destroyers were ordered out to round up the possible strays and return them to port. The *Emmons* was ordered to find convoy U2B and Minesweeping Flotilla 14 to insure they had received the recall message.

As the *Emmons* moved out to sea she was passed by a constant stream of ships heading into the shelter of Portland Harbor and Weymouth Roads. Out in the Channel it became abundantly clear why the invasion had been postponed. The weather was really foul. The smaller landing craft were having great difficulty holding to formations and most of the troops aboard were seasick. Low, scudding clouds and the sea seemed to meet in streaking, grey foam driven along by the fresh westerly winds. Visibility in the frequent rain squalls was poor, with only occasional clear patches. There was great concern as to whether the strays could be spotted in such weather. Thanks to radar, both groups assigned to the *Emmons* were found and the recall message delivered by signal light. Apparently it was not necessary as they were headed toward England when contacted.

When the *Emmons* returned to port she found a tangle of ships of all types vying for anchorages. She herself was ordered to anchor in the outer harbor off Portland wherever she could find an unoccupied spot. In spite of the confusion, the sudden influx of ships was gradually bedded down. Those that needed it were fueled and provisioned. The embarked troops tried to get a few hours sleep free of the rolling and pitching of the open sea. Each ship began preparations for picking up the next day's scheduled operations.

4

The weather was still bad during the midwatch, Monday, June 5th, but the chief meteorologist foresaw a break for at least two days beginning that day. Another agonizing early morning conference was held by the Supreme Commander. To cancel OVERLORD would mean regrouping and starting all over in about two weeks. By then the Germans would almost surely know of the plans. Momentum would be lost. General Eisenhower took a calculated risk and ordered the operation resumed. D-day was now set for June 6. The order was sent out. More than 4,000 naval ships, great and small, and 500,000 men picked up the threads of war which had been broken the preceding day.

The morning of the 5th the *Emmons'* crew enjoyed their second prebattle breakfast of steak and eggs. Since she had no assigned job until late afternoon she remained at anchor until 1300 when she and the *Doyle* got underway to rendezvous with Minesweeper Flotilla 31 south of Point Zed.

When the two destroyers got into the English Channel the weather had improved markedly although it was still rough and uncomfortable, even hazardous, for the hundreds of LCIs, LCTs, and similar landing craft heading toward their individual destinies. At this time the greatest worry for the destroyers was to avoid getting mixed up in the stream of ships strung along the route. By 1800 they had maneuvered through the pack and were well ahead. The rendezvous with the Canadian minesweepers south of Point Zed was made in good time and they began sweeping assault channel No. 3 through the German mine barrier protecting the French coast.

The sweeping operations started near the middle of the channel, approximately forty-five miles north of the French coast. As the sweeps worked steadily to the south in echelon, the *Emmons* with the *Doyle* took station behind the leading minesweeper, H.M.C.S. *Caraquet*. They were prepared to defend the formation against German E-boats, destroyers, and submarines known to be at Le Havre, Cherbourg and Brest. Before entering the German mine areas, about the middle of the English Channel, all hands were called to general quarters. They remained at battle stations until the afternoon of D+l, nearly forty-eight hours later.

Throughout the night the minesweepers slogged along toward the enemy coast ticking off one assignment after another, first the approach channel, then the transport area, and finally the fire support area. Fortunately no mines were found although the minesweepers to the westward, off Utah beach, dislodged a number. Around 0330 the job was finished and the flotilla withdrew to seaward. The *Emmons* and *Doyle* were left lying to about 3,000 yards offshore at the eastern end of the Omaha beaches. The destroyers had no specific assignment until the beginning of the shore bombardments at 0550, a few minutes before sunrise.

Psychologically, the period from the beginning of the minesweeping operation to daybreak of D-day was the worst of the entire operation for the *Emmons* because of the combination of darkness and the unknown. First, there was the possibility of mines. Second, German destroyers, or more likely E-boats, might come out of the night at any time. Above all, there was a heavily fortified enemy coast a few miles away. The coast was clearly outlined on the radar scope as the distance narrowed. The chance of detection grew as the hours and the minutes passed and the radar picture became sharper and sharper. There was little conversation among the men at general quarters. Some slept uneasily on their stations. After midnight the constant roar of planes crossing the Channel could be heard overhead. It was comforting to know that they were friendly. Sounds of bombing came from the southwest. Certainty by now the Germans must be alerted. Incredibly, there was no reaction along the Omaha beaches until after dawn.

5

The failure of the Germans to react more promptly against the invading fleet is all the more incredible when it is known from their war diary that reports of the paratrooper landings reached the command center of the Naval Staff between 0200 and 0300. At 0330 landing vessels were reported in the Bay of the Seine in the areas of Grandcamp, Port en Bessin, Ouistreham and the Channel Islands. At 0435 Naval Group West made additional reports on the air landing and advised that a PT-boat flotilla had been sent from Le Havre to reconnoiter the Grandcamp-Port-en-Bessin area. Six large ships had been reported lying to seven miles north of Port-en-Bessin since 0410. Presumably the report came from radar stations at Le Havre. Other reconnaissance craft were sent from Cherbourg to scout on either side of the Cotentin Peninsula. Curiously, they had nothing to report on their return to Cherbourg. On the other hand, the PT-boats from Le Havre ran into the British bombardment ships at the extreme eastern end of the British assault area about daybreak and were driven back after a brief encounter, not, however, before they torpedoed the Norwegian destroyer *Svenner.*

As daylight came, the reports became more frequent and the size of the invasion fleet became more apparent at Naval Staff Headquarters. There was disagreement between the Army and Navy Commands and the Armed Forces High Command as to whether the reports added up to the full-scale invasion which had been expected for so long. The Naval Staff had the advantage of frequent and largely accurate reports from subordinate commanders on the French Coast. At 0545 Naval Group West reported strong naval forces east of Barfleur and north of Port-en-Bessin and a patrol boat reported many vessels off the Bay of the Seine. Dense smoke screens were observed in the Cabourg-Houlgate area from Le Havre. Within a few minutes the invasion was well underway. By 0730 Naval Group West had defined the landing area as extending from St. Vaast on the west to Deauville on the east.

The Naval Staff still thought the weather was unsuitable for amphibious landings but correctly deduced that the Allies had gambled on an improvement over the forecasts. One of the earliest orders sent out was for U-boats on station in the Atlantic to send in frequent weather reports. They also initiated plans for countering the landings. Destroyer Flotilla 8 was moved from the Gironde to Brest to be in position to strike at the invaders. Submarines, which were counted on to disrupt the cross-Channel operations, were alerted to prepare for operations against the allied ships. Twelve were to take up attack positions in the Bay of Biscay. Six snorkel-equipped U-boats were ordered to leave Brest for operations in the western part of the Channel. Plans were activated to start mining the assault areas. Eventually the Germans hoped to use the new DM mines which were equipped with a pressure-activated firing device. Unfortunately for their plans, the highly secret new weapons were stored in the homeland and could not be brought to the scene of action for several days. Furthermore, they were in short supply.

By midmorning newscasts and statements from Allied leaders confirmed the magnitude of the attack. There was no doubt that the Germans faced a full scale invasion. But they had other areas to worry about as well. In Italy, their army had abandoned Rome and was in full retreat to the northward. Intelligence reports indicated that the Russian armies were ready for a major offensive. The Balkan satellites were showing signs of defection. There was much concern about the situation in the eastern Baltic where the Finns were showing signs of collapse. The immediate threat of new landings in the Mediterranean seemed to have eased, but still had to be reckoned with.

The Germans continued to worry about other landings along the western shores, a worry which was carefully fostered by allied counterintelligence. Even after the Normandy invasion had started the Germans were deluded into believing that a major army under General Patton was still left in England, prepared to strike at other areas. There was supposed to be another force in Scotland, capable of hitting Norway. The morning of D-day, decoy naval and merchant ships were deployed off other likely landing places in France to divert attention from the Normandy operation. As reports of activities in the Bay of the Seine reached the Naval Staff they were accompanied by reports of Allied ships off Boulogne, Pas-de-Calais, and the Channel Islands. The Pas-de-Calais coast had been considered by the Germans as a prime area for the Allied landing. So long as there was the threat of landings in other areas there was reluctance to shift forces to meet the emergency in Normandy.

The Naval Staff continued to believe that other landings would follow the one they were facing in Normandy. Shortly before noon a cautious message advised major commands that the landings between Le Havre and Barfleur was a major invasion, but that, based on pronouncements of allied leaders and disposition of their forces, other major operations could be expected to follow. The time and place could not be predicted. Hitler continued to be concerned about invasions in Norway, Denmark, and the German North Sea Coast. As late as June 10, after the commanders in the West had faced up to their grim situation in Normandy, he demurred at withdrawing divisions from Norway to Western Europe unless protection against allied landings on the coast was guaranteed by laying a minefield of the new pressure-activated DM 1 mines. In his report to the Naval Staff on the proviso, Captain Assman, of Hitler's staff, suggested that the Commander in Chief of the Navy, himself, advise the Fuehrer on the limitations of mines as a defense against enemy landings as he apparently expected too much from the new mines. The previous day Hitler had asked for an examination of the question of a protective minefield off the Jutland, Dutch, and Frisian coasts to prevent enemy warships from getting within range.

For whatever reasons, an armada of more than 4,000 ships was allowed to reach the landing beaches in the Bay of the Seine without opposition before daybreak on June 6. When the enemy did react, the *Emmons* was one of the first of the 4,000 to attract their attention.

Daylight found the *Emmons* and *Doyle* some 3,000 yards off Porten-Bessin, the dividing point between the American zone to the west and the British zone to the east, waiting to begin the scheduled shore bombardment. In the first light of day it was reassuring to see the heavy fire support ships of Task Group 124.9, including the *Texas,* flagship of Rear Admiral Carlton F. Bryant, commander of the Bombardment Group, standing down the swept channels to take their stations in the fire support areas. As they approached they split into two groups. To seaward of the *Emmons,* in the easternmost support area for Omaha, were the *Arkansas* and two Free French cruisers, the *Montcalm* and *Georges Leygues.*

Daylight was welcome. All hands were now wide awake and bracing for the inevitable discovery. It was not long in coming. It was almost a relief when at 0537 an enemy battery on the bluff east of Port-en-Bessin opened up on the *Emmons* with approximately ten rounds of medium caliber shells, registering several near misses. The last salvo was a straddle. About the same time the *Doyle* came under fire, probably from the same battery. Farther to seaward the *Arkansas* came under fire. The battle for Omaha beach had begun. The fire was promptly returned as the ship increased speed and began evasive maneuvers. Sixteen rounds from the 5" guns were expended. The *Doyle* took the same action. The counter-battery fire was effective. The enemy stopped firing—at least for a while. The duel lasted only a few minutes, but it broke the tension of waiting for the unknown. The *Emmons* had received her baptism of fire and had silenced the attacker.

6

A short time after the battle for Omaha beach was kicked off by the *Emmons* and her friends the scheduled pre-landing bombardment began, five minutes before the scheduled time. For forty minutes, two battleships, three cruisers, twelve destroyers, and a wide assortment of landing craft from the Close Gunfire Support Group pounded targets in and around the Omaha beaches. During the naval bombardment, wave after wave of Army bombers saturated the beaches to the east and west, but for some reason or other, probably the low lying clouds, the air bombardment scheduled for delivery on the Omaha beaches did not materialize. About five minutes before H-hour, 0630, the din slackened a little as the bombarding ships lifted their fire from the beach area to previously assigned inland targets. Rocket launchers approached the beaches and saturated them with several thousand rockets. At this point it was hard to believe that anything could survive the heavy pounding. Yet when the first wave of landing craft hit the beach they were met by a devastating fire from German batteries which very nearly stopped the landings at Omaha beach before the troops could get a toe hold.

The *Emmons'* assigned pre-landing targets were in the vicinity of Coleville-sur-Mer, back of Fox Green Beach. From a position 2,000 yards offshore to the east of the boat lanes she poured 258 rounds of 5" common and AA common into them without any casualties except for ruptures in the hydraulic lines of the rammers of No. 2 gun on the second round and of No. 1 on the sixtieth. Coxswain Edward N. Tostanoski, USNR, of No. 2 crew, rammed 65 rounds by hand. The gun didn't miss a single salvo. Both lines were promptly brazed during the first lull in the action and gave no further trouble.

After the first few rounds the targets were obscured by heavy clouds of smoke and dust. It became virtually impossible to spot. Reliance had to be placed on ranges and bearings transmitted to Control from a navigational plot maintained by CIC. In turn, navigational position was kept by radar bearings and ranges of points along the shore. Of these, the Port-en-Bessin breakwater was the sharpest. Indeed, that breakwater became the *Emmons*'s beacon for the next few days and nights. Because of the swift currents created by a tidal range of twenty-two feet, keeping an accurate position plot was a continuous chore. During low visibility it would have been impossible without radar.

Weather conditions around H-hour were satisfactory for ships the size of destroyers—less so for the landing craft which had to make a ten-mile run in from the Transport Area offshore. This, in spite of the fact that there had been a marked change in the weather in the last twenty-four hours. Winds had shifted to the southwest and were blowing offshore at a moderate Force 3. But the seas inshore were still very choppy with four to five foot breakers on the beach. Conditions were much worse to seaward. Visibility was about five miles where not affected by the smoke and dust of battle. H-hour had been chosen to take advantage of a rising tide. Low water came at about 0530, so during the bombardment period it was flooding and running eastward at about two knots. Throughout the morning it would pick up strength. The tides and currents continued to be a major problem off Omaha, a close second to the Germans.

According to plan, the *Emmons* ceased firing at targets in the Colleville five minutes before H-hour and began firing at designated target areas farther inland, using air bursts, to interdict possible troop movements into the landing beach areas. After twenty minutes of this fire it was stopped on the supposition that by that time our troops would be moving inland. That, unfortunately, was not the case at Omaha Beach.

7

After the smoke and dust settled the *Emmons* had an ideal position for observing the landings. There was one person aboard who not only had the time but was under orders to observe and record what he saw for posterity. For a week Lieutenant Dwight Shepler, USNR, Navy Combat Artist, on board for temporary duty, hopped about the ship recording his impressions on a seemingly inexhaustible series of sketch pads. His sketches were eventually incorporated in two forceful paintings of the happening at Omaha Beach. Both are now part of the Navy Combat Artists Exhibition and have been shown throughout the country. One portrays the *Emmons* with guns ablaze off the rugged cliffs to the east of the Omaha beaches. The other "The Battle for Fox Green Beach, Omaha" also features the DD457 in the midst of battle. It captures as nearly as any one medium can the grandeur and the near tragedy of the landing at Omaha. Shepler's painting has been widely used to illustrate books on the Normandy Invasion and before his death the artist reproduced "Battle for Fox Green Beach" as a mural on the wall of the midshipmen's mess at the Naval Academy.

While the shore bombardment was going on the assault waves could be seen circling near the line of departure waiting to make the run in. Some of the landing craft seemed to be having heavy going. A few were dead in the water, their motors drowned out. As the naval gunfire reached a crescendo the first wave was started toward the beaches. The touchdown was made on time but could not be clearly seen from the *Emmons*'s bridge because of the curtain of smoke drifting to seaward. Shortly after the landing craft disappeared in the smoke all hell seemed to break loose as revived German batteries and enfilading machine guns zeroed in on the beaches. The roar of exploding shells and detonation of ammunition indicated hits on landing craft and vehicles. The red glow of burning vessels and vehicles confirmed that the invaders were meeting heavy opposition. Later reports indicated a disaster was in the making.

The first wave consisted of light amphibious tanks followed by demolition teams and infantry. The tanks were to spearhead the attack while the demolition team cleared channels for succeeding waves through the mined obstacles between high and low water. Many of the tanks, destined for Easy and Fox beaches on the east, foundered before they ever reached land. Most of those which did make it were destroyed on the beaches. The demolition teams suffered heavy casualties and were unable to clear the obstacles from the required number of channels before high water. Many follow-up craft were destroyed trying to pick their own channels through the obstacles. Others were held up by wrecked craft blocking the cleared channels. Without tank support the troops were unable to advance against the carefully placed enemy guns.

When the smoke screen lifted it was apparent that the landing was not going according to plan. Burned out and burning tanks stood useless near the water's edge. Several landing craft were wrecks blocking access to the beach for others. Some were burning. Many others unable to land were milling about offshore trying to find an opening to the beaches. The rising tide was beginning to refloat other wrecks. Dead and wounded were scattered over the open beach. The men that had made it across the open beach were huddled behind a low stone wall. The Germans were still firing at the landing craft which were attempting to unload. Some stalled landing craft drifted helplessly to the eastward under the cliffs between Port-en-Bessin and the landing beaches, sitting ducks for any guns concealed on the cliffs. At this point the enemy was apparently more interested in the beaches than in disabled landing craft. Perhaps they couldn't bring their guns to bear. Maybe they considered the disabled craft harmless. At any rate they continued to concentrate fire on the beaches. Occasionally they would turn their sights seaward.

Following the bombardment the *Emmons* began to maneuver offshore searching for targets of opportunity while trying to contact her assigned shore fire control party. Repeated attempts throughout the day to raise them on authorized voice and CW circuits brought no results until late in the day when a test transmission on a CW auxiliary circuit was acknowledged and Easy Money was told to "Standby-wait." That was all. Attempts were continued for two more days with no return whatsoever. It is likely that the one transmission was by another party on the wrong circuit or it could have been German counterintelligence. If the latter, they failed to exploit the opening. The S.F.C.P. had been scheduled to land in an early wave at H+30 minutes while the going was the toughest. The simplest explanation is that their equipment was drowned out during the wet landing, but it is possible that the personnel were killed or wounded before their equipment could be started.

Whatever the reason, throughout the day the *Emmons* was obliged to confine her firing to targets of opportunity or those specifically designated by the commander of the Fire Support Group. Aboard ship the frustration at not being able to do more to relieve the pressure on the landing beaches was almost unbearable. Without positive knowledge of the location of the front line positions of our own troops considerable time was spent waiting for a target to reveal itself and then to positively identify it as enemy. During the morning of D-day the latter problem was not so great—the front lines were obviously the beaches. Later, as the troops began to push inland, greater care had to be taken not to fire on friendly formations.

Even without the benefit of a shore party to direct fire there was plenty to do. Throughout D-day 873 rounds of 5"/38 and 1,014 rounds of 40mm ammunition were expended on enemy targets. Of the 5" rounds, 574 were fired at targets of opportunity or as directed over voice circuits by the Fire Support Group Commander or his deputy for destroyers. Easy Money truly earned her money that day.

During most of the day the *Emmons* kept station 1,000 to 3,000 yards to seaward of the steep cliffs stretching about 2 1/2 miles, east to west, between Port-en-Bessin to the east and Fox Green beach to the west. From this area there was an excellent view of the fishing village and the beleaguered landing beaches. The view of the cliffs was not as good as the patrol area was too close in to see over the crest. Technically, Port-en-Bessin was in the British sector of responsibility, but in the natural course of events the town and its surroundings became the focal point of Easy Money's attention. Shortly after breakfast had been served at battle stations—no steak and eggs this time—shore batteries near Port-en-Bessin turned their attention to the *Emmons* and other destroyers near her. Again shells dropped uncomfortably close. Evasive maneuvers were started at once and fire on suspected sources on either side of Port-en-Bessin was initiated. The evasive action and the counter fire apparently were effective as each successive salvo fell farther from the ship. The most disconcerting part of the action was the whine of shells passing overhead or nearby. It must be admitted that there was a tendency to duck when the high pitched sound was heard, preferably behind some solid object. It is not known whether the counter fire found any German guns, but the exchange ended in victory for Easy Money, as the shelling stopped after counter fire was started.

Following this exchange the *Emmons* continued to patrol off the cliffs, firing occasionally at likely gun sites. During this period none were positively identified and the shore batteries paid little attention to the destroyers. The situation on the beach was still precarious. Attempts to land were actually stopped for an hour or so to regroup the waves of disorganized landing craft milling about offshore and to chart safe channels through the remaining underwater obstacles. During this period Captain Harry Sanders, Commander Destroyer Fire Support Group, ordered the destroyers to close in on the beaches to render close support for the troops. This was a difficult order to follow as most of them, including the *Emmons,* were already as close to the shore as they could get without danger of grounding. However, they pushed their luck even further and none ran aground. The order confirmed what most already knew—that the attack was bogged down. The Germans had their best chance of the invasion to drive the troops off the beach but were unable to bring up reinforcements because of naval gunfire. However, they could, and did, continue to prevent significant buildup at Omaha during the morning by concentrated heavy artillery and machinegun fire.

From time to time the shore batteries would turn their fire on the fire support ships offshore, much as one would occasionally take a slap at an annoying insect while concentrating on a more urgent task. For the most part their fire to seaward was sporadic and ineffective. For one thing, evasive action seemed to throw their aim off. For another, they were not persistent. Usually they ceased fire when their targets fired back. Only one destroyer off Omaha was hit. That was the *Baldwin,* and her damage was superficial.

Since a large amount of the fire in the *Emmons'* area came from around Port-en-Bessin, that town was closely watched for any signs of enemy activity. It was quiet until around noon when the 40mm battery officer reported that enemy troops were marching down the main street and requested permission to fire. The bridge confirmed the movement of a small formation of blue clad figures, probably naval personnel, and the battery was ordered to commence fire. The first shells fell behind the formation. This was sufficient. The sailors dived into alleys and houses as a few more salvoes dusted off the now empty street.

No further signs of life were observed in the town. The sailors either kept indoors or slipped away through the back streets. Later, high tide brought the upper part of a small patrol craft into view from the gun director. The craft had been hidden by the breakwater at low water and through most of the flood tide. Perhaps the sailors previously fired on were its crew abandoning ship. The *Emmons* and *Doyle* teamed up to render it harmless. Because of the breakwater, air bursts had to be used.

During the noon hour the *Emmons* was attacked a fourth time when a gun in what appeared to be a camouflaged casemate east of Port-en-Bessin tried to zero in on her. The emplacement had not been spotted by earlier visual checks of the area surrounding the town. Cleverly concealed in a fold of the hills it commanded a good view of the coast and could not be seen from seaward except from ships close to the shore. Conversely, its fire had to be confined to the beaches and targets close inshore. Its first few salvoes were close, but as soon as evasive action was taken they drifted away from the ship. As soon as the gun was located counter battery fire was opened and the firing stopped. Soon after, several men were seen disappearing behind a curve of the hill back of the target. Since it was not absolutely certain that the gun was disabled the *Arkansas* was called in to make doubly sure. With Easy Money spotting, the target was demolished with a few rounds from her 12" guns. When advised that the mission was a success the jovial reply from the old Arkie was "Roger, you do believe in Easy Money."

8

By noon the tide in the Bay of the Seine had turned and was beginning to set to the westward. Offshore observers could also detect a change in the tide of battle. Following the morning pause the regrouped landing craft resumed their landings in a more orderly fashion. But some of them never made it to the beach. Others were destroyed on the beach. The Germans were still capable of pouring murderous artillery and machine gun fire onto the landing areas. The underwater obstacles remained a hazard, but they too were being slowly eliminated as the tide ebbed. In the early afternoon observers on the *Emmons'* bridge could see small squads of troops moving out of their shelter behind the breakwater and disappearing up the draws leading inland from the seashore. One member of the director crew recounts seeing several army vehicles blown up at the same spot where the road from the beach curved around a spur in the hills. This problem was taken care of in good fashion by the well-trained GIs. The *Emmons'* observer saw a jeep approach the curve, but just before it got there its passengers bailed out and disappeared on either side of the road. Some minutes later other vehicles were negotiating the curve unmolested. Now, more than ever, the lack of a shore fire control party was felt. Extra care had to be taken before opening fire on suspected enemy positions.

Fewer disabled craft were noted in the Eastern Fire Support Area. One reason, of course, was that the ebbing tide was now carrying them to the west. The rescue craft were also catching up with their work. Shortly after noon the *Emmons* sighted a stalled Army Duck and took it in tow. Its engine had been drowned out and water had gotten into the gas. While the ship's engineers helped get the motor started the crew of the Duck was given sandwiches and fresh coffee. When the motor was started the craft was sent on its way.

In this case bread cast upon the waters was returned. One of the GIs aboard the Duck, Private First Class J. A. Bourgeois, had injured his ankle. It was decided that he should remain aboard the destroyer until he could be transferred to a medical facility. In spite of his injured ankle, Bourgeois climbed to the fire control director where he was of invaluable assistance in identifying friendly troops. The unofficial GI spotter was happy to be aboard ship except when shells were whistling by. Then he wished he were ashore because he "couldn't dig a fox hole in a steel deck."

Compared to the morning's activities the afternoon was relatively quiet. The situation was improving, but far too many shells were still finding the beaches from all directions except from seaward. Between 1300 and sunset the *Emmons* was involved in only three engagements with the enemy. The first came at 1537 when an enemy mortar post concealed at the intersection of two hedgerows behind Fox Beach was neutralized with 44 rounds of 5"/38. The mortar had revealed its position by puffs of smoke which synchronized with shells falling on the sand and water near the beaching points. No further fire was observed from this point.

Fire on the mortar had just been completed when an urgent message came in from the LCI 93 on nearby Fox Green beach. Disabled and under fire she wanted her wounded taken off. At the moment no targets were in view so a call for volunteers to man the whaleboat for the rescue mission was made over the intercom. The response was overwhelming. The exec selected a crew from men who could be spared from their battle stations if firing was renewed. The boat was gone from the ship only thirty-three minutes, but a lot was accomplished in that short time. As the boat neared the shore, the crew helped a number of troops struggling to get ashore under heavy packs. Some shells were still falling along the beaches. Fortunately, none fell near the whaleboat. Unable to locate the LCI 93 from close-in some of the crew went ashore to scout along the beach to locate her. Some of these men had the satisfaction of helping troops loosen the dogs on the hatch of what was apparently an abandoned casemated 3" gun. To everyone's amazement four German artillerymen emerged with their hands in the air. Once the LCI 93 was located her wounded and other survivors were picked up. All of them were Coast Guard men. Somewhere along the line three navy men from the LCI 487 were added. By the time the whaleboat returned to the ship they had on board six wounded and eighteen other survivors of the two LCIs. The medical officer, Lieutenant Charlie Williamson, and his assistants took care of the wounded while the others were given fresh clothing and a bunk to get a little rest. The most seriously wounded had had his throat torn open by shrapnel.

The next engagement was the high point of the day's action for the gunners. At 1815 Admiral Bryant announced that it was believed the tower of the Colleville-sur-Mer church was being used by the Germans as an observation post and asked if any of the destroyers were in good position to knock it out. Since it was clearly visible and within easy range, Easy Money eagerly volunteered for the task. The tower crumbled after sixty-six rounds—a remarkable bit of sharp shooting for such a target. Years later, on a wintry December day, the commanding officer of the *Emmons* at the time of the invasion, visited the Omaha beaches under the tutelage of a French taxi driver. Over Pernods at Colleville-sur-Mer, the cabbie pointed to the recently restored church tower and remarked that it had been destroyed by the Germans. It was not considered necessary to disillusion him. In a final analysis he was right.

The day's final engagement occurred just before nightfall. At 2100 while lying offshore west of Port-en-Bessin, an enemy battery believed to be four 88mm guns opened fire on the *Emmons* and *Doyle*. This fire was the most accurate yet. One four-gun salvo neatly outlined the *Emmons's* fantail, one to port, another to starboard and two close astern. The shells seemed to come from the top of the cliff. Since no emplacements could be located it is possible that the source was a battery of tanks at the crest. Both destroyers cruised along close to the face of the cliff peppering the crest with 5"/38 and 40mm. Results could not be observed, but no more shots were directed at the destroyers.

9

"The longest day in the year" as some have described D-day at Normandy was almost over. At dusk the ship moved a few hundred yards to seaward to the position she had occupied at first light, about 3,000 yards off Port-en-Bessin. There was less danger of grounding there with the rise and fall of the tides. As part of the Fire Support Group, she remained subject to call in support of the advancing troops or to repel any counterattacks on the beach positions. An appreciable number of men with the necessary support vehicles, including tanks and artillery, were now passing over the landing beaches. A few shells were still falling, but the great danger was now from Rommel's panzer divisions attempting to get up to the landing areas before they could be consolidated. Had Easy Money been called on to repel an attack she would have had to rely on some other ship's shore fire control party for target information or resort to star shells. Shore Fire Control Party No. 9 was still unaccounted for.

After dark the danger for the ships offshore from the sea and the sky increased. Throughout the day the weakened *Luftwaffe* had been unable to mount a significant attack. German submarines, destroyers, and E-boats had been unable to get near the invading fleet. Their chances were improved under cover of darkness, especially for the hit and run E-boats.

The *Emmons* settled down to a night of watchful waiting. In consideration of the possibility of air and sea attack and her somewhat lonesome position at the dividing line between British and American sectors the crew was kept at general quarters. After a long, active day most men stretched out as best they could to get a little rest before the next alert. By midnight most were asleep. Those who had to remain awake went over the day's events in their minds and wondered what the next few hours would bring.

They had every reason to be proud of their performance so far. The failure to contact the shore fire control party had been a major disappointment. Nevertheless, the ship had engaged the enemy at every possible opportunity. She had been attacked and had silenced the attackers without harm to herself. When conditions had permitted she had helped disabled craft—one was returned to battle. She had given medical help to the wounded.

There is no definitive way to evaluate the effect the *Emmons* had on the landings at Omaha, but there can be no doubt she contributed her share to keeping the attack going when the outcome was in the balance. Destroyers at Omaha Beach are credited with saving the landing. Gordon A. Harrison, the official Army Historian for World War II, records that the movement off the beaches at Omaha was "materially aided by the bold action of destroyers which came within a few hundred yards of the beach and delivered direct fire wherever they could observe enemy activity." Admiral John L. Hall, the commander of the assault force at Omaha, paid special tribute to the destroyers, including the *Emmons,* for their actions at Omaha.

The enemy also recognized the effects of naval gunfire. Many of the German generals in their current reports, and in later postmortem analyses, attributed their failure to stop the invasion to allied air superiority and the devastating and unexpected effects of naval gunfire on their defense plans, particularly in the inability to move up reinforcements within the range of naval guns. A June 11 assessment of the situation by Rommel noted the decisiveness of the extraordinarily strong and crushing superiority of the Allied Air Force and the effects of the heavy navy artillery. Several days later at a conference between the Fuehrer and his top commanders in the West, von Rundstedt and Rommel, one of the points made was the difficulty of bringing up reserves and supplies in the face of enemy air superiority and heavy artillery. It was noted that "our own attacks do not make any progress within the range of the enemy naval artillery." Hitler came to the conclusion that the elimination and impairment of the enemy naval forces, particularly of the battleships, was the only relief for the land front. His solution was the mining of the entire area by the German Air Force regardless of its effects on movements of their own surface ships. He asked for a report on the time the first mines using the DM 1 pressure firing device could be deployed.

Prisoners from the lower ranks captured at Normandy also acknowledged the demoralizing effects of naval gunfire to their interrogators. A *German Military Journal* broadcast of June 16, 1944, in an attempt to explain their failure at the beaches to the German people, stated that German troops were showing much more resistance now that the fighting was getting beyond the range of naval guns. The broadcast went on to explain that the fire curtain provided by the guns of the Navy so far had proven to be one of the best trump cards of the Anglo-American invasion.

10

About half an hour before midnight of D-day the Germans made a light air raid over the transport area to seaward. The sounds of battle could be heard. No plane approached the *Emmons* close enough to open fire.

But there was a follow-up to the air attack farther inshore. Shortly after midnight one of the lookouts reported a cry for help, in English, and spotted an object in the water. Assuming it was one of the many soldiers and sailors who had never made it to the beach that day, the captain ordered the engines reversed. The gig was lowered to investigate. Shortly, the boat came back to the ship, not with an American as expected, but a German aviator. By this time he was unconscious but still breathing. He must have made the call for help with his last conscious breath. As quickly as possible he was rushed to the battle dressing station in the wardroom. He was identified as Captain F. W. Waldemar Baetke, German Air Force. It is probable that he had been hit in the air action to the north and had bailed out closer to shore.

It is indicative of the kindness of the American sailor that there was as much concern for Baetke's survival as there would have been for one of our own. Doc Williamson and willing assistants worked as valiantly over him as they had over the crewmen from LCI 93 nine hours earlier. One of those assisting was Ensign J. J. Gilligan, later governor of Ohio, who even tried artificial resuscitation on the waterlogged aviator. But he had too many injuries and the efforts were in vain. Baetke expired on the wardroom table less than an hour after he had been fished from the water. There is an interesting note to this event. Ten months later, almost to the day, the *Emmons* was hit by five *kamikazes* off Okinawa and had to be abandoned. As the survivors abandoned the ship they saw one of the Japanese pilots, still strapped in his seat, wedged in the hatch leading to the after compartment. Thus, the survivors can take grim satisfaction in having served on a ship which had the unique experience of having both a German and a Japanese enemy aviator die on board.

11

Dawn of D+l found Easy Money in the same position off Port-en-Bessin. The usual morning muster was taken at 0800. The report of "no absentees" was not unexpected. The crew had had no chance to leave their battle stations for thirty-six hours except to relieve themselves or to fetch rations from the galley. The gig had left the ship on a rescue mission and had returned with more men than when it shoved off.

The enemy aviator had died during the midwatch. In the absence of proper morgue facilities his body was temporarily resting in the medical officer's stateroom awaiting removal and burial by the Graves Registration people ashore. For more than twenty-four hours he remained there, but the shore parties were too busy to respond to requests for removal. The morning of the second day the doctor informed the captain that some action had to be taken. The German aviator was buried at sea with appropriate Christian services a few thousand yards off the shores he had sought vainly to defend.

Eleven days later another casualty of the invasion was recovered from the sea some miles off the Utah beaches. This time it proved to be a fellow navy man, identified as W. F. Hopper, of Alabama. When no response was received from the Grave Registration Service to take charge of the body it was necessary to return it to the sea with a Christian burial service and full honors in accordance with Navy tradition.

Throughout D+l the *Emmons* remained on station in the fire support area near Port en Bessin, hoping in vain for a call from her missing shore fire control party. By now the fishing port was a familiar sight. It remained quiet throughout the day although it was not occupied by British troops until late in the evening.

In the meantime a few shots were taken on suspected enemy positions. Because the position of our own troops was now known only within broad limits fire was opened on these positions reluctantly and only after careful checking. For a few hours in the morning the *Baldwin*'s S.F.C.P. was turned over to Easy Money. Only one call for fire came in during the period. It was a real pleasure to fire on an enemy position near Mosles without having to check and double check as to its hostile character. It was doubly satisfying to have the spotters report destruction of the target after fifteen minutes and thirty rounds. The rest of the time was spent simply watching and waiting.

The last target ashore was a suspected mobile battery atop the cliffs west of Port-en-Bessin, engaged at about 1000. Thereafter no targets were spotted which could safely be assumed as enemy. Coleville was secured by troops of the First

Division around 1100 and it was assumed that they were expanding the bridgehead to the eastward as well. Sporadic shots were still falling on the beaches when the *Emmons* left the fire support area the morning of D+3.

Conditions had stabilized enough by 1300 on D+l that the ship secured from general quarters. The crew had been at battle stations since joining the minesweepers before sundown on D-l, the better part of two days. At that, they probably got as much rest on general quarters stations as they did for the next two days.

12

During the midwatch of D+2, Thursday, June 8, the *Emmons* was ordered to move to seaward to provide additional aircraft protection for the *Arkansas* against hostile aircraft in the vicinity. Twice between midnight and daybreak she laid down a smokescreen to hide the Arkie from unidentified aircraft detected on radar. None came close enough to present a profitable target. In fact, the almost nightly air raids were largely ineffective against the invasion fleet as far as bombing attacks were concerned. By far the greatest offshore damage was caused by mines dropped under cover of darkness by aircraft, E-boats and other fast craft operating out of Cherbourg and Le Havre.

The *Emmons* remained with the *Arkansas* during most of D+2, the 8th, but toward dusk was ordered to take a station on the "Dixie" line, a defensive picket line established to seaward of the assault area to guard against penetration by the few surface craft available to the enemy. Being near the middle of the assault area the Omaha area was less accessible to hit-and-run forays of E-boats and mine laying craft than those on the eastern and western flanks, adjacent to the German-held bases of Le Havre and Cherbourg. Continuous air and surface patrols to the east and west of the assault area prevented the sizeable submarine fleet, which the Germans had counted on to disrupt the build-up, from reaching the crucial parts of the Channel. Neither could the German destroyers based on ports of occupied France penetrate the protective barriers. Still there were plenty of alarms both day and night, most of them false. General quarters were sounded every two or three hours during the day and the ship stayed at battle stations from sunset to sunrise each night. It was not until the ship went back to Plymouth to replenish ammunition and fuel that anyone had a full rest. No matter how short the periods between alarms any chance to bathe and change into clean uniforms was welcomed. So were hot meals.

While she was on the Dixie line the night of June 8-9, or later for that matter, Easy Money did not encounter a single enemy ship. But, given the great number of ships entering or leaving the assault area, it is not surprising that there were frequent unidentified blips on the radar scopes. There was no assurance that a slow-moving contact which gave every indication of being harmless might not suddenly increase speed, change course, and dash in for an attack. Until a contact was positively identified by recognition signals or otherwise, it was necessary to be able to open fire at any time if it turned out to be hostile. Gun Control and the guns were always alerted and tracked the target along with the search radars, prepared to open fire if necessary.

In each instance the suspect was eventually identified as friendly. But there were many tense moments until the target gave the right answers to challenges. The question was when to stop tracking and start shooting. The ultimate test became illumination with star shells. On her first night on picket duty Easy Money was faced with the question when a small landing craft plowing blithely along approached the line oblivious to the fact that four guns were trained on it. After repeated failures to get a response the order to load and fire star shells went up to Control. The star shells revealed a small landing craft. Whatever the feeling may have been aboard the inbound craft, a sigh of relief went up from the bridge and control tower of Easy Money—more for the potential target than for the *Emmons* herself. On another occasion the target identified itself just before the order to fire star shells was given. The guns had to be unloaded through the muzzles.

The *Emmons* was not the only one to resort to illumination. Throughout the night illuminating shells were fired up and down the Dixie line. Several times she herself was caught in the light of descending star shells. It was assumed that the light came from friendly sources, but it gave a feeling of naked defenselessness to be caught in the glare of descending flares without knowing their source. The feeling was even worse whenever flares dropped by aircraft lighted the area.

Dixie line became a sort of halfway house for destroyers scheduled to return to England for replenishment. This was true for the *Emmons.* With the light of morning she, with the *Baldwin* and *Herndon,* joined the *Texas* to cross the Channel to Plymouth.

13

The stay in Plymouth was all too short, two nights and one day. While the ship was taking on fuel and ammunition, the LCI crews picked up off the French beaches were put ashore. Pfc. Bourgeois was sent to the Casualty Evacuation Center at Plymouth. The wounded Coast Guardsmen were turned over to the naval dispensary, while the other survivors of LCIs 93 and 487 were transferred back to the Eleventh Amphibious Force. With characteristic thoroughness, agents of the British Intelligence Service were among the first to board the ship when she docked. They wanted to know every minute detail of the rescue and death of the German aviator down to details of his uniform. There was really little to tell them beyond the fact that he was picked up and had died.

One section was lucky enough to get liberty on the afternoon and night of the tenth. There was not one absentee when the ship got underway bright and early the next morning to return to Normandy.

Back in the assault area the *Emmons* was once again assigned to picket duty on the Dixie line protecting the Omaha area. Compared to the first three days of the invasion this duty was quiet and unexciting, but hardly restful. During the day the ship would remain at anchor near the transport area, with half her guns manned, and prepared to get underway at short notice. Before sunset she got underway to patrol the picket line. From sunset to sunrise all hands remained on battle stations. At sunrise condition 2 watches would be set and she would return to her anchorage for what little rest and rudimentary upkeep could be had under the circumstances. This routine lasted until June 15, when she was ordered to report to Commander Task Force 129.

The commander of Task Force 129 was Rear Admiral Morton L. Deyo, the last commander of old Task Force 22 back in Casco Bay. His flagship was the cruiser *Tuscaloosa* which had been one of the heavy ships of that force. Whether by accident or design, all the ships of that force present at Normandy were being assembled to form a new gunfire support force for the Army as the old assault organization was being phased out. When the *Emmons* reported, Destroyer Squadron 10 was once more reunited, except for the *Macomb* and the *Corry*. The squadron commander, Captain Converse, was now Commander Task Group 129.3, the screen commander for Task Force 129. Twelve other destroyers in addition to the seven of Squadron 10 were assigned to the screening group. The *Macomb* was still in the Mediterranean and the *Corry* had been sunk by a mine off the Cotentin Peninsula on D-day.

By now most of the enemy targets were beyond the range of the destroyers' guns, so they were limited to escort duty and antiaircraft protection. The *Emmons* spent most of her time at the latter at the Utah beach anchorage. The routine was much the same as picket duty at Omaha except that the destroyers remained anchored in designated areas. During hours of darkness the anchor was kept at short stay and they were prepared to get underway at short notice. All battle stations were manned from sunset to sunrise. During the day condition watches were set and the anchor chain veered to normal. There was more threat from the air at Utah than at Omaha, probably because the area was so close to the battle going on for the strategic port of Cherbourg.

Nearly every night there were red alerts, warnings of unidentified aircraft in the area. Very few of them produced tangible targets. On two separate occasions the *Emmons* locked on potential enemy bogies. Once fire was withheld because there was doubt as to whether the plane was a friend or foe. The other time five rounds of five inch and several bursts of machine gun fire were let loose at a plane whose actions appeared to be anything but friendly. There were no signs of hits as the target moved out of range. It was possibly on a mine-laying mission.

Occasionally, the battleships and cruisers were called in to support the Army as it closed in on Cherbourg. From the beginning that city at the tip of the Cotentin Peninsula played an important part in the planning for OVERLORD. Its capture was essential as a safe, secure port through which troops and equipment could be moved in quantity under all weather conditions. During the assault phase of the invasion reliance was placed on artificial harbors made by sinking old hulks and concrete caissons to form a breakwater behind which floating piers from the beach were installed. These makeshift ports, or "Mulberries" and "Gooseberries" as they were called in the plans, served well during the opening phases of the invasion, but their capacity was limited, and cargo handling depended almost as much on muscle as on sophisticated equipment. Further, they were vulnerable to storms—operations could be slowed down or disrupted by adverse weather.

That is exactly what happened when an unexpected and unforecasted northeast gale struck the landing beaches on June 19. Just when supplies were beginning to flow over the beaches at a satisfactory and predictable pace they were halted for three days, until the 22nd. By then ammunition, fuel, and other supplies for the advancing army were beginning to get low. The Mulberries and the Gooseberries were left in a shambles. The largest Mulberry, in the Omaha sector was so badly damaged that it was deemed pointless to try to restore it to full capacity. After the storm abated, about 800 craft of all sizes, with various degrees of damage, were left stranded on the beaches. Emergency measures were taken to get them back into operation. About 600, including coasters and other small vessels, were repaired and refloated by the next spring tide, July 8. Another 100 were refloated later. In the meantime, in the absence of the essential small craft, LSTs, coasters, and similar ships were "dried out." That is, they were run on the beach on a high tide and were left high and dry to unload their cargoes directly onto the beach without benefit of boats while the tide was out. This unorthodox procedure proved so successful that it was adopted on a regular basis. However, at best, unloading on open beaches was precarious. Under these conditions the capture and rebuilding of the all-weather port installations at Cherbourg was all the more important.

12

Bombardment of Cherbourg

o o o o o o o o o o o o o o o o o o o o o o o o o o o o o o

12 to 16

.... 1210 enemy shore batteries opened fire on Allied Mine Sweepers. 1212 heavy ships opened fire on shore installations and selected gun emplacements. 1258 opened fire with main battery on enemy gun emplacements, bearing 200°(t), 15,000 yards, Fort de l'Est, Cherbourg, France. Unidentified enemy battery returned fire obtaining near misses. Retired to northward behind smoke laid by USS RODMAN. 1313 ceased firing...

—***Emmons*** *Log, June 25, 1944*

The capture of Cherbourg had been one of the first objectives of the invasion. The disruption of supplies through the makeshift harbors at the beaches made its capture all the more imperative. Before the gale the Army's VII Corps had reached the west coast of the Cotentin Peninsula, cutting off a part of the German Seventh Army, under General Karl-Wilhelm von Schlieben, in the northern part of the peninsula. The German general was authorized to withdraw to the prepared defenses of Cherbourg and given authority to take whatever steps he considered necessary to defend the port. During the gale the Americans reached the outer ring of Cherbourg's defenses four to six miles outside the city. By the 21st they were prepared for the final assault. First, however, they gave the Germans a chance to surrender—a chance which was ignored.

The Germans were well aware of the importance of Cherbourg's port to the Allies. Top ranking commanders early recognized this fact and were determined to make its capture as costly as possible. Field Marshal Rommel early listed the cutting of the Cotentin Peninsula and the capture of Cherbourg as one of the

Allies' primary objectives. After the Allied bridgehead was secure the Germans apparently recognized that Cherbourg's fall was likely and ordered systematic destruction of its harbor. After June 10, there are frequent progress reports of the demolition in the Naval Staff War Diaries. Even Hitler seemed reconciled to its eventual loss. After the VII Corps reached the city's outer defenses he sent von Schlieben a characteristically bombastic exhortation that even if it came to the worst he was to "defend even to the last dugout" and turn over to the enemy "not a harbor, but a field covered with ruins."

The German naval high command tried to assist their besieged forces in every way possible. An Allied naval bombardment of the port was considered inevitable and five submarines were ordered to shift their patrols to waters north of Cherbourg. Delivery of ammunition and critical supplies by PT boat and submarine was initiated. The destruction of port facilities continued. The port was used as a base for PT boats until the 24th, when all craft able to move, except four harbor patrol and sea rescue boats, were evacuated to ports in Brittany and the Channel Islands. Based on the pessimistic reports of General von Schlieben, the high command concluded the loss of Cherbourg unavoidable, but Grand Admiral Doenitz sent an encouraging message exhorting the defenders to hold out as long as possible. He told them that every day "gained in preventing the enemy from taking this large harbor will be of decisive importance." Hitler, with total disregard for the realities of the situation, directed the Commanding General of the West to investigate the possibility of an advance with forces "becoming available within the next few days" to annihilate the American forces attacking Cherbourg. A plan, including details of forces available and the time required for supplies was to be submitted immediately by teletype.

Cherbourg was doomed, but its final conquest was likely to prove costly. And the Germans were right that each day it held out would give them that much more time to strengthen their defenses against the Allied push to the French heartland. Although von Schlieben considered the situation hopeless, numerous isolated strong points remained, some heavily armed. About the only palatable reports reaching the high command from Cherbourg at this point were those of the Naval Commander, Normandy, who was charged with the naval defense of the city and the carrying out of the order to render the port useless to its captors. In addition to reporting the destruction of the port facilities and mining of the harbor, he reported on the 24th, that the coastal batteries and emergency antiaircraft guns were maintaining their harassing fire against American troops to landward. Obviously, he meant those which could be turned around. In a later report he stated that all the batteries of the northern front were practically undestroyed and ready for action. Unfortunately, he added, they were pointed in the wrong direction, that is, to seaward.

The inner defenses of Cherbourg consisted of both fixed and mobile batteries, ranging from 75 to 280mm. Most of the larger guns were fixed in heavily armored casemates and had limited arcs of fire, largely to seaward. Others were movable. One battery was reported as two 280mm railway guns on turntables, without tracks. As the VII Corps closed in, General Omar Bradley, Commander of the First Army, recognizing that these batteries would be costly to knock out, asked for a naval bombardment of Cherbourg and its defenses to be synchronized with the final assault. The task was assigned to Task Force 129 under Admiral Deyo who assembled the ships assigned at Portland, England, for planning and briefing. He left Utah anchorage late the 21st of June in his flagship, the *Tuscaloosa,* accompanied by the *Quincy,* the British cruisers *Enterprise* and *Glasgow,* and nine destroyers, including the *Emmons.* It was the last farewell to Normandy for Easy Money.

2

The cruisers and destroyers arrived at Portland the 22nd, where they were joined by Battleship Division 5, the *Texas, Nevada* and *Arkansas* and two additional destroyers. Three days were spent at Portland preparing for the operation. When the operation plan was completed and distributed it provided for two bombardment groups. The first was composed of the *Tuscaloosa, Quincy, Enterprise, Glasgow, Nevada, Ellyson, Emmons, Hambleton, Rodman, Murphy* and *Gherardi* under Admiral Deyo. The second was composed of two old battleships, the *Texas* and *Arkansas* with the destroyers *Barton, O'Brien, Laffey, Hobso,* and *Plunkett,* under Admiral Bryant. Each group was assigned a flotilla of minesweepers to clear the approaches and firing areas off Cherbourg.

The bombardment was set for June 25, when the Army was to begin its final push. The plan as originally drawn up was to have been carried out in three phases. During the first phase the ships were to remain between 20-25,000 yards offshore to take on the enemy's long range batteries which could challenge the bombardment groups. When those batteries were silenced or neutralized, range was to be closed to 8-12,000 yards for neutralization of medium range batteries. During the first two phases spotting for the heavy ships was to be by Royal Air Force planes. By the time the medium batteries were taken care of it was envisaged that the shore fire control parties with the troops would be in position to call for and direct the fire on targets as requested by the Army. During this phase,

phase THREE, the heavy ships were to take their assigned fire support stations off shore and provide direct support on call from the Army as long as required. During phase ONE the destroyers' role was necessarily confined to protective patrols. During phases TWO and THREE they were not assigned specific targets, but were to fire on targets of opportunity, positively identified as enemy, on the close flanks of the city, antiaircraft batteries, and the light batteries along the waterfront, concentrating on the latter. The destroyers were assigned neither air spotters nor shore fire control parties, but were prepared to fire under direction of the fire control parties if called upon.

H-hour originally had been set for 0600 on the 25th, about the time of sunrise. In the meantime, the Army had made such good progress that it looked for a while as if the operation might be called off. Final instructions from Admiral Alan G. Kirk, Commander Western Naval Task Force, received on the 24th, called for only ninety minutes of neutralization fire beginning at noon, the 25th. The Allied Naval Commander-in-Chief, Admiral Ramsey, indicated that the situation ashore was so favorable that the bombardment might not be needed at all.

3

So much for plans. The task force put to sea, Sunday morning, June 25, to carry out a plan drastically reduced in scope. Phases ONE and TWO, the neutralization phases of the original plan, were cancelled. During Phase ONE, intended to provide for the elimination of the heaviest German coastal batteries, the ships were to pause only long enough for the big ships to establish communications with spotter planes from the Royal Air Force. H-hour was changed from 0600 to 1030 and speeds adjusted to permit the two task groups to arrive in the close-in Fire Support Areas 3 and 4, 8,000 to 12,000 yards due north of Cherbourg, in time to begin ninety minutes of call fire as requested by the Army. The original plan underwent further alteration during the morning. The Commanding General, VII Corps, confirmed that he was expecting support fire about noon, but requested delivery only of such fire as was requested for fear of jeopardizing the attacking troops. Accordingly, Admiral Deyo directed Task Force 129 not to fire unless fired upon and not to fire at any target more than 2,000 yards in from the shoreline unless under direction of a shore fire control party.

Both task groups safely reached what, under the original plans, would have been their fire support areas for the neutralization fire against the strongest German batteries, Task Group 129.1 in Fire Support Area 1, almost due north of Cherbourg, and 129.2 in Fire Support Area 2, northeast of Cape Barfleur. They paused in their respective areas only long enough for the heavy ships to establish communications with their spotting planes and the shore fire control parties, before following their minesweepers down the approach channels to Fire Support Areas 3 and 4, north of Cherbourg. There each of the heavy ships was to take up its assigned position for the allotted ninety minutes of call fire. Under the revised plan the two groups were to converge in the call fire areas in time to begin fire about 1200.

Since the neutralization phases of the original plan had been omitted, some opposition from the still intact coastal batteries was anticipated. How much and from which batteries was a matter of conjecture. It was known that the target listed as No. 2 in the operation plan, situated about midway between Cherbourg and Cape Barfleur, had poured heavy fire on an allied formation of destroyers and minesweepers north of the Cape the previous day. This battery, called the "Hamburg" battery by the Germans, consisted of four turreted 280 mm. guns, protected in heavy concrete, steel-reinforced casemates. There were equally formidable batteries west of Cherbourg, but they were not so favorably situated to challenge the attacking ships. It was the Hamburg battery which caused the attacking ships the most trouble, particularly Task Group 129.2 which had to cross its arc of fire to reach assigned stations in Fire Support Area 3. Actually, the fire from "Hamburg" was so intense that the *Arkansas* and *Texas,* and their attendant destroyers, were never able to join the *Nevada* and cruisers in front of Cherbourg. Instead, they spent the allotted time for call fire alternately dueling with "Hamburg" and carrying out fire missions requested by the shore fire control parties from positions to the north and northeast of Cape Barfleur.

Since the *Emmons* was part of Task Group 129.1 the actions of that group will be followed rather than the *Texas-Arkansas* group. She kept station on the port flank of the heavy ships as they followed the minesweepers down the approach channel to Fire Support Area 3. The sweeps turned into the fire support area at 1155 followed closely by the bombarding ships. Up to this point there had been not the slightest hint of opposition. But as soon as the minesweepers steadied down and began sweeping the fire support area on a course parallel to the shore they came under heavy fire from shore batteries, apparently to the west of the city. The minesweepers doggedly continued their sweeping operations as shells fell around them. The motor launches with them and one of the destroyers laid down a heavy smoke screen between them and the beach which brought some relief. The smoke apparently threw off the Germans' aim, but it also obscured the view of the beach from seaward. Meanwhile the *Nevada* and the cruisers took the shore batteries under fire with the aid of air spotters. A short time later batteries to the east of Cherbourg opened fire on the minesweepers of 129.2 and that group went through much the same pattern as the group to the west, except the enemy fire was much more accurate to the east. During the early exchanges a shell hit in the *O'Brien's* superstructure, wrecking her CIC and much of the surrounding area. Thirteen men were killed and twenty wounded by this one hit. Although severely damaged she was not put out of action.

Back in Task Group 129.1's area the shore batteries continued to fire at the minesweepers and occasionally turned their guns on the cruisers. After the mine sweeps had covered about half of fire support area 3 without exploding any mines, the task force commander allowed them to retire to the north. For some reason the shore batteries did not fire on the destroyers during this period but seemed to concentrate on the minesweepers and the heavy ships, possibly because the destroyers were hard to pick out in the smoke. At least the *Emmons* found herself behind the smoke screen and was unable to take an active part in the action as her view of the beach was blocked out by the smoke. Under these circumstances she started to move to her previously assigned station in the southern part of the fire support area where it was hoped that a clear view of the beach could be had. During the move in the smoke a head-on collision with the *Gherardi* was narrowly missed by turning hard right while the *Gherardi* backed down.

Once clear of the smoke the *Emmons* took position about 16,000 yards north of Cap Levi and began to move slowly to the west scanning the shore for targets of opportunity. At the same time she tried to keep in position relative to the big ships to be able to lay down a smoke screen between them and the shore if it was required. The big ships were alternately dueling with the shore batteries and answering requests for fire from the shore fire control parties from positions partly in and partly to the north of the partially swept Fire Support Area 3.

Unlike Omaha Beach, details along the shore were difficult for Easy Money to make out because of the distance and the smoke and dust drifting to seaward along the waterfront. But perseverance finally paid off. At 1257 the gunnery officer reported flashes of fire from a small fort at the eastern end of the breakwater. It was later identified from grid coordinates as Fort de l'Est and appeared to be three small casemates. As the range was closed from 16,000 to 15,000 yards fire was opened. Opening fire was indirect with ranges and bearings fed into plot from C.I.C. As the range decreased, visibility improved to the extent that direct fire could be used. The fifth salvo was on target. Eleven more salvoes were fired using direct sight to spot. Many shells were seen to hit, but lasting effect was not known as Easy Money herself became the target of another battery. The source of the shells directed at her could not be located. They were all short, but as each successive salvo came closer it was thought best to retire behind the smoke screen from pots dropped by the *Rodman* before the hidden battery did find the range. Fire was continued on Fort de l'Est until it was blanked out by the smoke. It stopped firing when the first salvo from the *Emmons* fell near it and was never seen to resume fire before the bombarding force left the area.

The relative quiet behind the smokescreen did not last long. As the smoke blew out to sea the *Emmons* continued to search for targets along the shore while moving generally westward in conformance with the movements of the cruisers. At 1345 she was called on to provide a smokescreen for the *Glasgow* and *Quincy* which had come under heavy fire. This was an order to Easy Money's liking. At flank speed she laid down a beautiful blanket of chemical and smokestack smoke between the cruisers and the shore. The engineers were delighted to pour out the billowing black smoke without getting a call from the bridge to "knock it off." After the bombardment was over some of them gently chided the skipper for demanding what he had so often "chewed them out" for doing.

The smoke demonstration brought an unwelcome reaction from the German gunners. Frustrated in their attempts to get the cruisers they shifted their fire to the screening ship, firing several two-gun salvoes which at first were far astern. But when two shots landed close off the port quarter it was again time for Easy Money to duck behind a smokescreen. This time it was one she herself had laid down to hide the cruisers.

The allotted ninety minutes for the bombardment had expired at 1330. Obviously, the German batteries were still very active at that point although the shore fire control parties indicated that the Army was making good progress in the assault on the city from the landward side. In response to a query from Admiral Deyo whether he needed any further naval fire, General Collins requested a continuation until 1500. During the additional hour and a half the cruisers and battleships continued to respond to fire called for by the Army, but to protect them had to engage the still-active coastal batteries from time to time. Many of the latter would cease fire when fired upon, only to resume fire later when their targets were busy elsewhere—a tactic which the French had used successfully at Casablanca during Operation TORCH.

Because of the distance offshore and poor visibility in the target areas, the destroyers' role was largely passive during the last part of the engagement. Occasionally one of them would have an opportunity to fire on targets of opportunity as the *Emmons* had when it took on Fort de l'Est. Their main duty was to provide antisubmarine protection for the big ships. There had been reports of submarines off the Cotentin Peninsula and it is now known that submarines had been ordered into that part of the Channel in anticipation of a naval bombardment. Fortunately, none had been able to penetrate the extensive air and surface antisubmarine patrols guarding the busy Channel crossing areas. Perhaps the biggest service the tin cans rendered that day was to provide smokescreens as needed to shield the firing ships from the shore batteries and, incidentally, to act as a lightning rod to attract enemy fire away from the heavy ships as Easy Money had done for the *Glasgow* and *Quincy.*

Another function for the destroyers was to spot and destroy drifting mines. Although no mines had been found by the minesweepers, several floating mines were spotted around the task groups, and the destroyers were ordered to destroy them. This proved to be the *Emmons's* last significant act off Cherbourg. During the last half hour of the extended time period a lookout reported a mine dead ahead. Fortunately, the ship was making only ten knots at the time and the mine was missed by backing down and putting over the rudder. After warning the other ships she maneuvered to destroy it. Sinking it proved to be harder than expected. Slugs from a 20mm gun seemed to bounce off the casing without penetration. It was finally sunk, without exploding, by rifle fire in the hands of a sharp shooting gunner, just as the task group was forming up to return to Portland. The *Texas* group had been severely damaged—the *Texas, O'Brien, Barton,* and *Laffey* having sustained hits with fourteen killed and thirty-eight wounded. Damage to Task Group 129.1 was slight. The Glasgow had been hit twice. One shell had exploded in the captain's after cabin and another in the port hanger. The latter was a dud and had been lugged topside by hand to be heaved overboard.

Promptly at 1500 Admiral Deyo ordered all ships of Task Group 129.1 to withdraw by the same channel they had entered the firing area three hours earlier. Similar orders were given to Task Group 129.2 and the minesweeping units. The *Emmons* and the *Rodman* were the last to leave the bombardment area. Unlike some of the heavy ships, they drew no fire as they took up their screening stations on a northerly course.

5

It had been an exciting three hours but the results were in some respects disappointing. Some of the coastal guns were still firing as the task force withdrew. The *Texas* and the *Barton* to the east were straddled by the 11" guns of battery "Hamburg" a few minutes before the order to withdraw. The *Glasgow* reported enemy fire as the western group, Task Group 129.1, withdrew. On the other hand the air spotters reported many targets totally destroyed. Certainly, the Germans had used up a lot of their diminishing supply of ammunition. By their own admission the defenders of Cherbourg were running low on ammunition as the assault began.

The fire in support of the Army's advance was effective. Of twenty-one missions fired nineteen were reported as being successfully completed. And the support was not all physical. The naval support as they stormed the city was bound to have boosted the morale of the troops, most of whom had already seen the effects of naval gunfire at the beaches. General Collins wrote to Admiral Deyo shortly after the surrender of Cherbourg,

> I witnessed your naval bombardment of the coastal batteries and the enemy strong points around Cherbourg which were engaged by your guns on 25 June. The results were excellent and did much to engage the enemy's fire while our troops stormed into Cherbourg from the rear.

The effect of the naval guns on the trapped Germans was exactly opposite. The appearance of a strong naval force off the beleaguered city caused further deterioration in the spirits of the already demoralized defenders. General von Schlieben had, in effect, requested permission to surrender when, at 1209 on the 25th, he asked his superiors:

> ...Is it necessary, in view of the situation in general, to wait for the final annihilation of the remaining German troops which has to be expected because of the lack of effective defensive weapons? Relevant orders are urgently awaited.

At that time the duel between the coastal batteries and Task Force 129 had just begun. At 1254 the German general informed his superiors of "Enemy fire from ships firing from behind smoke screens on the open sea." At 1340 he made a further report:

> In addition to the overwhelming superiority in materials as far as artillery, air force and tanks are concerned, the enemy is now firing from the sea with heavy guns directed by artillery observation planes. It is our duty to report that further sacrifices cannot alter the situation.

The German Naval Staff War Diary noted at 1447 that "Bastion Cherbourg" was kept under naval gunfire. The naval commander at Cherbourg submitted laudatory accounts of the actions of his naval batteries, but was over-optimistic when he reported that the "Hamburg" battery had sunk one cruiser and severely damaged another.

Field Marshal Rommel could give no leeway to von Schlieben. At 1548, after the bombardment force was well on its way back to England, he sent the unhappy general a radiogram denying the privilege of surrender, but interestingly attributed the denial to Hitler:

> According to the order of the Fuehrer you have to continue to fight until the last round of ammunition is fired.

Regardless of the admonition General von Schlieben and Admiral Hennecke surrendered the following day, June 26. Although some of the forts in the outer harbor and at the northwest corner of the Cotentin Peninsula held out for several more days, clearance and rebuilding of the harbor began two days after the surrender. Within three weeks cargo was being discharged and by the end of July the port was almost up to the desired capacity. The first major army unit to be put ashore through the port was General George Patton's Armored Group which had been held in reserve in England and which was used so effectively in the drive through France.

The task force was back in Portland by sunset. As usual, the *Emmons* and *Rodman* were berthed together, this time alongside the *Glasgow,* with the *Emmons* outboard. The berthing assigned proved to be very convenient for the destroyers. On the way back across the channel a signal had been sent out to the commanding officers that the captain of the *Glasgow* had generously offered his cabin for a critique of the day's proceedings.

Without wondering why a critique would be held in the battled-damaged cabin of the British cruiser instead of aboard the flagship, the skipper of the *Emmons* climbed aboard the *Glasgow* at the appointed time, armed with pen and notebook, fully expecting to hear a discussion of the good and bad points of the day's action. He found the pen and notebook useless equipment for the business at hand. The meeting had been called for a post battle ceremony requiring no rehearsal or formal operating orders—splicing the main brace.

While the semiofficial "critique" was underway in the cabin country, the other messes of the *Glasgow* from the wardroom on down held their own celebrations to which their opposite numbers in the American destroyers alongside were welcomed. It was well past midnight before that particular nest of Anglo-American ships settled down for the night.

Joseph E. Woodnick, Jr. was the youngest of the crew. Typical of many who wanted to do their part, he falsified his enlistment age. He was two weeks shy of his 15th birthday when ordered to report to the *Emmons* in early 1943. He attained the rate of Gunner's Mate Third Class on board the ship.

Woodnick Family Collection

The Second Division (Fantail Division) posing while sweeping the deck. The ship was ordered into Mers-El-Kebir (Algeria)for maintenance and liberty after D Day. Note the other destroyers in the background receiving the same service. The ships were back in action in a month.

Korney Archives.

Six sailors on liberty, undated. The photo was taken while the ship served in the Atlantic. From L to R; Philip Jacoby (S); R.M. Diehl (S); Unknown;J.L. Donnelly; McMichael; unknown

Tostanoski Collection

Gun 2 Crew Left to Right: Roy O'Brien;J.A.Gocella (M); Philip Hebert (M); Wm. McConnell (M); John Malloway (M); J.R. Smith; Edward Tostanoski (W); J.P. Caracciolo (K)

Tostanoski Collection

13

Southern France

> To accomplish their various missions it was necessary for the destroyers to approach within point blank range of known enemy major and medium caliber coast defense batteries. The manner in which they did this and accomplished their various missions was an inspiration to all concerned. They knew thoroughly the part they had to play. They played it perfectly.
>
> —*CTG 85.12 Serial 0196 of 28 August 1944*

Cherbourg surrendered June 26. For all practical purposes its fall marked the end of the amphibious phase of the cross-Channel invasion. By July 3 it was agreed that the naval assault mission was completed and Task Force 122, the Western Naval Task Force, was withdrawn from the area, giving way to a permanent organization to support the growing expeditionary force and defend the conquered shores against any interference from the sea.

Even before Cherbourg, commands which had supplied ships on a loan basis for the Normandy operation were requesting return of their ships so they could get on with their own assigned tasks. Among these was a request for the return to the Mediterranean by July 1st of the *Texas, Nevada, Arkansas, Tuscaloosa, Augusta* and twenty-six destroyers, including the *Emmons.* They had been sent to the Mediterranean in the spring to take part in Operation ANVIL, the code name for the amphibious assault on the shores of Provence, between Toulon and Nice. The landings in Southern France had been given the blessings of the Big Three at the Teheran-Cairo Conference and were to have been executed simultaneously with the cross-Channel operation. However, when the landings in Normandy were expanded to include the Utah beaches, it had been necessary to scrape up additional naval support. The ships assigned to ANVIL proved to be the most convenient source. As a result ANVIL was temporarily postponed in favor of the expanded NEPTUNE landings. At the time of the request for the return of the Mediterranean ships, most of them had been assigned to Task Force 129, then being readied for the bombardment of Cherbourg. Since Admiral Ramsey did not want to lose any ships until Cherbourg was secured, no action was taken to send them back to the south until after the fall of the port city.

The invasion of Southern France had merely been postponed, not cancelled. It remained important in the overall planning of General Eisenhower and most of the staff. He was anxious to have the postponed operation executed as soon as possible for a number of reasons. Not only would it provide one arm of a pincers movement against the German Army in France, but most importantly, it would provide a major port, Marseilles, through which to pour men and materials to build up the Allied Armies in France. It was doubtful if Cherbourg, even when fully operational, could sustain an army of the magnitude required to regain France and conquer Germany. And it was not at all certain when additional ports on the west coast of Europe could be secured and rebuilt. Eisenhower estimated that the forces in Europe could be increased by as many as twelve divisions over those scheduled, if Marseilles was made available. Another important reason for carrying out the landings in Southern France as planned was that a French Army Corps was slated to play an important part in the assault. The II Corps, under General de Lattre de Tassigny, had been training in Northern Africa for some months. It was important politically, as well as militarily, that the French troops be committed to the liberation of France at the earliest possible moment.

The British, who had never been very enthusiastic about the landings in Southern France, considered that the forces earmarked for ANVIL could be put to better use. Prime Minister Churchill, preoccupied with the Balkans and Middle Europe, favored landings at the head of the Adriatic and a push through the Alps to Vienna. He was supported by the British Chiefs of Staff and to a lesser degree by General Sir Henry M. Wilson, the Supreme Allied Commander in the Mediterranean. After the initial successes in Western France, the British suggested cancellation of ANVIL and shifting the forces assigned to it elsewhere. Eisenhower held out for the execution of the landings as planned. In this he was backed by President Roosevelt and the U.S. Joint Chiefs of Staff. After several sharp exchanges between Roosevelt and Churchill the matter was apparently settled when Churchill phoned Eisenhower's headquarters to inform him that General Wilson would be given a clear-cut directive to attack Southern France as quickly as possible. A formal directive from the Combined Chiefs of Staff to Wilson on July 2 directed him to start ANVIL by August 15. About this time, the code name for ANVIL was changed to DRAGOON. It is reported that Churchill suggested the latter name because he had been "dragooned" into going along with the operation.

The fate of newly-christened DRAGOON was far from settled. Churchill and the British Chiefs of Staff continued efforts to have the operation changed, while Eisenhower and the U.S. Chiefs of Staff stood firm in their insistence that it be carried out as planned. As late as August 5, at a conference at Eisenhower's headquarters, Churchill tried to convince the general that DRAGOON should be cancelled and the troops involved put ashore through ports in Brittany or along the English Channel. In the meantime the British Chiefs of Staff alerted General Wilson to the possibility of a change in plans for the invasion. Such a drastic change on the eve of execution was too much for the Supreme Commander Mediterranean. He now advised against such action in face of the fact that some of the landing craft were already loaded and were scheduled to sail within a few days. A change at this stage of the game would mean unloading and reloading the craft already set to go, and would mean considerable delay in getting the troops involved from the Mediterranean to France via the western ports. There was also the fact that the ports to be used in Brittany were still in German hands and would have to be rebuilt before they could be used. The U.S. Joint Chiefs of Staff continued to disapprove any change in the plans.

While the discussions were in progress, preparations were going on in the Mediterranean for execution of the ANVIL-DRAGOON plan. In the long run the American view prevailed and the execution of DRAGOON remained targeted for August 15.

2

As previously mentioned, an important part of the naval forces slated for DRAGOON had been sent north to help out with NEPTUNE. At the end of the assault phase of the latter, little time was lost in getting them back to the Mediterranean. It was highly important that they have a few weeks to get fitted back into their assigned roles—although most would be repeating their Normandy jobs under a new set of commanders in a new setting.

Most of the attack transports which had helped lift the combat-loaded American divisions to Omaha and Utah beaches were scheduled to perform the same services in Southern France. As they completed their assignments at Normandy they were assembled at Belfast, Ireland, to await the move to the Mediterranean. The battleships, cruisers, and destroyers were not made available for the shift until after the surrender of Cherbourg. Most of the latter, assigned to Task Force 129, were waiting at Portland for the next move when Cherbourg fell. The American ships of the task force, with the exception of those which had suffered damage during the bombardment, and a few of the destroyers, were promptly ordered to Belfast to join the transports. They arrived at the Irish city June 30, and a new task group, 120.6, which included the transports and most of the ships of old task force 129, was formed for the voyage back to the Mediterranean. Admiral Deyo in the *Tuscaloosa* was placed in command.

The *Emmons* and *Rodman* did not accompany the rest of the task force to Belfast. While the other ships remained at anchor in Portland, they were involved in coastal escort duty. First, they were detailed to take the damaged *Texas* to Plymouth and, after a few hours there, to bring the USS *Tarazed,* a stores ship, back to Portland. After a day at rest they took the *Tarazed* back to Plymouth—the same day the task force got underway for Belfast. From Plymouth they were sailed independently to Ireland. The two destroyers arrived eight hours later than the other ships, but thanks to the long hours of daylight in early summer were able to anchor safely in Belfast Lough before dark.

The peace and quiet of Belfast Lough was in marked contrast to the noise and strain of the invasion and the almost constant alerts of the past month. Even in the invasion ports of Southern England there had been the constant threat of the rocket bombs which the Germans let loose in a desperate attempt to stop the invasion at its source. Belfast was far beyond the range of the bombs. There was very little possibility that the hard-pressed enemy air force could muster the strength for a conventional air raid against such a distant target. Besides, there were far more profitable targets within the battle zones. There was always a chance that some adventurous U-boat skipper could sneak through antisubmarine defenses, but even that possibility was remote. The odds against the submarines had changed so radically since early 1943 that the increasingly young and inexperienced German crews were concerned about whether they would return from a patrol at all, much less be victorious.

The crew of the *Emmons* took advantage of the three-day interlude to catch up on lost rest and to accomplish some of the housekeeping repairs which had accumulated during the invasion. Condition watches still had to be stood, but it was a luxury to turn in without expecting to have to rush to general quarter's stations every few hours. Everyone had a chance to go on liberty in Belfast although the distance from the anchorage to the port was so great that some of the destroyers had to be detailed as liberty boats. For once, the *Emmons* did not draw this duty. Some men were granted overnight liberty. The people of Belfast welcomed all the sailors as heroes, but those with Irish names received an especially warm greeting. There were many men of Irish extraction aboard the *Emmons,* although most of their families had gone to America from southern Ireland. It didn't matter whether they had come from the Irish Republic, south of the border, or from Ulster. In 1944, in Belfast, to be American with an Irish name was sufficient. One of the big events of the visit was a luncheon hosted by the city fathers for the commanding officers of the American ships jointly celebrating the victory at Normandy and the upcoming United States Independence Day.

3

Spirits were high when Task Group 120.6, consisting of the battleships *Arkansas* and *Nevada,* the cruisers *Quincy* and *Tuscaloosa,* the attack transports *Barnett, Samuel Chase, Charles Carroll Joseph T. Dickman* and *Thomas Jefferson,* the transports *Anne Arundel* and *Thurston,* escorted by Destroyer Squadron 10, less the *Macomb* and *Corry,* plus the *Plunkett,* left Belfast the morning of the Fourth of July. Altogether, the task group represented the major part of the assault transports and a sizeable part of the gunfire support ships destined for action in the invasion of Southern France.

For most of them DRAGOON would be their last action in the Atlantic theater against the weakening German arm of the Axis. From the makeup of the task group everyone aboard the ships assumed that they were headed for a landing operation in the Mediterranean—the exact time and place remained a secret. Aboard the *Emmons* there was little curiosity or conjecture as to where or when. Nor was there much concern at this time as to what her assignment would be. After Normandy, all hands were confident Easy Money could handle any task she was given.

To minimize the chances of running into submarines the group was routed to the north of Ireland and well off its west coast instead of the more direct passage to the south through St. George's Channel. For the same reason the route was kept well off the Bay of Biscay and the Spanish coast until it was necessary to turn shoreward to make the passage through the Strait of Gibraltar. The strategy was effective. The six-day voyage was made without any interference, although the second day out, about 125 miles west of Ireland, the *Hambleton* reported a sound contact which was believed good enough to be depth charged. A few minutes later she reported a torpedo wake. While the main body made an emergency turn away from the contact, the *Emmons* and *Rodman* were ordered to go to *Hambleton's* assistance. Contact was not regained and, after a few minutes, the *Hamble-*

ton decided the torpedo wake was merely a streak of foam. The destroyers were recalled to their screening stations and the formation returned to the base course. A day later, the *Augusta,* with the attack transport *Bayfield* and attack cargo ship *Achernar,* out of England, joined the task group almost due west of Land's End. After shepherding their charges into the formation, the four escorting destroyers high-tailed it over the horizon at high speed, bound on some other mission.

The formation passed through the Strait of Gibraltar during the midwatch on July 10, and arrived at Oran the afternoon of the same day. The destroyers were berthed at Mers-el-Kebir. There was little change in the base since their departures in May with the exception that fewer crippled ships were in evidence. Some of the damaged ships had been patched up locally, but most had been towed back to the United States for repairs.

At Oran, Task Group 120.6 was dissolved and its ships parceled out to various units of the Eighth Fleet according to the roles they were to play in the coming invasion. There was no great change for the *Emmons.* The destroyers of Squadron 10 spent the next month with the cruisers slated for the gunfire support groups. The destroyers not only acted as escorts but also received their share of training. The exercises reflected the lessons of Normandy: first and foremost, shore bombardment, then repelling surprise attacks by surface ships, damage control and antisubmarine defense, communications, and, significantly, the laying of smoke screens. The last part of July was spent at Palermo with the heavy cruisers. Around the 1st of August, as the different attack elements of the assault plan took up positions at their assigned staging ports, the squadron shifted its activities to Taranto, Italy. It was there that they received the signal to execute Operation DRAGOON.

4

After four days at Mers-el-Kebir for logistics, the *Emmons,* with the *Ellyson* and *Rodman,* was ordered to escort the *Tuscaloosa* and *Quincy* to Palermo. The ships were routed via the Gulf of Arzeu where they fired a shore bombardment exercise. The exercise was the most elaborate the DD457 had yet participated in. Each ship was required to fire on a target designated by a spotter plane and then to fire on a target selected by itself with spots from the spotting plane. The latter was designed to simulate firing on targets of opportunity as the destroyers had had to do at Normandy. The firing was successfully completed. It served to remind some of the old-timers aboard of the advancements made in shore bombardment equipment and techniques since the *Emmons* had gone through her first shore bombardment exercise at Bloodsworth Island before the African invasion.

The group arrived at Palermo the 18th. After its capture in July, 1943, that Sicilian city had become an important naval operating base. Furthermore, it had excellent beaches and was large enough to provide a wide variety of entertainment for visiting sailors, all the way from barber shops, which sometimes doubled as brothels, to an opera house. The trouble was there was very little time to enjoy either the fleshpots or the cultural offerings of the town. The checkerboard moves required positioning the many ships and men for DRAGOON were in full swing. Every few days some of the destroyers would be required to escort the larger ships from one port to another. When not out on escort duty or antisubmarine patrol there were the essential training exercises.

The first day of arrival at Palermo, while the other ships enjoyed liberty, the *Emmons* was detailed to take Admiral Deyo and some of his staff to Naples for a planning conference. Although this was in the nature of extra duty, it proved to be a very pleasant diversion. The weather was good, seas calm, and there were no other ships to watch out for. The trip across the Tyrrhenian Sea was made entirely at night at twenty knots. By daybreak the ship was standing into Naples. As soon as the admiral and his staff left the ship, she got underway again for Castellamare to take on fuel and a few stores, returning to Naples early in the afternoon. As the Admiral and his staff were not due back aboard until evening, limited liberty was granted to visit Naples only. Vesuvius loomed ominously above the Gulf but was too far from the docks for any sightseeing. According to later accounts, Naples was a far more interesting liberty port than Palermo, although no one aboard the DD457 had enough knowledge at that time to make an objective comparison. Its main drawbacks were that it was crowded with American servicemen and the Neapolitans had already learned what a soft touch the Yankees were.

As soon as the planning party reported aboard, the ship was underway for Palermo. She arrived early in the morning and went directly to the fueling pier, expecting to secure for the day after taking on fuel. However, it didn't work out that way. While she was still taking on fuel, the *Ellyson* and *Rodman,* escorting the *Omaha,* came in. Because of lack of space at the fuel pier, they were ordered to their regular berths, and old reliable, the *Emmons,* was ordered to top them off from her tanks before she could secure for the day. Shades of Argentia of 1942!

The following day, the *Emmons* put to sea for a day's exercise with the Italian submarine *Cagni,* returning to port in the afternoon. Most of the Italian navy was now cooperating wholeheartedly with their former enemies. There was little danger from submarines in the Mediterranean at this time, but the Germans were known to have a few at Toulon and in the Eastern Mediterranean. There was always the chance that one might get into the shipping lanes or get into position to disrupt an invasion fleet. Regardless of the threat, or lack thereof, it was always the practice to keep the destroyers sharp in what was essentially their primary function, antisubmarine action.

Nonetheless, antisubmarine work was only one of many tasks for which the destroyers would be responsible off the French coast. More and more reliance was being placed on their work as close-in fire support ships while the larger ships remained responsible for the heavier targets and those beyond the destroyer's range. Because of the importance of naval fire support in the planning for the upcoming invasion it is not surprising that the cruisers and destroyers at Palermo were scheduled for their second shore bombardment exercise in less than ten days. The exercise was scheduled for July 24, utilizing one of the craggy islets in the training area of the Lipari (Aeolian) Islands north of Sicily.

The *Tuscaloosa, Omaha, Quincy, Ellyson, Emmons,* and *Rodman* left port shortly before midnight July 23. The weather was fair. Because of the short distance from Palermo to the firing range, a leisurely speed of fifteen knots was maintained on a roundabout track which led northwest and north of the islands before curving south to enter the exercise area. During the midwatch the calm of the voyage was upset when one of the *Emmons'* lookouts reported sighting what appeared to be rockets or flares off the starboard bow to the east. Other lookouts also reported the fire. There was considerable conjecture as to what the display meant until someone noted that they were occurring at regular intervals. This, coupled with a series of bearings on the flares, led to the conclusion that the fire had nothing to do with men, ships or war. It was the volcano of Stromboli carrying out its normal routine.

The following morning's firing exercise was slow and deliberate with sixteen Hellcats from VOF-1 providing the spotting service. While one ship was firing the others engaged in individual ship exercises such as damage control exercises. The next day the entire group engaged in machine gun antiaircraft practice, firing at sleeves towed by three planes from VCS 7 out of Sicily before returning to Palermo.

The training phases of DRAGOON were just about finished. Within the next few days the group at Palermo was broken up and the individual ships dispersed to the ports throughout the Western Mediterranean from which they would sortie for the landing beaches of Southern France.

As part of the general pre-invasion positioning, the *Emmons* and *Rodman* were ordered to escort the *Quincy to* Malta. Just before midnight they navigated the Straits of Messina solely with the aid of radar. Ulysses would have marveled at the ease with which the warships scooted between Scylla and Charybdis with nothing but an electronic eye to guide them. The major worry for the warships was the unpredictable currents in the strait.

The destroyers delivered the *Quincy* safely to her destination and remained long enough to fuel. The battle-scarred harbor seemed carved out of solid rock which towered on either side of the ships as they stood down the main channel to the fueling facilities. The men aboard the ships could not help but think of the magnificent defense of Malta against everything the Axis forces could throw at it for four years. During the critical period of the North African campaign it had been a major factor in disrupting the Axis supply lines. This at a time when it appeared that the Axis would gain complete control of the Mediterranean from Gibraltar to Suez. Truly, its defenders were as granite-like as its foundations. Now the tables were turned and the Germans were on the defensive.

The destroyers had only a few hours in Malta before heading back to Palermo via the Strait of Messina. The passage through the strait was again made in the middle of the night. They arrived in the Sicilian port early in the morning and had nearly twenty-four hours at anchor before their next assignments. The *Emmons* sailed alone at 0200 on the 29th to rendezvous with the *Macomb* and *Texas* northwest of Malta. For the third time in less than fifty-six hours she scooted through the Strait of Messina, this time after daylight on the morning watch. In the light of day, the famous waterway was far more fascinating and somehow seemed more formidable than a narrow slot between two lines on the radar screen of the night passages.

For the *Emmons* it was the last of the checkerboard moves before the invasion. Although the operation plans had not yet been issued to individual ships and subordinate commanders, the 880 seagoing ships and craft involved were quietly being assembled in Allied ports throughout the Western Mediterranean, from Oran in Algieria to Brindisi on Italy's Adriatic coast. In some ports attack cargo ships had already been combat loaded. In others, attack transports were standing by to receive the assault troops converging on the staging areas. Special attack groups, support groups, minesweepers and gunfire support task groups were being gathered in still other ports.

Taranto was the assembly point for Task Group 85.12, the gunfire support group of the central assault task force. Rear Admiral Bryant, in the *Texas,* was its commander. As finally deployed on D-day, his task group was organized into five subordinate units according to types: 85.12.1, Battleship Unit, the *Texas* and *Nevada;* 85.12.2, Light Cruiser Unit, the *Philadelphia* and the Frenchmen *Montcalm* and *Georges Leygues;* 85.12.3, French Destroyer Leaders, *Le Terrible, Le Fantasque,* and *LeMalin;* 85.12.4, Destroyer Unit, the eight destroyers of DesRon 10; and 85.12.5, Close Support Unit, LCG 12, LCG 14, LCF 10, and LCF 14. All of the group except the French destroyer leaders, and the four gunfire support craft were at Taranto when the order to execute the operation plan for DRAGOON was executed. Of the group, the *Emmons, Texas, Montcalm* and *Georges Leygues* had served under Admiral Bryant at Omaha in Normandy, during the initial landings there.

5

In theory the waiting period at Taranto was to be devoted to last minute preparations for the assault. That was accomplished, but as usual there were many diversions. Sandwiched between routine tasks, such as landing unneeded publications and excess gear, the DD457 underwent a two-day annual military inspection and engaged in a sub hunt in the Adriatic.

With the gear put ashore under the care of the Naval Officer in Charge, Taranto, all the ships of the squadron sent their torpedoes to the torpedo station for safekeeping until after the invasion. Tony Esposito, then S1C, was sent ashore to help guard and maintain the fish. Because he spoke Italian he was also given liaison duty with the naval post office. To old destroyer men it was almost sacrilege to strip away a destroyer's torpedoes, once their primary weapon. But the later stages of the war had changed armament requirements drastically. In the upcoming invasion there was no probability of opposition from heavy surface ships for which torpedoes were designed. Air and submarine attacks were a possibility, and the Germans were known to have a number of fast small craft, similar to the E-boats used in the Channel, and small one-man submarines based on French and Italian ports along the Ligurian Sea. However, the greatest threat remained the formidable coastal defense batteries mounted along the southern coast. Hence the decision to land the torpedoes and have the destroyers utilize the saving in weight to take aboard more ammunition for use against shore defenses, including 1,000 rounds each of 40mm designed for fire against pill boxes, machine gun nests, and minor defenses which could be observed from close inshore.

Two entire days were devoted to the annual military inspection. Personnel and material inspections were held on August 2nd. The ship put to sea for battle and emergency drills on the 4th. Although there was as yet no official word as to what was to happen next, most men aboard sensed that something big was coming up soon. Here, within sight of what had been enemy territory a few months before, the exercises took on a realism which could never have been duplicated in a peaceful setting. All hands approached the drills as if their lives depended on them; as well they might in a few days. It is not surprising that the DD457 received good marks on her annual military inspection.

The arrival of the *Philadelphia* escorted by the *Ellyson* and *Rodman* from Palermo during the forenoon of August 5, completed the assembly of all the ships of Task Group 85.12 at Taranto except the French destroyer leaders and the gun support craft. They were not, however, to complete their preparations without interruption. Late in the afternoon all the ships of DesRon 10, except the *Ellyson* and *Rodman* received urgent orders to get underway without delay to try to intercept an enemy submarine reported to be trying to escape from the Adriatic. Accordingly, the *Emmons, Macomb* and *Hambleton* of DesDiv 19, and the *Forrest, Hobson* and *Fitch* of DesDiv 20, under the command of Commander Destroyer Division 20 in the *Hobson,* got underway in a hurry to carry out the orders. In fact, they left Taranto so hurriedly that many men of their liberty and recreation parties were left stranded. The *Emmons* left seventy-two men on the beach.

The sub hunters wasted no time rounding the heel of Italy and setting up a scouting line across the Strait of Otranto between the Italian mainland and the Greek island of Othonoi, northwest of Corfu. The Greek islands were still held by the enemy, but apparently they had nothing with which to challenge the destroyers which remained on the search for two nights and a day. There either was no submarine or it made good its escape. The search was called off the morning of the 7th, and the squadron returned to Taranto to resume preparations for the invasion.

Meanwhile, the men left behind had to shift for themselves. Some found lodgings with Italian families, but most simply reported themselves to one of the American ships still in port. One member of the abandoned swimming party ran across an old shipmate on the ship he reported to and rented his dress whites to join an *Emmons* buddy on regular liberty. When the two returned to their emergency quarters at the end of liberty they were invited to join a crap game going on below. They had less than $10.00 between them but decided to pool their resources and get into the game. One handled the dice while the other cheered him on. Luck was with them. While the shorthanded *Emmons* was methodically patrolling the entrance to the Adriatic her stranded sons cleaned out the game.

The men from Easy Money were four or five hundred dollars better off for being abandoned. Being aboard a stranger ship with so much money made them nervous, so they spent the next day and a half hiding out, mostly behind one of the cold boilers, until they got word their own ship had returned to port.

During the next four days the preparations for the invasion were completed. Among other things Shore Fire Control Party 25, assigned to the *Emmons,* came aboard for three days to go over communication, spotting and fire control procedures, and generally to get acquainted—a big improvement over time allotted for mutual understanding before NEPTUNE. Operation plans were given limited distribution to those who needed to know, including ComDesRon 10's (Commander Task Unit 85.12.4) Gunfire Support Plan 1-44, applicable to Destroyer Squadron 10 during the move to and at the assault area. The ship was sealed on the 10th, meaning no more intercourse with the shore was permitted. A priest came aboard the morning of the 11th to hold communion and hear confessions. At 1400 that afternoon Task Group 85.12 got underway from Taranto for the invasion area. H-hour was set for 0800, August 15.

6

The invasion of Southern France was not nearly on the grand scale of the Normandy operation, nor was it beset by the manifold problems which plagued NEPTUNE. Nevertheless DRAGOON was a major undertaking involving 880 seagoing ships and the United States Seventh Army under General Alexander M. Patch. Under him was the U.S. VI Corps consisting of three divisions commanded by Major General Lucian K. Truscott, and the French II Corps of two divisions under the command of General de Lattre de Tassigny. All the army divisions were veterans of the Italian campaign. The majority of the ships involved were from the U.S. Navy, but the Royal Navy provided a goodly share, as did the Free French. A few Canadian and Netherlands ships were present. Several destroyers manned by Poles and Greeks represented their governments in exile.

The plans called for the initial assault to be made by the three American divisions over three sets of beaches along the Provence coast between Rade de Hyeres and Cannes, each landed and supported by a naval task force. The landing areas were designated Alpha, Delta, and Camel from west to east. The naval task forces responsible for each area were also called the Alpha, Delta, and Camel forces. We are most concerned with the central, or Delta Force (TF 85), responsible for landing the 45th Division in the Baie de Bougnon, because the *Emmons* was part of Task Group 85.12, its fire support group.

The Southern France operation has become a classic example of a well-planned, beautifully executed, amphibious operation, where everything clicked. Its success is attributable partially to thorough, realistic planning, partially to the unexpected weakness of the enemy opposition, and partially to the tractability of the Mediterranean Sea as compared to the excesses of the English Channel.

The assault phase of the Mediterranean invasion of France was the responsibility of Vice Admiral H. Kent Hewitt, USN, who was designated Commander Western Naval Task Force—not to be confused with the task force of the same name for Normandy—for the operation. He was charged with planning the initial landings as far back as December, 1943, long before the name of the operation was changed from ANVIL to DRAGOON. Admiral Hewitt's regular command was the Eighth Fleet, the United States naval forces operating in Northwest African and Mediterranean waters.

The Germans were fully aware of the buildup in the Mediterranean and expected new action there. However, as with TORCH they were uncertain as to what the target would be. They were inclined to believe that landings would be in Southern France, although they could not rule out additional landings in Northern Italy or along the Istrian coast. For a few days around August 5, based on reports of movements of Free French troops from the Mediterranean to England, the Naval Staff concluded that Allied plans to land in Southern France had been postponed. As there were no indications of further amphibious landings in the north of France, the conclusion was reached that all Allied forces for France would be channeled through the Normandy beachheads. They did not hold to this idea very long. By the 8th, reports of troop concentrations in the Western Mediterranean convinced them otherwise. A concentration of American close combat troops was noted in Corsica. General de Gaulle had remarked in a radio address at Algiers on the 7th that soon a powerful, experienced French army would be fighting in France. Since there was then only one French tank division operating with the British in the West, and there was no confirmation of further withdrawal of French troops from the Mediterranean, the Germans concluded that the French Mediterranean would be the area of any new activity by the Free French. Accordingly, the Naval Staff informed subordinate commands that "a larger enemy landing operation must be expected daily at the French southern coast."

By now the Naval Staff deliberations were wholly pessimistic and confined almost entirely to defensive measures. German withdrawals in Western France were recognized as tactical necessities, but the staff tried to pretend they were of no consequence. The loss of Brittany ports was imminent—some ports had only three days ammunition left. The army was using up its reserves against the Russians on the Eastern Front. The city of Warsaw was in open revolt. Submarines could no longer cross the Bay of Biscay safely—plans were being made to shift their operations to Norway. If Sweden could not guarantee the neutrality of the Aaland Islands they stood to lose fifty percent of their iron ore imports. One solution was to seize the islands, but they concluded that they would lose more than they gained by alienating the Swedes. The Balkan satellites were restive and there was doubt as to Finland's continuation in the war. There was still some hope for improvement of the war at sea from submarine action and every effort was being made to equip active U-boats with snorkels. Another hope was in the deterring effect of the V1 bombs—as of August 2nd, 6,300 had been launched against England.

At a conference at Naval Headquarters on August 12, the Chief of the German Naval Intelligence Division advised that reports from the Mediterranean indicated an impending attack on Southern France. This conclusion was based, among other things, on Allied air attacks on radar installations along the coast. An unknown quantity was the arrival of Churchill in Rome. It was considered that the operation might be expected to begin on August 13. Further reports on the 13th and 14th strengthened the probability that the expected blow would be aimed at Southern France. These included the presence of strong French forces at Corsica where extensive material was stockpiled, strong naval activity off Corsica, the sighting of several convoys, and continued heavy air attack along the coast, particularly at Marseilles, Saint-Tropez and Nice. The Chief of Naval Intelligence reiterated his belief that Southern France was the most likely target, but would not rule out simultaneous, limited operations in the Adriatic, aimed at the Balkans. The German Army Command in Italy agreed, and added some information of its own. A count of convoys departing the Mediterranean was 125 ships short of the corresponding arriving convoys. Presumably those left behind were to be used in the attack. That command also noted the unusual activity off Corsica, as well as the heavy air raids against the French coast between the Rhone and Saint-Tropez, from which it was concluded that a landing in that area was more probable than one against the Ligurian coast which had been one of the possibilities under review.

From the above it is evident that the Germans were not caught napping. They knew for some time in advance that a major move was coming and had pretty well pinpointed the point of attack. When the German Chief of Naval Intelligence guessed that the operation would begin on August 13, he was not too far wrong. Many of the elements of the invading forces were already underway at that time. During the waning hours of the 14th reports began to trickle in to the Staff Headquarters of activity off the French coast which indicated that the awaited attack was beginning. Besides heavy air raids on Marseilles, the reports mentioned dropping of parachutists in the vicinity, and the detection of "numerous sea targets southerly of Ciotat." These alarms may well have been caused by diversionary efforts taken by the Allied forces at the Baie de la Ciotat, between Marseilles and Toulon, to divert attention from the real landing beaches farther to the east. Among other things booby-trapped dummy paratroopers were dropped and the planes leaving the area dropped extensive "windows," radar reflecting metal strips, to give the impression of large aircraft formations off shore. Shortly afterward the *Endicott* and a number of torpedo-boat types, trailing reflector balloons, passed along the coast within radar range to attract attention. The attention of the defenders was certainly attracted. Whatever the sources of their reports the Naval Staff concluded that enemy landings along the coast could be expected in the early morning hours.

From the viewpoint of intelligence evaluation, one significant input usually counted on by the Germans was denied them in the invasion of Southern France. At a conference with the Commander in Chief, Navy, at Staff Headquarters, the morning of August 15, after the landings between Toulon and Nice had been confirmed, their War Diary records, "This time the enemy news service did not supply us with particulars which might be of value to us."

While the Germans were wrestling with incoming alarms, the 880 ships of the invasion fleet were quietly approaching the designated transport areas off the Provence coast. Since the *Emmons* was a part of Task Group 85.12 the movements and action of that group will be followed in more detail than other segments of the fleet.

7

Orders to put DRAGOON into effect were issued August 9. H-Hour was set at 0800 on August 15. From the 9th to the 14th there was great activity in the assembly ports of the Western Mediterranean. One by one the various assault and support convoys got underway according to an elaborate movement schedule designed to get them to the landing area at the right time, in the proper sequence, to carry out their prescribed tasks. Each was assigned a speed of advance and a specific route to prevent interference with other convoys as they closed in on their destinations. The first to move were the slow convoys with the greatest distances to go, such as a 5 1/2 knot convoy composed largely of supply and ammunition ships and LSTs out of Oran. The last to get moving were those assembled at Corsica. Most of the transports and troop-carrying landing craft left the Naples staging ports on the 13th to proceed through the Strait of Bonifacio, between Corsica and Sardinia, on a staggered schedule. Some of the short-legged convoys had to put in to Corsican ports to replenish fuel, water and other essential supplies. All convoys were routed to the west of Corsica before making the final run to the landing areas.

Shriven, and in all other respects ready for combat, the *Emmons* joined the other destroyers of the squadron in the screen of Task Group 85.12 as it sortied from Taranto on the 11th for the invasion. It took better than three days to arrive at the Delta landing area, the task force having been assigned one of the longest approach routes of any group. The route led between Malta and Sicily and south of Sardinia before turning north to join the parade to the west of Corsica. One reason for the extended route was to go by Bizerte to pick up the three missing French destroyer leaders. Besides, so many troop convoys were being routed through Bonifacio that it was desirable to have the more self-sufficient convoys take longer routes to avoid a bottleneck at the Strait.

The French destroyers joined the formation around noon on the 13th. Late that evening course was changed to the northward to pass to the west of Sardinia. About twenty-four hours later rendezvous was made with assault convoy SF-1A carrying troops of the famous 45th Division, the Indian Division, responsible for securing the beachhead at the Delta area. The destroyer screen and the heavy gunfire support ships were re-stationed to give the troopships maximum protection as the augmented formation shaped course for the Delta assault area. The formation arrived in the assault area at 0417, August 15, 1944, where the transports anchored and began preparation for offloading the troops. At the inner transport area the destroyers of the gunfire support group left the transports under the protection of their regular escorts and headed without signal for their assigned fire support stations.

The approach phase of the assault had been executed without a hitch. Before leaving Taranto, Commodore Converse had held several briefing sessions with his skippers and had drawn up a fire support plan for the squadron to supplement the plans of Task Group 85.12. The plans had been thoroughly discussed and digested so that each ship knew its job and that of its neighbors as well. Under the plans, the five destroyers of DesDiv 19 were to deliver close-in support for the troops from Fire Support Area No. 6, 3,000 yards offshore. The three destroyers of DesDiv 20 were to remain in the outer fire support areas in the vicinity of the heavy ships, prepared to make smoke, spot for the heavies, or relieve the close-in destroyers, if necessary. On paper the situation at the Delta beaches seemed to pose far more hazards than had the situation at Omaha in Normandy. The Delta area sandwiched between Alpha to the west and Camel to the east, led into the Gulf of St. Tropez and the Baie de Bougnon, with Point Sardineau jutting out between them, was very narrow and restricted compared to the other landing areas. All the landing beaches were in the Baie de Bougnon, and boat lanes leading in to them further restricted maneuverability of the close-in destroyers. There was little danger from mines in the deep waters offshore, but inside the 100 fathom curve, where part of the fire support area of the destroyers lay, there was high probability of mines. There was no great fear of submarine or air interference, although both were possible. Nor was there much to be feared in the Delta area from hit-and-run sneak attacks. The assault areas of Alpha and Camel on either side acted as a buffer to absorb any sneak attacks originating east or west of the landing area, much as Omaha had been protected by Utah on the west and the British beaches on the east at Normandy. The cause for greatest concern was the possibility of fire from many coast defense batteries along the shore and inland. Fire was possible on the Delta area from at least eight 220mm coast defense guns, plus many more of smaller caliber. Five of the 220mm guns were mounted on Cape Saint Tropez overlooking the Delta area. This particular battery was designated P-39 in the Operation Plans, and was given extraordinary attention in the gunfire support plans.

After leaving Taranto the crew of Easy Money—much to everyone's delight the pseudonym for the *Emmons* at Normandy was retained in the new plans—had been assembled and given a thorough briefing on what to expect. There was little cheering this time; but neither was there any reluctance to face the formidable opposition possible in the upcoming operation. Her gunfire support duties were much the same as they had been at Omaha. She, with the *Ellyson* and *Hambleton* was to precede the first wave down the boat lanes on the heels of the *Rodman* and *Macomb*. The latter two were assigned to guard the minesweepers as they cleared the boat lanes and Fire Support Area No. 6. All ships were to be prepared to open counter-battery fire at any time and to arrive in the fire support area by H-70. On arrival in the fire support area the *Emmons* and the *Rodman* were to take stations south of the boat lanes near the entrance to the Gulf of Saint Tropez, while the others took stations north of the boat lanes. At H-70 saturation fire was to be directed against prearranged targets along the beachfront until seven minutes before touchdown of the first wave. Easy Money's area of responsibility for this fire, shared with the *Rodman,* covered Point Sardineau. Following touchdown the destroyers were to deliver counter battery fire as seen to be necessary or as requested by their shore fire control parties. The latter were to go ashore with the second wave. In addition to their other duties the destroyers were to continually observe selected targets, nominally the responsibility of the battleships and cruisers, to see that they did not menace the landing. If one did open fire, they were to keep it under fire until one of the heavy ships engaged. If necessary they were to act as close-in spotters for the big ships. Among the targets assigned to Easy Money for observation was P-39, the formidable 220mm. battery located on Cape Saint Tropez.

The actual assault went as smoothly as the approach. Indeed, instead of the hazardous undertaking envisaged in the plans, it proved to be a "piece of cake" as one member of the *Emmons's* crew described it. Not a single shot was fired at the destroyers or the boat waves as they approached the shore in broad daylight. Easy Money opened fire a few minutes ahead of the scheduled bombardment due to commence at H-70. As she was approaching her firing station 3,200 yards east of Point Sardineau the *Rodman* reported that P-39 was firing. Although no signs of activity by that battery could be observed from DD457, fire was opened on it anyway, as it was one of her principal responsibilities. In addition, the *Rodman, Montcalm* and *Georges Leygues* were directed to take the target under fire. Easy-Money expended twelve rounds of 5"/38, deliberate fire before the *Rodman* reported the target was quiet at 0644. However, at 0647 she reported that it had again opened fire. In the meantime the *Montcalm* and *Georges Leygues* kept P-39 under fire until the general bombardment began when the *Texas* assumed responsibility for that potentially dangerous battery and kept it under fire until H+14. After the touchdown of the first wave, both the *Emmons* and the *Fitch* reported no activity around the target. The *Emmons* added that the battleship's shells were right on target. There were no further reports on this target until 1037 when the *Emmons* reported troops in the vicinity which could well be our own.

The scheduled bombardment was started at H-70 and ended seven minutes before touchdown. The destroyers were so near the beach that targets were easy to locate, and direct fire could be used effectively. The larger ships offshore had more difficulty with their spotting because of the haze and the dust and smoke generated in the target area. About midway through the bombardment aircraft from bases in Italy and Corsica laid down a beautiful pattern of bombs along the beaches which also was very effective in keeping the enemy away from his prepared defenses. It is just as well that the enemy could not fire at such close range. It would have been difficult to take evasive action in the restricted waters of the fire support area. The destroyers would have had to go through the boat lanes, retire to seaward, or go into unswept waters of the Gulf of Saint Tropez. It is also just as well that the bombers were right on target—an error of a few yards offshore could have been disastrous.

Easy Money's primary targets along Point Sardineau were well taken care of. Twenty-two minutes after touchdown the Army requested no further fire on Point Sardineau except on call. The restriction was extended to the entire landing area a few minutes later.

The first wave of assault troops hit the beach precisely at H-hour, 0800, virtually unopposed; thanks to the tremendous pounding the defenses had taken during the prelanding bombardment. As soon as they landed, the troops formed up and fanned out inland against light opposition. One by one, the enemy strong points were taken over by the advancing troops. There appeared to be more activity in the areas assigned to the destroyers north of the boat lanes. They reported splashes in their vicinity and machine gun fire on the beaches in that area, both of which were taken care of. Things remained quiet in the areas assigned to the *Emmons* and *Rodman.* The *Emmons* continued to keep a watchful eye on P-39, which remained quiet. That battery was in the hands of our troops by noon. About the only things to do was watch and wait and keep an eye on the busy boat lanes down which reinforcements were streaming. At 1425 minesweepers working inside the Gulf of Saint Tropez reported they were under fire by guns believed to be 88mm. Neither the minesweepers nor the *Emmons* could locate the source, which ceased firing shortly afterward. It could have been a mobile battery which had to move on before it could do any damage.

Elaborate plans had been made to support the advance inland with naval gunfire directed by shore fire control parties. Each of the destroyers had a party assigned, and nearly all of them responded to calls for fire on enemy targets some time during the day. However, such calls were few and far between. Shore Fire Control Party No. 25, assigned to Easy Money, landed with the second wave. After setting up their equipment and establishing communication with the ship, they proceeded rapidly inland with their troop units. They were almost apologetic at lack of targets as they moved forward. Finally at 1526, the gunnery department was alerted by a call for fire on a suspected enemy observation post in front of their lines. After expenditure of thirty rounds of AA common from Easy Money's 5" battery, the shore party announced that the target was destroyed. Almost as an afterthought they added: "Just wanted to see how well you could shoot." Apparently they were satisfied. There were no more calls for fire support and by nightfall the front lines were beyond the ship's range.

After destruction of the observation post, Easy Money idled along the boat lanes off Point Sardineau, keeping an eye on the shore for possible trouble and waiting in vain for another firing mission. One fascinating pastime for that topside was watching successive waves of follow-up troops land on the beaches, form up, and march inland in battle array.

At 2030 Task Group 85.12 left the assault area for their assigned night retirement area. What had appeared to be a dangerous mission had been extraordinarily easy. The destroyers were especially grateful that their efforts had been successful without the penalty of sacrifice. For most of the ships of the task group the closest thing to genuine alarm for the day came as two JU88s approached the formation as it left the fire support area. One of them paralleled the formation for a few minutes before disappearing from sight. The other stayed at high altitude and never got within practical range. The first was taken under fire by ships which had visual contact, but suffered no apparent damage before sheering off. Easy Money expended forty-four rounds of 5" and forty-eight rounds of 40mm. with no observable damage. It is probable that the two enemy planes were a team of radio control bombers, as two bombs were seen to fall between the advance picket destroyer and the center destroyer of the antisubmarine screen.

After a quiet night the fire support ships returned to the assault area at daybreak to resume their stations of the previous day. Only a few requests for fire were received up to mid-morning. All of them were on targets in the Camel assault area to the right, where greater enemy resistance had been encountered. After clearance from the Camel fire support group all were undertaken. To her great disappointment, Easy Money was not involved in any of the morning's shoots. By noon it was obvious that there was no further need for fire support for the troops ashore in the Delta area. At 1405 Task Group 85.12 was released from further gunfire support duties. However, it remained in the area until nearly sunset to provide surface and air protection, if needed.

During the waiting period permission was granted to allow swimming over the side. The *Emmons* held swimming call for the port and starboard watches within sight of the beaches where U.S. troops had stormed ashore the day before. It was a fine August day, nearly perfect for swimming in the Mediterranean. In spite of the salubrious weather, few men remained for long in the water—jellyfish were far more numerous and menacing than human enemies at that point.

At 1900 the task group formed up and retired to the southward from assault area Delta, headed for designated ports in Corsica and Sicily. The *Philadelphia* and the French ships were to go to Propriano and the *Texas* and American destroyers were to retire to Palermo. Enroute the different ships were to report to other forces of the invasion fleet for further duty.

As they left the assault area the ships of the task group had every right to be both proud and thankful. Proud that they had accomplished their assigned missions in a professional manner Thankful that what could easily have been a vicious, bloody confrontation had, thanks to a combination of enemy weakness and our own careful planning and preparation, turned out to be a walkover. Not a ship in the task group had been touched. In his endorsement to Captain Converse's action report of the invasion, Admiral Bryant was unstinting in his praise of the destroyers, which had occupied the point positions.

9

The task group remained together until the following day when the *Philadelphia* and the French ships left the formation to go in to Propriano. The *Texas* and the American destroyers continued on through the Strait of Bonifacio en route to Palermo. On the way, Commodore Converse reported by dispatch for duty to Commander Task Group 80.6, the Antisubmarine and Convoy Control Group for the Western Naval Task Force, and recommended that Squadron 10 proceed to Taranto to recover torpedoes left there in preparation for the invasion.

The recommendation was approved. After a day at Palermo to replenish fuel and ammunition used during the assault phase of the invasion, the squadron, less the *Fitch,* proceeded to Taranto, where they took aboard the torpedoes and the personnel who had been left there to take care of them. Communications publications and other strip ship gear were also retrieved.

The squadron left Taranto the same day it arrived, August 20, for the assault area via Palermo and Ajaccio. The stop at the former was to take aboard more star shells as directed by the commander of the new task group, which foreshadowed the type of duty to be expected for the next month and a half. The stop at Ajaccio was to top off on fuel before reporting to the beach area.

The squadron arrived off the beaches in the Saint-Tropez area on the 23rd and the ships were immediately assigned stations on the picket lines set up around the landing areas to prevent surprise attacks from seaward. The new assignments marked the return of DesRon 10 to the destroyer workaday world of patrol and screening duties.

They were kept busy. The original beaches were still in use to augment and supply the Seventh Army and continued to be used until late September. As the beachheads were expanded to the west and northeast the picket lines had to be expanded to match. The beaches had to be guarded against attacks by the German small battle units—one and two-man submarines—as well as regular submarines, torpedo boats, and possible air attacks. Several new convoys entered and left the area every day. By the time the *Emmons* and her sisters returned to the assault area there was no longer any threat from the enemy on shore back of the landing beaches. That very day the Seventh Army reached Grenoble and the French II Corps captured Marseilles. Cannes would be occupied the following day, and Toulon would surrender within four days. The situation was favorable on all fronts. Much of the interior of France was under the control of partisans. The Allies were on the verge of entering Paris where partisans were already in control of many of the public buildings. In spite of the rosy outlook, the war in Europe was far from over. The day DesRon 10 returned to the French beaches, 211 people were killed by V-l bombs at East Barnet, part of London.

The capture of Marseilles and Toulon relieved the pressure on the beach unloading zones, although it would be several weeks before their port facilities could be returned to use. One thing their capture did was to virtually eliminate any orthodox submarine threat. The enemy had been forced to disable the few operable submarines left at Toulon. One, however, the U-230, tried to make good its escape and spent several days offshore before running aground in the Gulf of Hyeres. Its crew blew it up and commandeered a fishing boat. They were intercepted by the *Ellyson, Hambleton,* and *Ericson* while trying to get through the area screen and were taken into port as prisoners by the latter. This was the only action on the picket line involving the destroyers of DesRon 10.

The *Emmons* spent her share of time on the picket line, which was expanded with the fall of Marseilles and Toulon. She, in common with the other destroyers, would spend approximately one day at anchor in the Gulf of Saint Tropez for each day on the picket line. Saint Tropez, that jewel of the French Riviera and resort of the international set, showed the ravages of five years of war in 1944. Many of its villas had been taken over by the Allies and converted into recreation centers for service people fortunate enough to get ashore there. On one of their visits to the officers' club, several junior officers of the *Emmons* met some off-duty army nurses. They found out that one thing the nurses craved more than anything else was a hot shower with real, honest-to-goodness soap. They were quick to offer the facilities of Easy Money, such as they were, and thereafter, the nurses were extended a standing invitation to come aboard whenever she anchored in the gulf. Some of the men on liberty had an opportunity to talk with a group of German prisoners being held for further transportation. They exchanged cigarettes for German uniform emblems and later described the prisoners as showing no signs of fear, being quite friendly and pleasant, and apparently relieved to leave the fighting behind them.

The *Emmons* remained on patrol duty until September 5, when she and the *Ellyson* were sent to Oran for a five-day upkeep period at Mers-el-Kebir. The same day, under a reorganization of Task Group 80.6, ComDesRon 10 was made commander of Task Unit 80.6.7, the DRAGOON Escort and Convoy Control and Screen unit, with responsibility for protection of Allied forces at the beachheads from attacks by enemy surface forces, submarines and aircraft. He was also responsible for organizing, sailing, and providing escorts for convoys departing from the southern coast of France. To accomplish this formidable task he was given sixty-seven patrol and screening vessels ranging from destroyers through destroyer escorts to sloops and PC-boats. Most of them were American but there was a good representation of British and French ships in the group. Of Commodore Converse's own squadron, DesDiv 19 was assigned to the unit, but DesDiv 20 was more or less permanently assigned to escort Transport Division 3, busy plying between the out-ports and Southern France.

The *Emmons,* as a member of the Escort and Convoy Control and Screen Unit, was liable for escort duty when she, with the *Ellyson,* reported back from Oran. However, she continued on patrol duty off the original landing beaches until September 21, when she was directed to relieve the *Doyle* of patrol duty off Marseilles, incident to the departure of that ship to Oran. The *Ericson* was already assigned to Toulon. The two destroyers were to patrol at night off the harbors. In addition they coordinated the activities of other patrol craft assigned to their ports. Although most incoming convoys were scheduled to arrive during daylight hours, some did come in after dark, in which case the destroyers were to assist them in finding safe channels. When not involved with patrols or convoys, the destroyers were authorized to anchor near the harbor entrances.

By the time Easy Money took up her new duties off Marseilles, both that port and Toulon had been partially cleared and was handling the bulk of the incoming troops and supplies headed for the northern front. There the U.S. Seventh Army and the French First Army had already been absorbed into the Sixth Army Group operating directly under General Eisenhower in the drive toward the Rhine. The southern ports were now major supply points for all Allied troops in France. A week after the *Emmons* arrived off Marseilles the original DRAGOON beaches were closed for operations, having served their purpose well.

Because of the relaxed daytime schedule, a limited amount of liberty could be granted during the daylight hours in the liberated French city. The area around the ancient "old port" proved to be a favorite haunt of the liberty parties. There a few small bars and cafes had managed to survive the German occupation. It was there that the incoming LSTs were offloaded directly to the quay, sometimes three or more abreast. It was thrilling to sit at a small sidewalk cafe and watch the assortment of jeeps, trucks, and other vehicles come clanking off the ramps and go lumbering over the ancient cobblestones toward the front and their individual destinies. The sailors were not the only ones to get a thrill out of this demonstration of might. There was nearly always a rapt group of Frenchmen watching the parade with wide-eyed admiration. The tanks were especially fascinating for the Marseillais. Whenever several tanks would form up on the quay there would be spontaneous applause.

Although it had been several weeks since Marseilles was freed, the partisans were still very much in evidence. From time to time a jeep filled with exuberant young men, brandishing rifles and machine guns, would go careening through the streets with scant regard for the safety of pedestrians. Perhaps they were on their way to mete out justice to accused collaborators. Some members of an *Emmons* liberty party witnessed the shaving of the heads of several young women before a jeering crowd in one of the public squares. They had been accused of fraternizing with the enemy.

There was no mention of fraternization by the women in the houses of prostitution. Apparently to French logic there was a difference between voluntary fraternization and economic necessity. If this question was researched by the men on liberty, no evidence, one way or the other, was reported. The engineer office yeoman, responsible for compiling the shore patrol lists, was mystified by an unaccountably large number of volunteers for shore patrol duty—normally a duty to be shunned. When he got to the bottom of the mystery, he learned that some of the astute madams of Marseilles were offering the shore patrolmen, as a public relations gesture, choice of the best in the house.

Easy Money alternated between nights on patrol and daytimes at anchor off Marseilles until September 29, when she was ordered to Toulon. There she was assigned much the same type of duty off the naval port. The major difference was that there was more time at anchor inside the sheltered harbor, as the ancient French naval base had become the *de facto* base for Allied naval ships operating along the Southern French coast and there were more vessels to share the load. The base was a shambles and the harbor was littered with the hulks of a once mighty fleet, scuttled to prevent it from falling into the hands of the Nazis. The disabled guns of battleships, cruisers, and destroyers pointed grotesquely in all directions, some just above, and some half under the water. The harbor did provide shelter from the storms which were becoming more frequent as the autumn advanced.

The French Navy provided what services it could, but most had to be obtained from ships of the invasion fleet brought along to provide fuel, supplies and repair services. The inhabitants of Toulon were also generous in sharing what they had with the liberating fleet. If there were any friends of the Nazis left they maintained a discreetly low profile, although French and American sailors alike responded to the plaintive lyrics of "Lilli Marlene" in the few shabby nightclubs which were able to open. There was little these places could serve except nostalgic music, wine and a few bottles of *eau de vie.*

Since there was little else to do the liberty parties spent some time exploring the ruins, looking for souvenirs, or haggling with the French over whatever they could produce for sale. One crewman brought back a magnificent set of dueling pistols, which were really museum pieces. Others purchased small pieces of jewelry, some good, some not so good. There was an abundance of antique furniture, some of which had been exposed to the elements by the bombing and shelling—unfortunately, these items had to be passed up—there was no space to store antique furniture aboard a destroyer.

The mania for war souvenirs brought about the only casualty of the invasion aboard Easy Money. Many men brought back pieces of bombs, shells, shell cases, and some small caliber ammunition, not all of which had been detonated. One gunner's mate, who, of all people, should have known better, tried to disarm a small machine gun shell. Somehow, the primer went off in his hand. Result, loss of one finger. Inevitably, this brought about an attempt to lock the barn door after the horse was stolen. A thorough locker inspection produced enough military hardware to arm a small detachment—some of it potentially lethal.

The *Emmons* arrived at Toulon in time to welcome a new division and squadron commander. The last day of September, Captain Converse was relieved to return to the United States and a new assignment. His duties as convoy and screen commander for Southern France were assumed by Captain Valery Havard, Jr. of Destroyer Division 14. Captain Richard A. Larkin took over the dual role of Commander Division 19 and Squadron 10, and thus became the immediate superior of the *Emmons.*

9

September shaded into October as the *Emmons* continued to alternate on patrol duty between Marseilles and Toulon. A welcome break from the monotonous in-

and-out routine came in mid-October when she was detailed to escort the SS *Surprise* from Marseilles to Leghorn, Italy, via the Strait of Bonifacio. The trip was without incident, but it gave an opportunity to spend most of the daylight hours of the 15th in the Italian port. Leghorn had been captured in July and was now a supply port for the Fifth Army which was in the process of cracking the Germans' Gothic Line, some forty-five miles to the northeast. In spite of the nearness to German-held territory there were no air raids against Leghorn while the *Emmons* was there. A few people managed to catch rides to Pisa, about twenty miles to the north, to check on the famous leaning tower. The tower had been spared, as had the cathedral, but few other structures had been left intact by the Germans as they retreated.

The ship sailed alone back to Toulon, arriving there early in the morning of the 16th. Changes in the Convoy Escort and Screen for the Southern France coast were in the making. The morning of October 20, Easy Money was relieved of the patrol off Toulon, but instead of returning to the port as usual, she was directed to rendezvous with the *Rodman* and *Forrest* south of Marseilles to proceed to Oran. There was a great deal of conjecture as to what the move meant. Most people aboard guessed that it was the first leg of the homeward voyage.

They were right. Although the individual ships had not yet been informed, the squadron commander had on file among his secret dispatches, one which directed him to get the squadron ready for "distant duty" by the 23rd. All of his ships had arrived at Mers-el-Kebir by October 22. For short-term application, distant duty proved to be the United States, but it didn't take much imagination to jump from there to the Pacific.

Also assembled at Oran and Mers-el-Kebir were the transports of the Eighth Amphibious Force. Their assault missions at Normandy and Southern France completed, they, too, were heading back to the States for new assignments. The destroyers were ordered to escort the transports, accompanied by one ocean-going rescue tug, back across the ocean. Thus it was that the last important duty of the squadron with the Atlantic Fleet was to see a formation of twenty transports safely across the ocean from the Mediterranean to their home ports. The group left Oran the 25th and transited the Strait of Gibraltar the 26th, in broad daylight.

When the formation departed the Strait of Gibraltar it marked the end of an exciting period in the career of the *Emmons.* It had been just a few days short of six months since she had entered the Mediterranean with Task Group 27.4 on April 30. Most of the six months had been routine destroyer duty: training, escort, patrol, and just plain waiting. But there had been a few exciting days of actual combat. She had participated in the kill of an enemy submarine. At Normandy, at Omaha beach, she had been the first to be fired on and the first to fire back. She had drawn fire at Cherbourg and given back better than she received. Southern France had turned out to be far tamer than expected, but she had been in the forefront of the attack.

The Officers of the USS Emmons
Officers of the USS Emmons, DD457. Picture taken in August or September 1944 after invasion of Southern France.

Menaugh Collection

Front Row, L to R: Victor Jones, Lt. USNR (M), H Francis, William Warner (S), S.L. Fisher, Lt., (jg) (M), James Sheeran, Ens. (W), Ross Elliot, Ens. (K), H.F. Nelson, Lt.(jg) (S).

Middle Row, L to R: George Kennedy, Lt. (jg); T. H. Menaugh, Lt.(jg) (W); Earl Blake, Lt. (jg); E. B.Billingsley, Cmdr.; E.N. Foss, Lt. Cmdr. (W) ; J.J. Griffin, Lt.(S) ; R.F. Merrill, Lt.(jg) (S)

Back Row, L to R: D. Horwitz, Lt.(jg) (K); H.B. Smith, Lt.(jg) (W); J. Gilligan; K.F. Sweeney, Lt. (jg) (M); C.R. Williamson, Lt. (S); A.W. Steadman,Lt.(jg) (M)

The following officers were not on the ship at the time of the April 6th attack: H. Francis; G. Kennedy, Earl Blake. J Gilligan was detached to the USS Rodman DD456

The following officers were added to the Emmons Roster before going to the Pacific Theater: T.J.Lynds, Lt. (M); M.C. Minton, Lt. (S); R. M. Davenport, Lt (jg)(W); G.L.Theiss, Ens. (M).

Identification Key

(K) Killed in action

(W) Wounded

(M) Missing in Action. Declared dead July 1945

(S) Survivor

Dwight C. Shepler, June 6, 1944 (D Day). The scene shows officers on the bridge of another destroyer observing the USS Emmons shelling the landing beach. This is Fox Green Beach on D Day, June 6, 1944. The Emmons was ordered to destroy any structure standing that could be used as a spotter's post, and to eliminate enemy artillery locations shooting at the landing beach. The destroyers were trying to protect and help the jam of landing craft that was created by the German defense of the beaches. The USS Emmons also dispatched medical aid to the survivors of the two landing craft that had suffered direct hits.

The cover of this book was also done by the same artist. It shows the USS Emmons (DD457) in an artillery duel with the German 88's on top of the cliffs near Point-En-Bessin at Omaha Beach. The gunners of the Emmons won this battle quickly.

The church at Colleville-sur-mer was identified as a German observation post, directing fire on the troops attempting to land at Omaha Beach on D-Day. When called upon, Emmons destroyed the steeple with pin-point sharpshooting by its five-inch battery. This photograph shows the rebuilt spire.

Billingsley Collection

Life on a destroyer meant having days at sea like this. The picture shows the waves breaking over the bow of the USS Emmons. This is a view from the starboard wing of the bridge. Looking forward, the structures on the left side of the photo are number one and two guns, the two forward 5 inch gun turrets.

Tostanoski Collection

USS Emmons DD457

The ship was a sleek, fast fighting machine. Its speed and maneuverability made it a devastating opponent for any enemy. This photograph was taken while the ship was in service during the battle for the Atlantic. The transformation to a Destroyer Mine Sweep (DMS 22) necessitated the removal of the five inch gun turret (Gun 4) closest to the stern. The torpedo tubes and some of the anti submarine equipment were removed to make room for mine sweeping gear. John Griffin, SSO always made a point that their last battle with the Kamikazes was fought with the lack of 25% of their fire power with the loss of Gun 4.

The *USS Emmons* (DD457) lays down a smoke screen to protect the *USS Quincy* and the *HMS Glasgow* both of which had come under straddling fire from German Shore batteries. The Naval task force effectively neutralized the German defenses, allowing our troops to enter Cherbourg from the rear.

14

From Destroyer to High Speed Minesweeper

Moored Boston Navy Yard, Charleston, Mass.... this vessel's classification changed from DD457 to DMS22.

—***Emmons*** *War Diary, November 15, 1944*

The fourteen-day trip across the Atlantic was routine. The destroyers fueled from the transports twice and conducted the usual underway training exercises. There was not the slightest hint of the once troublesome submarines along the route. The only event out of the ordinary was connected with the upcoming presidential election, scheduled for November 7, in which President Roosevelt was seeking an unprecedented fourth term against Thomas E. Dewey, the young governor of New York. An indication that the armed forces were determined that the eligible voters serving their country away from home not be deprived of their vote because of that service came in a dispatch from the Commander-in-chief, U.S. Atlantic Fleet, directing that one destroyer be detached in time to go to Bermuda to pick up war ballots for distribution to all ships of the formation in time to be post-marked by election day. The *Hobson* was detailed to perform this service. There is no way of knowing how many voters got their ballots in the mail. Probably not many. If the *Emmons* was typical, the thought uppermost in everyone's mind was not politics, but the prospects of a few days at home.

Actually, they were to have six weeks in the navy yard. Not many aboard the destroyers knew it at the time, but they were to undergo a major change before putting to sea again. The entire squadron was to be converted to destroyer minesweepers (DMS) when it reached the States. The war against the Japanese in the Pacific was going well. The liberation of the Philippines had started with the Battle of Leyte Gulf which ended with complete victory for the American fleet. That battle was drawing to a close as DesRon 10 left Oran with the transports homeward bound. Looking beyond the Philippines to an amphibious assault on the Japanese homeland, the high-level planners in Washington realized that keeping the relatively shallow waters between the Japanese Islands and the Yellow and China seas free of mines would be a major task, requiring more minesweepers than were currently available. Some of them needed to be capable of high speed and of protecting themselves as well as the more conventional sweepers from air and surface attack. Earlier some of the old, flush deck destroyers had been converted to high speed sweepers but casualties had been high among them. Decision was made to augment those which were still afloat with twenty-four destroyers of the Benson-Gleaves class, which were no longer needed in the Atlantic.

The eight destroyers of DesRon 10 were among those designated for conversion. The day the squadron started back home, the squadron commander received a secret dispatch assigning his ships to the Service Force, Atlantic Fleet, for administration and naming the navy yards for accomplishment of the conversion. Logically, most of them were assigned to their home yards. The *Emmons,* along with the *Ellyson, Rodman,* and *Hambleton,* was to be sent to Boston.

2

Once past Bermuda the formation began to break up. Each of the transport divisions, escorted by two or three destroyers, headed for their home ports. The *Emmons, Rodman,* and *Forrest* took Transport Division 99 to the entrance of the swept channel to New *York* when they were released to go on to their own navy yards. The *Forrest* headed south for Norfolk, while the *Emmons* and *Rodman* proceeded to Boston around Cape Cod, arriving at the Charlestown Navy Yard the morning of November 9 to begin the six-week yard period during which the DD457 became the DMS22.

The six weeks were hectic. The yard crew worked around the clock to prepare the stern for handling the gear for sweeping all types of mines, from the old moored mines to the newer acoustic and magnetic mines. When they finished the area abaft No. 3 five-inch gun, it bore no resemblance to that of the old *Emmons.* Gone was gun mount No.4 and its associated ammunition handling equipment. Gone were most of the side-throwing K-guns with their depth charges. The long depth charge launching tracks had been shortened and moved outboard to make room for a bewildering jumble of reels, winches, and the complicated gear for launching and retrieving the sweeping gear. Farther forward there was not much change, except that amidships the torpedo tube and torpedoes had vanished in the constant struggle to control the topside weight. Much of the weight was taken up by a heavy, powerful motor generator needed to produce the current for activating some types of mines.

In spite of the drastic changes, the ship retained the basic characteristics of a destroyer. While a new and important function had been laid on her, she was still supposed to perform as a destroyer, although with fewer guns and depth charges than before the conversion.

The added function necessitated some changes in personnel. As there had been very few changes of personnel during the six months in Europe, a large turnover had been expected upon return to the States. That proved to be the case. During the fourth quarter of 1944, almost thirty percent of the old crew was shipped off to other duty. Because of a reduction in the allowed complement from 275 to 234 there was a net loss overall. Only thirty-nine men reported aboard during the quarter, while eighty were transferred. Most of the losses were from the petty officer ranks while most of the newcomers were seamen or firemen. Only a handful of petty officers, needed to manage the new minesweeping gear, or to fill key vacancies, were among those received on board. The new firemen outnumbered the seamen by three to two.

The more leisurely and efficient pace of getting the new recruits and draftees into uniform and off to the fighting ships was an indication that the situation at sea was now firmly in hand. The construction of new ships and the training of new men to man them had leveled off and were in much better balance than during the first precarious years of the war. Since the first of the year the *Emmons* had been receiving men with letter additions to their seamen's ratings indicating the specialties they had already started training in. Many had already been selected for engineering duty and rated as firemen second or first class. Even so, the ship, as always, relied heavily on its own training program, and continued to send many of its brightest petty officers and seamen ashore for advanced training whenever there was a chance to do so.

Inevitably, there were comparable changes in the wardroom. The *Emmons* returned from Europe with twenty-two officers aboard and ended the quarter with twenty. During the quarter, seven were ordered to other duties, while only five reported on board. Among the newcomers was Lieutenant (jg) Ralph M. Davenport, Jr., ordered aboard as minesweeping officer, and Lieutenant Temple J. Lynds, who became the new executive officer, relieving Lieutenant Commander Foss. Foss became the commanding officer when Commander Billingsley was detached to take command of a new 2200-ton destroyer building at Staten Island. Thus, the pattern of replacing the commanding officers by the executive officers at regular intervals was continued. With the departure of Billingsley, Foss became the sole remaining officer of the commissioning complement of December 5, 1941. He had reported for duty at Bath as a reserve ensign while the ship was still on the building ways.

The classification of the *Emmons* was officially changed from DD457 to DMS22 on November 15 by order of the Chief of Naval Operations, although at that point it would have been hard to distinguish her as anything but a destroyer with her after gun and depth charges missing. Other directives reorganized the first twelve destroyers undergoing change into a minesweeping squadron. The eight ships of Destroyer Squadron 10 were among the twelve which became Mine Squadron 20, subdivided into three divisions of four ships each. Captain Larkin became the squadron commander. The *Emmons* was assigned to Mine Division 59, along with the *Ellyson,* flagship of the squadron, the *Hambleton,* and the *Rodman.*

The six weeks at the Boston Navy Yard was a period cherished in the memories of the old-timers aboard. It was the longest continuous time in port since commissioning. With the ship torn up by the conversion work and the attendant noise by day and night, living conditions were far from pleasant. No one objected. They were on their home grounds, although the predominantly New England-New York composition of the commissioning crew had been considerably diluted. Three years of wartime operations had brought many changes. When the DMS22 left for the Pacific, only thirty-two of the original crew was still on board. The inexperienced apprentice seamen of 1941 were now in their early twenties, three years older, three years more experienced. Most of them had been advanced in rating and were shouldering responsibilities far beyond their years. Another striking change in the crew was the proportion of regular navy men to the reservists, those in only for the duration of the war. In December, 1941, 80.5 percent of the crew had been regulars. In December, 1944, the percentages were reversed. Only 53 of 235, or 22.5 percent, were classified as regulars. Of the officers only one was a career officer.

During the yard period, everyone aboard, not under a disciplinary cloud, was given a leave long enough to have a few days at home, regardless of the distance. Over the three years, several of the young recruits of 1941 had started families during their brief visits home. During the conversion period a few more joined their ranks. But for the most part, they chose to remain single. For the unattached, Boston's Scollay Square remained a magnet for those without personal ties in the area. There, some of them occasionally ran into a former shipmate who had been given a dishonorable discharge after the South American shakedown cruise. He had been unwilling, or unable, to shape up since then, and apparently existed by panhandling from the sailors who frequented the Square. His former shipmates pitied him, but none would have exchanged the discipline which regulated their lives for his style of freedom. This, in spite of the fact that there was a deep realization that their own days to roam about Boston were limited and that they faced a new and dangerous field of activity in the Pacific.

3

The relaxed days at Boston were soon left behind. Because the destroyers undergoing conversion were assigned to different shipyards there was no uniformity in their completion dates. As the ships were ready for sea in their new status, little time was wasted in sending them to the Pacific, where they were scheduled to take part in the upcoming Okinawa campaign. After a few days for post conversion trials and logistics they were headed south for the Canal Zone and the Pacific. Once through the Canal, the new minesweepers were routed to San Diego for a rugged inspection and several days' intensive training in the Pacific Fleet way of doing things. Between ports they were made available as escorts and routed singly, or in small groups, as circumstances dictated. No attempt was made to keep them together as a squadron until after February 10, when they were scheduled to assemble at Pearl Harbor for concentrated training in minesweeping tactics before going to the Western Pacific.

As for the *Emmons*, her conversion work was completed December 18 and she was given a few days for post-repair trials and logistics before going to Norfolk where she arrived Christmas Eve to join the *Ellyson* and the *Rodman*. Christmas day was spent quietly alongside a pier at the Naval Operating Base, but the following day she was underway with other ships of MinRon 20 present at Norfolk for exercises in Chesapeake Bay. New Year's Eve she and the *Rodman* spent all day at the base taking fuel and provisions for distant duty. One section of the crew was able to go on liberty and welcome the New Year in traditional fashion, but the remainder had to listen to the revelry secondhand over the radio. At any rate they were clear-eyed when the *Emmons* and *Rodman* got underway on New Year's Day for the Canal Zone. En route they acted as escorts for the new light cruiser *Vicksburg,* also bound for the Pacific. A few days later ComMinRon 20 in the *Ellyson* left Chesapeake Bay for the canal zone with the *Butler, Fitch, Hobson, Macomb, Jeffers,* and *Gherardi.* Within three hours of entering Limon Bay, January 5, the *Emmons* and *Rodman,* their escort duty completed, were headed through the big ditch for the Pacific. By dusk they were snugly moored in Balboa with two other ships of MinRon 20, the *Hambleton* and the *Harding,* awaiting further orders. They were now part of the Pacific Fleet. They were starting an entirely new ballgame, in a new arena, in playing positions far different from those to which they had been assigned in the Atlantic for the past three years. And, as the DMS22 was soon to learn to her consternation, under a new set of coaches.

4

New orders came quickly. After a day for logistics at Balboa, the four destroyer minesweepers were underway for San Diego. Thanks to the characteristically fine Pacific weather the eight-day voyage was uneventful. Advantage was taken of the good weather to make up some of the ground which had been lost during the hectic conversion period in the shipyards, both in upkeep and training, but because of the time involved, little could be scheduled by way of training in their new specialty, minesweeping.

The group pulled in to San Diego before noon on January 15. The *Emmons* had hardly moored alongside the *Rodman* when a boat from the Amphibious Training Command came alongside. Much to everyone's surprise, a starch-stiff four-striper, Captain R. W. Simpson, Senior Member of the San Diego Shakedown Group, came aboard and inquired if the ship was ready for inspection. Of course she was not. When Captain Foss explained that the *Emmons* had had no notice of an arrival inspection, the visitor's ire was wonderful to behold—and to hear. Part of the heat was taken off the *Emmons* and directed at his own staff when it was learned that the message advising of the inspection had been sent out on a communication circuit which the minesweepers had not been required to guard.

The upshot was that the inspection was delayed until mid-afternoon, when Captain Simpson came aboard with his party and held a personnel and below-decks inspection. It was far from satisfactory. Members of the crew still speak with bitterness—and some awe—of that inspection. Some considered it as mere nitpicking by a shore-based staff. In retrospect, they recognized that the inspectors were only carrying out their duty. Somewhere along the line there was need for professional nitpicking to prepare newcomers for the worst possible situations. Their objection was not to the objectives, but to the methods used.

DMS 22 rebounded from the shock of the unexpected inspection in characteristic style. After a week of intensive exercises with MinRon 20, under the aegis of the San Diego shakedown group, she was given an up check and left to join the *Ellyson* at San Francisco for the move to Pearl Harbor. The entire squadron underwent the most rigorous training period it had ever experienced, either as destroyers or minesweeps. Days and nights were filled with every conceivable type of casualty and gunnery drill. The gunnery exercises included surface action, night action, star shell illumination, anti-aircraft firing against drones, shore bombardment and calibration of fire control and radar equipment. One exercise which everyone enjoyed was receiving mail from a blimp off San Clemente and distributing it to other ships of the squadron. The grand finale for the *Emmons* was a battle problem exercise observed by the San Diego Shakedown Group, headed by none other than Captain Simpson. He returned to San Diego aboard, with a somewhat more favorable view of the DMS 22 than that of seven days before. Two days later the *Emmons* was underway independently for San Francisco.

The stay at San Francisco was brief. She entered the Bay early in the morning of January 26 and was ordered to be ready for sea by 1600. By sunset, she and the *Ellyson* were standing out the Golden Gate with the attack transport *Granville* on the way to Pearl Harbor as Task Unit 16.1.9.

The second day out of San Francisco a dispatch from Commander Western Sea Frontier designated the *Emmons* as Task Unit 16.1.12 and ordered her detached to rendezvous with the S.S. *Weltevreden,* then some 200 miles astern of the naval formation. After rendezvous, the *Emmons* was to escort the merchantman to Hawaii. The rendezvous was made without any difficulty the following morning and the *Weltevreden* delivered safely to Honolulu on February 2, only one day after the arrival of the *Ellyson* and *Granville.*

5

One by one, the ships of MinRon 20 reported to Pearl Harbor for several weeks of intensive training in minesweeping and regular destroyer offensive-defensive exercises under the direction of ComMinPac and ComDesPac. It was the first time the squadron had been together since leaving the conversion ship yards. In effect it was a shakedown for both the squadron and the individual ships. Even so, it was difficult to get them together for divisional exercises as most of them required upkeep time after their hurried departure from the East Coast and the long voyage to Pearl. The *Emmons* was no exception. She had to be docked on a marine railway for repairs to nicked propellers and realignment of her sonar dome. Advantage was taken of the upkeep time to work on her electronic equipment and the new minesweeping gear. As she had been designated as fighter-director ship for MinDiv 59 special attention was paid to radio equipment used for that function.

As the month of February neared its end, the training had to give way to preparations for moving the squadron on to Ulithi, the main staging point for the assault on Okinawa. Eight of the ships were formed up as Task Unit 18.2.3 and sailed for Ulithi on February 24 via Eniwetok. The *Emmons, Rodman, Macomb,* and *Jeffers* were held at Pearl to become the escorts of convoy PD-312-T consisting of the transport *General Taylor,* the attack transports *Colusa* and *Bland,* and the cargo ship *Sea Flier.* The convoy sailed February 27 as Task Unit 16.8.1 and, after an uneventful voyage of eight days arrived at Eniwetok where the ships spent the better part of two days before going on to Ulithi.

Since its capture in February, 1944, Eniwetok, westernmost of the Marshall Islands, had become a major base and stopping point for ships bound to or from the Western Pacific. From a distance, the low-lying atolls ringing the protected lagoon looked like a picture postcard. Close up, they offered little of interest to the crew of the *Emmons* except as a source of fuel, food, and supplies before they plunged into the Western Pacific. By now the crew had grown used to the benign climate of the Pacific and liked it in comparison to the rugged weather they had had to fight in the Atlantic. But they would gladly have exchanged the fine weather for the frequent returns to the East Coast ports of the United States and the visits to the cosmopolitan ports of Great Britain and the Mediterranean which had been part of the Atlantic duty. Since reporting to the Pacific they had been too busy to sample the attractions of the West Coast ports or the Hawaiian Islands to any great degree. Now those were far behind them. Few had any opportunity to add to the huge pile of empty beer cans which plainly marked Mog-Mog, the atoll set aside for recreation parties.

One man aboard had good reason to remember the brief visit to Eniwetok with pleasure. Fred Igou was tending the laundry machinery when he heard a voice he could not associate with any of his shipmates calling his name. Whirling around he was amazed to see his own brother, Bob, whom he had not seen since the beginning of the war. The fortunes of war had brought the brothers together for a few hours in the same Central Pacific lagoon more than a quarter of the way around the globe from their home. The elder brother was serving as a signalman aboard the tanker *Armadillo* and happened to have the watch on the bridge when the *Emmons* entered the lagoon. He immediately got permission to visit the minesweeper and was able to surprise his younger brother at work in the laundry room. The latter took pride in showing off his home to the visitor. A special feature was offering him ice cream fresh from the *Emmons* ice cream machine—a recent acquisition and a luxury of which few small ships in the forward areas could boast. The next day Fred spent with his brother on the *Armadillo* until just before time for the *Emmons* to get underway for Ulithi.

The Task Unit arrived at Ulithi, March 12, to find the lagoon crowded with ships of all descriptions, from giant carriers to tugs, preparing for the attack on Okinawa.

Ulithi had become an advanced base for operations in the Western Pacific almost from the time of its occupation by United States forces in September, 1944. The fast carriers of the Third Fleet had retired there for rest and reorganization after they were no longer needed in the Philippines. There, when the Third Fleet became the Fifth Fleet under Admiral Raymond A. Spruance, and Task Force 38, the Fast Carrier Force, became Task Force 58 under Vice Admiral Marc A. Mitscher, Ulithi lagoon became the base for fast carrier strikes against the Japanese home islands and much of the supporting forces for the attack on Iwo Jima in February, 1945. Now, in early March, it had become the main staging point for Operation ICEBERG, the assault on Okinawa, the last, and one of the grandest, amphibious operations of World War II.

6

The Okinawa operation originated in a directive dated October 3, 1944, to Admiral Nimitz, the Commander in Chief of the Pacific Ocean Area, at a time when the buildup for the landings at Leyte Gulf was well underway. Once the Philippines were liberated the quickest and surest way to bring the war to an end seemed to be a direct attack on the Japanese homeland. But there were several possible approaches to the home islands. One was through China, another through the Ryukus, the chain of islands between Formosa and Japan proper, and the third was up through the Bonins. All of them would involve amphibious assaults and all would be sure to bring high casualties. The directive of the Joint Chiefs of Staff ordered the seizure of one or more islands in the Bonins and one or more in the Ryukus in preparation for an attack on the Japanese home islands.

Iwo Jima in the Bonins and Okinawa in the Ryukus were chosen by the Central Pacific planners. The choice of Iwo Jima was dictated by the need for an intermediate airfield between the Marianas and Japan to provide fighter protection for Super Fortresses attacking the islands, as well as to provide an emergency landing field for the bombers in case of necessity. Okinawa, central and largest of the Ryukus, and almost equi-distant from Kyushu, the southernmost of the Japanese islands, the coast of China, and Formosa, was chosen as a stepping stone for any future attack on Japan itself. Further, it and its satellite island of Ie Shima had several good airfields capable of expansion. Of course, those same airfields were a menace to invasion forces up until such time as they could be captured and converted to use against the enemy.

One disadvantage of Okinawa as a target was its great distance from friendly bases, which posed enormous logistical problems. Its distance from Ulithi, which became the principal staging area for the attack, was 1,180 miles. Iwo Jima was secured shortly before the date for the invasion, but it would hardly have qualified as a base for resupply and support forces even if it had been available earlier. Leyte, slightly nearer than Ulithi, became another staging area, but the Philippines were still in the process of liberation when the Okinawa campaign started. Other bases from Guadalcanal to the Aleutians, were used as assembly points for men and material for the initial attack, and the replacement pipe lines extended all the way back through the Pacific to the continental United States. After the initial attack, most men and supplies were funneled through Ulithi, which served very well, but the fact remains that Okinawa was uncomfortably far from supply and support bases.

7

The plans for Operation ICEBERG, as the invasion of Okinawa was designated, were completed in record time in comparison with the planning periods for the African and European invasions and some of the Pacific operations. The accelerated pace of the war had the Japanese as well as the Germans on the run. It was imperative that the Japanese not be given a breather to dig in for the defense of their homeland.

Several factors facilitated the planning. One was the dual system of command of the Pacific Fleet, whereby the commanders and staffs of the Third Fleet and Fifth Fleet alternated between actual operations with the fighting ships at sea and planning duties ashore. Thus, Admiral Spruance, commander of the Fifth Fleet, and his staff had time to devote to planning for ICEBERG, while Admiral Halsey and his staff took the ships to sea as the Third Fleet in support of the repatriation of the Philippines. Another factor was that the successes in Europe and the Atlantic, combined with the outpouring of men and material from the United States, made it possible to allocate more men, ships and planes to the Pacific area than ever before. The commanders of a projected operation no longer had to wait months, even years, for the allocation and accumulation of enough men and material to proceed with reasonable assurance of success. The collapse of German opposition at sea was particularly helpful in building up naval forces in the Pacific Fleet, as witness the conversion and assignment to the Pacific of the *Emmons* and her sisters to supply the acute need for high speed minesweepers.

The principal commanders for Operation ICEBERG met at Pearl Harbor in November, 1944, to produce operational plans for the invasion. Admiral Spruance, in overall command, under Nimitz, of all forces engaged in the operation, issued his plan on January 3, 1945. It was followed on February 9, by the detailed plans of Vice Admiral Richmond Kelly Turner, who, as Commander of the Joint Expeditionary Force, Task Force 51, was responsible for all phases of the landings, except for operations of the fast carrier task force. The fast carriers remained directly under Admiral Spruance.

For sheer size the operation dwarfed previous amphibious operations in the Pacific. The plans for the most part followed the pattern which had been developed throughout the war with a few differences dictated by the geographic location of Okinawa. The main landings were to be made by the Tenth Army under General Simon Bolivar Buckner over five miles of beaches on the west coast, on either side of the Bisha River, named the Hagushi beaches after a village at the mouth of the river. The initial landings were to be made by two divisions of the Marine III Amphibious Corps north of the river and two from the XXIV Army Corps south of the river. The Marines were to drive to the east and north while the Army divisions were to push east and south. First objectives were to capture two airfields back of the landing beaches and the southern part of the island where the greatest opposition was anticipated. After southern Okinawa was secured attention was to be paid to northern Okinawa and the large island of Ie Shima with its valuable airfields. The third phase was to be a drive up the Ryukus chain to the Japanese homeland.

Two features of the assault plans are worthy of special attention. Because of the distance from friendly territory, protective air and surface coverage had to be provided by two fast carrier task forces. The first was the Fast Carrier Task Force, Pacific Fleet, TF 58, commanded by Vice Admiral Marc A. Mitscher, subdivided into four task groups, each composed of fast carriers, new battleships and cruisers, and one or more squadrons of destroyers. After raids on air and naval stations on Kyushu and a raid on Okinawa itself, TF 58 was to be stationed to the east and northeast of the target area to prevent interference with the invasion by Japanese forces from the home islands, the Chinese mainland and air stations in the northern Ryukus. The other carrier task force was the British Carrier Force, Task Force 57, under the command of Vice Admiral Sir H. B. Rawlings, RN. It was composed of their newest carriers, battleships, and cruisers, plus destroyers, most of which had recently been sent to the Pacific as the sea war in the Atlantic wound down. Among them were the *Illustrious, Victorious* and other old friends of the *Emmons* from Home Fleet days. The British task force was responsible for preventing any disruption of Operation ICEBERG from Formosa and the southern Ryukus.

Another variation was the early seizure and occupation of a cluster of lightly held islands, collectively known as Kerama Rhetto, about fifteen miles west of Naha. The islands were to be taken by Task Group 51.1, the Western Island Task Group, under Rear Admiral I. N. Kiland, a week before the main landings on Okinawa. The purpose was to provide a sheltered, defensible anchorage nearby, where fuel, ammunition, and provisions could be transferred from bulk carriers in relative safety from both enemy attacks and the hazards of the sea. It was also to become a seaplane base for long-range search and antisubmarine patrol planes, an anchorage for repair ships, hospitals, and a haven for ships whose missions were completed or which suffered battle damage. In effect, it became a local advanced base until such time as Naha, or other sheltered harbors in Okinawa could be secured.

A less important variation from previous assault plans was the substitution of "L-day" to replace the customary "D-day" to designate the date the troops were actually to hit the beaches on Okinawa itself. It is possible the substitution was made to prevent confusion of the date for the main landings with the preliminary seizure of Kerama Rhetto. L-day was eventually set for April 1 after it was clear that all forces, such as those assigned for the capture of Iwo Jima and to support the liberation of the Philippines, would be available for ICEBERG by that date.

Besides the Western Island Attack Group the Joint Expeditionary Force was organized along the usual lines for an amphibious expedition. The Northern Attack Force (TF 53) was responsible for landing the Marines on the northern part of Hagushi beaches while the Southern Attack Force put the Army troops ashore over the southern part. A Gunfire and Covering Force (TF 54) was to provide close gunfire support and protect the beach areas from enemy intrusions. Its backbone was old battleships supported by a mixture of light and heavy cruisers and, of course, destroyers. It was commanded by Rear Admiral Deyo, under whom the *Emmons* had operated at Normandy and Cherbourg.

The Amphibious Support Force (TF 52), commanded by Rear Admiral W. H. P. Blandy, was charged with a wide variety of support functions. Among its diverse groups was a Support Carrier Group (TG 52.1) of eighteen escort carriers which shared air support duties in the target area with Task Force 58. Of most interest to the *Emmons*, Task Group 52.2, commanded by Rear Admiral Alexander Sharp, was responsible for clearing enemy mines in the target area and anything else having to do with mine warfare. The twelve ships of Mine Squadron 20, plus three destroyer minelayers, became Task Group 52.3, the Destroyer Minesweeper Group, under the overall command of Admiral Sharp, but under the direct command of Captain Larkin. This group was further subdivided into three task units, 52.3.2, 52.3.3, and 52.3.4, also called Sweep units TWO, THREE, and FOUR on the operation plans. Each of the sweep units consisted of four destroyer minesweepers corresponding to the sweepers of Mine Divisions 58, 59, and 60 and one destroyer minelayer. The latter were destroyers of the *Sumner* class which had been converted to high-speed minelayers while still under construction. Mine Division 59, including the *Emmons*, became Task Unit 52.3.3 and Sweep Unit THREE. The *Lindsey* (DM32) was the fast minelayer attached to the unit. Captain Larkin wore two hats, one as Commander Task Group 52.3, the other as Commander Task Unit 52.3.3 and Sweep Unit THREE.

8

As for the Japanese, their dreams of an empire in the Pacific had vanished long before 1945. For the last two years they had been on the defensive and by the end of 1944 were standing on the last defense line of the homeland which they were preparing to hold at all costs. In the summer of 1944 they had drawn up plans for the defense of the homeland on the assumption that any attack would come either by way of Formosa and the Ryukus, or the Chinese mainland. The defense plans were called Operation TENGO and depended heavily on massed air attacks, including extensive use of kamikaze, or suicide, planes.

At the beginning of March, 1945, with the Americans in control of most of the Philippines and the fall of Iwo Jima imminent, the day of reckoning for the Japanese was at hand. It was obvious that the next move would be in the direction of the homeland. They correctly estimated that Okinawa was to be the target and desperately tried to bolster the defenses of that island, including the concentration of all available aircraft at airfields within striking distance from Kyushu to Formosa.

Neither the Japanese political nor military leaders had illusions about the gravity of the situation. Given the disparity between their depleted resources and widely scattered forces and those of the United States, they knew that ultimate defeat was inevitable. In fact there was a strong peace faction among their leaders, many of whom would gladly have negotiated a peace treaty on what they could consider honorable terms—continued Japanese independence and preservation of her institutions, including retention of the "divine" Emperor. Incidentally, Emperor Hirohito himself favored the peace faction and eventually, after the fighting on Okinawa had begun, approved the reshuffling of the cabinet to pave the way for negotiations. He even sanctioned a move to appeal to Russia to intercede with the United States on Japan's behalf—this, in spite of the fact that it was generally believed that Russia had agreed at the Yalta Conference to enter the war on the side of the Allies after the defeat of Germany. Before Okinawa the unconditional surrender edict of the Allies and the fanatical pride of the Japanese precluded a negotiated peace. This impasse continued until the dropping of the atomic bomb. At the beginning of the Okinawa campaign it appeared to Allied planners that the only way to bring the war to an end was to physically overrun and occupy the Japanese islands regardless of the cost. Planning was going ahead on that assumption. The Japanese leaders realized that their only hope of saving the homeland and preserving their institutions was to stop the Americans at Okinawa, or, failing that, to make its capture so costly that the Americans would be willing to make peace rather than face an even costlier invasion of the homeland.

9

When the *Emmons, Rodman,* and *Jeffers* arrived at Ulithi on March 12, most of the forces scheduled for the opening phases of Operation ICEBERG were in place at the staging ports, waiting for the signal to converge on Okinawa. A large part of the ships waiting in the lagoon were scheduled to take part in the preliminary operations off the target as well as in the actual landings on L-day. Among them were the other nine ships of MinRon 20 which had reached the port three days earlier, but were at sea engaged in exercises and the calibration of minesweeping equipment when the last three entered port.

The late arrivals put to sea the next day to join in the exercises. They got in two days of profitable training before returning to the lagoon for final preparations for the invasion. The *Fitch* was unlucky enough to wreck both her propellers on a concealed reef on the last day at sea and had to be towed back to port. Decision was finally made to send her back to Pearl for permanent repairs. Thus, when MinRon 20 set out for Okinawa, the squadron had only eleven rather than twelve sweepers.

The remainder of the squadron spent four days at anchor before leaving for Okinawa. Much time was spent studying and digesting the plans issued by the various task forces and groups. The minesweeping plans were of immediate concern, but as the high speed minesweepers were still as much destroyers as they were minesweepers they could be called on at any time to perform the duties of either. So they had to master the details of the plans of other task forces as well as those of the Mine Force. Actually, during the operation they spent as much time, or more, performing escort, screen, and patrol duties as they did sweeping for mines. While the officers and men responsible for executing the plans were busy digesting them, the rest of the crews were kept busy readying the ships and equipment for action.

One by one the first groups to kick off the Okinawa campaign left Ulithi. As one group of ships left, their place in the lagoon would be taken by others moving up from the rear to wait their turn. The first major group to sortie was the Fast Carrier Force which was to make air strikes against airfields and naval bases in Japan and finally on Okinawa itself before taking station to provide air support and cover for the invasion.

The carriers left Ulithi on March 14. They were followed on the 19th by the minesweepers. By the very nature of their task the minesweepers had to be the first surface vessels at the target area. Unlike the carriers they set course directly to the objective. The voyage took only four days and, as far as the destroyer minesweepers were concerned, was largely uneventful. Nonetheless, there was considerable concern over two threats. One was the deteriorating weather and the other was enemy air attacks.

The usually placid Pacific showed signs of anger at the massive invasion of its privacy. A typhoon was threatened but failed to reach full strength. In fact, the rough seas did more damage to later formations headed for Okinawa than it did to the minesweepers. The latter were able to fuel at sea with only minor casualties two days before beginning sweeping operations. Aboard the *Emmons,* Fireman First Class Bill Boyle suffered several fractured ribs when a huge wave slammed him against the bulkhead at the amidships fueling station as the ship pulled away from the tanker. Doc Williamson taped up the broken ribs and gave up his own bunk to the patient so that he might rest easier. Later, Boyle credited the cracked ribs with saving his life. His battle station was on the fantail, but because he could not go to his general quarters station, he escaped almost certain death on April 6, when the first kamikaze to zero in on the *Emmons* hit the stern.

There was no direct attack on the mine force during the four-day voyage to Okinawa. Although the Japanese had correctly pinpointed the target and their naval staff had even predicted the date with remarkable accuracy, they made no attempts against the approaching formations. This may be attributed to their preoccupation with the threat of Task Force 58 off the home islands. Moreover, they were still demoralized by fire-bombing B-29 raids earlier in March. Continued attacks by carrier-based planes and the heavy bombers from the Mariana area served to keep them off balance.

As the minesweepers neared Okinawa on the 23rd, the danger of an air attack became more likely. No real attack developed, but during the afternoon and early evening several bogies, the code word for unidentified aircraft, was picked up by radar. The formation took up a special defense disposition to be ready. Near sunset the *Hambleton* reported an enemy plane flying about fifty feet off the water. It disappeared without attempting to attack. Shortly before midnight several bogies closed the formation from starboard, crossed ahead and disappeared to the southwest without hostile action. Several ships in the screen to port took them under fire without any discernable results. Two night fighters from a nearby carrier group were vectored on the formation but the bogies were not intercepted. Throughout the night a Combat Air Patrol (CAP) remained overhead.

At 0300 on the 24th the destroyer minesweepers were detached from the formation to begin sweeping area V-4, to the south of Okinawa, at sunrise. For them operation ICEBERG had started, although the operation plans did not become effective until two hours later.

10

The actual sweeping operations were anticlimactic for the destroyer minesweepers. Task Group 52.3 spent all day, the 24th, plodding along within the assigned areas to the south and southwest of Okinawa. Largely because the sweep areas were outside the 100 fathom curve, no mines were encountered. The Japanese had not yet progressed beyond the moored mines which they used extensively in more shallow waters, mostly off potential landing beaches. It fell to the lot of the smaller minesweepers, the AMs and the YMSs, to clear the shallow waters. Throughout the operation the fast minesweepers made exploratory sweeps for moored and acoustic mines in deep water while the AMs and YMSs swept right up to the limits for their drafts. As the exploratory sweeps established that an assigned area was clear of mines the DMSs were frequently moved inshore to ride shotgun on the smaller units.

After the first day's sweep the *Emmons,* with TG 52.3, retired to the south with TG 52.2. Thereafter, as other elements of the assault force, such as the fire support units of Task Force 54, arrived in the target area, the destroyer minesweepers were either ordered to augment their screens at night or to man patrol stations off target areas. By day they functioned as minesweepers. By night they performed the duties of destroyers.

The sweeps scheduled for March 25, L-day minus 7, were among the most crucial of the entire operation. The next day, L-day minus 6, the fire support units of Task Force 54 were to move into position off the west coast to begin the first of six days' bombardment of the defenses in the vicinity of the Hagushi beaches preceding the landings on April 1. The same day the Western Island Attack Group was to occupy the Kerama Rhetto islands. Neither could start until the approaches and offshore areas were free of mines. Task Group 52.3 was given the task of clearing and buoying Channel A-1, the approach channel to the Hagushi beaches, which ran northwest and north of Kerama Rhetto. The destroyer sweep units were to be followed by AM sweep units to widen the channel on either side. At the eastern end all units were to sweep large areas off shore to provide maneuvering room for the fire support ships, and later on the assault ships. While the approaches to the main landing beaches on Okinawa were being swept, other sweep units were clearing the area around Kerama Rhetto for the Western Island Attack Group (TF 51.1) the following morning.

No mines were dislodged by the DMSs, but during the forenoon, the *Emmons* sighted a floating mine close aboard which was destroyed by the *Wiley* (DM-29). On completion of the day's sweeps the destroyer minesweepers took up patrol stations to prevent remaining of the newly swept area. The *Emmons* and *Rodman* shared a patrol line northwest of Kerama Rhetto.

Both the bombardment and landing operations scheduled for the 26th were carried out smoothly and with negligible opposition. While Task Force 54 was taking position to bombard the Hagushi beach area and Task Group 51.1 was landing on the islands, the *Emmons* with the rest of Sweep Unit THREE and Sweep Unit FOUR was engaged in a clearance sweep of the area to the north of Kerama Rhetto with negative results. After sweeping gear had been recovered the sweeps took night screening stations around the Kerama Rhetto transport area. Although the occupation of the islands had gone remarkably well, there were still many troops and much material aboard the transports in the anchorage area. There had been reports of unidentified aircraft to the north during the day and the ships of the bombardment force had reported sighting torpedoes. Further, a number of inactive suicide boats had been found on the occupied islands. There was every expectation of some sort of enemy action during the night. It came early in the evening when many unidentified planes were picked up approaching from the west. Several of the screening ships opened fire and one plane was seen to burst into flames before it turned away. None of the attacking planes came within range of the screen sector manned by TU 52.3.3. A more serious attack came the next morning when the *Gilmer*, at the anchorage, and the *Kimberly*, on radar picket station to the southwest, were hit by "Vals" in separate, uncoordinated attacks.

The ships of Sweep Units THREE and FOUR were aware that the attacks were going on, but took no part in the actions. At the time they were streaming sweeping gear at the entrance to Channel A-l, preparatory to a check sweep to make sure that the enemy had laid no mines in the vital channel during the night. After assuring that no mines were present the sweep units proceeded to an entirely new area, far to the west of Ie Shima, to conduct an exploratory sweep which produced no mines.

That night, instead of taking up patrol stations, the minesweepers joined the screen around heavy ships of Task Force 54 for their nightly retirement.

11

The foregoing account of the activities of the destroyer minesweepers during the first four days of the Okinawa campaign will give some idea of the variety of duties they were required to perform. Bouncing from task to task each day and night called for the utmost versatility and flexibility to adjust to the demands of each new situation. As L-day approached, the tempo of action off the beaches increased. So, too, did the frequency of the enemy air attacks, although they were still relatively weak. There was more and more need for destroyer types to augment the regularly assigned destroyers for patrol, picket, and screening duties. The fast minesweepers proved to be a natural reservoir of ships to fill additional requirements.

After the day's sweep of March 27, Task Unit 52.3.3 virtually ceased operations as a minesweeping unit for a few days and the individual ships were assigned to other duties as needed, largely with various fire support groups of Task Force 54. When that force returned to the Hagushi beaches the morning of the 28th to resume the shore bombardment, TU 52.3.3 remained in its destroyer screen instead of breaking off to begin scheduled minesweeping assignments as usual. After beating off a weak enemy suicide attack at dawn, the various fire support units, each composed of two old battleships, two or three cruisers, and four or five destroyers, were released to go to their bombardment stations.

Sweep Unit THREE was directed to accompany Fire Support Unit THREE, led by the battleship *Idaho,* as screen. The fire support ships, screened by the minesweepers, cruised off the Hagushi beaches all day, pounding enemy strong points from Point Zama Misaka to Naha. There were no further air attacks, and enemy shore batteries remained silent. The only casualty to U.S. ships in the area was the *Skylark* (AM 63), which hit a mine while sweeping near Point Zama Misaki. She sank within minutes. Fortunately, most of her crew was saved.

After the day's work TU 52.3.3 received new orders requiring them to join Fire Support Unit ONE for night retirement east of Okinawa. Two of the heavies in that group, the *Tuscaloosa* and the *Texas,* were old friends from the Atlantic and Mediterranean days. During the night the *Emmons* was charged with tracking the PBMs on antisubmarine and reconnaissance patrol out of Kerama Rhetto to insure that no one fired on them because of mistaken identity.

The morning of March 29, Fire Support Unit ONE with most of Sweep Unit THREE proceeded to the Demonstration beaches on the southeast coast of Okinawa to begin a series of operations designed to give the Japanese the impression that the assault, when it came, would be made over those beaches.

The *Emmons* was not with the Demonstration Group when it took station to begin the scheduled operations. By that time she was north of Okinawa, preparing to begin sweeping operations with Sweep Unit TWO near Yoron Shima. Sometime during the night she had been detached to report to ComMinDiv 58 of Sweep Unit TWO as relief for the *Macomb* so that the latter could get to Kerama Rhetto for fuel and other logistics. With the *Fitch* on the way back to Pearl Harbor, Sweep Unit TWO was already short-handed. With the *Macomb* gone it would have been down to two effective minesweepers, the *Forrest* and the *Hobson.* Another reason for substituting the *Emmons* for the *Macomb* was that the latter was fighter-direction ship for MinDiv 58 and it was desirable to replace her with another designated fighter director.

12

When the *Emmons* relieved the *Macomb* about 0500 the 29th, Unit TWO was engaged in sweeping an extensive area between Yoron Shima and Okino Erabu Shima, the first two islands north of Okinawa along the Ryukus chain in the direction of Kyushu. The center of the sweep area was about twenty nautical miles from the northernmost tip of Okinawa. The minesweepers, supported by the minelayer *Gwin* with ComMinRon 3 embarked, had been ordered to sweep for moored and acoustic mines during the day and patrol the area by night. With the exception of a few radar pickets and, at times, the widely-ranging fast carrier task force to the east, they were farther north and more isolated than any other units of the invasion fleet. In effect, besides sweeping for mines, they were point unit on the most direct route by surface or air from Japan to Okinawa. They were anything but bored in this exposed position.

Every day and night many aircraft, both friendly and enemy, were picked up by radar. By far the greater numbers of the latter were picked up during hours of darkness, and most were headed south. Fortunately, most of them stayed on course. They either were unaware of the minesweepers or ignored them. Occasionally one would come close enough to make it worth while to open fire. That happened the morning the *Emmons* joined the unit. Both ComMinRon 3 and ComMinDiv 58 noted a large movement of unidentified planes heading south between midnight and dawn on that date. Both reported that the ships of the formation opened fire on one which came within range without any apparent results. In his action report for the invasion ComMinDiv 58 stated: "This night and each following night while the unit was operating in this area, bogies passed from north to south, over land when at all possible. It looked like the main highway from the north leading to Okinawa airfields." The sweep unit had better results when another bogie was splashed by collective fire just before midnight on March 31.

At night, the formation was plagued by frequent surface radar contacts, all of which proved to be false. Nonetheless they had to be treated as real contacts until actually proven false. Air and surface contacts were so frequent that the *Emmons* adopted condition watches of six hours on and six hours off for half the crew. Apparently the false contacts were caused by some unusual atmospheric conditions. Lieutenant Commander Foss, skipper of the *Emmons,* described the radar conditions as "spooky." There was no obvious cause—the weather was mild, clouds were light, and visibility ranged from ten miles to unlimited. The ships of the unit began to refer to the false contacts as "The Galloping Ghost of Nansei Shoto." ComMinDiv 58 in his war diary reported that one night the *Hobson* "had a surface engagement with the Galloping Ghost." Another night the *Gwin* tried to illuminate the ghost without success.

Fortunately the ghost phenomenon did not affect the air search radars. The planes in the area were real enough. Not all of them were enemy. Many friendlies crossed over the sweep area. Their presences required extra precaution to determine the friendly or enemy character of each air contact by exchange of electronic signals before opening fire. Foss remembers one particularly troublesome night when a slow moving aerial contact came directly toward the *Emmons* but failed to show identification signals. It made no hostile moves—still its identification equipment was silent and that alone was sufficient to warrant opening fire. The gunnery officer reported the director and guns locked on the target and begged for permission to open fire. However, the skipper sensed that this was not the usual pattern and withheld permission, waiting for the last minute to give the order. As the slow-moving plane came within visual range it was obviously one of our own clumsy patrol PBMs. As it flew serenely on into the night its identification signals, which had been silent from head on, came in loud and clear from astern. There is no way of knowing whether or not its crew was ever aware of the *Emmons,* but they can thank the patience of her skipper that they didn't run into a lot of friendly, but deadly, flak that night.

There were several sonar contacts which could have been Japanese U-boats, but all proved to be non-submarine after thorough investigation. One submarine alert stemmed from the report of a possible periscope on the port beam by the *Forrest.* As the three minesweepers were in sweeping formation with gear streamed they could not respond immediately, so the *Gwin* was detached to investigate while the sweepers went about their business. The *Emmons* as fighter director ship vectored a nearby combat air patrol to the scene. Both the *Gwin* and the CAP reported no evidence of a sub. This incident occurred during the last pass of the scheduled sweep of the area on March 31. At 1249 that date sweeping operations were completed, gear recovered, and patrol of the newly swept area started pending new orders. Three of the ships had been sweeping and patrolling for a week. The *Emmons* had shared their vigil for the last three days. No mines had been found, but they had verified that none were present, if and when the fleet needed to cross those waters, and, of equal importance, they had supplied valuable information on air traffic in that area to the fleet to the south.

The waiting period was tense. Everyone aboard the ships of the sweep unit was aware that the actual landings on Okinawa would be kicked off within a few hours and everyone expected the enemy to pull up everything he had to stop it. Although a considerable distance from the landing area they knew that they were along the route of anything sent down from Japan. Naturally, the waiting period was enlivened by several alarms, most of them false, but some real enough.

Just before sunset the *Hobson* picked up a sonar contact which was eventually evaluated as no submarine. During the evening watch the patrolling ships had two encounters with the "Galloping Ghost of Nansei Shoto," both of them near the western end of their patrol. Just before midnight air search radars picked up several bogies in the vicinity which were real. One was seen to crash when fire was opened on them.

13

The midwatch of L-day opened with the four patrolling ships shadow boxing with several enemy aircraft which intermittently came and went between midnight and 0130. They made no attempt to attack the formation, but evasive action was taken to confuse them in case they did. Fire was opened on them several times with no observable results. After the bogies had disappeared the *Gwin* and *Forrest* left the formation in obedience to previous orders to set up an antisubmarine patrol east of Okinawa. In recognition of the strategic location of the newly swept area, the *Emmons* was ordered to remain as radar picket with *Hobson* as fire support ship.

To the south, the ships of the Joint Expeditionary Force were taking station to begin what was to be the last major amphibious action of World War ll.

The old battleships and cruisers of the Gunfire and Covering Force, with attendant destroyers, were plodding up the approach channel to the fire support areas off the Hagushi beaches. Following them were the transports and landing craft of the Northern and Southern Attack Forces, bound for their designated anchorages or assembly points in the transport areas. The time for each unit to move up the channel was carefully coordinated so that each ship would be on station and ready to offload its boats, troops, tanks, vehicles—whatever it carried—in time to meet the requirements of H-hour. H-hour was set for 0830. Similar activity was going on off the Demonstration beaches on the southeastern coast.

Aboard the fast carriers of Task Force 58 and the escort carriers of Task Group 52.1 fighters and bombers were being readied for the coming battle. Some were being prepared for combat air patrol over the assault beaches and the fleet concentrations. Others were being loaded with bombs and rockets for a final aerial bombardment of the landing beaches. Others would be prepared to provide tactical support on call from the ground forces after the touchdown. A few would become observers and spotters for the gunfire support ships or the artillery with the troops.

The ships of the Logistic Support Group, Task Group 50.8, rode quietly at anchor at Kerama Rhetto ready to provide their varied services as the battle developed. Some were prepared to go to the beach area, if necessary. They included tankers, ammunition a ships, reefers and stores ship, repair ships, floating drydocks, tugs, and, ominously, hospital ships and rescue tugs.

The minesweepers of the Mine Flotilla, Task Group 52.2, were the most widely scattered of all during the small hours of L-day. A few, such as the

Emmons and *Hobson,* were on radar picket duty. Others were on antisubmarine patrol. Most of the smaller minesweepers were with various retirement groups and would resume sweeping duties in the morning. Many of the destroyer minesweepers were escorting combat units. This was true of Sweep Unit THREE, to which the *Emmons* nominally belonged. During the midwatch, ships of the unit were screening Fire Support Unit ONE, but when that unit took station off the Demonstration beaches at daybreak, they were detached to proceed to an area northwest of Kerama Rhetto, there to standby for any emergency service ordered. Actually, they were not used until after sunset, L-day, when the unit was ordered to establish an antisubmarine patrol northwest of Ie Shima.

It was expected that the Japanese would oppose the landings with everything they could possibly muster up. There was not too much concern over their decimated surface fleet. There was more concern for the damage stray submarines could inflict if they managed to penetrate to the transport areas. But the greatest concern was over Japanese aircraft, particularly their increasing use of suicide planes. The preliminary operations had already resulted in a number of painful losses inflicted by a relatively few kamikazes. And it was known that the enemy was concentrating a large number of miscellaneous aircraft on the fields of Kyushu and the Ryukus, obviously with the intention of hurling them at the invaders.

Much to everyone's surprise, from Admiral Turner on down to the marines and soldiers who made the original landings, there was virtually no opposition on L-day and for several days thereafter. The defenders of Okinawa had made the decision not to try to stop the invasion at the beaches. Rather, they concentrated on strong defense positions inland, primarily in the mountains of southern Okinawa, hoping to stop reinforcement and supply of the troops by massive suicide attacks on the invading fleet, thus leaving the vanguard of the assault troops to wither on the vine. As a result the Army troops and Marines marched inland with little opposition during the first few days. Both Kadena and Yontan airfields were captured on L-day and rapidly converted for use against the entrenched Japanese. Originally it had been estimated that it would take three days to overrun them. However, the massive planned air attacks could not be mounted until five days after the landings. It took the Japanese that long to prepare and position the planes they had pulled together to execute TENGO.

The benign neglect of the Japanese of the invading forces on L-day was shared by the *Emmons* and *Hobson* on their northern radar picket station. However, they were not left on the isolated duty for long. About midmorning, when it became apparent that the enemy was not going to mount the massive counterattack expected, the *Gwin* and *Forrest* were ordered from their antisubmarine patrol to Kerama Rhetto for logistics. Some time during the afternoon they were joined at the anchorage by the *Emmons* and *Hobson.*

About sundown Commander Task Group 52.2 called a conference of the senior officers of the destroyer minesweepers in the vicinity aboard his flagship, the *Terror,* in Kerama Rhetto, to discuss plans for sweeping the waters east of Okinawa. Captain Larkin came in from the standby station of Sweep Unit THREE aboard the *Ellyson* for the conference. Orders for the new sweep operations were actually distributed by hand to the commanders present.

In the meantime, however, higher command decided that the best use for the destroyer minesweepers at that stage of the invasion was as antisubmarine patrols. Such patrols would serve the double purpose of protecting the fleet concentrations from submarines and augmenting the network of radar pickets already in place on the approaches to Okinawa. Before the conference of mine sweep commanders broke up, the plans they had agreed on for sweeping the eastern coastal waters were cancelled, at least temporarily, when orders from Commander Task Force 51 were received to set up two antisubmarine patrols. Sweep Unit THREE was to set up a patrol line northwest of Ie Shima while Unit TWO established one southeast of Hedo Saki, the northern tip of Okinawa.

The conference aboard the *Terror* broke up shortly after midnight and the minesweepers concerned started to get underway for their latest assignment. Just as Sweep Unit TWO, with the *Emmons* still substituting for the *Macomb,* got underway, condition RED, meaning enemy aircraft were in the vicinity, was announced for Kerama Rhetto. Under threat of an air attack, all the ships in the anchorage capable of doing so made smoke. The first three ships of Unit TWO got through the antisubmarine gate safely before the smoke closed in, but the *Emmons,* being the last to sortie, was so engulfed in smoke that she was ordered to anchor and wait for the smoke to clear before attempting to get out through the narrow gate. Condition WHITE, all clear, was announced in less than an hour and the *Emmons* easily overhauled the unit in time to take station at the seaward end of a patrol line extending between fifteen and thirty-one miles from Hedo Saki, on a bearing of 112°.

If any one feature characterized the duty assignments of destroyer minesweepers, it was the rapid change from one day to the next. After a day and night of unexciting beating back and forth along the patrol line, CTF 51 ordered the patrol terminated and the ships of Unit TWO were directed to screen the *Minneapolis* and *Wadsworth,* which in turn were acting as fire support ships for Sweep Unit FOUR off Kakagusuka Wan, later to be renamed Buckner Bay. The move was significant for several reasons. For one, the invasion was going very well—there was little to fear from submarines, and at that time, L-day plus 2, not much more from the air. For another, the minesweepers were returning to their normal business of minesweeping. And, of major importance, preparations were underway to make Nakagusuka Wan into a support base for operations ashore.

Much the same thing was going on with Sweep Unit THREE on the other side of the island except that Unit THREE had more interference from enemy air than the ships to the east of the island. In her war diary for April 4, the *Hambleton* recorded that sixteen suicide attacks had been witnessed in the last four days, six of them against Sweep Unit THREE. CTF 51 ordered the patrol line northwest of Ie Shima terminated on April 3 and Sweep Unit THREE took up screening duties for two AM sweep units and their fire support ships. The AMs were clearing the area north of Motobu Peninsula. Further evidence that things for the minesweepers were returning to normal came when the *Emmons* and *Macomb* were ordered to return to their regular units. Since the establishment of the Ie Shima antisubmarine patrol the *Macomb* had been operating with Unit THREE in what should have been the *Emmons's* position.

The *Emmons* left Unit TWO at midnight on the 3rd and joined up with Unit THREE north of Motobu Peninsula before the next day's sweeping operations started. The remainder of the day was spent with the unit screening the *Wichita, Beale,* and Sweep Unit ELEVEN while the AMs of the latter swept the bight formed by Okinawa proper and the peninsula. That night the destroyer minesweepers took up stations on the patrol line near Tonaki Shima, west of the assault beaches.

The following day, the 5th, the four destroyer sweepers themselves conducted an exploratory sweep of the broad channels between Okinawa and Iheya Rhetto to the northwest and Yoron Shima to the north. The sweep was done without benefit of gunfire support ships. Although the weather had been deteriorating for the last two days the day passed quietly enough. No mines were encountered and there was no harassment by enemy aircraft all day. The quietness was just the lull before the storm. The Japanese had been building up their air forces on Kyushu, Formosa, and in the Ryukus since they had decided that Okinawa was to be the next big target. By April 6 they had concentrated enough planes within striking distance of Okinawa to mount the first all-out air attack on the invading forces.

15

The Last Battle at Okinawa

o o o o o o o o o o o o o o o o o o o o o o o o o o o o o o o o o

The wounded were cared for at the scene to the best of the ability of those aboard and acts of heroism were seen on every side.

—*U.S.S. EMMONS Action Report, 12 April 1945*

Friday, April 6, started out much the same as the other days since L-day. The weather, which had been boisterous the last few days, was calming down. It was cloudy, but visibility was eight to ten miles. Winds were northerly at ten to fifteen knots. During the midwatch and morning watches the ships of Sweep Unit THREE manning the outer patrol stations off the landing beaches detected a number of bogies. The *Emmons* fired at three between 0330 and 0700. The last came at sunrise when the ships were leaving their patrol stations to take up daytime assignments. As they were leaving the patrol line a single-engine enemy plane made an attack approach from the north. The *Emmons* and *Ellyson,* which were nearest, opened fire as the plane started a steep dive. Surprisingly, it abruptly turned away to the north and disappeared. There was no way of knowing if it had been hit. It is possible that it was a reconnaissance plane for the attacks which were to follow.

This morning the four destroyer minesweepers of MinDiv 59 were split up to provide fire support for two widely separated AM sweep units. The *Emmons* and *Rodman* were detailed to provide gunfire support for Sweep Unit ELEVEN for a sweep northwest of Okinawa. The *Ellyson* and *Hambleton* drew support for Sweep Unit SIX south of Ie Shima for a close-in sweep.

2

While the small groups of minesweepers were en route to the assigned sweep areas there was extraordinary activity on the enemy airfields within striking distance of Okinawa. The Japanese were preparing to launch the first of a series of massive air attacks featuring the suicide planes which had been seized upon as the best hope of the Japanese to stop the invasion. Since the approval of Operation TENGO as the basis for defense of the homeland, the Japanese had been scrapping together aircraft to counter the expected move against the Ryukus. Originally, it had been planned to make more than 4,000 aircraft of all types available for the showdown at Okinawa. But, thanks to the activities of TF58 prior to and during the opening phases of the invasion, nowhere near that number was ever achieved. It was neither feasible nor planned to use all available planes in one massive attack. Rather, they were to be committed in several successive massed attacks designed to so cripple the American fleet that troops landed on Okinawa would wither on the vine for lack of adequate supplies. Typically, the Japanese gave the series of projected attacks the poetic name of *Kikusui,* or "Floating Chrysanthemums" in translation.

Most of the aircraft committed to the defense of Okinawa were naval planes based on southern Kyushu under the command of Vice Admiral Matome Ugaki, commander of the Fifth Air Fleet, but other planes of the First, Third, and Tenth Air Fleets, as well as Army planes of the Sixth and Eighth Air Armies were available in varying degrees. A large part of the Sixth Air Army, based on Kyushu, was reserved for the defense of the homeland. The Third and Tenth Air Fleets were training commands, but could provide replacements, particularly in the category of suicide pilots, who obviously did not require as extensive training as the regular combat pilots. The First Air Fleet and Eighth Air Army were based on Formosa and did not have as great a role in the Okinawa campaign as the units in Kyushu and the Ryukus, although they were involved. Admiral Ugaki of the Fifth Air Fleet appears to have been responsible for coordinating the attacks on the invading forces.

The seizure of Kerama Rhetto confirmed the belief of the Japanese high command that the showdown was at hand at Okinawa. Accordingly, the Commander in Chief of the Japanese Combined Navy directed Admiral Ugaki to attack with combined naval air forces under his command. These then amounted to about 1,185 planes, including 540 suicider planes. The Sixth Air Army was ordered to cooperate. However, it took several days to complete preparations for the attack. The Fifth Air Fleet had just come out of a four-day battle with TF58 during which it had lost 161 aircraft. Those which returned to Kyushu were widely scattered. Very few landed at their home fields and all were badly disorganized. Furthermore, their communication network had been disrupted by the carrier planes' attacks.

In the meantime, the American landings were made as planned at the Hagushi beaches on April 1. Troops were being reinforced and supplies were piling up at the beachheads at a satisfactory rate. There was little the Japanese could do to hinder the buildup except for a few scattered kamikaze attacks mounted by available planes in the Ryukus or an occasional attempt to sneak a suicide boat through the protective patrol lines. For their part, the American commanders hurried the buildup all they could as they kept a watchful eye on the skies for the inevitable counterattack from the air.

The Japanese were finally prepared to launch *Kikusui* Number 1 on April 6. It was the largest and most successful of ten large kamikaze attacks they mounted before Okinawa was surrendered. Around 450 planes were committed in the main attacks on that date, about 296 of them from the suicide corps. Most of them were from Kyushu commands, but some came up from Formosa.

The attack was opened in the morning when 120 dive bombers, fighter bombers, and fighters, half of them suicider planes, took off to attack Task Force 58, which had been spotted south of Amami Oshimi earlier in the day. Their mission was to disable the carrier force so that its planes could not interfere with the attacks to follow on naval forces off Okinawa. During the noon hour they were followed by around a hundred fighters which were to converge directly on Okinawa to clear the air of fighter opposition over the target while the kamikazes swept in from all directions to finish off the ships of the amphibious assault force. Three reconnaissance planes were to drop "window," radar-reflecting metal decoys, near Amami Oshima, designed to lure any American fighters remaining in the air away from the actual target area.

Kikusui No. 1 was carried out substantially as planned. On April 6 the air-sea battles lasted until well after sunset and continued on a diminished scale throughout the night and the following day. Based on reports of returning pilots, who tended to count each hit observed, and each fire sighted, as an American warship sunk, the Japanese proclaimed a resounding victory. Even the 32nd Army, Japanese defenders of Okinawa, watching the battle from their strong points ashore, reported thirty American ships sinking and twenty burning, including cruisers and battleships.

American losses were nowhere near the numbers claimed. Thanks to the heroic work of the Combat Air Patrols and the protective screens of destroyer types thrown up around the area, few of the marauders got into the transport area. Those which did get through did little damage except at Kerama Rhetto where two valuable ammunition ships and an LST were hit and lost. No major warship was hit during the battles of April 6. Indeed, it was not until the following day that a suicider managed to hit the battleship *Maryland*, severely damaging her. Nonetheless, it was a day of desperate anxiety for the Americans.

Credit must be given the destroyers and similar types manning the defensive screens and isolated stations around the fleet concentrations and Okinawa for absorbing and blunting the full fury of the attack, especially those to the north, along the approach route of enemy formations flying down from Kyushu. The attack would have been much more effective had the enemy ignored such outposts and driven straight to the transport area. However, they chose not to do so, and for reasons best known to them, expended much of their effective strength on isolated ships, such as the radar pickets *Bush, Calhoun,* and *Cassin Young,* some fifty miles north of the main target area, and the *Emmons* and *Rodman* to the northwest of Okinawa in the Iheya Rhetto Channel.

The Japanese were turned back with great loss in pilots and planes. But it was a costly victory for the United States Fleet, especially in destroyer types. Of the twenty-one vessels reported as hit on April 6 by Commander Task Force 51, fifteen were destroyer types, three were light minesweepers, two were ammunition ships, and one an LST. Six of the twenty-one were sunk. Of those, three were destroyer types on isolated duty north and northwest of Okinawa. One was the *Emmons.*

3.

Because of the distance involved it was late morning before the *Emmons* joined the *Rodman* and Sweep Unit ELEVEN in the assigned area northwest of Okinawa to begin the day's sweeping operation. The deeper portions had been the subject of an exploratory sweep by Sweep Unit THREE the day before. This time, however, five AMs of Sweep Unit ELEVEN, the *Ransom, Density, Facility, Rebel,* and *Recruit* were under orders to conduct a clearance sweep "as close to the beach as possible." While the *PGM-ll* tagged along as mine disposal vessel, the *Emmons* and *Rodman* took station to seaward as fire support ships. The *Rodman* was OTC.

The area to be swept lay in the channel between Iheya Rhetto and Okinawa. Its center was about thirty-five miles northeast of the landing beaches, and between twenty and twenty-five miles south of radar picket stations Nos. 1 and 2.

It was not far distant from the area north of Yoron Shima where the *Emmons* and Sweep Unit TWO had operated during the period preceding L-day, and where the *Emmons* had acted as radar picket on the eve of L-day. Situated as it was directly along the route of aircraft coming down from Kyushu, the *Emmons* and her group shared with radar picket stations 1,2, and 3 the dubious honor of being the first American warships to come within the sights of Japanese planes approaching from the north on April 6.

A few minutes before sweeping operations began at 1239, ships of the group went to general quarters in response to a Flash RED signal caused by enemy planes in the vicinity. They probably were strays from the earlier battle between the Japanese and Task Force 58 to the northeast or possibly the advance guard of the fighter formations heading for the transport area. Wherever they came from they did not bother the ships of the sweeping group and operations continued as scheduled. "All Clear" was in effect by 1335.

The lull did not last long. About 1500 the first of several waves of suicide planes and traditional bombers attacked the *Bush* and *Cassin Young* on radar picket stations Nos. 1 and 3 to the north. The *Calhoun* on station No. 2 went to the aid of *Bush* to her west. Eventually both the *Bush* and *Calhoun* were sunk. The *Cassin Young* was able to beat off her attackers and proceeded to the scene of the attack on the *Bush* and *Calhoun* to assist in the rescue of survivors.

Not long after the picket stations were hit, another swarm of Japanese planes, or possibly some of the same group moving farther south, discovered and attacked the *Emmons* and *Rodman.* First warning came when Combat Information Center (CIC) picked up a warning of enemy aircraft in the vicinity. Searching on the indicated bearing, CIC located two bogies closing in on the port quarter. At that time the sweep formation was on course 065 approaching the northern tip of Okinawa. The *Emmons* was on the port bow of the sweep formation and the *Rodman* on the port quarter, some four miles apart.

Apparently the enemy planes were stalking the *Rodman,* for at 1532 that ship spotted not two, but three planes diving out of the clouds, two on her port bow and one on her starboard. In spite of the fire of both ships, one crashed the *Rodman's* forecastle, starting huge fires, which shot sheets of flame as high as the director. Another dropped a bomb which missed to starboard. A third either dropped a bomb or crashed close aboard to starboard, rupturing the hull and causing flooding of several compartments. She temporarily lost power and steering control but was able to report the attack to CTF 51 and request air support.

As soon as he saw the hit on the *Rodman,* Captain Foss turned the *Emmons* toward the burning ship with the intention of going alongside to help fight the fires. He also called for air support. Damage control parties, already at general quarters, were alerted to make preparations for boarding her. However, as the *Emmons* got near the wounded ship it appeared that the fires were being brought under control. Furthermore, by that time the ships were surrounded by enemy aircraft distant from twenty to seventy miles. Later, it was estimated that they numbered between fifty and seventy-five. Some were visible. Bettys, Tonys, Vals, and Zekes were identified. In view of this threat, plans to go alongside were abandoned. Instead, the *Emmons* began to circle the *Rodman* at twenty-five knots to provide maximum fire support.

The *Emmons* now became a target as well as the *Rodman,* although it was nearly an hour before she was attacked directly. The two ships did not have to fight off the attackers alone. Shortly after the *Rodman* was hit a combat air patrol of Marine Corsairs came by and pitched into the fight. Around 1600 a patrol of sixteen Hellcats checked in and began to pick off enemy aircraft jockeying for position to get at the minesweepers. To observers on the *Emmons* it appeared that the Japanese pilots were more intent on getting at the ships than they were on engaging the fighters. Dogfights filled the sky on all sides. The crew of the *Emmons* was unstinting in praise of the carrier pilots who time and again stayed on the tail of diving would-be suiciders right on down through the ship's antiaircraft fire in an attempt to polish them off before they could complete their missions of self destruction. Estimates vary as to the number of enemy planes shot down by the fighters. The *Emmons* action report estimates that they accounted for fifty of the suicider planes. She herself got six before the action ended. Four more crashed close aboard after narrowly missing the ship. It is not known whether they had been hit or just simply missed their target.

The air-sea battle of Iheya Rhetto Channel lasted nearly four hours. On the surface the *Emmons,* as long as she was able, continued to circle the stricken *Rodman* while the latter fought to gain the upper hand over her fires and shored up her buckled bulkheads. Both ships took on enemy planes which eluded the combat air patrols. Above, the Corsairs and Hellcats had a field day chasing down enemy planes trying to get into position to attack the surface ships.

The first hour of the battle was largely confined to the skies. Those aboard the *Emmons* who could see what was going on from their battle stations watched the many dogfights with fascination and cheered whenever an enemy crashed harmlessly into the sea. But superior numbers began to tell. A few suicider planes eluded the Corsairs and Hellcats in the clouds from where they made diving attacks on their primary targets, the destroyer minesweepers. These attacks at first appeared haphazard, as might be expected from pilots on their last mortal mission, but during the progress of the fight the Japanese appeared to get smarter. The attacks became deliberate and well-coordinated. Several kamikazes would team up to strike at the same time from different points of the compass, coming in low over the water, thus preventing the ships from concentrating their fire. Apparently all of them carried bombs, and some strafed the decks as soon as they got within machine gun range. The planes themselves became deadly missiles at the hands of desperate men. The ruptured gasoline tanks fed the fires started by the explosion of the bombs.

The first direct attack on the *Emmons* came about 1630 when a Betty broke through the clouds to port and dived on the ship through a hail of fire. He missed, but pulled up on the starboard side, banked, and headed back toward the ship, only to miss again, probably because the ship was in a tight turn to port. He was smoking as he missed the starboard 40mm and mount 3 by inches to crash close aboard the port quarter. Two others followed. One was a Zero which was hit and crashed about 500 yards on the starboard beam. The third, a Tony, dived out of the clouds to port. For a few seconds it seemed that he would hit the director, but he missed it by about sixteen feet before crashing opposite gun 1 to starboard. The pilot must have been dead as he was seen by the director crew to be slumped forward in his seat as he passed the director.

Following the third there was a brief lull in the attacks on the surface ships during which the crew had time to relax, tidy up around their battle stations, and prepare for the next go-round. All hands were elated and there was much self-congratulation over the last set-to. The lull didn't last long. Overhead the dogfights continued and more enemy planes were shot down. But not nearly enough—the Japanese still outnumbered the carrier fighters and soon renewed their attacks on the two minesweepers with the *Emmons* receiving the most attention because she was still fully operational.

This time numerous Japanese, mostly Tonys' and Vals, came at the *Emmons* and *Rodman* flying low over the water. The main director spotted six coming in low off the starboard bow. The Mark 51 director for the starboard 40mm reported at least ten coming in from all angles, probably including those spotted by the main director. The *Rodman* counted ten. It wasn't long before every gun on the *Emmons* was firing. At least three more enemies were downed by her gunfire, bringing her total to six. Others simply crashed. Hellcats coming in right behind them accounted for others. The *Rodman* brought her total up to five. For some reason or other the 5" shells of the *Emmons* were falling short. One Val was seen to run into the splash thrown up by one of the shorts and nosed over—finished. Still they came. The Japanese who missed on their first run either crashed or turned around to try again. A Val missed and roared between the stacks carrying away the antennas strung between them. He crashed close aboard to port. A Hellcat following closely on his tail was able to pull up in time to avoid the same fate.

There seemed to be an inexhaustible supply of Vals and Tonys to replace those shot down or crashing. They kept coming in spite of their losses. One survivor of the *Emmons* described watching the planes coming at the ship as like being stranded in the middle of a superhighway with trucks and automobiles bearing down on him from either side—and wondering how long it would be before one got him.

There is no way of knowing how long this particular phase of the action lasted, but by the time it was over the *Emmons*'s ammunition was running low. She had only enough left for one more attack when the 5" guns were put out of commission. As antiaircraft ammunition was expended the magazine handling rooms were beginning to send up star shells, common, white phosphorous—anything they could get their hands on. Such was the condition of gun 3 just before the ship received its first hit. The gun was firing to port when someone on the 40mm yelled down to the gun captain and pointed out an enemy plane coming in almost directly astern. The gun captain immediately instructed his crew to shift to local control and get on the new target. It seemed to him that it took too long to fire. Just as he ducked down from the gun captain's hatch to see what the delay was the gun was loaded and fired. As he looked out the hatch, he was amazed to see the incoming plane disintegrate in midair as the shell hit it right on the nose. This was remarkable shooting in any league. The gun captain's evaluation changed from extraordinary to miraculous when he learned that that single shot was an armor piercing projectile.

All guns continued to fire with whatever ammunition was available, but the end was near. For two hours the combined fire of the two ships and the unrelenting support of the carrier fighters had prevented any damage to the *Emmons* and any further damage to the *Rodman.* But persistence and sheer numbers—plus the fanatical disregard for personal consequences of the kamikaze pilots—finally paid off for the enemy. At 1732 the first of five Japanese kamikazes, which ploughed into the *Emmons* in quick succession, struck. Simultaneously, another hit the *Rodman,* starting new fires in her superstructure, although the bomb it carried landed unexploded in the galley passageway. Both ships were now disabled and afire. After five hits within a period of two minutes, the *Emmons* was in worse condition than the *Rodman.* Although her fire rooms and engine rooms were still intact, she was unable to maneuver. The steering engine room was destroyed and the rudder gone. Fires were raging in her nerve centers. All 5" guns were disabled and on fire. Many of their crews were casualties. Most of the machine guns were out, largely because of fires and casualties among their crews. There was little she could do to defend herself with the few remaining machine guns as the attacks continued. The carrier planes continued their heroic defense of the crippled ships and probably prevented the kamikazes from finishing them off then and there. But they had to be back aboard their home carriers before dark. Fortunately, the Japanese decided to move on about the same time and the minesweepers were left alone to try to repair their damage. The last attack, according to the *Rodman's* log came at 1850. It was beaten off and two of the attackers were shot down by the American fighters as they were preparing to leave the scene.

4.

The first blow came shortly after gun 3 registered its direct hit on the attacking plane coming in from dead astern, when an enemy fighter sneaked in and crash dived into the fantail, just forward of the depth charge racks over the steering engine room. The pilot strafed gun 3 as he came in causing considerable damage. Several fires were started on the fantail and the depth charges were blown clear. These things were bad enough, but more serious were the destruction of the steering engine room and the loss of the rudder. Furthermore, the port propeller was so badly damaged that the port engine could not be used. Robbed of any chance of evasive action, the *Emmons* fell prey to other attacks which came immediately after the first. All men aft of gun 3 who had not taken cover as the kamikaze came in were either killed or missing.

The next hit aft came almost immediately. It was delivered by a Val that came in from the starboard quarter and slammed into the huge magnetic mine sweep reel just aft and below gun 3. The destruction of the fantail was now complete. The magnetic reel was blown sky high and all the rest of the mine sweeping gear cleared off the deck. Fragments of steel showered down as far forward as the stacks causing many casualties on the 40mm batteries and the men stationed at secondary conn. Gun 3 was put out of action. Flames, which momentarily engulfed the gun, entered the mount through the ports and hatches and got down to the upper handling room. Several of the gun's crew were burned and wounded. The second explosion threw the gun off its track, rendering it useless. It had to be evacuated.

Captain Foss was still trying to find out if the ship had steerageway and had just tried in vain to shift steering aft when two more planes slammed into the superstructure. The first hit on the starboard side, below the bridge in the vicinity of the radio shack. A few seconds later a second plane hit the port side at the combat information center. The first blasted away most of the starboard wing of the bridge and made a shambles of the pilot house. The entire side of the superstructure was blown open. Captain Foss was blown from the bridge by the blast and landed, badly burned and temporarily blinded, in the water. The plane which hit to port completely demolished the CIC, killing all hands on watch there, including the executive officer. Gasoline from both planes ignited, spreading fierce fires throughout the superstructure which extended from the plotting room up to the pilot house. Flames reached as high as the base of the director. Gun 2 was knocked out and fires started in the upper handling room. Crews of the 20mm guns around the superstructure and on the bridge who survived the immediate blasts were driven from their stations by the intense heat. Many men not otherwise injured had to jump overboard to escape the flames. Others were blown off the ship.

The first hit, according to the plotting room watch, had come at fifteen seconds after 1732. Within two minutes the fifth and last came on the starboard bow. Members of the starboard 40mm crew claim this plane was hit before it crashed, but it managed to stay up long enough to crash into the bow near the waterline, forward of No. 1 gun. Gun 1 was knocked out by the explosion and fires started in the upper handling room and the gun room.

Whether by design or pure luck, the Japanese had been remarkably successful in getting at the nerve centers of the *Emmons.* Certainly the aircraft expended were disproportionate to the task, but they could have hardly been more effective in destroying the control points of a destroyer minesweeper if they had practiced for weeks on a model safely anchored somewhere in the Inland Sea. After the last hit the entire main battery and most of the machine guns were out of action. With the rudder gone the ship was helpless to maneuver. The port screw was so badly damaged that the port engine could not be used. The entire stern from the after living quarters aft was missing. Sporadic fires breaking out around gun 3 hindered damage control efforts. The entire superstructure with its vital communication and control equipment was a shambles and that area was ablaze from the main deck to the flying bridge. Fires reached as far forward as gun 1 and effectively isolated the forecastle from the rest of the ship. The fire rooms and engine rooms were the only spaces which had not been damaged, but damage to the port screw prohibited use of the after engine. The ship was listing to starboard and settling in the water. With the captain wounded and in the water, the executive officer dead, secondary conn in a shambles, and all communications cut, men of each station still operational were thrown back on their own initiative to contain and repair the damage without guidance from any central point. The surviving officers and men responded magnificently. Months of training showed their worth as they worked to save their ship against insurmountable odds. Of necessity, first efforts were directed toward extinguishing fires and taking care of the wounded.

Many men of the damage control parties had been killed or wounded, but men from other stations, now inoperable, pitched in to help out. Fire hoses were started aft immediately after the first blast on the fantail.

Fire fighting was hampered by low water pressure. Although the fire and bilge pumps were intact and steam pressure to operate them was available, full pressure on deck could not be reached because of damage to the fire mains and topside fire hoses. The latter were full of holes from pieces of flying metal and the strafing of the attack planes. A member of the amidships damage control party, Steven Synosky, reports that a hose he was dragging forward was cut in two, inches from his hand, by machine gun fire from an attacking plane. Some water pressure was restored on deck by leading long sections of hose directly from the engine room, but it could never be brought above sixty pounds. There was no way of reaching the forecastle through the fire in the superstructure. Exploding ready ammunition boxes near the machine gun mounts on the bridge and around the superstructure made any place on the decks hazardous. The recurrence of small fires aft, even after they had apparently been put out, added to the problems.

The hardest part of the efforts was to ignore a wounded shipmate, sometimes a close buddy, to carry on the business at hand. Some of them were silent, beyond help. But the wounded did not go without help. Although the main battle dressing station, the wardroom, and the after dressing station, the crew's head, were afire, the wounded men on the main deck were carefully carried to the deck amidships, near the loading machine, where the only pharmacist's mate still on his feet, George T. Kennedy, PhM3C, dressed their wounds and made them as comfortable as possible. Volunteers, dislodged from their regular battle stations, helped with the dressings and administration of morphine. Kennedy himself was hit in the right knee and thigh by fragments of metal during the attack on the superstructure but continued to take care of others without regard to his own wounds. One of his patients was the chief pharmacist's mate, Lafayette C. Eaton, among the first to be hit. Later, some of the wounded were put overboard on life rafts and floats in case the situation worsened. The more seriously wounded were kept on board to take advantage of whatever meager medical care could be provided. Up forward the wounded were taken care of by the surviving guns' crews until "Doc" Williamson, who had been driven from the wardroom battle dressing station by the fire, made his way to the forecastle and took charge.

After the superstructure was hit the word spread around the main deck to abandon ship. It is not known where the misunderstanding originated. Most likely it just grew and was passed by word of mouth. A number of people had been blown off the ship from the bridge area and others had been forced to jump to escape the flames. Seeing a number of men in the water may have given the men on deck the idea that abandon ship was in progress. At that point there was no one person in command and no communications to countermand such an order if there had been.

There was no panic. As it was not an organized move with officers and petty officers in control, it became a matter of personal choice whether to go over the side or not; if so, when and in what manner. Most men chose to remain on board and continue to try to contain the damage. However, some men did choose to abandon ship under the impression it had been ordered. When the "order" was countermanded an estimated sixty to eighty were overboard, some through no choice of their own. Most men trapped on the forecastle had no choice. With little water pressure they were unable to make progress against the fires and there was always the fear that one of the magazines would blow, carrying away the entire forecastle. They chose to take their chances in the water. One indirect benefit of the premature abandon ship amidships was that the life rafts and floats were put over early and thus were available in the water to the men who later left the ship, deliberately or otherwise, as well as the wounded.

After the blasts in the superstructure the main battery director was without power and had no communication with the guns it was designed to control. The gunnery officer, Lieutenant Griffin, decided it would serve no purpose to remain in the useless director and carefully led his crew down to the flying bridge, from there down to the bridge proper, and, finally, to the main deck via the ladder on the foremast abaft the bridge. On the way down, Griffin stopped on the flying bridge long enough to try to help Ensign Ross T. Elliot, Jr., the assistant gunnery officer and machine gun control officer, who had been mortally wounded trying to protect his crew by shielding them with his own body from a strafing attack. But the young officer expired as he was trying to help. When he was certain that Elliot was beyond help the gunnery officer went on to the bridge below. There, on the after part of the bridge, the director crew ran into Edwin Hoffman, Jr., QM3C, who had managed to get out of the pilot house, but had been unable to get down the mainmast because of a broken leg. All the regular ladders were either carried away entirely or blocked by sheets of fire. The gunnery officer, a powerful man, put his arms under Hoffman's shoulders and helped him down the ladder one rung at a time. At the bottom, where the rungs ran out, he dropped to the deck below and caught Hoffman in his arms when the latter let go. Other members of the director crew checked out CIC as they went by and reported that its door was open and flames were coming out. Several bodies were lying near the door, obviously beyond help.

During the torturous climb down from the director, Griffin had seen enough to realize that he was senior uninjured surviving officer left on board. This was confirmed when he reached the main deck. Unhesitatingly he announced that he was in command and began to direct the damage control efforts. One of his first orders was to countermand the abandon ship "order" and direct all hands to stay on board until the situation was fully investigated. Evacuation of the wounded to life rafts and floats already in the water was continued. The more seriously wounded were kept on board and one life raft kept alongside in case of sudden need to get them off the ship. Because of the pronounced starboard list and the gradual settling aft there was concern over foundering. All loose gear was jettisoned and the disabled machine guns were cast loose from the deck and thrown overboard.

Some of the engineers went back down into the engineering spaces to increase the steam pressure for fire fighting. They succeeded in bringing up the pressure at the fire and bilge pumps but there was little effect on the hose pressure on deck. Handy billies were started and helped some, but were hard to keep running. Progress was made against the fires aft. They were gradually extinguished. However, they kept popping out again as soon as attention was diverted to other problems.

The fire in the superstructure was brought under partial control long enough to permit launching the whaleboat. Previous attempts to get to the boat had been driven back by the heat in the vicinity. Several men, including Frank Basile, the coxswain, Anthony Esposito, Paul Delve, Robert Reid, and James Stanton got to the boat and with great difficulty got it in the water. For one thing, the falls jammed, leaving the boat dangling several feet above the water. Taking a chance at wrecking the boat, the men cut it loose. It stayed afloat and they scrambled down the lines before it drifted away from the ship. Once afloat and clear, their troubles were not over, the hull was full of machine gun holes from the strafing. Vigorous bailing was required to keep it afloat. Reid attributes the fact that it was kept afloat as long as it was to the fact that it had a smokestack-type exhaust which exhausted upward rather than through the stern. The crew started picking up survivors from the water and delivering them to the *Recruit* which had just arrived on the scene with the other vessels of Sweep Unit ELEVEN. As they were taking their second load of survivors to the AM, two Japanese kamikazes started a pass at the *Emmons*, but suddenly changed course to attack the AM instead. One flew so low over the whaleboat that the occupants had to duck. One of the planes was splashed by the *Recruit* and the other by the combined fire of the *Recruit* and the *Ransom*. Once alongside the *Recruit* the whaleboat was so waterlogged that the skipper forbade the crew to go out again. He proved to be right. Within a few minutes it sank alongside the minesweeper. It was now dusk and boats of the newly arrived minesweepers had taken over the rescue work.

When the *Rodman* received her first hit the sweep formation had been on the last lap of the day's assignment on a course of 065°, northwest of the northern tip of Okinawa. After the *Emmons* left the formation to help her sister ship, the ships of Sweep Unit ELEVEN continued the last pass with the *PGM-11* as the sole fire support ship. They watched from a distance as the kamikazes gathered and the battle over the DMSs developed. The easterly course gradually opened the distance between the embattled ships and themselves. When they completed the day's sweep and began recovering gear they were about eight miles east of where the *Emmons* and *Rodman* and the carrier planes were fighting it out with the Japanese planes. Perhaps it is just as well they were not in the middle of the fight at that time as the destroyer minesweepers absorbed most of the kamikaze fury at a time when the small minesweepers were most vulnerable. Besides, at that time, the *Emmons* and *Rodman*, with the support of the CAP were more than holding their own. As it was, Sweep Unit ELEVEN did not entirely escape the attention of the Japanese. They repulsed several suicide attacks before joining the main battle a little before sunset. Before the end of the day they had accounted for four or five enemy planes.

While they were still recovering their sweep gear, twelve to fifteen low-flying Vals were observed to their north, heading west. Doubtless it was part of the group which finally broke through the *Emmons* defense. While they watched one was shot down by 5" fire from the *Emmons* and others came under attack by friendly fighters as they started runs on the DMSs. As the Vals headed west, several broke off to attack the *Rebel* and *Density*, but did not persist when two of their numbers were splashed. The remainder turned away and headed west to join the battle there. In the meantime, sweeps of Unit ELEVEN completed recovery of their gear by 1716, formed column, and headed for the *Emmons* and *Rodman* at maximum speed. On the way the formation was attacked by a Zeke which crashed close aboard the *Ransom*. During the violent maneuvering to avoid him, the *Rebel* parted her steering cable. As a result she had to drop out of formation and continue on emergency steering with *PGM-11* standing by. Both ships arrived at the scene of action slightly behind the other four AMs of the sweep unit. The brush with the Zeke occurred just about the same time the Japanese pushed home their fatal attack on the *Emmons.*

The leading AMs of Sweep Unit ELEVEN reached the *Emmons* and *Rodman* a little after 1800 and began rescue operations for men struggling in the water. The operations were hampered by the Japanese who now turned their attention to the newcomers. Earlier in the day the destroyer minesweepers had absorbed the attention of the enemy to the advantage of the AMs to the east. The latter now more than repaid the favor by acting as lightning rods to attract any kamikazes which got past the CAP over the disabled pair. The AMs were interrupted by attacks several times before the Japanese decided to call it a day around sundown. The AMs claimed a Zeke and two Vals before the enemy left the scene. It was one of the Vals which came near clipping the *Emmons'* whaleboat while it was approaching the *Recruit.*

As the AMs were coming up, Lieutenant Griffin had directed William J. Roberts, QM2C, one of the survivors of the secondary conn station, to signal one of the approaching ships to come alongside. He hoped to get assistance in fighting fires and more medical help for the wounded. Roberts was able to reach only two of them by flashing light. One replied that they would come alongside after they had finished picking up men from the water. The other did not reply.

About 1800, after consultation with the other officers left aboard, Griffin made the agonizing decision that the ship would have to be abandoned. Reasons for the decision are summarized in the *Emmons*'s Action Report.

a. The port main engine was inoperable.

b. There was no means of steering the ship as the rudder had been blown off.

c. The fire forward could not be controlled due to the combination of its intensity and the low pressure on the main.

d. The ship continued to take more water and settle perceptibly.

e. There was imminent danger of explosion in both magazines and fuel tanks.

f. The entire battery with the exception of two 20mm guns was inoperable.

One of the big concerns connected with abandoning ship, provision for the safety of the disabled, was alleviated with the arrival of Sweep Unit ELEVEN.

Evacuation of the wounded to the *Facility,* lying to off the starboard side, was started. Two life rafts crowded with wounded were dispatched from the port side under the guidance of uninjured men. Others still on board were loaded into a whaleboat sent over by one of the AMs. Some were near death, others were ambulatory, many were badly burned. Although little more than an hour had passed since the first kamikaze struck the *Emmons* it had seemed like an eternity to those waiting and still conscious. The loading into the boat over the starboard side was supervised by "Doc" Kennedy. The whaleboat used probably came from the *Facility,* although some accounts claim it was the *Emmons* gig after it had been cut from its falls. The *PGM-11* came alongside to port just as a boatload of wounded was ready to shove off from the starboard. Decision was made to send the loaded boat on to the *Facility* and put the remainder on the gunboat.

Kennedy went with the last boatload of wounded to the *Facility.* He worked all night with that vessel's medical personnel taking care of his patients. Of fifty-one men from the *Emmons* on board, including those rescued from the water, only ten were without injuries. Three men died during the night. The medical personnel were assisted by volunteers from both ships. Some of those from the *Emmons* were themselves wounded. One of them was Chief Petty Officer Martin R. Kiser who, although burned about the face and arms, worked into the morning hours until exhausted. The men of the *Facility* unselfishly gave up their own bunks and provided clothing to make the refugees as comfortable as possible under the circumstances.

Dusk was fading into darkness when the *PGM-11* came alongside the *Emmons* to port and prepared to send over a fire-fighting party. The burning superstructure gave ample light to work by—too much light. The fire provided a highly visible reference mark for any kamikazes roaming the skies over Iheya Rhetto Channel. A few miles to the south the *Rodman* was making painfully slow progress out of the area toward the haven of Kerama Rhetto under the guidance of the *Density. YMS 341* had come alongside at 1830 and taken off her wounded and about sixty other men, leaving a salvage crew of fifty-eight men aboard. The rest of her crew had been forced to take to the water by the Japanese planes and were now being picked up by the ships of Sweep Unit ELEVEN along with the men of the *Emmons.* The *Rodman* had subdued her fires by sunset and therefore bent every effort to getting to Kerama Rhetto under her own power, although limited to six knots because of her damage. She made it before the end of the midwatch.

Long before the gunboat came alongside everyone left alive aboard the *Emmons* had reported topside. The only men who went below were engineers sent to check up on the machinery, damage control personnel, and, toward sunset, men to bring up portable battle lanterns. Work at putting out the fires forward was going on as vigorously as water pressure and fire hose capacity permitted. There now was not too much fear of air attacks—those ceased after sunset. However, exploding 20mm ammunition around the bridge was a constant threat. The forward 5" mounts were still burning with the attendant danger of touching off the magazines. The firefighters had been able to push three fire hoses forward as far as the forecastle deck, but could not reach gun 2.

As soon as the *PGM-11* came alongside the remaining wounded were sent aboard. While they were being sent over a final inspection was made of the engineering spaces and all other accessible spaces. Meanwhile, the *PGM-11* managed to get a stream of water on the superstructure fire when an explosion in the handling room of gun 2 convinced the gunboat's skipper that it would be unsafe to stay alongside. Aboard the *Emmons,* Lieutenant Griffin ordered all hands still on board to abandon ship. The last of the firefighters dropped their hoses and followed the wounded aboard the rescue vessel. Lieutenant Griffin was the last of five officers and fifty-seven men to go aboard. In order to get away quickly the lines to the *Emmons* were ordered cut. In the haste someone failed to cut one line. It was as if she were reluctant to let go of the men who had been part of her life for better than three years. It fell to Gerard Simoneau, a plank owner, to cut the last line between the ship and her men.

Meanwhile the minesweepers of Sweep Unit ELEVEN were busy combing the waters for men from both the *Emmons* and *Rodman.* Many of the crew of the latter had also been forced overboard by fires and low flying aircraft. The five small minesweepers rescued over 200 men from the water besides the wounded taken directly from the *Emmons.* The *Density* accounted for sixteen of the *Rodman's* men before leaving the scene to escort her to Kerama Rhetto. The *Facility* received fifty-one men from the *Emmons* alone, which included the wounded transferred from the ship just before she was finally abandoned. The *Ransom* saved fifty-two from the water from both ships. Many of the men who had had to jump from the forecastle of the *Emmons* ended up aboard the *Ransom.* Among them was the medical officer, Dr. Williamson. Another was the supply officer, Lieutenant (jg) H. F. Nelson. The *Rebel* took aboard thirty-four men from both ships. The *Recruit* recovered no less than eighty altogether. One, brought aboard from a life raft, was the skipper of the *Emmons,* Lieutenant Commander Foss. He was conscious when carried aboard, but severely wounded, with terrible burns about his face and hands. He was temporarily blinded. It was two weeks before he recovered sight and months before careful skin grafts restored his face and hands to normal. Another member of the *Emmons's* crew swept off the bridge was Chief Quartermaster Henry O. Thompson. He expired shortly after being brought on board the *Recruit.*

When darkness prevented further rescue operations, CTU 52.5.3 ordered the four minesweepers left in the area to proceed independently at best speed to Kerama Rhetto where complete medical services were available. *PGM-11* was also ordered to proceed to the haven when she cleared the burning *Emmons.* En route to Kerama Rhetto, Lieutenant Griffin advised higher authority by voice radio that there was still possibility of salvage if proper equipment was made available by daylight. The *Ellyson,* with ComMinRon 20 aboard, and the *Hambleton,* were already on the way and salvage tugs had been requested. At that time he did not believe there was immediate danger of the hull drifting onto enemy beaches and if it should start in the direction of Japanese territory it could be sunk by the many friendly units approaching the area.

5

The account of the last battle of the *Emmons* up to this point has been primarily concerned with the overall action. It has been based largely on official reports and records. By their very nature such reports and records are concise and brief. Naturally, they are sparing in details concerning individuals except in the most extraordinary cases.

The section following is an attempt to relate the experiences of representative individuals from different battle stations in widely different parts of the ship from the time she went to the aid of the *Rodman* about 1530 on April 6, to the time she herself had to be abandoned around 1900 the same day. The sources are sixty handwritten accounts of the battle written by survivors of the *Emmons* at the request of Lieutenant Griffin. They were written aboard the transport *Wayne* within four days of the sinking as the survivors were preparing to begin the long voyage home.

As might be expected from any event reported by sixty different men from almost as many different locations aboard ship there is far from unanimity, especially as to the exact sequence of events, and the times of the five hits inflicted on the *Emmons,* There is, however, surprising agreement on essential facts. Some recall the previous seemingly endless days of tedious training and credit it with saving their lives. Others ruefully recall violations of training rules which caused them needless trouble. If there is anything that stands out above all else it is the concern that every man displayed for his shipmates—a willingness to share, if need be to sacrifice self to help someone else. And, of course, there was always a burning desire to save their ship.

There were 254 officers and men aboard at the start of the battle. It would be impossible to give a complete account of each man through the fight in a single volume, even if there was enough information on each to do so. A few typical examples from each group must suffice to represent the experiences of all.

In the interest of brevity and simplicity the custom of using only surnames, as men do in conversation aboard ship, is followed below. Formal ratings and titles are used only when necessary to indicate military relationships within a group or to distinguish between individuals.

6

The control center of the ship, the bridge, suffered heavy casualties. Only a few men escaped, and those who did were either blown or jumped clear, or found some way to climb down outside the fires which were blocking the regular ladders between the bridge and the main deck.

Captain Foss was one of those who was blown clear. For two hours before the first hit on the fantail he had prevented any damage to the *Emmons* and any further damage to the *Rodman* by circling the latter at flank speed and maneuvering wildly while engaging any of the kamikazes which came within gun range. It appeared to Foss during this period that the kamikazes deliberately milled about out of gun range until the pilot got up enough courage to dash in for a diving attack from 6 or 7,000 feet. The Japanese got smart somewhere along the line and changed these unproductive tactics to a more dangerous one for the *Emmons.* Instead of isolated diving attacks they shifted to coordinated, multiple attacks coming in low over the water. The new tactics proved to be more difficult to defend against. It was especially difficult for the CAP planes to spot the Japanese down low.

The skipper watched the attack develop which finally penetrated the *Emmons*'s defense. A large group of kamikazes came in simultaneously. A number missed or crashed near the ship and he saw three or four shot down by the CAP. But finally one crashed into the fantail, followed in quick succession by four more which rendered his ship helpless to maneuver or defend itself.

Foss was standing on the port wing of the bridge when the first blow in the bridge area came. He doesn't recall exactly what happened to him but he was in effect blown into the water, badly burned about the face and hands and blinded. Near him in the water was the chief quartermaster, Thompson. The two stayed together until taken aboard a life raft. Eventually, a boat took the raft to the *Recruit* where all the occupants were taken aboard and given medical attention. Thompson did not survive the night. Foss was conscious when he was taken on board and was transferred to the *Crescent City* at Kerama Rhetto for further treatment the following day.

From Kerama Rhetto to St. Albans, the last hospital before his discharge, Captain Foss's journey sounds like a medical Odyssey. Evacuated on the hospital ship *Hope* to Saipan he spent nearly a month at the military hospital there. Penicillin was just then coming into use and was administered every three hours because that was the length of its effectiveness. Each three hours the nurse would appear in the ward and bellow in a commanding voice, "Bottoms up, boys!" whereupon some thirty to forty obedient males would turn on their stomachs to receive a shot in the rear from indifferently sharp needles. At Saipan Foss's eye bandages were gradually removed and he learned his sight would be alright. From Saipan he moved on for a month at Aiea Naval Hospital outside of Pearl Harbor. The next stop was a crucial one. At Oak Knoll Naval Hospital he underwent plastic surgery and began a long series of skin grafts to restore his face and hands to normal. The last hospital before discharge was St. Albans at Jamaica, New York. The trip from California to New York was by train. In order to see his family, the skipper took advantage of the delay feature of "proceed" orders to go by Boston for three days.

Other men with bad wounds, particularly those with burns, went through similar routines. Several of them were at Oak Knoll at the same time. Men who went through extensive treatment were strong in their praise for the painstaking medical attention they received at the hands of medical personnel, both afloat and ashore. Many, especially those with severe burns, attributed their lack of permanent disfigurement to the dedicated care of medical personnel, in the forward areas as well as in the better equipped rear areas. There was less enthusiasm for the psychiatric examinations all were obliged to undergo. Some considered it a waste of time—others thought it beneficial.

Several men from the area of the bridge got clear by climbing over the railings and down outside the burning areas. Some found their way down the ladder on the foremast as Hoffman and the director crew did.

One of the signalmen, Keller, on the port side, was one of the latter. He watched the kamikaze which finally ploughed into CIC coming in and realized that it was going to hit in spite of the shells thrown at it. When he realized it wasn't going to be stopped he hit the deck by the flag bags, or possibly was knocked down by the impact. This, however, did not prevent him from getting severe burns when the elasticized bands around the neck and wrists of the jacket he was wearing under his life jacket caught fire from the flash fire. He tried to get off the bridge by the normal ladders but found the way barred by roaring fires and had to climb down the ladder on the foremast. He barely made it down when he found that he was unable to see to get around. He had to depend on others to help him get off the ship when the bogus abandon ship was circulated. Someone—he doesn't know who—guided him down the deck and told him to jump when they were opposite a life raft. Helpful hands hauled him in. After some difficulty the raft was paddled away from the ship's side. It was subsequently picked up by one of the AMs and the men taken aboard for delivery to Kerama Rhetto. A haunting memory that Keller carried with him was seeing his friend, Horvatin, still strapped in one of the bridge 20mm guns, dead.

Esposito's general quartes station was depth charge release on the bridge. As no submarines were involved he had plenty of opportunity to observe the air action. He, too, saw the Japanese mass attack after their change of tactics and watched those coming in from starboard with fascination. He didn't see the first hits on the fantail. About that time he was watching two fairly large planes coming in from starboard. One was hit by our machine gunners and disintegrated in the air so close to the ship that he could see the pilot. He doesn't know what happened to the other plane—it may have been the one which hit under the *Emmons*'s bridge, because he heard a violent explosion and found himself flattened against a 20mm ready ammunition box. Dazed, he pushed himself off the ammunition box and somehow managed to climb down to the main deck where he started to look for his buddies, Basile and Monte, who had been stationed forward. He saw Basile running through the flames down the starboard side of the deck. Later they found Monte. After the fires around the whale-boat were brought under partial control, Esposito was one of the men who helped get it launched and became part of its crew as it started to rescue survivors from the water.

Hairston, on the 20mm machine gun on the port wing of the bridge, had a field day until the tide of battle turned against the *Emmons.* The last target his gun opened up on came right in through the stream of shells and crashed into the superstructure at CIC. The explosion and ignited gasoline sent flames shooting up to the bridge. Hairston was forced to go over to the starboard side which he found as bad, or worse. There was no way down by the normal ladders so he climbed over the railing and down to the main deck where he helped the damage control parties and worked with the wounded until time to abandon ship.

During the conversion to minesweeper a new Mark 51 Director had been installed on the flying bridge over the pilot house. It was designed to control the fire of the machine gun batteries and, if necessary, the main battery guns. There, the assistant gunnery officer and machine gun officer, Ensign Ross T. Elliott, Jr., U.S.N.R., with a crew consisting of a director operator, lookouts, and the tele phone talkers, had his battle station. Among the crew were Coppola, Heck, Palicki, Picketts, and Ringenberger.

During the first part of the fight the machine guns accounted for two of the six planes claimed by the *Emmons,* possibly more. Ensign Elliott moved constantly from one side of the flying bridge to the other checking on lookout reports and designating targets to the eager gunners until the telephones went out. He then had to point out targets by any means he could, including yelling and pointing. During the main push of the kamikazes, he spotted the plane which hit under the bridge. In spite of all efforts, the plane kept coming in. When it became apparent that the plane would crash into the bridge he ordered his crew to lie down as close as possible to the main director barbette. Just before the plane crashed into the side he threw his own body over the men providing a shield against the strafing and shrapnel which subsequently showered the bridge. After the crash, all five of the sky director crew were able to carry on, thanks to the self-sacrifice of the sky control officer, but Elliott was mortally wounded.

He died in the arms of Palicki who later wrote to a kinswoman of the young officer that he broke down and cried as he tried in vain to bring life back to the body. Lieutenant Griffin also did all he could for the dying officer. When he was certain that Elliott was beyond human help he ordered the men in the machine gun control crew to go on down to the main deck to get away from the flames licking at the bridge below. In recognition of his unselfish self-sacrifice Ensign Elliott was posthumously awarded the Navy Cross.

Diehl, the range finder operator in the main battery director, and Robinson, the radar operator, were kept busy tracking enemy targets right up to the time power was lost to the director. Up to that point, the director crew had been successful in keeping targets separated and under fire, except for the plane which sneaked in undetected on the fantail. When Robinson first reported to his general quarters station, the director was tracking a plane, later identified as a Betty, in a cloud cover, near land, about 14,000 yards away. After they had tracked him a few minutes he broke through the clouds and made a run on the *Emmons.* The first of many, he was splashed.

Thereafter, numerous Vals and Tonys were fired on, using both radar and range finder ranges, depending on the visibility. After the enemy changed tactics to use multiple attacks, coming in just above the water, all planes were visible during their entire approach, so range finder ranges could be used continuously. Diehl and the rest of the crew were kept humping shifting from one target to the next. In spite of some difficulty with the cross level and a difference in elevation between the director and plot, they did alright. Of six Tonys and Vals closing from starboard during the biggest attack of the day—the one which eventually resulted in the loss of the *Emmons*—four planes were downed or crashed close aboard. Shortly after Japanese, chased by a Hellcat, roared between the stacks and crashed on the port side, Robinson felt a crash aft. He looked in that direction in time to see flames engulf gun 3 and secondary conn. Soon after that he and Diehl and most of the others in the director were knocked down to the director pit by the two explosions against the superstructure. When they climbed back to their stations they found there was no power. It was then that Lieutenant Griffin made the decision to evacuate the director.

On the way down, Robinson stopped off on the landing outside CIC to see if he could help anyone there. Roaring flames coming out the open door and several dead bodies nearby convinced him that there was no chance of anyone remaining alive there, so he jumped down to the deckhouse where he joined Ayer in cutting loose and throwing overboard the dan buoys. He and Ayer then helped Diehl, Leistman, and Jacoby throw over all the empty powder cans and anything else that would float. Two attempts to get up to launch the boat were driven back by exploding 20mm ammunition from the forward machine guns. When he and Leistman spotted a Val closing several miles out, Leistman jumped into the harness of the starboard midship 20mm while the others rounded up some ammunition drums. Before they had a chance to use them a Hellcat swooped down and dropped the Val about 5,500 yards out.

As the fantail was settling in the water, Lieutenant Warner told Ayer, Robinson and Leistman to abandon ship. They decided to make the jump from what was left of the fantail. On the way back to the jumping off point they stopped to look over the wreckage of a Japanese plane and the remains of its pilot piled up against the after deckhouse. They were careful to jump well clear of the starboard screw which could be clearly seen turning over very slowly in the clear water. An AM was lying off the starboard quarter and they started swimming toward that. It proved to be the *Ransom* which picked them up and gave them a bunk and dry clothing. They had barely gotten aboard when a kamikaze made a pass at the *Ransom,* but missed and crashed close aboard, doing only superficial damage. The rest of the night was taken up helping Doc Williamson care for the wounded aboard.

After throwing over floatable gear, Diehl held the portable signal lamp for Roberts trying to get through to the approaching AMs. Then he went down to the main deck to help with the wounded, many of whom were begging for cigarettes to help ease the pain. He got hold of a flashlight and went down through gun 3 and the head to his locker in "O" compartment. From there he brought up five cartons of cigarettes, which he turned over to the wounded, and a few towels he found hanging from the overhead. The latter were turned over to the men tending the wounded. He was able to report that he had seen no one in any of the spaces he had gone through, including gun 3 and its handling room. He had seen a Mark 40 projectile and powder on the loading tray of the gun and had thrown them overboard.

Diehl was helping man the forward hoses when the *PGM-11* came alongside. He had reached the forecastle deck on the starboard side, but was unable to push forward to mount 2 because there was nothing but wreckage where there once had been a deck. When word was passed up to get aboard the gunboat he left the hose still playing water on the fire and went aft to get aboard the rescue vessel.

There were no survivors from CIC or the radio shack to record their experience. The communications officer, Lieutenant (jg) Dave Horwitz, was seen on the main deck shortly after the explosions with his face, scalp, hands, and clothes horribly burned, but no one knows where he was when the planes hit. He was in such a state of shock that all he kept repeating was, "Those dirty Japs, they burned my mustache. Those dirty Japs, they burned my mustache." He was sedated and put over on a life raft with a number of other wounded, but it seemed to those on deck that he was either unable to hang on or had no will to do so. Anyway, he slipped off. Korney, who by this time had come up from the forward fire room with the rest of the engineers, jumped into the water and with the help of Taubert and Grieco helped get the officer back aboard the ship. He was later evacuated to the *Facility* and eventually wound up on board the *Gosper* with other wounded from the *Emmons.* There he seemed to have recovered his usual cheerfulness and became a source of strength and encouragement to the other *Emmons* survivors in the compartment. Although he, like many of them, could not move around nor see, he kept in voice contact, calling each man by name and offering encouragement. But the second morning no warm greetings and inquiries came from the direction of his bunk. They learned that he had died during the night.

The men manning the plotting room fared much better than men in battle stations immediately above them. Being beneath the main deck gave a little extra protection against blast and the spread of fire over that offered to the exposed stations. On the other hand they couldn't see what was going on except by means of their instruments and plotting equipment. And they always ran the risk of being trapped below decks. That is almost what happened on April 6.

The plotting room crew was working on the problems of the range finder cross level angle and the 10° minus elevation difference between the director and the computer when they felt a light jar coming from somewhere aft. Whether it was the first or second hit aft is not certain. It wasn't strong, but was duly recorded as coming at 1732 plus fifteen seconds by the clock on the bulkhead. There was little damage. One light bulb over the computer broke and the lights began to dim. The guns continued to fire. Then came three explosions forward in rapid successions which were far worse. The switchboard lit up like a Christmas tree. The fuse panel was shot. Almost immediately flames began to shoot out of the ventilation system. There was a strong smell of gasoline in the entire area. Fires started in plot and the IC room. When the crew left plot they found the ship's office and the entire surrounding area was ablaze. All fire control and communication circuits were out. Attempts to reach control, or any other station, by telephone were fruitless. While Hudson and Deverell stayed behind to try to fight the fire, the rest of the gang, including Blair, Zeringue, Cowley and Rea, went into the after mess hall intending to go topside by way of the galley passageway. They soon found that the passageway was blocked by fire and had to retrace their steps and go into the forward mess hall. There they joined a number of men from the lower handling rooms holding a council of war on what to do since they found their way blocked both forward and aft. Meanwhile, Hudson and Deverell had to give up on their attempts to put out the fires in plot and started out via the mess hall and the galley passageway. They, too, were turned back by the fires in the galley passageway and wound up in the forward mess hall where their efforts to find a way topside were merged with those of the men from the lower handling rooms.

The three 5" guns of the main battery kept up a nearly constant stream of fire for almost two hours before they were put out of action by the suiciders which hit the ship shortly after 1730. Most of the time their fire was director-controlled, but at times some guns had to go to local control when too many targets came in at one time for the director to handle. Casualties among the gun crews were heavy. The handling room crews fared much better although the below-decks crews of the forward guns faced incineration for a time when they were trapped in the wardroom passageway. Their experience will be described in greater detail below.

Gun 3 was the first to start firing and the first to be put out of action, although there was very little time between the knockout blows to the separate guns. The condition watch in gun 3 had already gotten off three rounds at the *Rodman's* attackers when the regular gun captain for the general quarters crew, Ayer, took over. Soon after general quarters was set, the *Emmons* received its first attack from a diving kamikaze, which, as we know, was hit and splashed near the port quarter. From then on the gun was kept busy swinging from port to starboard and back again as the enemy came from all sides. Ayer spent his time standing in the gun captain's hatch watching for incoming targets and alternately ducking down to check on the performance of his crew. He was well pleased. The gun was firing at a target to port when someone on the 40mms behind him called attention to a plane coming in from almost directly astern, just off the water. He yelled down for the crew to shift to local control and pick up the new target. After what seemed an interminable delay to the gun captain, the gun finally fired. This was the shot which, against all reasonable odds, brought the plane down—a single shot, and an armor-piercing projectile at that.

The crew didn't have time to gloat. While they had been busy,another kamikaze was sneaking in from the quarter. It crashed into the fantail, completely wrecking the steering engine room and knocking out the steering. Within seconds another hit to starboard just aft and below the gun mount. This was the blow that put gun 3 out of action, knocking the mount off the roller path and starting fires in and around the gun chamber. It was a complete surprise to the gun crew. According to McLean, the pointer, there was an awful explosion followed by flames shooting into the mount through the gun ports. He was dazed by the explosion, but recovered quickly. When he recovered his senses, he helped Madden, the trainer, who was wounded and blinded, out of the mount. Someone else helped Posey, the fuse setter, also wounded, get out and up to where other wounded were being collected near the 40mms. Beck, the shell loader, noted the wing of a Japanese plane draped over the muzzle of the gun as he left the mount.

Ayer's departure from the mount was unceremonious. He doesn't remember whether he ducked or was blown clear of his hatch. All he remembers is flying through the air trying to disentangle the telephone cords from around his neck. When he came to on deck under the hot shell scuttle the first thing he did was get up and look inside his gun. Everyone was already out. He heard a groan behind him and turning around saw Kubany, from secondary conn, behind him trying to move. He dragged him forward to join the other wounded near the 40mms. About then he felt a jolt but couldn't tell where it came from—it was probably the kamikaze which hit under the starboard side of the bridge. Just as he looked up another plane piled into the port side of the superstructure.

The men in the handling rooms of gun 3 fared relatively well. Ash, in the upper handling room, felt the first hit, but saw no more damage than the men in the gun chamber above. The second hit, just aft of the gun mount, was a different story. It caved in the bulkhead, the lights went out, and fires were started in the handling room. Ash intended to go out through the starboard side of the head but found fires blocking his way. Instead he went out through the 40mm clipping room. Cruz and Frampton in the lower handling room felt the concussion of the second hit, but weren't even sure the ship had been hit until someone reported smoke above. They went up the ladder to the head, and, unlike Ash, were able to get to the starboard main deck by that route.

With their gun disabled, the crew of gun 3 became active helping the damage control parties and tending to the wounded aboard ship and on the rafts. They soon found that because of low water pressure and the scarcity of watertight hose there wasn't too much need for them as fire fighters, so they kept busy at other activities. Before the *PGM-11* came alongside, Ash, Cruz, Frampton, and McLean helped to load two life rafts with wounded over the port side. When one of the rafts was almost drawn into the jagged edges of the hole in the fantail, these four pushed and pulled it away from the side by use of sheer physical strength. The only paddle was a board only 1 1/2" by 24". They were helped by Tostanoski, also wounded, who jumped off one of the rafts to lend a hand. Once clear of the side the men got them around the stern of the *Emmons* and, again with great difficulty, alongside the *Facility,* lying to off the starboard quarter. When one of them was having trouble getting to the *Facility,* Cruz swam to the AM, got a line, and swam back with it to the raft, which was then hauled in from the ship.

During his all-out efforts to save his ship Ayer spotted the American flag lying on deck in a pool of blood and water. He looked around for a halyard to hoist it back, but being unable to find one he tucked it inside his shirt rather than leave it lying there. He was awarded a Bronze Star for his work as gun captain as long as his gun was capable of firing, and for his leadership in efforts to save the ship after it was out of action.

When the time came to abandon ship, Ayer jumped over the fantail with Robinson and Liestman. The three found a seat cushion and hung on to it so they would be together. It was almost dusk when they were picked up by the *Ransom.*

Gun 2 was so near the radio shack and CIC that it had practically no chance when those centers were hit in one-two order by bomb-carrying kamikazes. The impact of the hits knocked the gun off its track and the flames roared into the mount from all sides, starting fires in the gun mount and upper handling room. The blows and flash fires were so sudden and unexpected that there was little time for the gun crew to get clear. There are no survivor accounts from men in the gun chamber. The gun captain, Malloway, was listed as missing in action. Those who did escape from the mount were wounded and burned. One who made it out of the mount was so severely wounded that he did not survive. He was T. H. Nichols and was in poor condition when the forecastle was abandoned. He was put aboard a raft, but was dead when carried aboard the *Ransom,* either from wounds or drowning.

The crew of No. 2 handling room faced almost as dangerous a situation as the men in the gun chamber above when fire broke out. However, thanks to the fact that two watertight access doors opened out directly to the forecastle deck to port and starboard, they found it much easier to escape when the fire hit the handling room. Cordrey, the ship's mailman, who was in charge of the handling room crew, and four other men, walked out the port door, shaken and singed, but otherwise alright. A fifth, Paterno, was wounded in the foot, but able to make it on his own. A sixth, Edelman, chose to leave by the starboard door. He must have been caught in an incoming Japanese attack, or some of our own exploding 20mm ammunition, which cost him a mangled arm.

The experience of gun 1 paralleled that of the other guns. The gun captain, Flanagan, and an eager crew kept it firing smoothly and rapidly except for the first few minutes of the engagement when ammunition was not coming up from below fast enough to suit the gun crew. The gun captain and Yecke, the powder loader, were loud in their exhortations for the handling room crews to speed things up. Jensen, the gun repairman, ducked below to check the hoists out. He found some maladjustment in the lower hoist which accounted for the problem. As soon as it was corrected the ammunition moved up as fast as the gun crew could handle it and continued at a satisfactory pace until the entire mount was disabled.

Gun 1 was the last of the 5" guns to cease fire. During most of the time it was under control of the director but when power went out the gun captain shifted the crew to local control and continued to fire in that condition until the kamikaze hit just forward of the gun, completely disabled it, and fires forced its evacuation. Casualties were heavy. Infanto, the hot shell man, was killed outright, Yecke died before he could be gotten to a hospital ship, and Tommy McConnell, the shell loader, was listed as missing in action. Benford, the fuse setter was wounded.

Another who was wounded was Jolly, the pointer. He recalls that he was off watch, but on deck when he saw the first attack on the *Rodman*. Without waiting for general quarters, he jumped into his gun and began preparations for firing. He remembers that they fired at many targets, some of them heading directly at the ship. As pointer it seemed to him that each was headed for him personally until it was hit or crashed. He doesn't know how many gun 1 accounted for, but is sure they got their share. When flames engulfed the mount he just barely got out and probably would not have if he had taken time to pick up his life jacket which had been taken off to give him more freedom of action—a fact which almost cost him his life when he had to abandon ship. As it was his face and hands were severely burned.

After the crew got out on deck they turned to under Flanagan tending to the wounded, trying to fight fires without adequate hoses and trying to help the men from the lower handling rooms that had been trapped below.

Flanagan was deeply concerned about the precarious situation of the men on the forecastle, especially the wounded. Against seemingly impossible odds he fought his way aft to consult with Lieutenant Griffin about some sort of help. Obviously, there was nothing to be done at that point, so he fought his way back to do the best he could under the circumstances. Later, he tried to get aft to launch the whaleboat but was unable to make it because of the fires. For his outstanding record as gun captain of gun 1 and his leadership of the little group of men stranded on the forecastle after the guns were disabled he was awarded the Silver Star. Years later he contended that he did no more than anyone else. What impressed him was that each and every man did his best and there was no panic.

Elsewhere in this history mention has been made of the sense of claustrophobia experienced by men at battle stations in the magazines and handling rooms deep in the ship. Cut off by steel bulkheads, watertight doors and hatches from the rest of the crew and surrounded by tons of powder and shell, there is little chance of survival if anything goes wrong. The sense of isolation is complete. The only way of knowing what is happening in the rest of the ship is over the telephones or the public announcing system.

General quarters for the handling rooms on April 6 was not much different from the many general quarters sounded since the ship had been in Okinawan waters, except that this time there were so many planes and the guns were shooting at such a pace that both upper and lower handling rooms for all the 5" guns were moving ammunition so fast the crews had no time to think about anything else. Toward the end of the first two hours some types of ammunition were beginning to run out in all mounts. The lower handling room of gun 1 had sent up all of its Mark 40s and was working on AA common. Mount 2 had emptied the upper handling room twice over and was working on its third refill when the Japanese struck.

From time to time news of downed enemy aircraft was relayed by telephone to the men toiling below. Each new announcement brought cheers and renewed energy to keep the powder and shells moving up. The ammo handlers were feeling proud of their performance when the tide of battle changed. They knew when the ship was hit on the fantail but had not learned the details when the Japanese shifted their attacks forward. There was no let-up of the pace in the forward handling rooms until the guns themselves were put out of commission.

The first inkling the upper handling room crew of gun 1 had of disaster was when they found themselves scrambling around on all fours amidst loose powder cans and shells on the deck. Then smoke and flame began to come in from the gun chamber and from forward. Some powder and a few shells began to burn. Mooney dived for the sprinkler valve and got it turned on. Jensen, right behind him, turned it on full. As there was fire in the gun chamber above them and fire forward of the handling room, they and the other men opened the watertight door to the wardroom passageway and started aft, expecting to go out through the wardroom. They ran into Doctor Williamson, Lieutenant (jg) Nelson and some men from the battle dressing station coming in the opposite direction, who reported that it was impossible to get out through the wardroom.

Miller, in the lower handling room, had just sent up the last of the Mark 40s and gone into the powder room to help out there when the Japanese hit aft. He isn't certain how many hits came thereafter, nor in what order, but there was no doubt about the one on the bow which put gun 1 out of action. Water began trickling in from the compartment just ahead of the magazines and smoke started coming down the hoist. Miller and the other men in lower 1 decided it was time to leave and, fearing fire above, chose to go aft into the lower handling room for gun 2 to find an exit. That area had received no damage, but just as the men from No. 1 came in, Brill, manning the telephone, heard someone say to abandon ship. Both crews then climbed up to the forward mess hall expecting to go aft and out through the galley passageway. As they left the handling room fire was beginning to come down the hoist. To their consternation they found the galley passageway blocked by fire. Nor could they get forward. After a consultation in the mess hall they decided the only way out was up through the provision hatch leading into the wardroom country. While they were discussing the problem they were joined by the first group from the plotting room. Someone had used a wrench to close the dogs on the provision hatch, so they could not be budged by hand. In the absence of a wrench a battle lantern was used to pound the dogs loose. While they were working on the hatch the remaining men from the plotting room came forward from the after mess hall and joined them. It was a sizeable group which crawled through the provision hatch to the wardroom passageway to join the men from the battle dressing station and the upper handling room of gun 1. Altogether twenty-two were now caught in the passageway.

Apparently, they had not improved their chances of escape by moving up a deck. Behind a watertight door aft of them the wardroom was a roaring furnace. Behind another one at the forward end of the passageway No. 1 upper handling room was still afire. The hatch to No. 2 upper handling room couldn't be budged, probably because of the weight of ammunition, or possibly water from the sprinkling system, on top of it. In the meantime the air in the passageway was becoming thinner and the smoke thicker. The temperature was almost unbearable. Some men were beginning to cough and wheeze and to wonder how long they could endure without fresh air. Some relief was found by opening ports in the officers' staterooms. Some tried to squeeze through them, but no one was small enough. Mooney got his head through one and got the attention of men on deck who could offer no help, not even a hose with water pressure. McClure found a 45 automatic in one of the officer rooms and kept it at hand, determined to kill himself before he would be roasted alive. He claims he was on the verge of pulling the trigger several times before relief came; the last time was just before he got the word that a way up through gun 1 was clear.

While the trapped men were frantically trying to find a way out, Hudson, one of the plotting room crew, decided to take matters into his own hands, although it involved going up and out through gun 1 at considerable personal risk. Accordingly, he left the group and went forward to the upper handling room. It was still burning, but apparently the sprinkler was beginning to have some effect, water on the deck was now ankle deep. Some powder cans and projectiles were still burning, as was the grease on the roller path, but less fiercely than before. He pulled his shirt over his head and started up. On the way he saw a projectile spitting in the fuse pot. Gun 1 was still burning briskly as he scrambled out the hatch. Hand holds and ladder rungs were so hot they could be grasped only briefly, but he made it safely to the open air.

On deck, he went to the upper handling room of gun 2 and tried to get to the hatch leading below to open it for the men in the wardroom country below. He noted that the sprinklers were turned on but the handling room was still afire and it was so hot he couldn't get near the hatch. He then tried to get the provision hatch open but failed without a wrench. Next he crawled down a hole in the forecastle to the chiefs quarters and tried to open the watertight door to the handling room. The dogs worked, but the door was so buckled it wouldn't move. Someone else had apparently returned to the handling room by now as he could hear them on the other side. Whoever it was, they still couldn't get the door open, so Hudson returned to the forecastle to try another gambit.

Back on deck after talking with Flanagan, the two got a fire extinguisher from the gun and played it into the chamber. It didn't put out the fire, but slowed it down and drove it to one side of the mount enough to leave a clear passage up through the other side. Hudson yelled down to the men trapped below to come up that way.

The reprieve came just in time for the trapped men. Some were nearly out from heat exhaustion and smoke inhalation. When they went through the handling room the sprinkler system had just about accomplished its purpose. Water from the sprinklers on deck was halfway to their knees and the fires were out. When the last of the twenty-two trapped men hopped out of gun 1 and announced that he was the last one of the group, Hudson stuck his head into the mount for a final check. The mount was still burning on the port side. A Mark 40 left on the loading tray was spitting and burning. Some months later Hudson was awarded a Silver Star for his efforts in saving the trapped men.

As soon as Doctor Williamson emerged from gun 1 he was rushed over to look at the wounded, which had been laid out near the forward deckhouse. He did what he could to make them comfortable, but there was little else to do except to administer morphine and have them moved farther up the forecastle to get them away from burning gun 2. With two burning guns and a blazing bridge structure as background for his exposed dressing station, the doctor was very much concerned for the safety of his patients, over and above the wounds they already suffered, if the fires in the guns should reach the magazines. His fears were shared by everyone on the forecastle in their right mind.

Williamson had no way of knowing when, if ever, his patients would be taken off the forecastle. He believed they would be safer waiting for rescue on board a life raft, or anything stable in the water, than staying aboard ship waiting for the whole thing to blow. Accordingly, he ordered the wounded put over the side. They were eased over as gently as possible and helped to the closest object which would support them comfortably. Nichols and Yecke, the worst off, and others who could not take care of themselves were gotten over to nearby life rafts and put on board. Yecke was later put back aboard the *Emmons* at the main deck to join the other seriously wounded waiting there for evacuation. In spite of all efforts, neither made it through the night.

After the wounded were put over, the uninjured men were told to abandon ship by Lieutenant Nelson. Many had already gone over the side to assist the wounded or to try to round up some of the life rafts and floats drifting in the vicinity of the ship. The men from the forecastle were in the water a relatively short time as the AMs of Sweep Unit ELEVEN were on the scene by that time and had begun rescue operations. The men who had been blown overboard or had abandoned ship earlier had to hang on quite a bit longer—not that it was easy for anyone. It wasn't long before the men from different parts of the ship were mingling in the water and providing mutual support. They tended to stay as near the ship as their physical condition and fear of a magazine explosion permitted.

Besides the life rafts and floats scattered around, there was plenty to hang on to—dan buoys, powder cans, shoring timbers, even some chair cushions—floatable gear which had been thrown overboard when the abandon ship "order" was first circulated. It was relatively simple for those men physically capable of swimming to a raft or other object to hang on until help arrived. But many of the men were so physically exhausted or weakened from wounds that they couldn't make it to a raft or other support, or hang on if they did make it. The badly burned couldn't use their hands. Many were unable to see. Some men, particularly those with burns, had gone overboard without life jackets. Still others found that their life jackets or belts would not inflate. Some had laid aside their cumbersome jackets in the heat of battle.

In true *Emmons* fashion, the good swimmers and the uninjured took it on themselves to look out for their shipmates who were unable to take care of themselves, sometimes at considerable personal risk. The men tried to stay close together for mutual support, so efforts to help the wounded became largely teamwork. Several examples will serve to illustrate the spirit of the men of the *Emmons* while they were drifting off the burning ship waiting for help. They are by no means exhaustive.

While the medical officer was trying to decide whether to put the wounded on the forecastle in the water, Hudson had spotted a life raft near the break of the deck and had jumped in, intending to bring it forward to receive them. There were no paddles, however, and he couldn't manage the awkward raft alone. Jensen, Deverell, and Cowley went to his help. They were making some progress when there was no longer need for the raft alongside, so they started toward Jolly who was calling for help. Without a life jacket he was struggling and in danger of drowning. Deverell swam out to help him, but found himself being pulled under, whereupon he called for help from Hudson, who came out, and getting his arm under Jolly's chin towed him to the raft. Between them the two got the drowning man safely aboard. This incident prompted Deverell to remark in his survivor's report, "I guess I can thank Hudson again," referring to his part in rescuing him and the others trapped below deck aboard ship such a short time before. With Jolly aboard the raft crew then began to pick up other men who were in less drastic trouble, but who were nonetheless happy to have something solid to hang on to. Before they were picked up by the *Facility* they joined two other rafts and the three were tied together for mutual support. One was full of wounded from the bridge, most of them burned. Cordrey and most of the crew of the upper handling room of gun 2 found a piece of raft which they found adequate, if not fancy. They, too, began to pick up other men in the water. One of the first they spotted was Captain Foss. By kicking and shoving their fragmented raft along they managed to get over to him and get him aboard. He still wore his life jacket. He was placed in the center and kept there until the. raft was picked up. They tried to make him comfortable but first aid on most of the rafts was virtually nonexistent. Another casualty of the hits on the superstructure they brought aboard was Chief Thompson. Wolf and Cordrey had to swim out from the raft to haul in Sofranko, the chief yeoman, who was struggling without a life jacket. The group was rescued by the *Recruit*.

"Pop" Ould and Whitson, from the after repair parties, formed the nucleus of a group which found temporary haven on and around a P-38 paravane. Whitson, badly burned, had jumped over and made it to the paravane. Ould joined him a few minutes later and helped him hang on. At that time Japanese planes were still active and when one would hit the water the concussion was actually painful to the men in the water. Somewhat later, when the group stranded on the forecastle abandoned ship, Blair and Hobart had gone over together, but Hobart had jumped over without a life jacket, so Blair struck out and found a powder can for him to hang on to. Somehow, however, he lost the can and then had to hang on to Blair's life jacket until something else could be found. The situation was complicated when Lucci, just ahead of them, called out that he was having problems with a life belt which wouldn't hold air. Blair invited him to hang on also. The three made it to where Ould was holding Whitson on their paravane and joined them. Whitson was saying he couldn't hold on much longer when Pease and Mooney came along and joined the group. While Lucci and Pease took over the job of holding Whitson on the paravane, Mooney kept blowing a whistle to attract the attention of the AMs now in the vicinity. He finally caught the attention of the *Recruit* which picked up all seven after stopping to rescue two other men from the water.

Costello, whose battle station was the generator room on the main deck, went over the side when he was assured by an officer that it was alright. Very quickly he found a dan buoy and grabbed on to it. An unidentified shipmate grabbed another and the two decided to stick together. The arrangement didn't last long; however, as they saw R. K. Baker, wounded, and another injured struggling to stay afloat. They turned their buoys over to the wounded men and they remained in the vicinity. Costello noted that Baker's life belt was not inflated and tried to blow it up himself without success. It had a leak somewhere. He and his former partner kept swimming and encouraging the two newcomers while the latter clung to the buoys. Then they saw an AM coming toward them and tried to swim toward it, but it was slow going. The supply officer came along and gave all four of them a hand. They managed to get alongside the AM, which helped them get Baker and the other man aboard before they themselves climbed on board. The rescue vessel was the *Recruit.*

Miller and Pease had said goodbye to each other on the forecastle of the *Emmons* and took the plunge. Miller had no life jacket and couldn't find one before he went over the side. In his case, it didn't seem to bother him as he was a good swimmer and very soon found an empty powder can which he clung to. He got separated from Pease, but ran into T. B. Baker and they teamed up to find a buoy which provided support for both until they were picked up by the *Recruit.*

Another team which tried to stay together was Brill and Coughennower who left the ship together and swam together until they came to a buoy already supporting six other men. Two more didn't seem to make much difference. They were all there when a boat from one of the AMs came along to take them off. On the way back to the mother ship they were strafed by a Japanese plane but escaped unharmed. Once on board the AM they almost got it again when an enemy attack was stopped thirty feet short of the ship. Brill recorded that all of his group were shaking like leaves during the attack, but got over it quickly when the plane was splashed.

Not all the heroism and self-sacrifice was attributable to teams or groups. Incidents of individual bravery were abundant. A case in point is that of "Pappy" Cole, one of those trapped below decks in the heat and smoke of the wardroom country for so long. He was still wheezing and coughing from smoke-clogged lungs when the forecastle abandoned ship. In the water he could hardly breathe. The effect was cumulative, the harder he fought to breathe the more salt water he took in. He was struggling to get to a life raft when Roberts aboard the *Emmons,* on the superstructure deck, noticed his predicament. The alert quartermaster jumped to the main deck and hit the water. Swimming to Cole, he helped the nearly drowned man to the nearest life raft and then returned to the ship to continue trying to signal the rescue craft.

The machine gun battery was, in every sense of the word, the last line of defense against kamikazes. The men who manned them, besides having strong nerves, had to have a keen sense of judgment on when to open fire in order to get optimum range, yet not waste ammunition. There wasn't that much problem about when to cease fire—they fired until the plane dropped—or else. Like the pointers on the five-inch guns the machine gunners usually had the feeling the planes were aiming for them personally—frequently they were. The machine guns of the *Emmons* got at least two planes, probably more. There is no way of accurately determining who was responsible when all guns were firing.

According to the survivor reports submitted after the battle there was very little for the machine guns to do during the early minutes of the action. During this period the Japanese kept a respectful distance. Several men on the machine gun crews mention watching the dogfights aloft between the combat air patrol and the kamikazes. Both Dodzik of the starboard amidships 20mm and Cassell of the port 20mm saw around six Japanese shot down by the Corsairs and Hellcats before the *Emmons* was subjected to its first dive bomb attack. The tempo increased as the enemy got his act together. By the second hour every gun on the ship was involved. The machine guns had as much, and more, as they could handle. They took care of close-in targets which couldn't be handled by the main battery. If the main battery was free they all joined in. Targets were engaged as designated by machine gun control or as spotted by the individual gun crews.

The machine guns claimed a number of hits, but crews were amazed at the amount of punishment the suicider planes could absorb before going down—sometimes just short of the ship. Dolasky, operator of the Mark 51 director for the starboard 40mm, described the splashing of an incoming plane about 500 yards off the starboard quarter by the 40mm the director was controlling. Another plane coming in off the starboard bow was shot down at the same time by the 5" guns. Flynn, first loader on the port 40mm, was watching as the plane on the starboard quarter came in. He identified it as a Val and says that only the starboard 40mm and one 20mm were firing on it. It seemed to him as if it would never be stopped. Finally, it crashed just short of the starboard quarter, much closer than Dolasky put it, an estimated ten yards.

There were just as close calls to port. Meyers, of the port 40mm, watched a plane continue to close through heavy fire until it crashed just a few feet off the ship. He also saw a Val on the starboard beam start strafing the ship before hitting the water.

Starting with the hits on the fantail everything changed. Flynn, as loader of the port 40mm, was facing aft when the Val hit the starboard quarter. Instinctively he ducked down by the mount when he saw the plane hit. It may well have saved his life. When he managed to stand up again most of the crew was gone. Chester Kennedy, who had been standing next to him was bent over in pain, mortally wounded. Ensign Sheeran was kneeling holding on to the loader's platform. Flynn helped him to his feet and across the catwalk to the area around the stacks where some of the men had taken shelter.

Dolasky, on the opposite side, strapped in the harness of the Mark 51 director, was spun completely around by the blast. It seemed to him that everyone had been pushed bodily forward. When he steadied down and looked around only one man was left on the starboard 40mm, Wilder, the trainer, still strapped to his seat, dead. Dolasky himself got out of the director harness and went down to the main deck because he thought No. 3 upper handling room had been hit. Many wounded were lying about the deck, some of them from the 40mm guns who had been hit by flying metal fragments from the magnetic reel and the mine sweeping gear. Some were burned.

Apparently no longer afraid of the upper handling room of gun 3 he returned to the 40mm gun and helped to throw the ammunition overboard. Eventually, he abandoned ship by taking to the water and was picked up by the *Facility.*

Hunkele's experience on the starboard 40mm was similar. He did not actually see the Val hit the starboard quarter, but felt the concussion and saw the mine sweeping gear go flying into the air. The pieces arced over the entire area, killing and wounding many men in exposed positions on the main and superstructure decks. There was no pattern to the way the deadly fragments fell. It was pure luck; one man would get hit while another next to him escaped without so much as a scratch. Hunkele joined the rest of the crew in seeking cover and went down to the main deck. When things calmed down a little he returned to the 40mm deck, but there was little he could do. Jacoby asked him to help get Chester Kennedy from the port 40s to the main deck and onto a raft which he did. He also helped get Borelli onto a raft. Earlier, he had heard the word to abandon ship, but paid little attention to it until someone yelled "No. 3 handling room is going to blow!" That was enough for Hunkele. He and Edgar Simoneau jumped over the side together. They were eventually picked up by the *Emmons*'s whaleboat and delivered aboard the *Recruit.*

The port 20mm was firing at a target to port when the blow came on the starboard quarter. Cassell was knocked off his feet and back between the stacks by the concussion. He was just getting back on his feet to return to his gun when two other explosions occurred around the bridge. When he got back to the gun he found it was no longer operative, so he turned to with other displaced gun crews trying to contain the damage and help the wounded lying around the decks. At that time many of the men were gathered around the break of the deck. It is probable that some of them had made their way there from the three machine guns clustered around the bridge structure or from some of the other battle stations on or around the bridge. Cassell, finding his 20mm useless, helped carry some of the wounded back aft to where "Doc" Kennedy had set up his temporary dressing station. The machine gun crewman estimated that seventy to eighty men were in the water off the starboard side and he was one of the men who helped get rafts and other floatable material over so they would have something to hang on to until help arrived. Near sunset, he watched helplessly as two kamikazes began a run on the ship with the intention of fulfilling their divine mission. There was nothing on board to stop them, but as he watched they abruptly shifted their attack to the AMs off the starboard side, giving the men on deck a few more minutes of grace to continue the fight to keep their ship afloat. About dusk the *PGM-11* came alongside and started to take on board the men still left on the *Emmons.* The process was speeded up as explosions were heard in the forward magazines. Cassell jumped aboard as she was backing off. He noted that at the time the water was about to the deck edge on the starboard side. The superstructure was still afire up to the director. As he left the ship he heard explosions which seemed to come from the forward magazines.

Dodzik, gunner on the starboard 20mm, missed getting in on the first suicider brought down by the *Emmons* because of a jam caused by a wet drum, but corrected it in time to take on any others which came within range of his gun until it was put out of action. One suicider crashed about a hundred yards in front of the gun with a terrific explosion. Once the air was so full of suicide planes closing in on the ship, the Hellcats from the CAP followed them right on in. Dodzik started firing on one of the Hellcats which appeared to be diving at him. He ceased fire when he recognized the diving plane as a Hellcat and shifted to one of the more appropriate targets. Dodzik remembers only four enemy hits on the *Emmons,* but isn't certain what time they came, nor the exact sequence. He saw the plane which crashed the fantail. The resulting explosion threw him out of his harness. Suddenly another terrific explosion sent the magnetic reel on the fantail flying skyward and showered the area with steel fragments. That one threw him to his knees and left some of the shrapnel in his right leg. A hit forward, apparently at CIC, threw a mass of debris around his gun, including what he believed were pieces of flesh and bone. The crew of the gun was sprayed with green marker dye, probably from one of the lockers in the bridge area. He saw another plane hit the forecastle, but couldn't say when. Some men began to abandon ship after the explosions on the fantail, but Dodzik decided to remain aboard and stayed until the *PGM-11* came alongside. As ship's service store operator, his last act aboard the *Emmons* was to break open the store room with the approval of Lieutenant Griffin and get some cigarettes for distribution to the men leaving the ship for the last time. He, too, heard explosions forward while the gunboat was alongside following which her skipper had the lines cut and backed away as quickly as possible. Dodzik's report ended with the note: "All hands performed splendidly from beginning to end."

Many men assigned to battle stations not directly involved with fighting the guns or minute-by-minute running of the ship were relegated to a more or less passive role during the first half of the battle. Most of them were stationed on the main and superstructure decks aft of the galley to the fantail. They found themselves helpless, but fascinated, onlookers of the deadly fight between the *Emmons's* guns and the combat air patrol on the one hand and the Japanese kamikazes on the other. For example, once battle stations were manned and battle condition AFFIRM, meaning all watertight doors and fittings not actually needed at general quarters were closed, was set throughout the ship, the men of the three repair parties had nothing to do but remain on station, check and recheck their damage control equipment, and hope that their services would not be needed. Similarly, men of the depth charge attack crews, the battle dressing stations, secondary conn, and mine sweeping units, having no immediate part in the action, were left in the role of spectators as long as the Japanese were held off. Those stationed topside were kept busy scurrying from one side of the ship to the other whenever an enemy plane appeared to be coming in. Some relieved the tensions by helping the machine gun crews load ammunition drums and clips.

Their roles changed drastically when the first Japanese plane managed to plunge into the fantail. With incredible swiftness the spectators became active participants along with the gunners and ship control people as they went into action to contain the damage. For some it was all over. Casualties were heavy among the men in exposed stations aft and on the superstructure deck near the machine guns and gun 3. Members of the repair parties suffered from machine gun strafing and flying debris as they began to fight the fires started by the rapid succession of hits. Later, exploding ammunition from the ready ammunition boxes became a hazard.

All of the battle stations aft of the stacks were wiped out and many men went with them. The steering engine room was one of the first to go. It was directly under the point of impact of the first kamikaze and was completely demolished. No one stationed there survived.

A one-man station, the chemical smoke generator on the fantail, would almost certainly have meant the death of Bill Boyle, who was normally assigned to it at general quarters, if he had been there on April 6. But on the big day he was on the sick list recovering from several broken ribs sustained two weeks earlier during fueling operations. By then he had recovered enough to walk around, so he watched the battle from amidships rather than from his battle station on the doomed fantail. Fortunately, it had not been deemed necessary to assign anyone else to the station.

Most of the men stationed on the fantail were casualties, including the men assigned to the general quarters minesweeping detail and the depth charge attack team. Tostanoski, the boatswain's mate of the minesweeping crew was one of the few to survive. When word came down from the bridge to take cover they all started forward. Tostanoski saw several men duck under the magnetic hose reel. He himself continued forward but got caught in the fire of the machine gun from the attacking kamikaze. He was severely wounded in the legs and one heel and to this day cannot wear regular oxfords. At that, he was luckier than the men who had stopped at the magnetic reel. They did not survive the hit which carried away the reel and started fires in and around gun 3.

Anderson, whose battle station was with the depth charge battery was one of the survivors of that group. He, with nearby members of repair party 3, was an interested spectator of the aerial battle overhead. The first real scare came when one of the planes broke through the CAP and dived on the ship. That plane crashed on the port quarter, but from then on attackers approaching the ship were more frequent. Even so there were short lulls in the action when the men discussed how lucky they had been so far. To them, everything seemed to be going well as one plane after another hit the water, some close to the ship, others several thousand yards away. Anderson was lying on the deck aft of the after fire room hatch when the first blow came. He felt a blow on the back of his head from something, but his helmet absorbed the impact and he was able to get up, uninjured, when "Pop" Ould, lying beside him, called for the repair party to man the fire hose. Anderson started aft with them, but didn't get far when he saw a plane fly into the port side of the superstructure at the CIC level. By then the firefighters realized that they had no pressure on the fire hoses. Someone gave the order to man the life rafts. He helped to launch the two after port rafts and helped lower wounded from the deck into one of them. When that was filled he was ordered to get into the other and help take other wounded aboard. Later he took to the water to get the first raft clear of the jagged fantail. He remained with that raft and was eventually picked up by the *Facility* along with the wounded it carried.

George Kennedy, the junior man in the medical department, was responsible for medical dressings topside during battle. Having nothing to do for the first two hours he helped the 20mm crews load ammunition drums on the superstructure deck, but started aft immediately when the first kamikaze crashed the fantail. He had not gone far before the second blow fell. After that he found several wounded men under the port 40mm, including his immediate superior, Chief Eaton, and Lieutenant Davenport. The regular after battle dressing station was afire, so he set up an improvised dressing station in the vicinity of the loading machine, on the port side. He found plenty of assistance from survivors of the repair parties and other battle stations, some of whom were wounded themselves. In his report Kennedy made special mention of Beck, Chara, Synosky, and Lieutenant Davenport. The latter was described as dragging himself along the deck to help the pharmacist's mate. Kennedy himself was wounded in the legs during the attacks on the bridge, but he continued to tend the wounded. After the original fires had almost died out he went forward and then aft looking for any wounded who might have been overlooked. He could not get into CIC because of the heat, nor could he get onto the forecastle because of the fire and debris. He found several bodies outside CIC, but no signs of life. Returning aft he found several more bodies near the depth charge racks. While there, he looked into the after passageway. All he saw was part of a plane at the foot of the double ladder. The wreckage of another was against the after deck house. Kennedy's last task aboard the *Emmons* was to evacuate some of the more seriously wounded to the *Facility.* He was awarded the bronze star medal for his dogged devotion to the wounded.

Synosky of repair party 2 saw gun 3 and the 40mm machine guns knock down four Japanese planes before the first ones got through to the ship. After that it seemed to him that planes were coming in from all sides. He saw one hit the port side of the bridge structure and another strike somewhere near gun 1, but missed the one which got the starboard side of the bridge. About that time he and other members of the repair party were getting a hose out of the electrical shop to lead forward. The hose was O.K. when they got it out of the shop, but a Japanese plane came in spraying the deck with machine gun bullets as they headed forward. The hose was left useless in their hands. It was then that it was cut in two within inches of Synosky's hands. The attacks lasted only a few minutes, but damaged fire hose and low pressure rendered their efforts futile. At that point the main deck was a shambles, and fires and exploding machine gun ammunition prevented attempts to get to the bridge for the time being. Synosky turned his attention to helping the wounded. After the more seriously wounded were cared for others renewed attempts to get to the bridge. Synosky and others searched accessible parts of the ship for wounded, but found no one alive.

Titko remained in the machine shop with other members of repair party 2 until they felt the impact of the first hit. He rushed out of the machine shop with the others as they started aft, grabbing fire hoses on the way. As they tried to get water pressure, a second hit drove them back into the machine shop where Titko saw Ensign Smith lying on the deck, wounded. He started aft a second time when he saw the bridge go up in flames. At the same time some men began to go over the side. When Titko asked if abandon ship had been ordered someone told him it had. Remembering Ensign Smith lying on the machine shop deck he turned back intending to help the officer get off the ship, but found the machine shop empty. As 20mm shells began to pop off from the bridge, he decided it was time for him to go. Once in the water, he helped Benford, who was without a life jacket, stay afloat until an AM came along and picked them both up.

For the men whose battle stations were in the engine rooms and fire rooms, the first part of the battle was routine as they kept the boilers and main engines operating smoothly in response to orders from the bridge while the *Emmons* circled the *Rodman* at flank speed. The men were acutely aware that they were in a life and death struggle, although, like the men in the ammunition handling rooms they were unable to see what was going on. Being shut off from visual contact with activities overhead, the black gang relied on information passed down from the bridge to the forward engine room, the engineering control station.

Although they could not see what was going on, the engineers needed no reminders to know when their ship was under direct attack. They were alerted by the roar of the guns and the violent maneuvers ordered from the bridge to throw the attacking planes off their stride. The orders incident to the radical maneuvering kept the black gang too busy adjusting steam pressure and engine speeds in response to the engine-order telegraph to worry about their own skins.

There were no direct hits on the engine rooms and fire rooms. As a result most damage in those spaces was indirect and largely confined to the after engine room through damage to the port propeller and reduction gear. Neither were there any casualties among the men manning them until they had secured and gone topside in obedience to orders.

In the forward engine room, the throttle man, Greico, reported that there was no damage after the first hits, but the ship seemed to vibrate when the engine was stopped. Mierzwa, the chief in charge, felt additional hits after the stop bell was received. At that time there was loss of steam pressure, the generator slowed to a stop, and the lights went out. While the engine room crew struggled to get machinery back into operation, the engineer officer, Lieutenant Minton, was receiving reports from other machinery spaces over the engineering circuit and trying in vain to contact the bridge over the maneuvering circuit. Tenerowicz, the talker on the latter circuit, was unable to reach any other station. After some time, the engineer officer, left in the dark, both literally and figuratively, decided to go topside himself to see what was going on. While he was gone, someone from topside called down through the hatch to abandon ship, an unofficial order which was ignored. The other engineering spaces also ignored the unofficial message.

After ten minutes or so the engineer officer returned to the forward engine room and issued orders to secure the engine rooms and fire rooms. The men were to take their life jackets and helmets and go aft. This had not been intended as an order to abandon ship, but unfortunately, unofficial word was passed at the same time that the forward engine room was abandoning ship.

In the after engine room, Heath, the chief in charge, realizing that the port engine was useless, and unable to find out what the true situation was, decided to go topside to check things out for himself. When he emerged from the engine room hatch he saw the bridge and superstructure ablaze and men abandoning ship. Some fifty or sixty men were in the water on the starboard side while men on the ship were throwing over all floatable gear. The stern was gone. When he got back to the engine room the steam pressure was dropping and he gave orders to secure all steam machinery except the fire and bilge pump. That was secured when pressure continued to drop but was started up again later by a party sent down from topside. When the order came from the forward engine room to go topside, the after engine room was already set to go. Heath's last order was for his men to take their helmets and life jackets and go topside.

According to the chief in charge of the forward fire room, Cooper, the crash of planes which hit other parts of the ship could hardly be felt in the fire room, except for the one which hit the starboard side of the bridge. That explosion was so violent that it popped open the fire room hatch. Small bits of the suicide plane fell into the fire room.

Sometime during the battle Korney, the telephone talker in the forward fire room was relieved to go topside. While topside he witnessed No. 3 gun knock down an attacking plane on the nose and saw another making a pass at the bridge as he returned to the fire room to resume the talker's duties. As he resumed his talker's duties he felt several severe hits. Unlike most people he believed the first hits were forward. After an especially strong shock the fire room filled with smoke and the machinery was fouled up for several minutes. Then there appeared to him to be a heavy hit aft which shook the whole ship. He heard over the phones from someone that they might have to abandon ship. Eventually word came to secure the fire room and prepare to abandon ship. When the fire room personnel went topside Korney assisted the firefighters and later the wounded. He left the *Emmons* aboard the PGM-11.

Sandwiched between the two engine rooms and not too close to the points of impact of the kamikaze attacks, the after fire room was least affected by the hits. Peters, on the feed checks thought there was only one explosion during the fight. Henwood, on the burners, wasn't sure how many, but it seemed to him that they all came at the same time. The only thing out of the ordinary noted was an excessive vibration of the starboard shaft running through the fireroom before it came to a stop. When orders came to secure and go topside the fireroom crew did so in an orderly fashion leaving enough burners in the boiler to keep 600 pounds pressure on the fire and bilge pumps.

It is not surprising that men in different spaces gained different impressions of the gravity of the situation, largely dependent on the location of their battle stations in relation to where the attacking planes struck. To most of them, as well as to the men topside, time became meaningless after the ship was stopped dead in the water and they were involved in nursing their machinery along as they waited for orders. Neither did most of the engine room and boiler room crews have any true idea of the damage which had been inflicted until they emerged onto the main deck in response to the orders to secure and go topside. They were shocked at the fires and wreckage, and seeing the bodies of their dead and wounded shipmates lying around the deck. Most had left their duty stations expecting to abandon ship. Appalled as they were by the wreckage and carnage they saw around them, few opted to do so. Instead, they pitched in to help the repair parties do what they could to save their ship. Most of them stayed aboard until the last men were taken off by the PGM-11 around dusk.

Among other tasks they performed they explored accessible parts of the ship to assess damage and look for any survivors who might have been trapped. One such party, led by Mierzwa and Stevenson, went forward to see if anyone was trapped in that area. During the search, Mierzwa was surprised to hear a reply from the bridge to his calls. Accompanied by Rush he tried to reach the bridge by means of an outside ladder, but they found the rungs so hot they could not hang on. After going back down to the engine room for asbestos gloves they managed to reach the bridge where they found Kohl, a sonar-man, by some miracle still alive, but mortally wounded. They lowered him to the main deck where he was given first aid, but he didn't survive long enough to be evacuated to the *Facility* with other seriously wounded men. Afterward, Mierzwa made another trip back to his engine room to make sure that all machinery except the fire and bilge pump was properly secured—someone had reported that the starboard propeller was turning over slowly. Both Mierzwa and Stevenson were awarded Bronze Stars for their outstanding work with the repair parties. They were among the last men to leave the *Emmons* aboard the PGM-11.

The last comment of Cooper, of the forward fireroom, in his informal report is applicable to all the black gang, "There was little or no excitement and crew carried out their duties very well."

8

The *Ellyson* and *Hambleton* had completed their day's sweeping assignment off Ie Shima early in the afternoon of April 6, and had gone down to Kerama Rhetto for routine logistics. They arrived off the north entrance to the anchorage during one of the heaviest enemy air raids of the day and had to remain outside waiting for the air raid to end. While waiting for the all-clear signal and permission to enter, ComMinRon 20 intercepted a message from the *Rodman* calling for help. She was under heavy air attack and had been hit. Some time later another message, presumably originated by one of the AMs approaching the two embattled ships, was intercepted. Both the *Emmons* and *Rodman* were under attack and had been severely damaged. The *Emmons* was reported as abandoning ship.

On receipt of the last message ComMinRon 20 ordered the *Ellyson* and *Hambleton* to reverse course and proceed at best speed to assist the *Emmons* and *Rodman.* Speed was restricted to nineteen knots by damage to one of the *Hambleton's* propellers.

At 2100 the two destroyer-minesweeps made contact with the mine sweeps of Unit 11 heading for Kerama Rhetto with survivors of the battle aboard. From the AMs it was learned that the *Rodman* was proceeding to the haven under her own power, escorted by the *Density,* also damaged. The *Hambleton* was detached to accompany them to the base. When she joined the two, the *Density* reported to her that the forward magazine of the *Emmons* had exploded and that she was unsalvageable.

In the meantime the *Ellyson* proceeded to the vicinity of the still burning, drifting hulk of the *Emmons* north of Motobu Peninsula. There she found the LCI (G) 558 and LCI (G) 559 standing by. They had been on patrol stations near Ie Shima and the Motobu Peninsula when ordered to go to the assistance of the *Emmons* and *Rodman* and to continue the search for survivors. They had arrived in the area as the AMs were heading south for Kerama Rhetto, and had renewed the search for survivors with negative results. The *Ellyson* arrived on the scene around 2155.

On arrival at the scene ComMinRon 20, with the aid of the LCIs and the *Ellyson,* began a survey to determine the condition of the *Emmons.* The LCIs reported that fires were raging below decks throughout her length—a fact confirmed by observers aboard the *Ellyson,* who could see fires through holes in the hull. The *Ellyson's* log records that cautious use of a twelve inch light revealed extensive topside damage. The fantail was demolished and the port side of the bridge blown off. She made no mention of the starboard wing which many of the survivors from the *Emmons* reported as having been blown away. Her log reported there was no list and the draft was about thirteen feet. The latter led the commodore to believe that there was little underwater damage and that the hull could be saved with the proper equipment—a conclusion in agreement with Lieutenant Griffin's earlier report, except that the *Emmons* was now drifting toward enemy territory. Attempts by a party from the *Ellyson* to get aboard the *Emmons* to secure a tow line were thwarted by darkness and fires.

Weighing against attempts at salvage was the fact that the hulk was only a few miles north of enemy-held Motobu Peninsula and was now drifting southward at one knot. The commodore decided it would be best to sink it before it got into shoal water. Some time before midnight he made the following report to CTF 51 summarizing his findings and recommendation regarding the *Emmons.* "About 30 feet of stern destroyed by explosion, fires burning in bow prevent running tow line, draft forward 15 feet indicating little underwater damage. Salvageable but drifting south at one knot toward enemy territory. Estimate EMMONS will reach shallow water within three or four hours. Permission to sink EMMONS requested."

In the meantime the *Ellyson* stood by the doomed *Emmons* waiting for a reply to the request to destroy her. Every hour she drifted closer to enemy territory. About 0200 information was received that two tugs were on the way to assist. Wherever they were, their orders were soon cancelled. At 0230 instructions were received from CTF 51 to sink the drifting ship. The *Ellyson* then closed and opened fire with her main battery. As crippled and defenseless as she was the *Emmons* refused to give up easily. After ninety-six rounds of 5"/38 caliber AA common she capsized and sank at 0318 on April 7, 1945, in twenty-five fathoms of water off the north coast of Motobu Peninsula of Okinawa. She had served her country faithfully and well for three years, four months, and a day.

Lt. Commander Eugene N. Foss II

Commander Foss was a plank owner of the USS Emmons, having joined the commissioning crew as an Ensign. He served as Executive Officer under Billingsley and replaced him as Captain. Foss was the first reserve officer to become Captain of the Emmons. On April 6, 1945, during the successive kamikaze strikes, he was blown off the bridge, landing in the water severely burned and temporarily blinded. Foss was awarded his second Bronze Star and the Silver Star for his action in the attack. He died in 1995.

Foss Family Collection

Lt. John J Griffin
Senior Surviving Officer

Griffin was the Emmons Gunnery Officer on April 6, 1945. When it was realized all senior officers were disabled, or missing, he assumed command as senior surviving officer. He tried to save the ship but the damage inflicted by the five kamikaze strikes was too extensive. He directed evacuation of the wounded still on board and then remaining able—bodied survivors. One of his most notable directives, issued later aboard an evacuation ship, required each survivor to record his account of events during and after the attack. These eyewitness reports were invaluable reference in accounting for crew and describing events. Griffin was awarded the Silver Star for his efforts during and following the attack. Once back in the states, he visited many casualty families. He died March 30, 2005.

Griffin Family Collection

Ensign Ross T. Elliott, Jr. (K)
Awarded the Navy Cross Posthumously

Ensign Elliot was assistant gunnery officer and machine gun officer on the Emmons. He was at his battle station on the flying bridge above the pilot house, with a crew of five men on April 6, 1945. When he saw that a strafiing kamikaze was going to crash the bridge, he ordered the men to lie down and threw his body over them as a shield. The men all survived, but Ensign Elliot was mortally wounded.

16

Honors

o o o o o o o o o o o o o o o o o o o o o o o o o o o o o o

By her own aggressiveness and the courage and skill of her officers and men, the U.S.S. EMMONS achieved a record of gallantry in combat reflecting the highest credit upon herself and the United States Naval Service.

—*Excerpt from the Navy Unit Commendation awarded the* ***Emmons***

The loss of the *Emmons* was announced by Fleet Admiral Chester W. Nimitz on April 22, 1945, while the survivors were still on the way home aboard the *Wayne.* It was June before accounts of her last battle appeared in newspapers throughout the United States. Most of the newspaper accounts followed closely the press release of the Navy's Public Information Service. The latter summarized the high points of her career, from her commissioning two days before Pearl Harbor to her loss to enemy action in the mass suicide attacks on April 6, 1945. The journalist who wrote the news release emphasized the fact that the *Emmons* was lost defending a sister ship from the enemy. He seemed to be unaware of the close relationship which had existed between the *Rodman* and the *Emmons* since the formation of Destroyer Squadron 10. He noted that between the commissioning and the end of Okinawa, the *Emmons* had steamed better than 300,000 miles hunting the enemy during more than three years of global war.

Another document hidden in the files of the Naval Historical Center at Washington is the official history of the *Emmons* compiled much later, in February, 1952. It covers much the same territory as the press release issued after her sinking. New material of interest included are a list of honors won by the DD457-DM522 during World War II and the text of the Navy Unit Commendation awarded for her role in the Okinawa campaign.

The *Emmons* earned four Battle Stars on the European-African-Middle Eastern Service Medal and one Star on the Pacific Area Service Medal for participation in the following engagements and operations:

1 Star North African Occupation
Algeria Morocco Landing—9-11 November 1942
1 Star Class "B" Submarine Assessment—14 May 1944
1Star Invasion of Normandy (Including the bombardment of Cherbourg)—6-25 June 1944
1 Star Invasion of Southern France—15 August to 25 September 1944
1 Star Okinawa Gunto Operation
Assault and Occupation of Okinawa Gunto—25 March to 6 April 1945

The text of the Navy Unit Commendation read as follows:

> For outstanding heroism in action while attached to Mine Squadron TWENTY, operating under Commander Mine Force, Pacific Fleet, from March 24 to 31; and thereafter under the operational control of Commander Transport Screen, from April 1 to 6, 1945, during operations for the seizure of enemy-held Okinawa, Ryuku Islands. Although lightly armed and highly vulnerable while operating in dangerous mined waters, the U.S.S. EMMONS rendered heroic service in minesweeping, fire support, radar picket, anti-suicide boat, antisubmarine and antiaircraft screen missions. A natural and frequent target for heavy Japanese aerial attack, she was constantly vigilant and ready for battle, fighting her guns valiantly against a group of Japanese suicide planes striking in force on April 6, and downing six of the attackers before five others crashed her in rapid succession, killing or wounding many personnel and inflicting damage which necessitated her sinking. By her own aggressiveness and the courage and skill of her officers and men, the U.S.S. EMMONS achieved a record of gallantry in combat reflecting the highest credit upon herself and the United States Naval Service. The Navy Unit Commendation was the Navy's way of recognizing the bravery and devotion to duty of an entire crew. It was impossible to recognize each one individually, so their performance as a group was highlighted. A few individuals were cited for and eventually received personal recognition. Altogether thirteen officers and crewmen were cited for outstanding performance of duty in battle against the enemy on April 6, 1945. Among them were one Navy Cross, four Silver Stars, and eight Bronze Stars.

2

In this history there has been much about watches, drills, false alarms, chow, liberty ports, and gambling, good and bad weather. There has been a little about operations, missions, submarine warfare, and invasions. A glance has been had of the privations and hardships inherent in a small warship under wartime routine. There has been some about training and the development of teamwork among youngsters of widely varying backgrounds under the tutelage of the older veterans. The accelerated development of a strong sense of personal responsibility and a corresponding sense of duty can be detected—a determination not to be the one to goof off, not to let their shipmates down. More than one man who has served aboard the *Emmons* has stated that he "grew up" in a hurry aboard the DD457-DMS22. Some of the things recorded here, such as the joyous free-for-all for possession of the last black bean in a packet of jelly beans, or a crap game in the engineer compartment, were trivial. Others, such as heel and toe watches in stormy, freezing weather north of the Arctic Circle, the stalking of submarines in the Mediterranean, or clearing of mines off Okinawa were of the utmost importance. Taken all together they spelled out life aboard a small warship under all sorts of conditions. No matter how trivial some may have appeared to others they were all of major importance to several hundred young men who left the comfortable routine and safety of their homes to serve their country during the war at one time or another aboard the *Emmons.*

It is not easy to record the affection and loyalty men sharing a common responsibility and a common danger develop for one another. Most men of the *Emmons* would scorn to try to put such sentiments in words. Nonetheless, they come shining through the events, great and trivial, which are recorded here.

Nor is it easy to describe the bonds between a sailor and his ship. Ray Quinn, gunner's mate 3c, and gun captain of the starboard 40mm machine guns on April 6, 1945, came aboard the *Emmons* as an apprentice seaman in June, 1942, and left her aboard the PGM-11 when she had to be abandoned, drifting and burning. He spoke for all when he said, "I know we griped and complained at just about everything, but as we sat in the rescue craft and took a look back at our proud ship, a part of each one of us stayed with her."

17

Rediscovery of the USS Emmons

By John W. Chandler, Lt. Col. (Ret.) USMC

In the fall of 1999, the island of Okinawa was pounded by a typhoon of horrifying strength. The island, 66 miles long and less then three miles wide at the narrowest point, was battered by the power of the sea and the wind. The storm was extreme in its force with winds howling past 234 miles an hour, literally rocking the island beneath its crashing waves.

Shortly after the typhoon receded, a group of diver friends and myself were chatting and perusing the local papers about the storm's damage. Rich Ruth, a fellow diver and good friend, pointed out an article that carried a special interest to all of us. The Japanese Coast Guard had received reports from fishermen that oil was bubbling and sheening the ocean's surface off the coast of Kouri-jima. The Coast Guard cutter dispatched to the scene employed side—scanning sonar to detect a vessel-like image on the bottom. It appeared to be a very large destroyer-like silhouette. The newspaper hypothesized that the ship on the bottom had been rolled by the typhoon and started to leak oil. This made sense to all of us divers who had just experienced the third most powerful storm to hit the island in recorded history.

Throughout 2000 Rich Ruth, I and several other divers continued to ponder the question: "Was there really a destroyer there"? We made trip after trip, diving time and again in a search pattern on the western side of Kouri-jima. Local archives had volumes of documentation on the ferocious Battle of Okinawa, which commenced Eastern Sunday, April 1, 1945. Everything indicated we must be searching for the *USS Emmons*. Research showed that the *Emmons* was hit very hard by the "typhoon of steel" that had flown from the Japanese mainland April 6th to disrupt the support and for the Marines and Army troops who had invaded Okinawa. As a group, we continued diving regularly until February 19th, 2001. On that date, a dive group comprised of Rich Ruth, Steve Tomlin, and Ms. Tami Clark swam up on the awesome mass of the *Emmons*. The ship was lying on its starboard side, her five-inch guns still pointing skyward as they had on April 6, 1945. That day her gun crews had fought fiercely against 75 to 90 attacking aircraft, splashing 10 of the enemy. Finally, however, the ship received five direct hits in succession within two minutes time. The *Emmons* lost its ability to control its movement or defend itself and had lost the senior officers. The senior surviving officer knew she had to be abandoned. Now, the *USS Emmons* was rediscovered.

My first visit to the *Emmons* was the following day. I carried my usual camera apparatus to record the find. I remember the excitement of the event as if it was yesterday, and I would learn later that the survivors' memories were etched deeply, as well. The images I recorded that day and on many subsequent days reveal the strength and depth of the American Spirit. Holes explosive scars and metal torn from its welds attest to the storm it had weathered the day of the attack. The damage shows the tenacity with which the crew had fought to protect the troops and support activity at the beaches just 30 miles to the south. Such an aerial assault on the landings would have killed thousands and severely jeopardized success of the American mission on Okinawa.

The divers that day were all active, retired or former US Marines. On surfacing, we were all speechless, and after viewing Rich Ruth's video-taped images were even quieter. Our excitement was tempered by a mixture of awe and respect for the ship, her crew and the shipmates who are still aboard. Less then two months later, on April 6, the anniversary of the ship's loss, we conducted the first memorial service at the site. With assistance from the Navy, we gathered local veterans and religious personnel to commemorate the lives lost 56 years earlier. For all the years since World WarII Okinawa had only one American memorial, Ernie Pyle's on Ie-shima. Now it has two.

In the present age of instantaneous, imbedded reporting, where we can actually maneuver with soldiers and marines on the battlefield, it is inconceivable that you had not heard about the *Emmons* and the horrendous losses of other Navy ships at Okinawa. I attribute this silence at the time to America's weariness from unending losses since December 7, 1941. Coming in the wake of devastating losses to Marines on Iwo Jima, our country was not made aware of severe losses once again being experienced at Okinawa. During the three months of the Okinawa campaign, President Roosevelt had died and the war in Europe had ended. Tired of the dying and with the anticipation building toward the invasion of Japan, the Battle of Okinawa and its bravery were moved t page two of the newspapers.

The crew of the *Emmons* has quietly endured and absorbed the passing of three wars since their ship was blown from under them. Their special relationship was formalized into an association which endured and strengthened through the years. Rich Ruth and I have been honored with invitations to join with them at reunions. Their annual meetings are events that I personally assess as quiet valor. With their wives, these men gather just to be together. They do not seek a hero's label; they simply seek and are consoled in each other's friendship and respect. They are Family

Rich Ruth and I pray our efforts in these few years have brought the image of their ship back to them. A ship without a crew is just a piece of steel. This ship still has her crew, and they know where their ship rests. My God bless the crew, the survivors and the family of the *USS Emmons.*

John Chandler entered the US Marine Corps at the age of seventeen, and rose to the rank of senior officer during his twenty-nine year career. During this time he was able too combine his love for photography and diving with his deployment throughout the U.S., Europe and Asia. He has earned renown as a professional underwater photographer and author. This career culminated at Okinawa where he was part of the group discovering the wreck of the Emmons and was a prime mover at protecting and commemorating the site. He has been honored by the Emmons Association as an honorary member of Ship's Company.

The Divers who discovered the *USS Emmons* wreck
Left to right: Rich Ruth, Jack Martin, Tami Clark, and Steve Tomlin

E-mail sent by Rich Ruth to Ed Hoffman on February 25th, 2001:

"Just a quick reply, but I will send more lately. I just (not more than two hours ago) finished some dives. The ship is pretty intact (considering what happened to it and the abuse she took). All the guns are intact and standing straight towards the sky, the props are still there and this proud ship really looks like she could just drive away. We are 100% certain that this is the Emmons.........."

(This note was sent before final identification of the *USS Emmons* as the wreck they discovered.)

Photo by John Howland

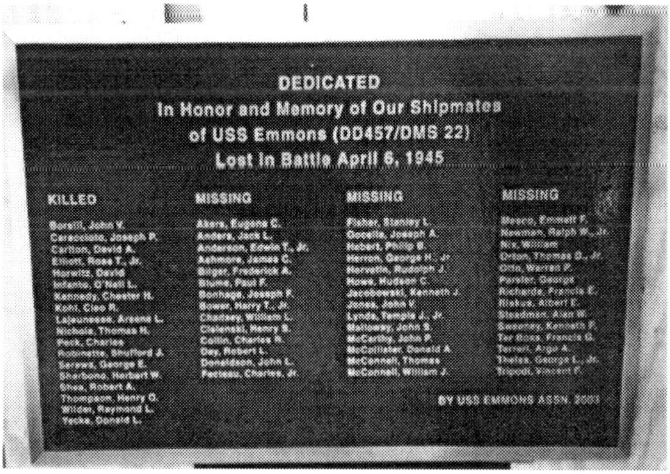

Acting on a proposal by John Chandler, Emmons Family members raised the funds and purchased a bronze plaque, to be placed on the ship's wreck as a permanent memorial to killed and missing shipmates.

The memorial plaque is shown attached to the *Emmons*' hull where it was affixed by Rich Ruth and fellow divers of Okinawa in May 2003.

18

A Special Bond

By Ed Hoffman

The Emmons Family, as members proudly identify themselves, did not take shape immediately after they returned home from WWII. Rather it developed over the years as an enfolding relationship, nurtured by continuing association and a growing appreciation of the historic role of their ship and shipmates during the *Emmons'* relatively short life.

The first effort to get back together was at a "crew only" reunion in Boston in 1953. This was followed the next two years with reunions in New York and Newark, NJ, with wives invited. These early get-togethers tended to replicate socially the organizational groupings of shipboard days. Deck divisions and bridge personnel knew each other while working together and constantly seeing each other. The engineers and other below-decks personnel were as familiar with each other on the same basis. The whole crew had a common meeting ground in the mess compartments and at movies, and could learn everyone's name from the ever-present laundry stencils on dungaree shirts. But close friendships and liberty buddies were pretty much confined to the respective gangs. These relationships still prevailed to a great degree at these early reunions.

After 1955, reunions were temporarily discontinued, for want of responsible organizers and everyone's preoccupation with earning a living and raising families. They were resumed in 1974 when aggressive drive of shipmates David "Moe" Jensen and Jerry McAlevey resulted in the first latter-day reunion. Most of the men by then established their careers and families and could devote time to getting back together. Reunions continued biannually, alternating north and south among eastern cities. In 2002, the crew voted to meet every year.

At the 1980 reunion in Wrightsville Beach, NC, attendees adopted the formal status of the Emmons Association. Successions of willing officers have ensured cohesive direction since that time.

As the group aged, renewal of relationships grew in importance. No longer was there a distinction between shipboard groupings or rank, nor did it matter whether a shipmate had been aboard at the beginning of the *Emmons'* life or at the end or at any time between—-they were all Men of the *Emmons.* With their wives, family members and special friends they became the Emmons family.

Significant interest and support came from our wartime leaders, especially Edward Baxter Billingsley and Eugene Noble Foss, II. Baxter as he was affectionately known by the crew, retired as rear admiral, but the *Emmons* was his first command and "dearest to his heart." Both he and Gene Foss, *Emmons*'s last skipper, maintained steady contact and attended every reunion until their passing. Mrs. Foss stayed in touch with the Association members, whom she called "her family,"until her death in 2005.

During the years after the war, no one from the *Emmons* sought publicity or felt a need to regale the ship's history publicly. Looking back to the past, we each recognize a special attachment with each other and with our ship. The crew had only done what all destroyer sailors were trained to do—meet every assignment and carry out orders to the best of each person's ability, quietly, and effectively.

Upon completeion of Adm. Billinglsy's history in 1989, *The Emmons Saga* was published privately by the Association.

In 1990, the Association acquired its own internet web site, affording unforeseen extension and strengthening of the Family. Numerous relatives of shipmates killed or missing in the final attack were able to make contact and learn for the first time, circumstances had befallen their loved ones. Children of other deceased crew members who had spoken only sparingly of their wartime experiences were able to learn details of their parents service. These searchers have been embraced by the Family and have become members of the Association.

Rediscovery of the *Emmons* wreck by Rich Ruth and his fellow divers in 2001 brought a heightened sense of attachment for our ship and our shipmates. Early on, Ruth and John Chandler ensured respectful regard for the wreck as the resting palce for 38 shipmates and protection against irresponsible visitation.

Rich Ruth hosted a group from the Association who journeyed to Okinawa for the second memorial service in 2002. Chandler was responsible for the idea of the Association's buying a bronze plaque, bearing names of lost shipmates, which has been permanently mounted on the ship by Ruth and fellow divers. Both Ruth and Chandler have attended recent reunions where they were gratefully welcomed as members of the Family.

There has been an increased recognition of the role of Navy destroyers, and the *USS Emmons* in particular, in World War II. This is all so vividly chronicled in "*The Emmons Saga*"—the life and deeds of a ship and its crew in an historic era, and an inspiring legacy for a family that proudly remembers.

Ed Hoffman enlisted in the Navy the day after graduating from high school, and went aboard the Emmons in August 1943. As a quartermaster, he was at his battle station on the bridge on April 6, 1945. Returning to civilian life, he graduated from Penn State. After a career in a management position in employee and labor relations with a national food company, he retired. Ed devotes his time and interest to maintaining contact among former shipmates and their families. He serves as the newsletter editor and correspondent for the Emmons Association. He and his wife Shirley, an enthusiastic supporter and co-worker in that effort, have been married 56 years. They have four children, nine grandchildren and two great-grandchildren.

The two sections of the above panoramic photo show the first get-together of the *USS Emmons* officers and crew after WWII, in 1953. Shipboard relationships were maintained and grew through the years. The *Emmons Family* now includes later generations, relatives of casualties, and members of the dive group who re-discovered the *Emmons* on the sea floor off Kouri-shima, Okinawa, in 2001.

The Donovan Family Collection

A photograph of the attendees for the second memorial service held over the USS Emmons on April 6, 2002. They represent a mixture of crew, survivor, and casualty families. Some are children of attendees.

L to R: Jerry Horwitz, AJ Cunningham, Jeffrey Horwitz, Leon Horwitz, Ed Tostanoski (Survivor), Ed Tostanoski Jr.,Robert Charoux (Crew), John Tostanoski, Joseph Woodnick (Crew).

A Marine Corps chaplain conducts service over the *Emmons* site on the 58th anniversary of its sinking. The flag being unfurled is one that was a steaming color of the *Emmons*. From left: Cmdr. Mike Hogg, Chaplain; Joe Woodnick; Ed Tostanoski(S); Harry Thomas, Cmdr. Okinawa VFW; Bob Charoux.

The Japanese Prefecture of Okinawa built a memorial to all who died in the Battle for Okinawa. Known as The *Cornerstone of Peace*, one section contains granite monuments, engraved with the names of all casualties: American, Allied, Japanese, and island natives. Ther group returned with photographs of engraved names of *Emmons* casualties for distribution to their families.

Bob Charoux on the left photographing Ed Tostanoski. The former Emmons crew members paid their respects to the memory of friends and shipmates. John Tostanoski stands left of his brother, Ed Tostanoski, Jr, watching their father as he looks for his friends' names.

APPENDIX A

Officers and Crew Serving On Board

DECEMBER 5, 1941–APRIL 6, 1945
(Asterisk Indicates Plank Owner)

OFFICERS

BEHAN, Joseph N, Jr.*

BILLINGSLEY, Edward B.*

BLAKE, Earl C.

DAVENPORT, Ralph M, Jr.

DAVIS, G. R.

DITZEK, J. F.

ELLIOTT, Ross T., Jr.

FISHER, S. L.

FOSS, Eugene N., 2nd*

FRANCIS, Herbert R.

GILLIGAN, John J.

GRIFFIN, John J. Jr.

GRUBER, Douglas L.

HALL, Thomas C.

HEMING, Harold M.*

HENESSEE, S. C.

HOLLINGSWORTH, Albert F.*

HORWITZ, David

JONES, Donald R.

JONES, J. V.

KEEGAN, Thomas F.*

KELLY, Edmond F.*

KENNEDY, George R.

KRECKEL, John P.*

LIEBSCHNER, Orville O.*

LEWIS, Malcom E *

LYNDS, Temple J.

MENAUGH, Thomas H.

MERRILL, Ralph F.

MINTON, M. C.

MORSE, Richard C, Jr.*
NELSON, H. F.
OLSON, O. E.
PIERCE, George E.*
RAGAN, Thomas C.*
SCHAULE, N.
SHEERAN, J. J.
SILL, J. "A"
SMITH, H. B.
STEADMAN, A. W.
SWEENEY, Kenneth F.
TAYLOR, B. W.
THEISS, G. L., Jr.
TRUDEAU, Edmond A.*
VINCENT, E. L.
WARNER, William J., Jr.
WHITE, R.
WILLIAMSON, Charles R

CREW

ABERNETHY, Ralph A., Jr.
AGEE, James M.*
AKERS, Eugene C.
AKSAMIT, Joseph J.*
ALEXANDER, Kenneth R.*
ALLBAUGH, Edward D.
ALLEN, Carl C.
ALMY, Guy, Jr.
ANDERS, Jack L.
ANDERSON, Conwell A.
ANDERSON, Edwin T., Jr.
ANDERSON, Robert G.
ANDERSON, WILLARD V.
ANDREWS, Charles E.
ANTHONY, James A.
ARINGDALE, Jesse W.
ARMBRUSTER, Harold W.
ARPAIA, Angelo E.
ARRENHOLZ, Frederick D.
ASH, Marvin H.
ASHCRAFT, Walter E.
ASHMORE, James C.
AVERY, George W., Jr.
AYER, Donald W.*
BAILEY, Leonard J., Jr.*
BAKER, Floyd W.
BAKER, Raymond K.
BAKER, Thomas B.
BALTHROPE, Marvin B.
BANDY, Owen L.*

BANG, Edward D.
BARNES, Bruce O.*
BARNING, Edward E.
BASILE, Frank J.
BATES, Rupert E.
BECK, Clifford W.*
BELANGER, Roger J.*
BENFORD, Michael W.
BERG, Norman H.*
BEST, Arthur L.
BEUKEMA, Donald R.*
BIGLER, R A.
BILGER, Frederick A.
BLAIR, Walter D.
BLAISDELL, George
BLEY, Henry C.*
BLOOM, Monroe H.
BLUME, Paul F.
BLUMER, Arthur L.
BLY, Zane R.
BOETTCHER, Herman M.*
BONHAGE, Joseph F.
BORDER, George C.
BORELLI, John V.
BOWER, Harry T., Jr.
BOYD, Harvey W.
BOYLE, William J.
BOYSIEWICK, Walter
BRANSOM, Richard K.*
BRAUM, Robert A.
BRETSCH, Stanley G.
BRIGGS, Andrew P.*
BRILL, David W.
BROOKS, Arthur L.*
BROWN, Bennie
BROWN, Eddie
BROWN, Elgie V.*
BRUMMETT, Willie*
BRYAN, Brady L.*
BUCKMAN, Lester W.*
BURTON, Maurice W.*
BUTLER, Owen B.
CAIRL, Frank R., Jr.
CALNAN, George E
CALVERT, Arthur K.*
CALVIN, Jessie
CAMPBELL, Robert L.
CARACCIOLO, Joseph P.
CARLTON, David A.
CARNELL, Franklin E.
CARNER, Robert L.
CARPENTER, Robert F.
CARTER, George P.
CASON, James F.

CASSELL, Joseph A.

CASTELLO, Domingues P.

CATANIA, Nunzio J.*

CAUDLE, Theodore F.

CAULFIELD, James F.*

CHADSEY, William L.*

CHARRON, Arthur W.*

CHANTLIN, Clarence

CHARA, Paul J.

CHAROUX, Robert W*

CIELENSKI, Henry S.

CLARK, Charles J.*

COATES, Thomas E., Jr.

COCKERAM, John G.*

COLE, Donald G.

COLLIN, Charles R.

COLWECK, Roy H.

COMALANDER, John S., Jr.

CONRAD, Herbert A.

COOPER, Louis A.*

COOPER, Russell F.*

COPELAND, William D.

COPPOLA, Arthur J.

CORDREY, Charles O.*

CORNETTA, Edwin J.

CORTISS, Warren W.

COTHRAN, Russell S.*

COUGHENNOWER, William E.

COWLE Y, Charles T.

COX, Gilbert R.*

COX, John C.*

CRAAYBEEK, Simon W.

CRAVER, Clarence H.*

CRAWLEY, William F.*

CREMEANS, Leonard Leo

CROFUT, George E.*

CRONN, Wilber C, Jr.*

CRUZ, Sherwood A.

CULKIN, Edward T.*

CURRIER, Mayo*

CURRY, Donald B.

DALTON, Harry S.*

DAUM, Warren I.*

DAVENPORT, O'Dell

DAVIS, William E.

DAY, Robert L.

DEANS, Bartley

D'ENTREMONT, Stanley J.

DEHART, Charles J., Jr.

DELVE, Paul H.

DELY, Anthony T.

DEMERS, Albert L.

DENNING, Charles, Jr.*

DERKACS, Charles, Jr.*

DERNANGO, Fred*
DESSE, Billy R.
DEVALENTINO, Nacey J.
DEVERELL, Roy I.
DEVERS, John H.
DIAMOND, Benjamin J.
DICARLO, Michael
DICKSON, Ray P.*
DIEHL, Raymond M.
DILLION, Christopher S., Jr.
DiRUBBIO, Anthony
DOBROVICH, Anthony
DODD, Paul F.
DODZIK, Andrew J.
DOERRER, George W.*
DOLASKY, William E.
DONAGHEY, William F.
DONALDSON, John L.
DONNELLY, James A., Jr.*
DONOHUE, George J.
DONOVAN, James F.
DOUGHERTY, John R.
DOWD, Charles W.*
DOWELL, Robert
DOWER, Warren T.
DOZIER, Jessie L.
DURELLA, Andrew
DUTTON, Guy D.*
DWYER, Harold B.*
EATON, Lafayette C.
EDELMAN, Jack
EDMUNDS, George R.
EDWARDS, Gilbert J.*
ELKIN, Jack B.
ELLSWORTH, Richard J.*
EPPERSON, Charles M.
ESPOSITO, Anthoney S.*
ESQUIVEL, Francisco S.
EVANS, Loyd R.*
EVANS, Reese A.*
FALLS, James M.*
FECTEAU, Charles, Jr.
FETTERHOFF, Charles B.
FINCH, Edwin L.*
FINLEY, Fred L.
FINNEY, Rex W.*
FLANAGAN, John J.
FLEMING, David G.
FLORY, George C.*
FLYNN, Patrick J.
FONTANA, Gregory A.
FOUST, James D.
FRAMPTON, Wayne E.
FRANGOWLAKIS, David W.

FRANKLIN, Edison E
FRANSECKY, Donald G.
FRYE, Ellsworth W., Jr.*
FYFE, Donald W.*
GAIDIS, Peter J.
GAINES, Joe T.
GANDY, Earl J.*
GARLINGTON, Walden B.*
GERVAIS, Daniel G.J.*
GINN, Leon E.*
GLUTTING, Robert J.*
GOCELLA, Joseph A.*
GOESEKE, Henry G.*
GORMAN, Thomas E., Jr.*
GOODMAN, George
GRACE, James E.*
GRANA, Louis*
GREENLAW, Edward E.
GRIBBINS, Phillip J.*
GRIECO, Julius R.*
GURSKI, Sigmund A.
GUTHRIE, Robert E.*
HAASE, Kenneth R.
HAIRSTON, Daniel W.
HAMMOND, Claude W.
HANNA, Floyd B.
HANSHAW, Everett A.
HARDY, Charles W.
HAMILTON, Thomas W.
HARRIS, Errol D.
HAUS, Clarence*
HAUGHNEY, Luke J.
HAWK, Horace R.
HAYES, William M.*
HEATH, Harold J.*
HEBERT, Philip D.
HECK, Kenneth E.
HEIN, Kenneth F.*
HENRY, Bernard J.
HENWOOD, William E.
HERLING, Edward H.
HERRON, George H., Jr.
HILL, Henry A.
HILLIARD, Robert B.
HINES, Joseph E.
HOBART, Earl C.
HOFFMAN, Edwin L.
HOLLAND, Conrad H.*
HOLLAND, Herbert F.*
HOLMES, Lloyd N.
HORVATIN, Rudolph J.
HOWE, Hudson G.
HOWE, Kenneth R.*
HUBAL, Joseph P.

HUBBARD, Leroy W.
HUCKER, Earl W.*
HUDSON, Louis P.
HUNKELE, George E., Jr.
HUNTER, Robert E.
IGOU, Frederick L.
INFANTO, O'Neil L.
IOVINO, Gene A.
IRISH, Vaughn L.
IRONS, Earl J., Jr.
IRVIN, Fredrick C.
JACOBOSKI, Kenneth J.
JACOBY, Philip A.*
JAMILA, Galicano A.*
JAMPOLSKY, Harold J.*
JENKINS, John
JENSEN, David*
JESSEN, Jes R.
JOHNSON, Joseph E.
JOHNSON, Dale E.*
JOHNSON, Arnold S.
JOHNSON, Lavern O.
JOLLY, Armand J.
JOY, Ellis F.*
KANARIAN, Paul
KAPFENBERG, Nicolas H.*
KELLER, Charles L.
KENNEDY, Chester H.*
KENNEDY, George T.
KESSLER, Jack L.
KICHLINE, John A.
KIDD, Richard E.*
KINNEY, Anthony R.*
KISER, Martin R.
KISSACK, Donald R.
KOHL, Cleo R.
KORNEY, James
KRAGTORP, Alvin O.
KRECKEL, John P.*
KROM, Edwin, J.
KUBANY, Milan J.
KUDRYK, Theodore W.*
KUKAKA, Thomas
KURTZMAN, Edward I.
KYLE, William H.*
LACKO, Edward J.*
LAJEUNESSE, Arsene L.
LAKIN, Louis E.*
LA ROCCA, Anthoney M.
LARSEN, Edward J.
LASAK, William G.
LASHOMB, Harlow W.
LAWLOR, Frank J.
LAZZATI, John L.

LEISTMAN, Harold R.*
LESWING, Edward C.
LETSON, Robert B.
LEWIS, Simeon C*
LILLIE, Charles L.*
LILLYBRIDGE, Kenneth C.*
LINDLEY, Carson*
LINDLEY, Joel R.*
LINDSEY, Milton W.*
LINKEWICZ, Peter A.
LITTLES, Johnnie
LONERGAN. John J.
LONG, Elmer R.*
LONG, William*
LOOKOSHUS, George C.*
LOUVAR, Orville L.
LOVELESS, Donald R.
LUCCI, Joseph A.
MacKINNON, John J.
MADDEN, Howard C.
MADOR, Allen A.
MAHONEY, William H.*
MALLOWAY, John S.*
MALONEY, Richard W.
MALSON, Robert O.
MANNINEN, Robert P.
MANNINO, John P.
MARKOWITZ, Stanley I.
MARTIN, Elzy B.*
MARTIN, Robert J.*
MARTIN, Robert V.
MARTONE, Joseph
MASSARO, Louis G.*
MAUGHMER, Major R.
MAY, Ernest
MAYER, Charles F.
MAYNARD, Arthur E.
McALEVEY, Jerome D.*
McALLISTER, Thomas N.*
McBRIDE, William M.
McCARTHY, John P.*
McCARTHY, Kenneth C*
McCARTHY, Thomas R.
McCLURE, Willie L.
McCOLLISTER, Donald A.
McCONNELL, Thomas
McCONNELL, William J.
McCORMICK, Joseph P.
McCULLOUGH, Russell H., Jr.
McDANIEL, Robert W.*
McGEOGH, Archibald W.
McGLAUGHLIN, Ira E.
MCLAUGHLIN, Michael J.
McLEAN, Burl D.*

McMANUS, Eugene R.
McMICHAEL, John L.
McMICHAEL, Grover T.
McRAE, John D.
MEADE, Gutherie P.
MEHLE, John C.
MELKUNAS, Charles P.
MELLEY, Harry J., Jr.
MERRICK, Maurice G.*
MESCO, Emmett F.
MEYERS, Arthur E., Jr.
MIERZWA, Stanley J.*
MILLER, Harold D.
MONAHAN, Edward T*
MOORE, Jack
MOORE, Raymond B.
MOORE, William A.*
MOONEY, James A., Jr.
MONTE, Joseph D.
MORLEY, James E.*
MOSLEY, Roosevelt
MOTT, John M.*
MOULTON, Donald H.
MUDGE, James M.*
MURPHY, Daniel
MURPHY, J. B.
MURPHY, James G.
MURRAY, James P.*
MURRAY, Paul J.*
MUTZABAUGH, Richard K.
NATZKE, Kenneth L., Jr.
NEEL, Allen P.
NEMES, Frank
NETTUNO, Daniel C.*
NEWELL, Donald J.
NEWMAN, Ralph W., Jr.
NEWTON, Richard M.
NICHOLS, Robert F.*
NICHOLS, Thomas H.*
NIEBLING, James M.
NITSCHE, Herman A.
NIX, William
NIXON, William R.*
NOLAN, Frederick V.*
NOLL, William F.
NUGENT, James L.
O'BRIEN, Eugene E.*
O'BRIEN, Roy W.*
O'CONNELL, Raymond E.
OEHLER, Edward G.*
O'LEARY, Patrick C
OLENDER, Edward F.*
OLOONEY, Bryan A.
OLZENSKI, James J.*

O'MALLEY, John E.*
ORTON, Thomas D., Jr.
OSBORNE, Richard W.*
OTTO, Fredrick G.
OTTO, Warren P.
OULD, William R.*
PACKERT, Albert R.*
PAGE, Elmo C.
PALICKI, Steven S.
PALMER, Charles A., Jr.
PANGBURN, Daniel H.
PAPISERGI, Sam
PARK, William G.
PARKER, Frank*
PARLETT, Russel F.
PARMENTER, Charles F.
PARMENTER, Stanley A.
PAROLA, Antonio H.
PARRINELLO, Frank
PARSLER, George
PASKI, Henry*
PASQUALE, Michael J.
PASTORE, Vincent J.
PATCH, Philip E.
PATERNITI, Joseph P.
PATERNO, Andrew P.
PATERNO, Salvatore
PATRINOS, Stephen
PATTERSON, William M.
PATTON, William R.
PAULIK, Andrew
PAYNE, Ralph L.
PEASE, Maurice E.
PECK, Charles
PETERS, Horace Q.
PFEUFFER, Henry W
PHELPS, Ivan V.*
PIATT, Harvy H.
PICKETTS, Howard L.
PIERCE, Raphael R.*
PIETROBONO, Louis J.
PIKE, Chester
PIRRELLO, Joseph S.
PISZCZEK, Joseph A.
PITTMAN, William T.
POMYKALA, Joseph P.
POOL, Robert A.
POOLE,Joseph W., Jr.
POPPITZ, Wilbur G.
POSEY, Eugene L.
POWELL, Martin S.
PRENTISS, Robert G.
PRESTON, Claude R.*
PUND, Gilbert E.*

QUAIL, Stanton E.
QUEEN, James G.
QUIER, Leon C.
QUINSEY, Joseph H.
QUINN Raymond F.
RAMIREZ, Federico*
RANSOM, Earl R.
RAY, Kenneth F.
REA, William J.
READ, Arthur R.
REED, Eugene J., Jr.
REED, Roger B.*
REESE, Clifford C*
REGISTER, Bert
REID, Harry M.
REID, Robert R.*
REILLY, John A.
REIMERS, John H.
REYNOLDS, Edward L., Jr.
RHUE, Clyde R.
RHYNE, Fred*
RICE, Archie W.*
RICHARDS, Francis E.
RICHARDSON, Francis E.
RICHARDSON, Jack*
RIEGER, Howard H.
RINGENBERG, James D.
RISKUS, Albert E.
ROBBINS, James E.
ROBERTS, William J.
ROBINETTE, Shufford J.
ROBINSON, Quentin E.
ROONEY, Edward J.*
RUSH, Kenneth E.
RUSSELL, Dilbert E.
RUSSO, J.
RUSSO, Vincinzo J.
RYAN, Lawrence P.
SACCO, Emil
SAUNDERS, Earl F.*
SCAMMACA, Salvatore J.*
SCHEEL, Ervin A.*
SCHIKORA, Raymand A.
SCHMIDT, Richard J.*
SCHRAFF, Robert P.*
SCHULTZ, Robert J.
SEREWA, George E.
SHARBONO, Herbert W.
SHEA, Robert A.
SHEPARD, George R.*
SHEPPARD, Thomas J.*
SHOTTS, Lewis E.*
SHUGREN, Glenn W.*
SILVA, Manuel C, Jr.

SIMONEAU, Edgar R.*
SIMONEAU, Gerard J.B.*
SIMS, Edward L.*
SINCLAIR, Theodore E.*
SIRAGUSA, Anthony J.*
SMERALDO, George W.*
SMILEY, William V.*
SMITH, Eugene C.*
SMITH, James S.*
SMITH, Ralph D.
SOFRANKO, Joseph P.
SORRELL, Cecil E.*
SOSENKO, John*
SPARKS, L. S.
SPARKS, Warren G.
SPENCER, J., Jr.
SPINA, F.
SPRING, I. S.
STAGER, I.I.
STALY, L. I.
STANLEY, Theodore R.*
STANTON, James R.
STEVENSON, Allen W.*
STEVENSON, Frederick C*
STICKER, M. J.
STOKES, Margil L.*
STONE, Hubert L.*
STREETS, Elwood R.
STUCZYNSKI, William*
SUMMERVILLE, Martin P.
SURETTE, Leonard J.*
SUTORIUS, Carl E.
SWAFFORD, James W.*
SYNOSKY, Steven
TAKACS, Laszlo A.*
TATAR, Julius
TAUB, Robert
TAUBERT, Gustave A., Jr.
TEMPONE, John F.*
TENEROWICZ, Thaddeus T.
TEODORCZYK, Sigismund S.
TER BOSS, Francis G.
TERENSKY, Joseph, Jr.*
TERRELONGE, Eugene G.*
TERRERI, Argo A.
THOM, Albert
THOMAS, William J.
THOMPSON, John B.
THOMPSON, Henry O.
TIERNEY, Raymond M.
TILLMAN, Eddie C.
TINKOVICZ, Peter J.
TISONY, Joseph J.
TITKO, Edward

TITTLE, Homer D.
TOMPKINS, Arthur O.
TOOHEY, Richard H.
TORRES, Philip L.
TOSTANOSKI, Edward N.
TRABERT, Donald C.
TRIPODI, Vincent F.
TROTTIER, Francis W.
TURNER, John R.
ULMER, Thomas J.
ULRICH, Arther G.
UNGER, Aaron
UNNERSTALL, Joseph L.*
UNTERBERGER, Charles E.
URBAS, Carl J.*
USHER, John D.
VEAL, Clyne C.
WAGNER, Robert C*
WALSH, Edward*
WALTER, BillieD.*
WARD, Leonard*
WEBB, William J.
WEBBER, Willis H.*
WEIMAR, VernerT.*
WELLS, Birt L.
WHITSON,LelandA.*
WHYNOT, Harold W.
WILCZWESKI, John P.
WILDER, Raymond L.
WILLIAMS, Benjamin H.
WILLIAMS, Don E.* WILLIAMS, Joel C.
WOLF, Kenneth E.
WOOD, Eugene W.
WOODS, Joseph R.*
WOODS, Morris M.*
WOODRUFF, Robert L. WOODSON, Lee*
WOODNICK, Joseph E., Jr.
WYATT, William H.*
WYNN, Harry W.*
YECKE, Donald L.
YOUNG, Harold W.*
ZACHA, James L.
ZERINGUE, James J.

APPENDIX B

List Of Killed, Missing In Action, Wounded And Other Survivors

o o o o o o o o o o o o o o o o o o o o o o o o o o o o o o

From Japanese Kamikaze Attack, 6 April 1945 (Principal Sources: EMMONS Action Report dated 12 April 1945 and Report of Changes for crew submitted 6 May 1945.)

OFFICERS

FOSS, E. N., 2nd, Lt. Cdr., USNR	WOUNDED
LYNDS, T. J., Jr., Lt., USNR	MISSING
WILLIAMSON, C. R., Lt, MC, USNR	SURVIVOR
WARNER, W. J., Jr., Lt., USNR	SURVIVOR
GRIFFIN, J. J., Jr., Lt., USNR	SURVIVOR
MINTON, M. C, Lt., USNR	SURVIVOR
FISHER, S. L., Lt., (jg), USNR	MISSING
MENAUGH, T. H., Lt., (jg), USNR	WOUNDED
HORWITZ, D., Lt., (jg), USNR	KILLED
MERRILL, R. F., Lt., (jg), USN	SURVIVOR
DAVENPORT, R. M., Jr., Lt., (jg), USNR	WOUNDED
SMITH, H. B., Lt., (jg), USNR	WOUNDED
SWEENEY, K. F., Lt., (jg), USNR	MISSING
JONES, J. V., Lt., (jg), USNR	MISSING
NELSON, H. F., Lt., (jg), SC, USNR	SURVIVOR
STEADMAN, A. W., Lt., (jg)	MISSING
SHEERAN, J. J., Ens., USNR	WOUNDED

ELLIOT, R. T., Jr., Ens., USNR	KILLED
THEISS, G. L., Jr., Ens., USNR	MISSING

CREW

AKERS, Eugene C.	WOUNDED
ALLBAUGH, Edward D.	WOUNDED
ALLEN, Carl C.	WOUNDED
ANDERS, Jack L.	MISSING
ANDERSON, Conwell A.	WOUNDED
ANDERSON, Edwin T., Jr.	MISSING
ANDERSON, Robert G.	WOUNDED
ANDERSON, Willard V.	WOUNDED
ARAPIA, Angelo E.	SURVIVOR
ARMBRUSTER, Harold W.	WOUNDED
ARRENHOLZ, Frederick D.	SURVIVOR
ASH, Marvin H.	SURVIVOR
ASHCRAFT, Walter E.	SURVIVOR
ASHMORE, James C.	MISSING
AVERY, George W, Jr.	SURVIVOR
AYER, Donald W.	SURVIVOR
BAKER, Floyd W.	SURVIVOR
BAKER, Raymond K.	WOUNDED
BAKER, Thomas B.	SURVIVOR
BALTHROPE, Marvin S.	SURVIVOR
BASILE, Frank J.	SURVIVOR
BATES, Rupert E.	SURVIVOR
BECK, Clifford W.	SURVIVOR
BENFORD, Michael W.	WOUNDED
BEST, Arthur L.	WOUNDED

BILGER, Federick A.	WOUNDED
BLAIR, Walter D.	SURVIVOR
BLOOM, Monroe H.	WOUNDED
BLUME, Paul F.	MISSING
BLUMER, Arthur L.	WOUNDED
BLY, Zane R.	WOUNDED
BOETTCHER, Herman M.	SURVIVOR
BONHAGE, Joseph F.	MISSING
BORDER, George C.	SURVIVOR
BORELLI, John V.	.KILLED
BOWER, Harry T., Jr.	MISSING
BOYLE, William J.	SURVIVOR
BOYSIEWICK, Walter	SURVIVOR
BRAUM, Robert A.	SURVIVOR
BRILL, David W.	SURVIVOR
CAIRL, Frank, Jr.	SURVIVOR
CAMPBELL, Robert L.	SURVIVOR
CARACCIOLO, Joseph P.	KILLED
CARLTON, David A.	KILLED
CARNER, Robert L.	SURVIVOR
CARTER, George P.	WOUNDED
CASSELL, Joseph A.	SURVIVOR
CASTELLO, Domingues R.	SURVIVOR
CAUDLE, Theodore F.	SURVIVOR
CHADSEY, William L.	MISSING
CHANTLIN, Clarence	WOUNDED
CHARA, Paul J.	WOUNDED
CIELENSKI, Henry S.	MISSING

COATES, Thomas E., Jr.	WOUNDED
COLE, Donald G.	SURVIVOR
COLLIN, Charles R.	MISSING
COLWECK, Roy H.	WOUNDED
COMALANDER, John S., Jr.	SURVIVOR
COOPER, Russell F..	SURVIVOR
COPPOLA, Arthur J.	WOUNDED
CORDREY, Charles O.	SURVIVOR
COUGHENNOWER, William E.	SURVIVOR
COWLEY, Charles T..	WOUNDED
CRAWLEY, William F.	SURVIVOR
CREAMEANS, Leonard L	SURVIVOR
CRUZ, Sherwood A.	WOUNDED
CURRY, Donald B.	WOUNDED
DAY, Robert L.	MISSING
DEANS, Bartiey	SURVIVOR
DEESE, Billy R.	SURVIVOR
DELVE, Paul H.	WOUNDED
DENTREMONT, Stanley J.	SURVIVOR
DEVERELL, Roy I.	SURVIVOR
DIEHL, Raymond M.	SURVIVOR
DODD, Paul F.	SURVIVOR
DODZIK, Andrew J.	WOUNDED
DOLASKY, William E.	SURVIVOR
DONALDSON, John L.	MISSING
DOWD, Charles W.	WOUNDED
DOWELL, Robert	SURVIVOR
DOZIER, Jessie L.	SURVIVOR

EATON, Lafayette C.	WOUNDED
EDLEMAN, Jack	WOUNDED
ESPOSITO, Anthony S.	SURVIVOR
ESQUIVEL, Francisco S.	SURVIVOR
FECTEAU, Charles, Jr.	MISSING
FETTERHOFF, Charles B.	SURVIVOR
FLANAGAN, John J.	WOUNDED
FLYNN, Patrick J.	SURVIVOR
FOUST, James D.	SURVIVOR
FRAMPTON, Wayne E.	SURVIVOR
FRANKLIN, Edison F.	SURVIVOR
GOCELLA, Joseph A.	MISSING
GRIECO, Julius R.	SURVIVOR
GUTHRIE, Robert E.	SURVIVOR
HAIRSTON, Daniel W.	SURVIVOR
HAMMOND, Claude W.	SURVIVOR
HARDY, Charles W.	WOUNDED
HAUGHNEY, Luke J.	SURVIVOR
HEATH, Harold J.	SURVIVOR
HEBERT, Philip B.	MISSING
HECK, Kenneth E.	SURVIVOR
HENWOOD, William E.	SURVIVOR
HERRON, George H., Jr.	MISSING
HILLIARD, Robert B.	SURVIVOR
HOBART, Earl C.	SURVIVOR
HOFFMAN, Edwin L.	WOUNDED
HORVATIN, Rudolph J.	MISSING
HOWE, Hudson C.	MISSING

HUBBARD, Leroy W.	WOUNDED
HUDSON, Louis P.	WOUNDED
HUNKELE, George E., Jr.	WOUNDED
HUNTER, Robert E.	WOUNDED
IGOU, Frederick L.	WOUNDED
INFANTO, O'Neil L.	KILLED
IRISH, Vaughn L.	SURVIVOR
IRONS, Earl J., Jr.	WOUNDED
JACOBOWSKI, Kenneth J.	MISSING
JACOBY, Philip A.	SURVIVOR
JENSEN, David	WOUNDED
JESSEN, Jes R.	WOUNDED
JOLLY, Armand J.	WOUNDED
KANARIAN, Paul	SURVIVOR
KELLER, Charles L.	WOUNDED
KENNEDY, Chester H.	KILLED
KENNEDY, George T.	WOUNDED
KICHLINE, John A.	WOUNDED
KISER, Martin	WOUNDED
KOHL, Cleo R.	KILLED
KORNEY, James	SURVIVOR
KROM, Edwin J.	SURVIVOR
KUBANY, Milan J.	WOUNDED
KURTZMAN, Edward I.	WOUNDED
LAJEUNESSE, Arsene L.	KILLED
LAKIN, Louis E.	WOUNDED
LARSEN, Edward J.	SURVIVOR
LAWLOR, Frank J.	SURVIVOR

LEISTMAN, Harold R.	SURVIVOR
LETSON, Robert B.	SURVIVOR
LUCCI, Joseph A.	SURVIVOR
MADDEN, Howard C.	WOUNDED
MALONEY, Richard W.	SURVIVOR
MALLOWAY, John S.	MISSING
MANNINEN, Robert P.	SURVIVOR
MANNINO, John P.	SURVIVOR
MARTIN, Robert V.	SURVIVOR
MCCARTHY, John P.	MISSING
McCLURE, Willie L	SURVIVOR
McCOLLISTER, Donald A.	MISSING
McCONNELL, Thomas	MISSING
McCONNELL, William J.	MISSING
McLAUGHLIN, Michael J.	SURVIVOR
McLEAN, Burl D.	SURVIVOR
McRAE, John D.	SURVIVOR
MEHLE, John C.	SURVIVOR
MELLEY, Harry J., Jr.	WOUNDED
MESCO, Emmett F.	MISSING
MEYERS, Arthur E., Jr.	SURVIVOR
MIERZWA, Stanley J.	SURVIVOR
MILLER, Harold D.	SURVIVOR
MONTE, Joseph D.	WOUNDED
MOONEY, James A., Jr.	SURVIVOR
MOORE, Raymond B.	WOUNDED
MOULTON, Donald H.	SURVIVOR
NATZKE, Kenneth L., Jr.	WOUNDED

NEMES, Frank	SURVIVOR
NEWMAN, Ralph W., Jr.	MISSING
NEWTON, Richard H.	SURVIVOR
NICHOLS, Robert F.	WOUNDED
NICHOLS, Thomas H.	KILLED
NIEBLING, James M.	SURVIVOR
NIX, William	MISSING
NUGENT, James L.	SURVIVOR
ORTON, Thomas D., Jr.	MISSING
OTTO, Warren P.	MISSING
OULD, William R.	SURVIVOR
PALICKI, Steven S.	WOUNDED
PARMENTER, Charles E.	SURVIVOR
PARMENTER, Stanley A.	SURVIVOR
PARRINELLO, Frank	WOUNDED
PARSLER, George	MISSING
PATERNO, Andrew P.	WOUNDED
PAULIK Andrew	WOUNDED
PEASE, Maurice E.	SURVIVOR
PECK, Charles.	KILLED
PETERS, Horace Q.	SURVIVOR
PICKETTS, Howard L.	SURVIVOR
PISZCZEK, Joseph A.	WOUNDED
POPPITZ, Wilbur G.	SURVIVOR
POSEY, Eugene L.	WOUNDED
QUINN, Raymond F.	SURVIVOR
QUINSEY, Joseph H.	SURVIVOR
REA, William J., Jr.	SURVIVOR

REID, Robert R.	SURVIVOR
RICHARDS, Francis E.	MISSING
RINGENBERG, James D.	SURVIVOR
RISKUS, Albert E.	MISSING
ROBBINS, James E.	SURVIVOR
ROBERTS, William J.	WOUNDED
ROBINETTE, Shufford J.	KILLED
ROBINSON, Quentin E.	WOUNDED
RUSH, Kenneth E.	SURVIVOR
RYAN, Laurence P.	SURVIVOR
SCHRAFF, Robert P.	SURVIVOR
SEREWA, George E.	KILLED
SHARBONO, Herbert W.	KILLED
SHEA, Robert A.	KILLED
SILVA, Manuel C, Jr.	SURVIVOR
SIMONEAU, Edger R.	SURVIVOR
SIMONEAU, Gerard J.B.	SURVIVOR
SOFRANKO, Joseph P.	WOUNDED
STANTON, James R.	WOUNDED
STEVENSON, Allen W.	SURVIVOR
SYNOSKY, Steven	SURVIVOR
TAUBERT, Gustave A., Jr.	SURVIVOR
TENEROWICZ, Thaddeus T.	SURVIVOR
TEODORCZYK, Sigismund S.	SURVIVOR
TER BOSS, Francis G.	MISSING
TERRERI, Argo A.	MISSING
THOM, Albert	WOUNDED
THOMAS, William J.	SURVIVOR

THOMPSON, Henry O.	KILLED
TILLMAN, Eddie C.	SURVIVOR
TITKO, Edward	SURVIVOR
TOMPKINS, Arthur O.	WOUNDED
TOSTANOSKI, Edward N.	WOUNDED
TRIPODI, Vincent F.	MISSING
VEAL, Clyne C.	SURVIVOR
WHITSON, Leland A.	WOUNDED
WILDER, Raymond L.	.KILLED
WOLF, Kenneth E.	SURVIVOR
YECKE, Donald L.	JCILLED
YOUNG, Harold	SURVIVOR
ZACHA, James M.	SURVIVOR
ZERINGUE, James J.	SURVIVOR

APPENDIX C

Employment Schedule

5 December 1941–6 April 1945

Dates	*Place and Employment*
1941	
5 Dec	Commissioned, Boston Navy Yard.
5-31 Dec	Fitting out at Boston Navy Yard.
1942	
1-22 Jan	Fitting out at Boston Navy Yard.
23-27 Jan	Newport. Degaussed. Loaded torpedoes.
28-29 Jan	Yorktown. Took aboard depth charges.
29-31 Jan	Norfolk. Preparations for shakedown cruise.
31 Jan	Underway with USS *Hambleton* (DD455) en route Cristobal, C.Z. Escorting SS *Robin Tugford.*
5-6 Feb	Cristobal, Canal Zone.
6 Feb	Transited Panama Canal.
6-7 Feb	Balboa, C.Z.
8 Feb	Crossed Equator.
11-14 Feb	Callao,Peru.
18-21 Feb	Valparaiso, Chile.
27 Feb-2 Mar	Guayaquil, Ecuador.
4-5 Mar	Balboa, C.Z.
5 Mar	Transited Canal.
6-9 Mar	Cartagena, Colombia.

11 Mar	Guantanamo Bay. Fueling. Interrupted by submarine alarm offshore. To sea.
13 Mar	Returned Guantanamo Bay to complete fueling. To sea to join TG 22.7, *Ranger, Augusta, Savannah,* four DDs.
20-21 Mar	CascoBay
21-29 Mar	Boston. Eight-day post-shakedown navy yard availability.
29-30 Mar	Newport
31 Mar	Transited Cape Cod Canal, northbound.
1 Apr	New York. Briefing for A/S patrol.
2-9 Apr	Antisubmarine patrol with *Hambleton* off Cape Hatteras.
9-13 Apr	Norfolk. Exercises Chesapeake Bay.
13-14 Apr	En route Newport. Escorting *Ranger.*
14-22 Apr	At Newport. Training exercises offshore.
22 Apr-10 May	En route Point "X," Gulf of Guinea, with TF 36 composed *of Ranger, Augusta,* and DesDiv 19.
28-29 Apr	Port of Spain, Trinadad. Logistics.
10 May	Arrived Point "X," Gulf of Guinea. *Ranger* launched sixty-eight fighter planes.
21-23 May	Port of Spain. Logistics.
28-29 May	Newport
29 May-2 Jun	Boston. Three-day navy yard availability.
5-20 Jun	Aigentia. Training exercises TF 22.
22-23 Jun	Newport
23-26 Jun	Boston, two-day overhaul Boston Navy Yard.
26 Jun-1 Jul	Newport
1 Jul	Rendezvoused with TF 37, a seven-ship troop ship convoy.
2 Jul	Returned Boston for emergency drydocking and replacement of starboard propellor.
4-5 Jul	Halifax

5-11 Jul	With *Macomb* and *Buck* escorting troop ships *Siboney* and *Aorangi*, part of TF 37, designated convoy AT17B. *Siboney* joined Rest of convoy continued on to Greenock.
12-14 Jul	Greenock. Assigned to U.S. Task Force 99 under command of British Home Fleet.
15-26 Jul	At Scapa Flow. Exercises with Home Fleet.
28-29 Jul	Hvalfjordur, Iceland.
31 JUL-10 Aug	Scapa Flow. Exercises with Home Fleet.
11-13 Aug	Greenock. Preparations for Murmansk Relief Expedition (code name: Easy Unit).
15-17 Aug	Scapa Flow. Preparations for Murmansk Relief Expedition.
18 Aug	Seydisfjordur, Iceland. Fueled.
20 Aug	Crossed Arctic Circle.
23 Aug	Murmansk, U.S.S.R. Delivered supplies. Took aboard survivors of Convoy PQ17.
28 Aug	Seydisfjordur. Fuel and provisions.
30 Aug-1 Sep	Greenock, Disembarked survivors Convoy PQ 17. Preparations for return to States.
1 Sep	Duty with British Home Fleet terminated. TF 99 dissolved.
3 Sep	Hvalfjordur. En route States.
9-10 Sep	New York. Overnight.
11-22 Sep	Boston. Navy yard availability.
23-26 Sep	Casco Bay. Training with heavy ships, TF 22.
28 Sep-3 Oct	Norfolk. Training exercises, Chesapeake Bay, including shore bombardment.
6-9 Oct	Portsmouth, Va. Navy yard availability.
9-13 Oct	Norfolk. Preparations for Operation TORCH.
15-25 Oct	Bermuda. Training with Air Group formed for TORCH.
8-13 Nov	Off Safi, Morocco. Operation TORCH.
11 Nov	Safi. *Emmons* and *Rodman* fueled.

21-22 Nov	Bermuda. Retrieved strip ship gear.
24-25 Nov	Norfolk. Escorting carrier group.
26 Nov-7Dec	Boston. Navy yard availability.
10-13 Dec	Key West. Antisubmarine exercises. Waiting to escort battle-damaged *South Dakota* to New York.
17-23 Dec	New York area. Exercises Long Island Sound.
22 Dec	Gardner's Bay. Overnight anchorage.
23 Dec	Hempstead Bay. Overnight anchorage.
24-25 Dec	New York City. Logistics.
26-27 Dec	Norfolk. Joined remainder of DesDiv 19 to escort troop convoy to Canal Zone.
1943	
2-9 Jan	Cristobal, C.Z. Antisubmarine and gunnery exercises.
9 Jan	Transited Canal
9 Jan-13 Jan	Balboa. Simulated battle practices on the 11 th and 12th, and night battle practice night of the 12th. Six Ecuadorian officers came aboard for the exercises the 12th.
13 Jan	Transited Canal
13-15 Jan	Coco Solo, C.Z. Toipedo Overhaul.
17-19 Jan	Cristobal, C.Z. Waiting for T.U. 91.1.4 {*Chester* and three troop transports} to escort to Miami.
26Jan-3Feb	New York. Availability, Brooklyn Navy Yard. Test fired new Bofors machine guns, Long Island Sound.
6-7 Feb	New York. Preparations join escorts troop convoys, TFs 35 and 36. After one day shifted from TF 35 to fast TF 36.
19-22 Feb	Fedhala, Morocco. Waiting for TF 36 to offload.
22-27 Feb	Casablanca. Fueled. Boat guard and picket duty off port.
11–23 Mar	New York. Nine-day availability at Brooklyn Navy Yard.
24 Mar-2 Apr	Casco Bay. Exercises with TF 22.

5 Apr-12 May	Aigentia. Operations with TF 22. *Alabama, South Dakota, Ellyson, Emmons, Rodman, Macomb,* and *Fitch,* formed as TF 61 and ordered to Scapa Flow to operate under British Home Fleet as U.S. TG 92.4.
19-31 May	Scapa Flow. Operations with British Home Fleet.
2-5 Jun	Hvalfjordur. Positioning for operations in Berents and Norwegian seas.
5 Jun	Reykjavik, Iceland. Transport TG92.4 liberty party from Hvalfjordur.
5-6 Jun	Hvalfjordur. Upkeep.
7-9 Jun	Akureyri, Iceland. On exercises.
13-16 Jun	Hvalfjordur. Upkeep.
16 Jun	Reykjavik. Liberty party.
17-19 Jun	Hvalfjordur. Upkeep.
21–22 Jun	Scapa Flow. Upkeep.
22-23 Jun	Invergordon, Scotland. Embarked First Sea Lord, Mr. A. V. Alexander, and Admiral H. R. Stark, and their staffs.
23 Jun-7 Jul	Scapa Flow. Disembarked First Sea Lord and Admiral Stark. In and out exercises with British.
7-9 Jul	Operation CAMERA. Fleet demonstration off Norwegian coast.
9-10 Jul	Scapa Flow. Operations with Home Fleet.
12-19 Jul	Hvalfjordur. Insure Germans did not sneak out via Denmark Strait. Patrol. Individual ship exercises at sea.
17 Jul	*Emmons* received surprise military inspection.
20 Jul	Reykjavik. Liberty party.
21-26 Jul	Hvalfjordur. Exercises and upkeep.
26-29 Jul	Operation GOVERNOR. Fleet demonstration off Norwegian Coast.
29 Jul-1 Aug	Scapa Flow. Preparations for return to States.
1 Aug	TG92.4 took departure for States. En route task group was dissolved.
9-10 Aug	Norfolk. Fuel and Provisions.

11-28 Aug	Boston. Twelve-day availability, South Boston Navy Yard. Dry-docked.
21 Aug	TF 22 reconstituted under Admiral Hustvedt, consisting of *Iowa, Ellyson, Emmons,* and *Rodman. New Jersey, Hambleton* and *Macomb* added later.
30 Aug-21 Oct	Argentia. Training with TF 22.
24 Oct-1 Nov	Portsmouth. Availability at navy yard.
1-3 Nov	Norfolk. Logistics.
5-6 Nov	Port Royal Bay, Bermuda. Fueled
11-15 Nov	Horta, Fayal, Azores. Fueled. Awaiting orders. Became TU 27.5.3.
17 Nov	Rendezvoused with *Iowa* with President Roosevelt and his party aboard. *Emmons* with *Ellyson* and *Rodman* escorted to Strait of Gibraltar.
20-21 Nov	Gibraltar. Fueled. Relieved screen *of Iowa,* outward bound, en route Brazil.
29-30 Nov	Bahia (Salvador). Fueled. Orders changed.
4-6 Dec	Freetown, British West Africa. Awaiting orders.
9 Dec	Dakar, French West Africa. Antisubmarine patrol while President Roosevelt and party boarded *Iowa.* TU 27.5.3 escorted *Iowa* first leg of President's homeward voyage.
16-17 Dec	Bermuda. Fueled.
19-31 Dec	Boston. Sixteen-day availability at Navy Yard, South Boston Annex. Major job: Installation of Combat Information Center.
1944	
1-5 Jan	Navy Yard Annex, South Boston
5-8 Jan	Casco Bay. At anchor. Part of TF 22
8-13 Jan	Casco Bay. Daily exercises off shore.
13-17 Jan	Flight operations south of Nantucket shoals. *Ranger* (CTF 22), *Emmons, Rodman.*
17-19 Jan	Quonset Point. Upkeep. DDs underway for antisubmarine exercise.

20-22 Jan	Newport. Upkeep. Shore leave. Underway for flight operations with *Ranger* south of Nantucket Shoals.
26 Jan-9 Feb	Casco Bay. In and out exercises offshore. Four days upkeep.
10-12 Feb	*Emmons* and *Rodman* flight training with *Ranger* and A/S exercise.
12-13 Feb	Newport. Anchored overnight. Underway A.M., 13th, for A/S exercise.
13-27 Feb	Quonset Point. In and out with *Ranger* every two or three days for flight training off Cape Cod.
28 Feb-1 Mar	Flight and task force operations south of Cape Cod. Entire TF 22 participating—*Ranger, Tuscaloosa, Augusta, Ellyson, Emmons, Macomb, Rodman.* Cruisers with *Emmons Rodman,* detached to proceed Casco Bay on 1 Mar.
1-16 Mar	Casco Bay. In and out exercises with destroyers and cruisers at Casco Bay. *Emmons* and *Rodman* detached for antisubmarine exercises off Narragansett Bay on 16 Mar.
16-17 Mar	Melville, R.I. Overnight.
17-25Mar	Quonset Point. On 22nd antisubmarine exercises off Block Island. Upkeep.
26-29 Mar	Flight operations and exercises for entire task force south of Cape Cod. End of exercise *Augusta, Emmons, Rodman, Humbleton,* detached for Navy Yard, Boston.
29 Mar-8 Apr	Boston. Navy Yard Annex, South Boston. Preparations for Mediterranean duty.
9-20 Apr	Casco Bay. In and out exercises off shore. Preparations for foreign duty.
15 Apr	Task Force 22 dissolved.
20 Apr	Underway for Mediterranean with Task Group 27.4, eleven DDs, including DesDiv 19, ComDesDiv 19, Capt. A.F. Converse, in *Ellyson,* OTC.
30 Apr	Transited Strait of Gibraltar.
1-3 May	Mers-el-Kebir, Algeria. Task Group 27.4 dissolved. Assigned to Destroyers, 8th Fleet to train for Invasion of Southern France and augment antisubmarine forces in the Mediterranean. Underway 3 May to assist in two different sub hunts.

7-14 May	Mers-el-Kebir. Upkeep alongside tender Vulcan. Underway 14 May participate in combined destroyer and shore-based aircraft submarine hunt. Hunt ended morning, 17 May, when U-616 surfaced, scuttled self. Second sub attacked homeward bound formation with acoustic torpedoes. Started new hunt. DesDivl9 relieved by new destroyers out of Mers-el-Kebir.
17-18 May	Mers-el-Kebir. Logistics. Preparation for voyage to England and Normandy. *Ellyson, Emmons, Hambleton, Rodman* underway for England.
22-28 May	Plymouth, England. Part of Task Force 122, Western Naval Task Force, for OPERATION NEPTUNE, naval phase of OVERLORD, Normandy Invasion. *Emmons's* original assignment Task Group 122.4, Assault Area Screen, changed to Bombardment Group, TG 124.9, Assault Force "O," Omaha Beach. Making preparations for the invasion, including shore bombardment at Slapton Sands.
28-29 May	Milford Haven. Loaded special ammunition.
29 May-5 Jun	Weymouth Roads, England. Awaiting D-day which was postponed one day. Conferences. Final preparations for invasions.
5 Jun	Underway with *Doyle* to support minesweepers clearing approach channels and assault areas off Omaha beach.
5-9 Jun	Off Omaha Beaches, Normandy, France. Shore bombardment. Close-in fire support. Night of8 June manned outer screen.
9-11 Jun	Plymouth. Logistics.
11-15 Jun	Off Omaha Beaches. Stationed on outer screen.
15-22 Jun	Off Utah Beaches. Reported to CTF 129 for duty. Antiaircraft screen, transport area.
22 Jun	With TF 129 underway for Portland, England.
22-25 Jun	Portland. Preparations for bombardment of Cherbourg.
25 Jun	Bombardment Cherbourg with TF 129.
25-26 Jun	Portland
26-27 Jun	Plymouth. With *Rodman* escorted *Texas* from Portland.
27-29 Jun	Portland. With *Rodman* escorted SS *Tarazed to* Portland. 29 Jun returned her to Plymouth. Proceed to Belfast, Ireland to join rest of TF 129.

30 Jun-4 Jul	Belfast, Ireland. Upkeep. Underway 4 Jul with TG 120.6 (ships being shifted from Normandy Invasion to Invasion of Southern France).
10-15 Jul	Mers-el-Kebir.Upkeep.Degaussing. Liberty.
16 Jul	Underway with *Tuscaloosa, Quincy,* and *Ellyson* for Palermo, Sicily. Shore bombardment exercise at Gulf of Arzeu.
18 Jul	Palermo, Sicily. Arrived, 1058. Underway, 2037, with ComCruDiv 7 and his staff on board for conference in Naples, Italy.
19 Jul	Naples. Arrived, 0556. Underway at 2200 with ComCruDiv 7 and staff aboard to return Palermo.
20-26 Jul	Palermo. In and out for exercises with cruisers and A/S patrols. 26th underway with *Rodman* to escort *Quincy* to Malta via Strait of Messina.
27 Jul	Valetta, Malta. Arrived 0700. Fueled. Underway with *Rodman* at 1739 for Palermo via the Strait.
28 Jul	Palermo. Underway at 0200,29th, to rendezvous with *Texas* NW of Malta to escort to Taranto, Italy, assembly point for Task Group 85.12, gunfire support group of the central assault force for the invasion. 30
Jul-11 Aug-30	Taranto. Final preparations for Invasion of Southern France. Annual military inspection. 5 Aug: Emergency sortie with five other destroyers of DesRon 10 for hunt of submarine reported in southern Adriatic. 7 Aug: returned Taranto.
11 Aug	Underway with TG 85.12 for Invasion Southern France (Operation DRAGOON).
15 Aug	D-day. Off Point Sardineau. Pre-landing bombardment of beaches and selected targets. Lying-to in fire support area after landing. On call from SFCP. Observing beaches for targets of opportunity. Retired to sea at night with TG 85.12.
16 Aug	Off Point Sardineau. Standing by for call fire. 1405 Task group released from further fire support duties.
18-19 Aug	Palermo. Logistics. Underway with DesRon 10 for Taranto.
20 Aug	Taranto. Took aboard torpedoes and liaison personnel left before invasion. Underway for Palermo.

21 Aug	Palermo. Took on additional star shells. Am 1326. Dep: with DesRon 10 at 1834.
22 Aug	Ajaccio, Corsica. Topped off fuel.
23 Aug-5 Sep	Saint-Tropez and assault area. With DesRon 10 assigned to Task Group 80.6, Antisubmarine and Convoy Control Group. Alternated between manning picket and patrol stations and periods at anchor in Gulf of Saint-Tropez. On 5 Sep. ComDes-Ron 10 assigned command Task unit 80.6.7, the DRAGOON Escort, Convoy Control and Screen Unit with sixty-seven patrol and screening vessels, including DesRon 10.
6-12 Sep	Mers-el-Kabir. Upkeep.
13-21 Sep	Gulf of Saint-Tropez. Picket and patrol duty.
21–29 Sep	Marsailles. Patrol duty. Underway at night, at anchor during daytime near harbor entrance.
29 Sep-7 Oct	Toulon. Patrol, alternating between patrol and periods in port.
7-13 Oct	Marsailles. Patrol and escort duty.
13-14 Oct	Escorting SS *Surprise* Marseilles to LeghoLrn, Italy, via Strait of Bonifacio.
14-15 Oct	Leghorn. Underway for Toulon at 1633 the 15th.
16-20 Oct	Toulon. Patrol. Relieved of patrol at 0825, 20 Oct. Proceeded Mers-el-Kebir with *Rodman* and *Forrest.*
20-25 Oct	Mers-el-Kebir. Preparations return to the United States.
25 Oct	Underway with DesRon 10 as screen for the Eighth Amphibi-ous Force, en route States.
9 Nov-22 Dec	Boston. Navy Yard, Charlestown. Conversion to highspeed minesweeper.
15 Nov	Classification changed from DD457 to DMS22. In the new organization, the *Emmons* became part of Mine Division 59 of Mine Squadron 20, along with the *Ellyson, Rodman* and *Hamb-leton.*
24-31 Dec	Norfolk. After Christmas day, exercises in Chesapeake Bay. Return to port at night.

1945

1 Jan	Norfolk. Underway with *Rodman,* en route Canal Zone, escorting *Vicksburg.*
5 Jan	Limon Bay, C.Z. Transited canal.
5-6 Jan	Balboa, C.Z. Underway 1305,6th, with *Rodman, Harding* en route San Diego.
15-16 Jan	San Diego. Arrival inspection by Amphibious Training Command.
16-22 Jan	Intensive training schedule conducted under supervision of ComPhibTraPac.
26 Jan	San Francisco: Arr. 0850. Departed 1800, with *Ellyson,* escorting *Granville* (APA-171). En route Hawaii. 28 Jan. *Emmons* designated TU 16.1.12, directed rendezvous with S.S. *Weltevreden* and escort to Hawaii. Arrived Honolulu 2 Feb.
2-17 Feb	Pearl Harbor Navy Yard. Voyage repairs. Drydocked marine railway for repairs to propeller blades and sound dome. Painted entire underwater body. Individual and team training at shore facilities.
17-27 Feb	Pearl Harbor. Individual ship and division training exercises offshore. Minesweeping, antiaircraft, shore bombardment. Under way with *Rodman, Jeffers, Macomb,* escorting Convoy PD 312-T to Eniewetok.
7-8 Mar	Eniewetok. Underway escorting EU49 to Ulithi.
12-19 Mar	Ulithi. Minesweeping exercises with Mine Squadron 20. Awaiting start of Operation ICEBERG, the invasion of Okinawa.
19 Mar	Underway for target area with minesweeping groups assigned Operation ICEBERG. Destroyer minesweepers of MinRon 20 designated TG 22.3. MinDiv 59 designated TU 22.3.3 arid Sweep Unit THREE. All under command CTG 22.2 (ComMinPac).
23 Mar	Arrived off Okinawa.

24 Mar	**OpPlans for ICEBERG effective at 0500. DMSs began sweeping operations at sunrise.**
24 Mar-6 Apr	**Off Okinawa. Minesweeping, fire support for small minesweepers, escort duty, patrol and picket duty. 6 Apr Iheya Retto Channel. With fire support ships for sweeping operations northwest of Okinawa. When *Rodman* hit by kamikazes, *Emmons* went to her assistance. Both ships now became targets massed enemy attack. *Emmons* sustained five hits during the four-hour battle—severe damage and uncontrollable fires. Fought to control until near dark when forced to abandon ship in face of threatening explosions in magazine forward. 7 Apr Off Mobotu Peninsula, Okinawa. Hulk sunk by *Ellyson* at 0318 to prevent drifting onto enemy territory.**

Bibliography

Books

Bailey, Thomas A. *A Diplomatic History of the American People.* Seventh Edition. New York: Meredith Publishing Company, 1964.

Beesly, Patrick. *Very Special Intelligence: The Story of the Admiralty's Operational Intelligence Center, 1939-1945.* Garden City, NY: Doubleday Company, Inc., 1978.

Belote, James, and Belote, William. *Typhoon of Steel: The Battle for Okinawa.* New York: Harper & Row, Publishers, 1970.

Bemis, Samuel Flagg. *The Latin American Policy of the United States.* The Norton Library. New York: W. W. Norton & Company, Inc., 1967.

Butcher, Harry G, Captain, USNR *My Three Years with Eisenhower.* New York: Simon and Schuster, 1946.

Campbell, Ian, Vice Admiral, R.N., and MacIntyre, Captain, R.N. *The Kola Run: A Record of Arctic Convoys, 1941-1945.* London: Frederick Muller, Limited, 1958.

Chandler, John, Lt. Col. USMC (Ret'd.) In Depth Photography, Richlands, NC 28278.

Churchill, Winston S. *The Second World War.* 6 vols. Boston: Houghton Mifflin Company, 1947-1953.

Dictionary of American Naval Fighting Ships. Vol. II of cight. Washington, D.C.: The Naval History Division of the Office of the Chief of Naval Operations and its Successors, 1959-1981.

Doenitz, Admiral Karl, German Navy. *Memoirs: Ten Years and Twenty Days.* Translated by R. H. Stevens in collaboration with David Woodward. Cleveland and New York: The World Publishing Company, 1959. (First published in Germany under title *Zehn Jare und Zwanzig Tage.)*

Eskew, Garnett Laidlaw. *Cradle of Ships.* New York: G. P. Putnam's Sons, 1958.

Friedman, Norman. *U. S. Destroyers: An Illustrated Design History.* Profile drawings by A. D. Baker III. Annapolis, MD: Naval Institute Press, 1982.

Gow, Ian. *Okinawa, 1945: Gateway to Japan.* Consultant, H. P. Wilmott. 2nd edition. Garden City, N. Y.: Doubleday & Company, Inc., 1985.

Harrison, Gordon A. *Cross-Channel Attack.* Vol. 3, part 2 of the *History of the European Theater of Operations* of the series *United States Army in World War II.* Washington, D.C.: Office of the Chief of Military History, Department of the Army, 1951.

Hinsley, Francis Harry. *British Intelligence in the Second World War: Its Influence on Strategy and Operations.* With R. E. Thomas, C. E G. Ransom, R. C. Knight. 3 vols. London and New York: Cambridge University Press, 1979-.

Hodges, Peter and Friedman, Norman. *Destroyer Weapons of World War 2.* London: Conway Maritime Press, Ltd; Annapolis, MD: Naval Institute Press, 1979.

Kimble, George H. T., and Good, Dorothy, eds. *Geography of the Northlands.* American Geographical Society Special Publication No. 32. New York: The American Geographical Society and John Wileys Sons, Inc., 1955.

Lott, Arnold S, *Most Dangerous Sea: A History of Mine Warfare, and an Account of U. S. Navy Mine Operations in World War II and Korea.* Annapolis, MD: U. S. Naval Institute, 1959.

Morison, Samuel Eliot. *History of United States Naval Operations in World War II.* 15 vols. Boston: Little Brown and Company, 1947-1962.

A Naval Encyclopedia: Comprising a Dictionary of Nautical Words and Phrases; Biographical Notices, and Records of Naval Officers. Philadelphia: L. R. Hamersley & Co., 1884. Republished Detroit: Gale Research Company, Book Tower, 1971.

Nichols, Charles S., Jr., USMC, and Shaw, Harry I., Jr. *Okinawa, Victory in the Pacific.* Under the auspices of the Historical Branch, G-3 Division, Headquarters, U. S. Marine Corps. Rutland, VT & Tokyo, Japan: Charles Tuttle Co., Publishers, 1966.

Rohwer, Juigen, and Hummelchen, Gerhard. *Chronology of the War at Sea, 1939-1945. 2* vols. Translated from the German by Derek Masters. New York: Arco, 1972-74.

Roskill, Stephen Wentworth, Captain, R.N. *The War at Sea, 1939-1945.* 3 vols. London: Her Majesty's Stationary Office, 1954-1961.

Ruge, Vice Admiral Fredrich. *Der Zeekrieg: The German Navy's Story 1939-1945.* Annapolis, MD: United States Naval Institute Press, 1957.

Rich Ruth, Fathoms Dive Shop, Okinawa, Japan

Schofield, Bryan B. *The* Russian *Convoys.* London: B. T. Batsford, Ltd., 1964.

Sherrod, Robert. *History of Marine Corps Aviation in World War II.* Washington, D.C.: Combat Forces Press, 1952.

Speidel, Hans. *Invasion 1944: Rommel and the Normandy Campaign.* Translated from the German by Theo R. Crevenna. Westport, CT: Greenwood Press, 1971.

Toland, John. *The Rising Sun: The Decline and Fall of the Japanese Empire, 1936-1945.2* vol. New York: Random House, Inc., 1970.

Van der Porten, Edward P. *The German Navy in World War II.* New York: Thomas Y. Crowell Company, 1969.

Wilt, Allen F. *The Atlantic Wall: Hitler's Defenses in the West.* Ames, IA: The Iowa State University Press, 1975.

Young, Peter, editor, and Natkiel, Richard, cartographer. *Atlas of the Second World War.* New York: G. P. Putnam's Sons, Paragon Books, 1979.

Newspapers

***Bath Daily Times.* Bath, ME. July 1-December 31,1941.**

***The Boston Daily Globe.* Boston, MA, 1944,1945.**

***LaCronica,* edition de la manana. Lima, Peru. February 11-14,1942.**

***Portland Sunday Telegram and Press Herald.* Portland, ME, 1941.**

***La Prensa,* Guayaquil, Equador. February 27-March 2,1942.**

"Scuttlebutt," mimeographed news sheet of USS *Emmons.* Irregular dates.

***ElSiglo.* Bogota, Colombia. March 6-7,1942.**

***New York Times.* New York, NY, 1941-1945.**

***La Union,* Valparaiso, Chile. February 18-19,1942.**

***The Daily News.* New York, NY, 1944.**

Periodical Articles

Carney, Robert B., Admiral, USN, (Ret.). "A Well-kept Secret; North Atlantic Operations, 1941-1942." *Shipmate,* June, 1983,27-28.

Yokoi, Toshiyuki, Rear Admiral, former Imperial Japanese Navy. "Kamikazes and the Okinawa Campaign," *U.S. Naval Institute Proceedings,* May, 1954, 505-513.

Government Documents

***Congressional Record,* 73rd Congress, 2nd Session, and 75th Con gress, 3rd Session. 1934, 1938. Washington: United States Printing Office, 1934,1938.**

***Dictionary of American Naval Fighting Ships.* 8 vols. Compiled by the Naval History Division, Office of the Chief of Naval Operations and its successors. Washington, 1959-1981.**

Foreign Relations of the United States: Diplomatic Papers, 1942. 7 vols. Washington: United States Government Printing Office, 1963.

Naval Records in National and Naval Archives, Washington, D.C.

Unpublished Administrative Histories of World War II, Navy Library Commander in Chief, US. Atlantic Fleet. "Commander in Chief, U.S. Atlantic Fleet." Volume I parts 1-2.1946.

Fifth Naval District. "War Record of the Fifth Naval District, 1942." Commanders U.S. Naval Forces Europe. "Administrative History, United States Naval Forces in Europe 1940-1946." 7 vols. London, n.d.

Ship's Logs, National Archives

USS *Ellyson* (DD454-DMS19)

USS *Emmons* (DD457-DMS22)

USS *Facility* (AM233)

USS *Hambleton* (DD455-DMS20)

USS *Hobson QMS 26)*

USSLCI(G)558

USSLCI(G)559

USS *Lindsey* (DM32)

USS-*Ransom*(AM283)

USS *Rodman* (DD456-DMS21)

Ship's War Diaries, Naval Operational Archives

USS *Beale (DD471)*

USS *Ellyson* (DD454-DMS19)

USS *Emmons* (DD457-DMS22)

USS *Forrest* (DMS24)

USS *Gwin* (DM33)

USS *Hambleton* (DD455-DMS20)

USS *Iowa (*BB61*)*

USS *Lindsey* (DM32)

USS PGM 11

USS *Ranger* (CV4)

USS *Recruit* (AM285)

USS *Rodman* (DD456-DMS21)

USS *Santee* (ACV-29)

USS *South Dakota* (BB55)

USS *Texas* (BB35)

USS *Tuscaloosa* (CA37)

Task Force and Administrative Command War Diaries, Naval Operational Archives

Commander Battleships, Atlantic Fleet (Rear Admiral Olaf M. Hustvedt). (Also Commander Task Force 22 and Task Group 92.4 parts of 1943.) 1943.

Commander Destroyer Division 19.

Commander Destroyer Squadron 10.

Commander Mine Division 58.

Commander Mine Squadron 20.

Commander Task Force 99 (Rear Admiral Robert C. Giffen, also Commander Cruiser Division 7).

German Naval Staff, Operations Division. Translated from the German. 1942-1944.

Action Reports, Naval Operational Archives

Amphibious Forces Pacific Fleet (Vice Admiral Richmond K. Turner, Commander Task Force 51). "Operation Plan No. Al-45." 9 February 1944 (Okinawa).

Commander Amphibious Forces Pacific Fleet (Vice Admiral Richmond K. Turner, Commander Task Force 51). "General Action Report—Capture of Okinawa Gunto—Phases I and II—17 February 1945 to 17 May 1945." 25 July 1945.

Commander Battleship Division 5 (Commander Task Group 124.9, Rear Admiral Carlton F. Bryant). "Action Report for Operation Period 3-17 June 1944." 10 July 1944.

Commander Battleship Division 5 (Commander Task Group 129.2, Rear Admiral Carlton F. Bryant). "Report of Action off Cher bouig, 25 June 1944." 15 July 1944.

Commander Cruiser Division 7 (Commander Task Force 129, Rear Admiral Morton L. Deyo). "Bombardment of Cherbourg, 25 June, 1944, Action Report On." 6 July, 1944.

Commander Destroyer Squadron 10 (Commander Task Unit 85.12.4). "Action Report, invasion of Southern France, period August 11-18, 1944, Task Unit EIGHTY-FIVE POINT TWELVE POINT FOUR (Destroyer Squadron TEN)." 18 August 1944.

Commander Mine Division 58 (Commander Task Unit 52.3.2). "Report of Action, Invasion of Okinawa Gunto, 19 March 1945 to 21 June 1945." 20 July 1945.

Commander Task Group 52.2 (Rear Admiral Alexander Sharp, Comman der Mine Craft Pacific Fleet). "Action Report—Okinawa Gunto—Phases one and two." 23 April 1945.

Commander Task Group 85.12 (Rear Admiral Carlton F. Bryant, Naval Gunfire Support Group, DELTA Force). "Report of Action, August

11-16,1944—During the Invasion of the Coast of Southern France." 24 August 1944.

Commanding Officer, USS *Iowa* (BB61). "Special employment of Task Group 27.5 during the period October 24,1943 to December 18, 1943, Report of." (President Roosevelt's trip to Africa and the Middle East.)

Commander Task Force THIRTY-SIX. "Report of Transportation of U. S. Army P-40-E aircraft from Naval Air Station, Quonsett Point, RI, to Accre, Gold Coast, Africa." 30 May 1942.

Deputy Commander Destroyer Fire Support Group, Force "OBOE" (Commander Destroyer Division 36). "Action Report 1100,5 June to 0800,15 June 1944." 23 June 1944.

Naval Commander, Western Naval Task Force (Vice Admiral H. Kent Hewitt). "Report of Invasion of Southern France." 15 November 1944.

Ramsey, Admiral Sir Bertram H., RN. "Report by the Allied Com-mander-in-Chief Expeditionary Force on Operation 'NEPTUNE.'" 16 October 1944. 3 Vols. Volume III contains reports of the principal United States naval commanders in the American sector, "OMAHA" and "UTAH" beaches.

USS *Emmons* (DD457-DMS22). "Action Report and Sinking of USS EMMONS (DMS 22), 6 April 1945." 12 April 1945.

USS *Emmons* (DD457-DMS22). "Action Report for USS *Emmons* for Period 14 August through 16 August." 17 August 1944.

USS *Emmons.* "Narrative Action Report of Bombardment of Cherbourg, Normandy, France, 25 June 1944, with Task Force 129." 26 June 1944.

USS *Emmons* (DD457-DMS22). "Narrative Report of Mission Fire off Cherbourg, Report of." 25 June 1944.

USS *Emmons* (DD457). "Report on Narrative of Operations of USS EMMONS (DD457) during operation 'Neptune' from 5 June 1944 to 17 June 1944." 22 June 1944.

USS PGM 11. "Aircraft Action Report off Okinawa Shima Island 6 April 1945." 11 April 1945.

USS *Rodman* (DD456-DMS21). "Action Report—USS RODMAN—(DMS21), off Okinawa, 6 April 1945." 28 April 1945.

USS *Santee* (ACV-29). "Action Report. Participation in Torch Operation. Report of Operations from 13 October 1942 to 20 November 1942." 21 November 1942.

Miscellaneous

Correspondence concerning construction, acceptance, final armament, and shipyard overhauls of USS *Emmons* (DD457-DMS11). Bureau of Ships files, Washington National Records Center, National Archives, Suitland, MD.

Correspondence and conversations with former officers and crewmen of the USS *Emmons.*

"Log of President's Trip to Africa and the Middle East, September-December, 1943." Kept by his Naval Aide. Franklin D. Roosevelt Library, Hyde Park, NY.

McCrea, John L., Vice Admiral, USN "Draft Memoir Number 9. *Iowa*–President and Joint Chiefs of Staff to Africa and Back." Unpublished memoirs in Franklin D. Roosevelt Library, Hyde Park, NY.

Muster Rolls, Recapitulation Sheets and Reports of Changes for USS *Emmons* (DD457-DMS22). Microfilm. Washington National Records Center, National Archives, Suitland, MD.

Responses to two questionnaires addressed to members of the USS *Emmons* Association in 1982.

Roosevelt, Franklin D. "Diary kept during trip to Africa and Middle East, November-December, 1943." Franklin D. Roosevelt Library, Hyde Park, NY.

Taped interviews with former *Emmons* crew members recorded at biennial reunions at Portland, ME, 1982, and Wrightsville Beach, NC, 1984.

"USS *Emmons* (Hull No. DD457)." Card file of historical data maintained for naval vessels in Navy Library, Naval Historical Center, Washington, D.C.

978-0-595-36299-8
0-595-36299-0

Lightning Source UK Ltd.
Milton Keynes UK
UKOW04f1544010915

257879UK00002B/759/P

9 780595 362998